Federalism and Internal Conflicts

Series Editors

Soeren Keil, University of Fribourg, Fribourg, Switzerland

Eva Maria Belser, University of Fribourg, Fribourg, Switzerland

This series engages in the discussions on federalism as a tool of internal conflict resolution. Building on a growing body of literature on the use of federalism and territorial autonomy to solve ethnic, cultural, linguistic and identity conflicts, both in the West and in non-Western countries, this global series assesses to what extent different forms of federalism and territorial autonomy are being used as tools of conflict resolution and how successful these approaches are.

We welcome proposals on theoretical debates, single case studies and short comparative pieces covering topics such as:

- Federalism and peace-making in contemporary intra-state conflicts
- The link between federalism and democratization in countries facing intra-state conflict
- Secessionism, separatism, self-determination and power-sharing
- Inter-group violence and the potential of federalism to transform conflicts
- Successes and failures of federalism and other forms of territorial autonomy in post-conflict countries
- Federalism, decentralisation and resource conflicts
- Peace treaties, interim constitutions and permanent power sharing arrangements
- The role of international actors in the promotion of federalism (and other forms of territorial autonomy) as tools of internal conflict resolution
- Federalism and state-building
- Federalism, democracy and minority protection

For further information on the series and to submit a proposal for consideration, please get in touch with Ambra Finotello ambra.finotello@palgrave.com, or series editors Soeren Keil soeren.keil@unifr.ch and Eva Maria Belser evamaria.belser@unifr.ch.

Eduardo Wassim Aboultaif · Soeren Keil ·
Allison McCulloch
Editors

Power-Sharing in the Global South

Patterns, Practices and Potentials

palgrave
macmillan

Editors
Eduardo Wassim Aboultaif
School of Law & Political Sciences
Holy Spirit University of Kaslik
(USEK)
Jounieh, Lebanon

Soeren Keil
Institute of Federalism
University of Fribourg
Fribourg, Switzerland

Allison McCulloch
Department of Political Science
Brandon University
Brandon, MB, Canada

ISSN 2946-5370 ISSN 2946-5389 (electronic)
Federalism and Internal Conflicts
ISBN 978-3-031-45720-3 ISBN 978-3-031-45721-0 (eBook)
https://doi.org/10.1007/978-3-031-45721-0

© The Editor(s) (if applicable) and The Author(s), under exclusive license to Springer
Nature Switzerland AG 2024

This work is subject to copyright. All rights are solely and exclusively licensed by the
Publisher, whether the whole or part of the material is concerned, specifically the rights
of translation, reprinting, reuse of illustrations, recitation, broadcasting, reproduction on
microfilms or in any other physical way, and transmission or information storage and
retrieval, electronic adaptation, computer software, or by similar or dissimilar methodology
now known or hereafter developed.
The use of general descriptive names, registered names, trademarks, service marks, etc.
in this publication does not imply, even in the absence of a specific statement, that such
names are exempt from the relevant protective laws and regulations and therefore free for
general use.
The publisher, the authors, and the editors are safe to assume that the advice and information in this book are believed to be true and accurate at the date of publication. Neither
the publisher nor the authors or the editors give a warranty, expressed or implied, with
respect to the material contained herein or for any errors or omissions that may have been
made. The publisher remains neutral with regard to jurisdictional claims in published maps
and institutional affiliations.

Cover credit: Westend61/Getty Images

This Palgrave Macmillan imprint is published by the registered company Springer Nature
Switzerland AG
The registered company address is: Gewerbestrasse 11, 6330 Cham, Switzerland

Paper in this product is recyclable.

ACKNOWLEDGEMENTS

Finalizing a book is no easy feat. This project has been ongoing for several years, inviting authors to contribute, reading drafts, providing feedback, working and finalizing our own contributions, revisiting the different contributions, and asking for updates, all while aiming to realize, what is in our understanding one of the first comprehensive edited collections on power-sharing arrangements across the Global South.

This would not have been possible without the support of numerous people and institutions. First and foremost, we would like to thank the authors and contributors for their insights, their hard work, and their patience with us. We, as editors, have learned a lot in the process of compiling this book, and we could not be more pleased with the cooperation and engagement with the contributors, their speedy response to feedback, their engagement with discussions and questions we had, and their willingness to work with us in order to make this edited volume possible. We would also like to thank Ambra Finotello, the Senior Commissioning Editor at Palgrave, as well as Hemapriya Eswanth from Palgrave's production team for their support, their encouragement, and their patience. We would like to thank our three academic institutions, the Holy Spirit University of Kaslik in Lebanon, the University of Fribourg in Switzerland, and Brandon University in Canada.

There are a number of academic colleagues, who have supported, encouraged, and/or inspired us throughout this project. These include, in no particular order, John McGarry, Siobhan Byrne, Timofey Agarin,

vi ACKNOWLEDGEMENTS

Brendan O'Leary, Joanne McEvoy, Dawn Walsh, and Neophytos Loizides. Arend Lijphart has been an inspiration to all of us. His work on consociationalism continues to inspire researchers across the world and has been widely cited in the contributions to this book. We are grateful for his support and endorsement of this publication. Liam Nohr at Brandon University provided excellent research assistance, for which we are grateful. A special thank you to Ines Marchand.

Eduardo Wassim Aboultaif would like to thank Dalia al-Jawhary for continuously providing abundant support for his work, prioritizing his well-being at the expense of everything else, making the burden of academic publication possible and smooth. His parents are of great support to his work. He also extends his gratitude to the President of the Holy Spirit University of Kaslik, Fr. Talal Hachem, for having insightful and deep conversations about power-sharing and consociationalism, as a legal expert himself and previous dean of the School of Law and Political Science. Moreover, the newly appointed dean of the School, Fr. Wissam Khoury, has brought a lot of needed energy to faculty and staff members, and having a very calm leader amidst everything going on in Lebanon is a blessing for employees. In addition, Aboultaif would like to thank the Library of his University for providing the essential material for researching this topic. Finally, he is thankful for interesting talks with William Harris, Akram Kashee, Bechara Karam, and colleagues at the Higher Institute of Political and Administrative Sciences for being supportive in stimulating academic inquiry at the department.

Soeren Keil would like to thank his two co-editors for the discussions, the hard work and the many things he has learned in the making of this book. He would also like to thank his colleagues at the Institute of Federalism of the University of Fribourg for their support and encouragement. They continue to inspire and motivate him every day. He is grateful to wonderful academic friends, for their discussions, the laughs, and the mutual support, including Paul Anderson, Jelena Dzankic, Zeynep Arkan, and Bernhard Stahl. Finally, he would like to thank Claire for her patience and support, Malindi for making it all worthwhile and Thomas, Athena, and Lilly, as well as Cloe and Chica for the good company, the love, and for reminding him that occasionally there are more important things than work.

Allison McCulloch would like to thank David and Xavier, as always, who make this all worth it. She is also fortunate to have Liz, Ray, Ange, and Jen as her family. She owes a deep appreciation to Josie, Fionn, and

Swift who were always there to remind her that regular breaks are a good idea, and are even better when accompanied by treats. Ongoing collaborations with Siobhan Byrne, Joanne McEvoy, and Tamirace Fakhoury have informed, cohered, and refined her thinking about power-sharing, as have debates and exchanges with students at Brandon University. Long chats over Zoom or Teams, as well as in Beirut, with Soeren and Eduardo, were always welcome and enlightening. Thanks for going on this adventure together!

Finally, we would like to dedicate this book to our families, who have always supported us, encouraged us to do what we love doing, and who have given us the space, time, and support needed to complete this book.

This volume was a collective effort and the names of the editors appear in alphabetical order.

CONTENTS

1 **Introduction: Power-Sharing in the Global South**   1
Soeren Keil and Eduardo Wassim Aboultaif

2 **Power-Sharing in the Global South in Comparative Perspective: Patterns and Practices**   17
Caroline A. Hartzell

3 **The Idea of Power-Sharing in South Africa's Transition from Apartheid to Constitutional Democracy (1983–1993)**   37
Derek M. Powell

4 **Power-Sharing in Colombia: Bipartisanship, Leftist Insurgencies, and Beyond**   63
Ana Sánchez Ramírez and Madhav Joshi

5 **Power-Sharing Processes in Post-Arab Spring Tunisia: From Elite Compromise to Presidential Monopolization**   85
Julius Dihstelhoff and Moritz Simon

6 **The Limits of Territorial Arrangements and the Relevance of Consociationalism for India**   121
Harihar Bhattacharyya

ix

x CONTENTS

7 Power-Sharing in Nigeria's Divided Society: Structures, Conflicts and Challenges   145
Dele Babalola and Hakeem Onapajo

8 Power-Sharing in Malaysia: Coalition Politics and the Social Contract   169
Andrew Harding

9 The Paradox of Power-Sharing in Mauritius   189
Sheetal Sheena Sookrajowa

10 Lebanon: Consociationalism Between Immobilism and Reform   215
Drew Mikhael and Allison McCulloch

11 Consociational Democracy Without Minority Veto? Power-sharing in Ethiopia   237
Yonatan T. Fessha and Biniyam N. Bezabih

12 The Power-Sharing Arrangements in Iraq: The Instability Within   261
Farah Shakir

13 "The Unloved Child Matures": Power-Sharing in Burundi   285
Réginas Ndayiragije and Alexandre Wadih Raffoul

14 On the Adoptability of Power-sharing in Syria   309
Eduardo Wassim Aboultaif

15 The Pacific Islands: The Centrality of Context for Power-Sharing in the Global South   327
Jon Fraenkel

16 Conclusion: The Power-Sharing Lifecycle across the Global South   353
Allison McCulloch and Joanne McEvoy

Index   375

Notes on Contributors

Eduardo Wassim Aboultaif holds a Ph.D. in politics from the University of Otago, New Zealand. He is an Assistant Professor of politics at the Holy Spirit University of Kaslik, Lebanon. His work focuses on power-sharing democracies in a post-war environment as a mechanism of conflict resolution. He has extensive publications on power-sharing democracies, consociationalism, armed forces, and Middle East affairs. He has studied different characteristics of deeply divided societies, including securitizing identity, mobilization of ethnic communities, collective memory, and trauma.

Dele Babalola is Senior Lecturer in Politics and International Relations at Canterbury Christ Church University, UK. He formerly taught at Baze University, Nigeria and the University of Kent, UK. He holds a Ph.D. in Politics and Government from the University of Kent, UK. His research interests include federalism, political economy, ethnicity, and terrorism in Nigeria. He has published articles in notable journals and contributed chapters in several edited books. He is the author of *The Political Economy of Federalism in Nigeria* (Palgrave, 2019).

Biniyam N. Bezabih obtained his M.A. in Federal Studies from Addis Ababa University. His research interests include multinational federalism, democratization, fragile states, and international security. He has

xii NOTES ON CONTRIBUTORS

published on Ethiopian federalism. He is a regular commentator on political affairs and federalism in Ethiopia. He is currently pursuing a doctoral study on federalism at the University of the Western Cape.

Harihar Bhattacharyya Ph.D. (LSE) works as the Professor of Political Science at the University of Burdwan, West Bengal, India. His research focuses on comparative federalism, ethnic conflict resolution, constitution making, and power-sharing in India. His latest publications include *Asymmetric Federalism in India: Ethnicity, Development and Governance,* Palgrave Macmillan, 2023); *Federalism in Asia: India, Pakistan, Malaysia, Nepal and Myanmar* (Routledge, 2021), *Radical Politics and Governance in India's North East: the Case of Tripura* (Routledge 2018); (jointly authored) *Politics and Governance in Indian States: Bihar, West Bengal and Tripura* (Routledge, 2018); "Rethinking Indian Federalism: Consequences of Diversity Promoting Governing Practices," *Economic and Political Weekly,* April 2021; and "Limits of Ethno-territorial Model of Ethnic Conflict Resolution in India: Tension between ethnicity and Territory in India's North East" (*Ethnopolitics* 2019). He has taken part in international ethnic peace conferences for many countries.

Julius Dihstelhoff has served since May 2020 as Academic Coordinator for the international "Merian Centre for Advanced Studies in the Maghreb (MECAM)" which is based in Tunis. He is also Postdoctoral Research Fellow in the Department of Politics at the Centre for Near and Middle Eastern Studies (CNMS) at Philipps University Marburg. His research focuses on Political Islam and German foreign policy in the Arab world since the so-called Arab Spring, with a special focus on Tunisian transformation processes. His recent publications also include *Entanglements of the Maghreb—Cultural and Political Aspects of a Region in Motion* (Transkript, 2021—co-edited with Pardey, C./Ouaissa, R./Pannewick, F.), "German approaches to the Muslim Brotherhood between domestic and foreign policy" (Vernon Press, Forthcoming), and "Political Islam as an ordering factor? The reconfiguration of the regional order in the Middle East since the 'Arab Spring'" (Palgrave Macmillan, 2020).

Yonatan T. Fessha is Professor of Law and Research Chair in Constitutional Design and divided societies at the University of the Western Cape. His teaching and research focus on examining the relevance of constitutional design in dealing with the challenges of divided societies.

He has published widely on matters pertaining to but not limited to federalism, constitutional design, autonomy, intergovernmental relations, and politicized ethnicity. His publications include books on *Intergovernmental Relations in Divided Societies* (Palgrave, 2022, co-edited), *Courts and Federalism in Africa: Design and Impact in Comparative Perspective* (Routledge, 2020, co-edited), and *Ethnic Diversity and Federalism: Constitution Making in South Africa and Ethiopia* (Ashgate, 2010). He was a Michigan Grotius Research Scholar and recipient of the Marie-Curie fellowship.

Jon Fraenkel is a Professor of Comparative Politics in the School of History, Philosophy, Political Science, and International Relations at Victoria University of Wellington. He was formerly a Senior Research Fellow based at the Australian National University (2007–2012) and the University of the South Pacific in Fiji (1995–2007). He is the Pacific correspondent for *The Economist* and has published extensively on the politics of Fiji, Solomon Islands, Vanuatu, New Caledonia, Republic of the Marshall Islands, Nauru, Kiribati, Tonga, Samoa, and Papua New Guinea.

Caroline A. Hartzell is a Professor in the Political Science Department at Gettysburg College. Her research focuses on the termination of civil wars, the effects power-sharing mechanisms have on the duration and quality of the peace, and the roles of citizens in peace processes. Her recent publications include *Power Sharing and Democracy in Post-Civil War States: The Art of the Possible*, co-authored with Matthew Hoddie, and a special feature in the *Journal of Conflict Resolution* on Citizens in Peace Processes, co-edited with Felix Haass and Martin Ottmann.

Andrew Harding is a Leading Scholar in Asian Legal Studies and Comparative Constitutional Law. At the National University of Singapore, he has held the positions of founding Director of the Centre for Asian Legal Studies and Chief Editor of the Asian Journal of Comparative Law. He is now a Visiting Research Professor attached to the Centre for Asian Legal Studies, and a Professor of Law at the University of Reading Malaysia. He has worked extensively on constitutional law in Southeast Asia, especially Malaysia and Thailand, and has made extensive contributions to scholarship in comparative law, and law and development, having published 25 books as author or editor. He is co-founding-editor of Hart/Bloomsbury's book series "Constitutional Systems of the World," and has authored three books in that series. His most recent book is *The Constitution of Malaysia: A Contextual Analysis* (2nd ed., 2022). Currently, he is working on a book on *Territorial Governance in Southeast Asia*.

Vanessa Igras is a student at Gettysburg College where she is pursuing a degree in International Affairs and Anthropology with a minor in Middle Eastern & Islamic Studies. Her research interests include Islamic extremism, sub-state violence, and power-sharing mechanisms as a means of reducing violence. She will be graduating from Gettysburg College in the Fall of 2023.

Madhav Joshi is a Research Professor and Associate Director of the Peace Accords Matrix project at the Kroc Institute for International Peace Studies in the Keough School of Global Affairs at the University of Notre Dame. He is a faculty fellow at the Pulte Institute for Global Development and Liu Institute for Asia and Asian Studies. His research focuses on comparative peace processes, peace agreement design and implementation, post-war peacebuilding and social, political, and economic changes, and the Maoist insurgency in Nepal. He holds a Ph.D. in political science from the University of North Texas.

Soeren Keil is the Academic Head of the International Research and Consulting Center at the Institute of Federalism, University of Fribourg, Switzerland. He was formerly Associate Professor in Politics and International Relations at Canterbury Christ Church University in the UK. He has written, edited, and co-edited eleven books, as well as numerous articles in leading journals and book chapters focusing mainly on Eastern European countries, democratization, decentralization, and federalization. He has served as an international consultant for several programmes on decentralization and good governance and is currently involved in processes of power-sharing debates in varied contexts such as in Myanmar, Syria, Nepal, Lebanon but also Bosnia and Herzegovina, North Macedonia, and Armenia. His latest publications include *Emerging Federal Structures in the Post-Cold War Era* (2022, co-edited with Sabine Kropp) and *A New Eastern Question?—Great Powers and the Post-Yugoslav States* (co-edited with Bernhard Stahl). He is also the Scientific Coordinator of the EU and SERI-sponsored Horizon Europe Project "Legitimate Crisis Governance in Multilevel Systems – LEGITIMULT."

Allison McCulloch is a Professor in the Department of Political Science at Brandon University, Canada. Her research considers how power-sharing governments handle political crises, the incentive structures for ethnopolitical moderation and extremism that power-sharing offers, and how power-sharing arrangements can be made more inclusive of identities beyond the ethnonational divide. She is the author of *Power-Sharing and Political Stability in Deeply Divided Societies* and the co-editor of several books on power-sharing performance.

Joanne McEvoy is Senior Lecturer in the Department of Politics and International Relations at the University of Aberdeen. She has published widely on post-conflict power-sharing democracy and has comparative expertise across cases including Northern Ireland, Bosnia and Herzegovina, and Iraq. She is the author of several books, including *Power-Sharing Executives*, as well as the co-editor (with Brendan O'Leary) of *Power Sharing in Deeply Divided Places*.

Drew Mikhael is a Visiting Scholar at the Centre for the Study of Ethnic Conflict at Queen's University Belfast. His primary research interests are focused on ethnic conflict management, post-conflict peacebuilding, and the exclusion of marginalized groups in post-conflict settings in the Middle East and Great Lakes Africa. He is an experienced consultant across a nexus of development issues, advising large and small international organizations such as UNHCR, EEAS, and OECD, among others.

Réginas Ndayiragije is a Teaching Assistant and Ph.D. candidate at the Institute of Development Policy (IOB), University of Antwerp. His doctoral research investigates how ethnic power-sharing in Burundi has evolved over time, and how it influences citizens' experiences and perceptions of political representation.

Hakeem Onapajo is Senior Lecturer in the Department of Political Science and International Relations at Nile University of Nigeria, Abuja. He has held research and lecturing positions at the University of Zululand and University of KwaZulu-Natal, both in South Africa. He is a Fellow of the African Humanities Programme of the American Council of Learned Societies. He researches in the areas of elections and democratization in Africa and conflict and terrorism in the Sahel region. His publications have appeared in reputable international journals and other reputable book publishing outlets.

Derek M. Powell is an Associate Professor at the Dullah Omar Institute of Constitutional Law, Good Governance, and Human Rights at the University of the Western Cape, South Africa. He was formerly a Deputy Director-General and Senior Official in South Africa's post-apartheid government (1996–2009) and head of the research department at the Constitutional Assembly during South Africa's two-year constituting-making process (1994–1996). He is the author or editor of three books and publishes in the areas of constitutional law, comparative constitutional law, international law, federalism, and local government.

Alexandre Wadih Raffoul is Ph.D. candidate at the Department of Peace and Conflict Studies at Uppsala University. His research interests include constitutionalism, political parties, and power-sharing as a tool for conflict transformation in multi-ethnic societies. His dissertation project focuses on the causes and consequences of "associational" power-sharing.

Ana Sánchez Ramírez is a Peace Studies and History doctoral candidate at the University of Notre Dame's Kroc Institute for International Peace Studies. She holds an M.A. in History from the University of Notre Dame, an M.A. in Ethnic Studies, and a graduate certificate in Women Studies and Gender Research from Colorado State University, and a B.A in Anthropology from the National University of Colombia. Her research focuses on the political and intellectual histories of peacebuilding in late twentieth-century Colombia. Her dissertation project examines the development of "violentology" in Colombia—an expert knowledge that emerged at the intersection of violence studies and the government's peace initiatives from the late 1980s onwards.

Farah Shakir Ph.D. is a Research Fellow at Centre for Federal Studies at the University of Kent. Her research focuses on federalism and Iraq's political system. Her experience also encompasses projects that dealt with internal displacement and forced migration and the survivors of conflict-related sexual violence in Iraq. Currently, she is working on building a global database of IDP returns in federal systems. Her Ph.D. thesis was published in English in 2017 and translated into Arabic and published in 2021.

Moritz Simon (M.A.) completed his Master's in Political Science at Goethe University Frankfurt am Main. He served as a research assistant for the project "Re-thinking Multilateralism" and interned at the "Merian Centre for Advanced Studies in the Maghreb (MECAM)" in Tunis. His research focuses on Theories of International Relations. Currently, he is working on his doctoral thesis titled "World Order Conceptions of a 'New (global) Far-Right.'"

Sheetal Sheena Sookrajowa is a Senior Lecturer in Political Science in the Department of History and Political Science at the University of Mauritius. Her main research interests are ethnicity, political parties, elections, nationalism, and power-sharing. She is currently a Doctoral Candidate at the University of Cape Town, South Africa. She is the Chair of Research Committee 14 Politics and Ethnicity of the International Political Science Association.

LIST OF FIGURES

Fig. 4.1 Number of active armed groups with stated political incompatibility 70

Fig. 9.1 Map of Mauritius's 20 constituencies (*Source* Couacaud, L., Sookrajowa, S. S., & Narsoo, J. [2022]. The Vicious Circle that is Mauritian Politics: The Legacy of Mauritius's Electoral Boundaries. *Ethnopolitics, 22*(1), 48–67) 200

Fig. 13.1 Number of political parties in government (*Source* Compilation by Réginas Ndayiragije) 300

LIST OF TABLES

Table 4.1	List of Peace Agreements negotiated with armed insurgent groups in Colombia	72
Table 6.1	Religious composition of India's population (2011)	127
Table 6.2	India's official languages (2011) (8th schedule)	129
Table 6.3	Distribution of tribes and their percentage contribution to the total population in States and Union Territories (2011)	131
Table 9.1	The number of voters per ethnic group and the ratio of the members of the Legislative Council following the 1948 election	195
Table 15.1	Pacific Islands population, land area, GDP *per Capita*, languages and institutions	331

CHAPTER 1

Introduction: Power-Sharing in the Global South

Soeren Keil and Eduardo Wassim Aboultaif

INTRODUCTION

Examining power-sharing in the Global South posed three major considerations for the editors of this volume. First, conceptual clarification was required about what is meant by both the Global South and power-sharing. The "Global South" has nowadays become widely used in academic scholarship as a conceptual, geographic and political term—yet its definition has remained challenging, both in contrast toward the Global North and when discussing different dynamics in the Global South. Our understanding of geography, of power relations or of epistemological frameworks and newer questions related to the decolonization of academic research have all raised important dimensions in the study

---

S. Keil (✉)
Institute of Federalism, University of Fribourg, Fribourg, Switzerland
e-mail: soeren.keil@unifr.ch

E. W. Aboultaif
Holy Spirit University of Kaslik, Jounieh, Lebanon
e-mail: eduardoaboultaif@usek.edu.lb

© The Author(s), under exclusive license to Springer Nature
Switzerland AG 2024
E. Wassim Aboultaif et al. (eds.), *Power-Sharing in the Global South*,
Federalism and Internal Conflicts,
https://doi.org/10.1007/978-3-031-45721-0_1

1

of the Global South as a term and a concept. We treat it in this book in the first place as a geographic term, one defined by countries positioned in Africa, Latin America, Asia, and Oceania. However, the fact that not all of our case studies are located in the Southern Hemisphere demonstrates the limits of the term in geographical categories. Indeed, as the contributions in this volume highlight, using the term "Global South" should not give the impression that there are not substantial differences between the cases studied in this book, a "heterogeneity of 'Southern' realities and increasing levels of complexity" as highlighted by Haug et al. (2021: 1923). Conceptually, then, the Global South should be understood in political and economic terms—countries not at the core of global power relations but with specific relevance for global dynamics, and with important developments within them—often affected by previous colonial legacies (Levander & Mignolo, 2011). The term power-sharing is equally challenging to define. While previous research pointed to the origins of the term in Arend Lijphart's work and the use of consociationalism mainly in continental Europe (McCulloch, 2021), situating power-sharing outside of Europe, and the Global North more widely, comes with additional complexities. As will be elaborated below, power-sharing in the Global South is much more diverse, going beyond consociational institutional arrangements and demonstrating a variety of mechanisms, institutional choices and formal and informal processes in different political systems.

In addition to the challenges of discussing power-sharing and its many uses across the Global South, it is also important to contextualize the performance of these power-sharing systems. Power-sharing is often a compromise solution—as demonstrated in many case studies across this book, it is an acceptable agreement between parties who previously were in conflict with each other, often characterized by significant intra- and inter-group violence. However, while there might be a lot of similarities in the reasons that countries' elites choose for the implementation of power-sharing, be they violent conflict, secessionist demands, economic oppression and exclusion, recognition of cultural, linguistic and religious diversity or pressure from external actors to share powers with different groups, there are also significant differences between the power-sharing systems discussed in this book. For one, some of them, such as South Africa, had limited and temporary power-sharing arrangements. In others, power-sharing became heavily routinized, for example in Lebanon. Likewise, in cases such as Burundi and India, changes to the power-sharing arrangements can be observed over time. These different forms of implementation and their change over time allowed for an insightful framing of our discussion. We therefore followed the lifecycle approach to the study of power-sharing (McCulloch & McEvoy, 2020), asking the contributors to look at the coming-into-being of these systems (their adoptability, often after conflict), as well as their potential for change over time (adaptability) and their ability to evolve and move beyond a simple tool of peace-building and conflict resolution to become a framework for good governance. In some cases, even the end-ability of power-sharing has to be mentioned. In South Africa, the original agreement was designed to be temporary, but in other cases, the power-sharing framework eroded over time, as is highlighted in the case of Burundi. Hence, all contributors were asked to link their analysis broadly to the lifecycle framework, and particularly to questions of adoptability and adaptability.

The final challenge for the editors was the question of case selection. Because of the wide territorial interpretation of the Global South, and the wide conceptual interpretation of power-sharing, narrowing our case selection to a manageable number of chapters was a straightforward task. Difficult choices had to be made about which cases to include. Several guiding principles informed case selection. First, it was important to ensure geographical representation across different continents. Hence, from Colombia to India, from Nigeria to Fiji and from Ethiopia to Lebanon, all continents bar Europe and North America were covered. Naturally, other cases could have been included. From Suriname to Yemen, from Zimbabwe to Myanmar, forms of power-sharing—some temporary and limited, others more long-lasting—exist in many other contexts. However, a second important selection criteria helped sharpen the case selection—temporality. Since the lifecycle approach requires a focus from adoption to end, cases were selected that were at the very beginning of their power-sharing journey (e.g., Syria), those where power-sharing had only recently been installed (e.g., Iraq, Burundi, Tunisia) and cases with long histories of power-sharing (e.g., India, Mauritius, Malaysia, Lebanon). Some cases featured only temporary power-sharing arrangements, such as South Africa after the end of apartheid, while in other power-sharing became less important, in most cases as a result of authoritarian revivals (such as in Burundi, Iraq or Tunisia). A third criteria, closely linked to the temporal dimension, was the performance of power-sharing. While it is difficult to assess as system as performing "well," not only because of complex evaluation criteria and changes over time, but also because of the sheer variation in the power-sharing designs, it was nevertheless necessary to include systems which are considered as relatively successful (such as India and Malaysia) to those with a degree of instability (Nigeria, Ethiopia, Burundi), and cases in which power-sharing is considered performing poorly at best, and a failure at worst (Iraq, but also the failure of agreement on power-sharing in Syria). These criteria allowed for the following chapters to be based on a wide geographical spread, with different forms of power-sharing and ultimately with different performance trajectories in the implementation of power-sharing provisions.

ONE FORM OF POWER-SHARING OR MANY?

Power-sharing as an academic topic emerged with the work of Arend Lijphart (1969, 1977). Studying his native The Netherlands, Lijphart (1968) concluded that the cooperation between representatives of the different "pillars" of Dutch society represented a case separate from traditional majoritarian democracies, but which was nonetheless able to maintain democratic stability. In his later work, he observed similar processes in Belgium, Switzerland and Austria, all characterized by the four main elements of consociational theory. These are: (1) a grand coalition government in which all major segments are represented; (2) proportional representation of different groups in parliament, the civil service and the wider administration of the state, including the security apparatus; (3) veto rights for minorities on specific issues that affect their "vital interests" such as language, religion, territorial organization, cultural questions and education; and (4) autonomy for different groups, either through territorial autonomy when groups are territorially concentrated (for example through federalism, devolution or other forms of territorial decentralization) or through cultural autonomy by providing groups with specific cultural and identity rights independent of where they live in a country. These tools are specifically designed to ensure stability and democracy in divided societies—states characterized by different groups claiming these countries as their homeland and demanding recognition and inclusion. In these systems, so Lijphart's argument goes, majoritarian democracy would not work as it would lead to a permanent dictatorship of the majority, turning numerically smaller ethnic, religious and linguistic communities into permanent political minorities (Lijphart, 2008).

Consociational democracy can come in two forms: liberal or corporate. A liberal consociational arrangement does not specify what offices or seats a political community receives in the system. The ethnic, linguistic, religious or ideological distribution of parliamentary and executive seats, in addition to bureaucratic and security appointments, are left open to electoral alliances (McGarry & O'Leary, 2007). In this way, the system creates a balance between group and individual rights, and the former is not superior in status to that of the latter. Therefore, as McCulloch notes, liberal consociations are more likely to allow identities to develop and change rather than freeze in time (McCulloch, 2014). Only a few countries apply the liberal consociational model like Iraq and Malaysia. On the other hand, the corporate model is more rigid in its design. Corporate consociations have ascriptive identity-based criteria for the distribution of posts in the executive, legislative and public sector (McGarry & O'Leary, 2007). Once the corporate system is established, it is hard to move beyond the identity labels, and hence new identities cannot be formed easily, and if they are, there is always a challenge for them to be acknowledged by the state.

In his later work, Lijphart highlighted more strongly how consociational power-sharing can also be applied outside of Europe. While he also studied cases in the Global South in his 1977 book, it is remarkable that these discussions on cases such as Lebanon, Malaysia and Nigeria have been mainly overlooked in academic discussions in favor of his work on power-sharing in Europe.[1] He also studied South Africa (Lijphart, 1985a) and India (1996) as possible examples for consociational power-sharing outside of its original cradle in Western Europe. In line with Lijphart's work, other scholars have looked at the use of consociational power-sharing outside of Europe. Hartzell and Hoddie (2015), for example, examine how power-sharing, referring specifically to elite cooperation, has contributed to conflict resolution in 34 out of 46 peace agreements in the 1990s alone (Hartzell & Hoddie, 2015). The cases they examine include Lebanon, South Africa, Burundi, Ethiopia and Fiji—all cases studied in more detailed in this book. According to their argument, power-sharing has mainly been used in non-Western contexts to pacify war-torn societies

---

[1] We are grateful to Allison McCulloch for pointing this out to us and highlighting that Lijphart has had a much longer interest in the study of consociationalism in the Global South than is often recognized in the discussions of his work.

and bring enemy parties together. They, however, highlight that power-sharing, as used in the peace agreements they study, has taken on a wider meaning than Lijphart's consociationalism.

In fact, in the 1980s and 1990s, as consociationalism became used more widely not just in the established European democracies, but in conflict-torn societies in Europe (such as Bosnia & Herzegovina, North Macedonia, Northern Ireland and Kosovo) and beyond, an increasing number of skeptics voiced criticism of the consociational framework. Most notably, Donald Horowitz pointed to consociational power-sharing as an institutional framework that would reward radicalization and further separates different communities from each other (Horowitz, 1985). The required willingness of cooperation among elites would be limited, because segregation and group autonomy would favor ethnic outbidding, which in turn would limit any chances for cooperation (Horowitz, 1993). In contrast, the Horowitzian school of thought represents the opposite pole of the spectrum in power-sharing with an integrationist or centripetal characteristic. This approach relies on the integration of ethnic groups at the center by creating a strong presidency which oversees the executive, and where the winning candidate must rely on vote pooling from all communities. To win, candidates need to present themselves as ethnically moderate. Horowitz argues that the system would avoid immobilism because there is no veto power, and a strong presidential system with limited veto powers will ensure sufficient policy output (Horowitz, 2014). Aspects of the integrationist or centripetalist approach has found support in systems such as Nigeria, Malaysia and the Indian state of Kerala, though consociational power-sharing has remained the most important framework for conflict resolution in civil war situations.

In addition to Horowitz's discussion on centripetalist approaches, there have been other discussions on power-sharing and conflict resolution. Lijphart (1985b) and Daniel Elazar (1985) shared an important debate in the mid-1980s about the use of consociationalism and federalism as tools of non-majoritarian democracy. While they did not agree on the best framework for the management of diversity in divided societies, they nevertheless laid the foundations for an ongoing debate between federalism scholars and those interested in power-sharing. As is expressed in detail in the chapters on India and Ethiopia, federalism has been at the heart of power-sharing in these two systems. In Nigeria, Malaysia, Iraq and South Africa, too, forms of federalism and territorial autonomy are significant as tools to manage diversity, support democratization and ensure power-sharing between different groups. While more research is needed on the relationship between federalism and power-sharing—and their interplay in post-conflict societies—what is visible when looking at the case studies examined in this book is their strong connection. Even in cases in which federalism was not adopted, there remain important discussions on territorial reorganization, including in Tunisia, Lebanon, Syria and Colombia, where strangely decentralization did not feature much as an issue of negotiations in the latest peace-building efforts with FARC rebels.

In addition to the ongoing debates about the linkages of federalism and different forms of power-sharing, there is also a growing recognition in the academic literature that international actors play a greater role not only in the adoptability of any power-sharing agreement, but also in relation to their adaptability over time (McCulloch & McEvoy, 2018; Walsh & Doyle, 2018). As Caroline Hartzell and Vanessa Igras point out in their chapter in this volume, international actors matter: They have promoted power-sharing solutions in many Global South contexts, including through UN mediation processes, constitution-building support or direct imposition of specific power-sharing frameworks, as was the case in Iraq and to some extent also in Mauritius at the time of its independence. International actors are often fundamentally important in the adoption of a power-sharing system, as well as their preferences and involvement over time in the functioning of these systems. As is visible in numerous cases, power-sharing would not have been implemented, were it not for American support for a power-sharing solution in Iraq, British pressure on Mauritian elites to choose inclusive institutions, and the role of France in New Caledonia. UN constitution-makers also played an important role in countries such as Tunisia and Sudan, where constitutional negotiations relied on external expert input. As will be seen throughout the chapters of this book, international actors are an important feature in many power-sharing systems in the Global South, and while their role has changed over time, their influence in many contexts needs to be examined and further elaborated. This is not only important in order to understand the adoptability and adaptability of the studied power-sharing systems, but also the non-adoptability in cases such as Syria, where Russian, Iranian and Turkish involvement helps to explain the lack of a stronger push for a power-sharing solution.

If one wants to understand the different forms of power-sharing applied in the Global South, and studied throughout this book, it is important to understand the literature on "complex power-sharing" solutions (Walsh, 2018; Wolff, 2009). In the 1990s, much of the academic debate on institutional design for divided societies was dominated by the consociationalism vs. centripetalism debate. More recently, there has been a much more inclusive strand of research, which has pointed out that for policy-makers, international peace-builders and political elites, it is often important to have the greatest selection of institutional tools in order to find solutions to end violent conflict (Cederman et al., 2022). Instead of focusing simply on consociationalism, or integration, or federalism, or an alternative approach, authors such as Stefan Wolff (2009) have highlighted the advantages of using power-sharing as a toolbox (see also McCulloch & Aboultaif, 2023). In it, institutional mechanisms from different frameworks—consociationalism, integration, etc.—can be found and used in order to satisfy opposing elite agendas and reach agreement on peaceful conflict settlements. While this literature was initially welcomed by scholars and policy-makers alike, some scholars claim that consociationalism works best when implemented coherently instead of partially and as part of a wider package (Bogaards et al., 2019; Schulte & Trinn, 2021). The evidence in our case studies is mixed. Partial implementation of consociationalism has contributed to flawed systems in Iraq and Burundi. However, Lebanon, which has implemented all aspects of consociational democracy, has nevertheless been unable to transform into a stable and functioning democracy in the post-civil war period. The contributions in this book allow for one important observation in this regard: It might not even be most important what kind of institutional design is adopted at the beginning of a power-sharing regime, but it might be substantially more important how power-sharing institutions and the elites that give life to them, change, adapt and evolve over time. Adoptability will often be flawed, because these systems come into being in moments of crisis, either after conflict (such as in Lebanon, Burundi and Iraq), or as a result of regime change (as was the case in South Africa in the early 1990s and Nigeria in 1999 for example). Some power-sharing systems are adopted when states become independent in the process of decolonialization, as seen in India and Mauritius. Yet, for all of these states, a common denominator can be detected—while they had very different institutional frameworks when adopting power-sharing, those that ended up stabilizing as functioning democracies were able to adapt and evolve their initial power-sharing institutional frameworks.

Organization of the Book

This book follows in its organization the above-described lifecycle approach. After this Introduction, a global snapshot of power-sharing challenges and performance in the Global South is provided by Caroline Hartzell and Vanessa Igras. The authors pinpoint the success and failure of power-sharing in the Global South by comparing the use of power-sharing institutions in post-conflict provisions based on consociational and consensus models, with a rich study on power-sharing according to the following criteria: who has power; the effects of exercising power through power-sharing institutions; and the trends in the adoption and evolution of power-sharing in the Global South. They also ask what factors explain the absence of major power-sharing solutions being adopted in the last decade by looking at geopolitics and the changing nature of insurgencies in different countries. Their results are mixed; clearly power-sharing does not solve all problems, but it is often better than its reputation, and in the last decade we have seen the absence of major power-sharing solutions thereby demonstrating that prolonged conflict or continued authoritarian rule is often the alternative when no power-sharing deal can be reached.

The next section looks at cases which have had limited and short-lived power-sharing experiments. These past cases of power-sharing include South Africa, Colombia and Tunisia. Derek Powell's chapter on the consociational arrangement in South Africa argues that some power-sharing was necessary in order to oversee the transition to majoritarian democracy—but that policy debates both within the African National Congress and within the White minority did not per se favor strict institutionalized form of power-sharing. Powell argues that the consociational principles guiding the Government of National Unity (GNU) which brought together previous protagonists (the African National Congress, the National Party and Inkhata Freedom Party) paved the way for a peaceful transition from what he calls the undemocratic political negotiations to the democratic constitutional negotiations. However, these arrangements, so Powell's argument goes, were always intended to be limited and temporary. South Africa thus serves as an example of where sunset clauses enabled the end-ability of the power-sharing system.

In Chapter 4, Ana Sánchez Ramírez and Madhav Joshi study the evolution and institutionalization of power-sharing arrangements in Colombia in the last century. They divide power-sharing into two phases, one that began in the early twentieth century until the 1970s, and the second after 2016 with the peace agreement between the government and the Revolutionary Alternative Common Force (FARC Party). They argue that power-sharing is not a new concept in Colombia, but that it is surprising how little previous historical experience is reflected in the most recent peace agreements.

In the next contribution, Julius Dihstelhoff and Moritz Simon analyze the transition to democracy in Tunisia between 2011 and 2018 as a result of the Arab Spring. Here power-sharing was a compromise between two ideological pillars, the secular bloc led by Nidaa Tunis Party and the Islamist bloc led by Annahda Party. The 2011–2018 period demonstrated signs of elite compromise and fragmentation of power, though this arrangement began to wither away in favor of a strong presidential monopoly of power after the election of Kais Saied in 2019. The emergence of a key institutional player in Saied, who did not believe in power-sharing, or parliamentary democracy for that matter, highlights the limits of power-sharing systems. For, when a major actor—in the Tunisian case, a directly elected President does not believe in the principles of parliamentary democracy and party coalitions and consensus-building, and when he is supported by other major actors, including the security services, it becomes relatively easy to undermine, and in the Tunisian case, to completely stop power-sharing institutions and democratic decision-making. Dihstelhoff and Simon's chapter thus opens the door to the study of Tunisia as a case in which power-sharing has ended due to a presidential coup d'état or autogolpe.

The next section of the book includes cases that already have power-sharing provisions, and where those institutions are still in place, but where they are not necessarily performing as intended: India, Nigeria, Malaysia, Mauritius, Lebanon, Ethiopia, Iraq and Burundi. These cases offer an important lens as to the functionality of different forms of power-sharing. Harihar Bhattacharyya argues that Indian power-sharing is based on territorially based federal arrangements with dozens of non-territorial issues remaining unresolved. One of the main problems that the Indian system faces is the exclusion of minorities who are too territorially dispersed or too small to be represented in a specific geographical area. With respect to Nigeria, Dele Babalola and Hakeem Onapajo assess the elite's lack of commitment to power-sharing, which leads to phases of instability despite structural and informal power-sharing mechanisms. The federal nature of the state faces many problems including unequal representation in offices, along with favoritism in the distribution of posts or lack of commitment to rotation of offices as in the case of previous President Goodluck Jonathan. This has led to extensive calls to restructure the federal formula in the country, but where the adaptability of the system remains contested.

In the Malaysian case, Andrew Harding looks at power-sharing through the lens of social contract theory. Stability in Malaysia has been maintained as a result of a social contract whereby minorities recognize the special position of the majority. In return, minorities have their own special interests protected and are allowed to participate in the state and its public life. Ethnic party coalitions play a vital role in the discussions on Malaysian power-sharing as they ensure stability on the one hand, and protect Malay dominance while also ensuring minority inclusion. However, Harding points out that it is becoming more challenging to sustain this social contract as there are increasing social tensions and inter- and in-group conflicts, which cannot be managed anymore by the existing institutional arrangements.

In Mauritius, Sheetal Sheena Sookrajowa explains the evolution of power-sharing since independence. Despite coalition governments and some consociational features, Sookrajowa argues that Mauritius delivers majoritarian outcomes due to its electoral design that provides a clear Hindu majority, along with a weak veto system and segmental autonomy that strengthens the power of the prime minister and power concentration in the Executive. While there have been many discussions on reforming the system, so far it has remained reasonably stable, despite contestation from a variety of groups, parties and actors.

Regarding Lebanon, Drew Mikhael and Allison McCulloch shed light on the prospect of reform in the system. The authors' extensive fieldwork and interviews with civil society actors regarding the successful attempt to repeal "marry your rapist" laws and ongoing discussions about the nationality law, to allow Lebanese women to provide their nationality to their partners and offspring, signals that the adaptability of the system is slowed or even stopped by elites when they feel that their interests are threatened. Mikhael and McCulloch therefore ask important questions about power-sharing adaptability: What (and who) is power-sharing for in Lebanon beyond elite rule and peace? How can power-sharing ensure inclusion even if the groups that want to be included were not part of the initial power-sharing adoption process? The ongoing political, economic and social crisis in Lebanon therefore offers a good example for the study of the performance of power-sharing and its ability to adapt and reform as well as analysis of its capacity to deliver public goods.

In Chapter 11, Yonatan Fessha and Biniyam Bezabih explain how law and politics are interrelated in Ethiopia according to the demographic and historical context, territorial autonomy, executive power-sharing and the impact of party politics on accommodation. While federalism and cross-party coalitions have been vital to governance in post-1995 Ethiopia, the subsequent stability was bought by one-party dominance and rule through an elite cartel. Recent power shifts have opened the door to new unrest and demands for a reorganization and renegotiation of power-sharing in the country, as well as to a protracted civil war in Tigray region.

In the next chapter, Farah Shakir details the problems of Iraq's liberal consociational system. Shakir discusses the sources of instability and exclusion, the formation of identity-based parties and how the problems of corporate arrangements are repeated in the liberal approach of power-sharing in Iraq. She raises the important question of flawed adoption and a subsequent lack of adaption of the power-sharing arrangement, which has contributed to the ongoing instability in the country.

The final chapter in this part covers the case of Burundi, which is addressed by Réginas Ndayiragije and Alexandre Wadih Raffoul. The authors look at the case of Burundi through the institutional design of power-sharing, its evolution over time and the preferences of major political partners and their influence on power-sharing institutions. Their conclusions highlight how power-sharing has eroded over time in Burundi, partly due to democratic decline and authoritarian revival. They teach us important lessons about making power-sharing work and upholding the commitment to power-sharing beyond the point of adoption.

The final empirical part that deals with future prospects for power-sharing as a method of conflict resolution and regulation includes two chapters. Eduardo Wassim Aboultaif writes about the possible adoption of power-sharing in Syria to end the civil war. In contrast to prevailing scholarship which tends to support liberal consociation, Aboultaif argues in favor of a corporate consociational arrangement in Syria. His argument is premised on the way by which identities have been sharpened amidst insecurity and lack of trust. Alongside his recommendations for corporate institutions, Aboultaif discusses the need to reform the armed forces of Syria to avoid using it as an instrument of oppression in the future.

The last empirical chapter is that of Jon Fraenkel who writes on power-sharing in the Pacific Islands, zeroing in on Fiji and New Caledonia. Fiji, which had a brief but high-profile experience with a form of power-sharing that showed aspects of both consociationalism and centripetalism, has subsequently moved on from power-sharing, in another instance of power-sharing ended by coup d'état. New Caledonia's "classically consociational" arrangement, as detailed in the Nouméa Accords persists, still under French tutelage, though negotiations between the French state and local actors, including the Kanak Indigenous people, have begun again. Fraenkel emphasizes the need to take into consideration "the context," which he defines as the character of the cleavages, and the specificities of the cases. He argues for a more codified and institutionalized version of power-sharing in the cases he compares, suggesting that this will be important to avoid future abuses of power.

The book concludes with a chapter by Allison McCulloch and Joanne McEvoy. They apply the lifecycle approach to the chapters, revisiting the themes of adoptability, functionality, adaptability and end-ability of power-sharing and applying these to selected cases from the book in a more comparative perspective. In doing so, they highlight some of the convergences and divergences in the origins, performance and challenges of power-sharing across the broad remit of the Global South.

BIBLIOGRAPHY

Bogaards, M., Helms, L., & Lijphart, A. (2019). The Importance of Consociationalism for Twenty-First Century Politics and Political Science. *Swiss Political Science Review, 25*(4), 341–356.

Cederman, L., Hug, S., & Wucherpfennig, J. (2022). *Sharing Power, Securing Peace? Ethnic Inclusion and Civil War.* Cambridge University Press.

Elazar, D. (1985). Federalism and Consociational Regimes. *Publius—The Journal of Federalism, 15*(2), 17–34.

Levander, C., & Mignolo, W. (2011). Introduction: The Global South and World Dis/Order. *The Global South, 5*(1), 1–11.

Lijphart, A. (1968). *The Politics of Accommodation: Pluralism and Democracy in The Netherlands.* University of California Press.

Lijphart, A. (1969). Consociational Democracy. *World Politics, 21*(2), 207–225.

Lijphart, A. (1977). *Democracy in Plural Societies: A Comparative Exploration.* Yale University Press.

Lijphart, A. (1985a). *Power-Sharing in South Africa* (Policy Papers in International Affairs no. 24). Institute of International Studies at Berkeley.

Lijphart, A. (1985b). Non-majoritarian Democracy: A Comparison of Federal and Consociational Theories. *Publius—The Journal of Federalism, 15*(2), 3–15.

Lijphart, A. (1996). The Puzzle of Indian Democracy: A Consociational Interpretation. *American Political Science Review, 90*(2), 258–268.

Lijphart, A. (2008). *Thinking About Democracy. Power-Sharing and Majority Rule in Theory and Practice.* Routledge.

Hartzell, C., & Hoddie, M. (2015). The Art of the Possible: Power-Sharing and Post-Civil War Democracy. *World Politics, 67*(1), 37–71.

Haug, S., Braveboy-Wagner, J., & Maihold, G. (2021). The 'Global South' in the Study of World Politics: Examining a Meta Category. *Third World Quarterly, 42*(9), 1923–1944.

Horowitz, D. (1985). *Ethnic Groups in Conflict.* University of California Press.

Horowitz, D. (1993). Democracy in Divided Societies. *Journal of Democracy, 4*(4), 18–38.

Horowitz, D. (2014). Ethnic Power Sharing: Three Big Problems. *Journal of Democracy, 25*(2), 5–20.

McCulloch, A. (2014). Consociational Settlements in Deeply Divided Societies: The Liberal-Corporate Distinction. *Democratization, 21*(3), 501–518.

McCulloch, A. (2021). Introduction: Power-Sharing in Europe—From Adoptability to End-Ability. In S. Keil & A. McCulloch (Eds.), *Power-Sharing in Europe—Past Practice, Present Cases and Future Directions* (1st ed., pp. 1–18). Palgrave Macmillan.

McCulloch, A., & Aboultaif, E. W. (2023). *Territorial and Institutional Settlements in the Global South.* Oxford Research Encyclopedia of International Studies. Oxford University Press.

McCulloch, A., & McEvoy, J. (2020). Understanding Power-Sharing Performance: A Lifecycle Approach. *Studies in Ethnicity and Nationalism, 20*(2), 109–116.

McCulloch, A., & McEvoy, J. (2018). The International Mediation of Power-Sharing Settlements. *Cooperation and Conflict, 53*(4), 467–485.

McGarry, J., & O'Leary, B. (2007). Iraq's Constitution of 2005: Liberal Consociation as Political Prescription. *International Journal of Constitutional Law, 5*(2), 670–698.

Schulte, F., & Trinn, C. (2021). *Why We Should Stop Cherry-Picking in the Analysis of Consociational Institutions.* 50 Shades of Federalism. http://50shadesoffederalism.com/theory/why-we-should-stop-cherry-picking-in-the-analysis-of-consociational-institutions/

Walsh, D. (2018). *Territorial Self-Government as a Conflict Management Tool.* Palgrave Macmillan.

Walsh, D., & Doyle, J. (2018). External Actors in Consociational Settlements: A Re-examination of Lijphart's Negative Assumptions. *Ethnopolitics, 17*(1), 21–36.

Wolff, S. (2009). Complex Power-Sharing and the Centrality of Territorial Self-Governance in Contemporary Conflict Settlements. *Ethnopolitics, 8*(1), 27–45.

CHAPTER 2

Power-Sharing in the Global South in Comparative Perspective: Patterns and Practices

Caroline A. Hartzell

INTRODUCTION

Power-sharing institutions, arrangements designed to help manage conflict in divided societies, have played a prominent role in the governance of numerous Global South countries. Although countries of the Global South have been using power-sharing for several decades, the reasons that they have adopted these institutions, the forms that power-sharing has taken, and the consequences that these measures have produced often have been overshadowed by the study of power-sharing

---

Vanessa Igras (Gettysburg College, Gettysburg, PA, USA) has contributed to this chapter along with the author.

C. A. Hartzell (✉)
Gettysburg College, Gettysburg, PA, USA
e-mail: chartzel@gettsburg.edu

© The Author(s), under exclusive license to Springer Nature Switzerland AG 2024
E. Wassim Aboultaif et al. (eds.), *Power-Sharing in the Global South*, Federalism and Internal Conflicts,
https://doi.org/10.1007/978-3-031-45721-0_2

as a European phenomenon. Accordingly, the goal of this chapter is to analyze the practice of power-sharing in the Global South. By putting power-sharing in a comparative perspective, we hope to facilitate a clearer understanding of the successes—and failures—associated with the use of this form of conflict management by countries of the Global South.

Our analysis of power-sharing in this chapter begins by comparing the understanding of the use of power-sharing institutions that stems from consociational and consensus models of conflict management to one rooted in the way that countries of the Global South have most commonly used power-sharing, which is as a means of ending civil wars. Focusing on the role that intrastate conflict has played in shaping the Global South's approach to power-sharing, we describe the types of power-sharing measures that have been adopted by a variety of countries in the Global South. We then discuss the implications that power-sharing arrangements have had for who exercises power as well as some of the political and economic effects they have generated. We conclude the chapter by describing trends in the adoption and evolution of power-sharing institutions in the Global South, noting what these might imply for the future of power-sharing in the Global South.

COMPARATIVE PERSPECTIVES ON POWER-SHARING: FROM CONSOCIATIONAL AND CONSENSUS MODELS OF DEMOCRACY TO POST-CIVIL WAR CONFLICT MANAGEMENT

Although different interpretations of the nature and utility of power-sharing institutions exist within the scholarly and policy communities, power-sharing is generally understood as a tool for managing conflict within societies in which one or more cleavages exist. Initial scholarship on power-sharing was motivated by a body of work that advanced a pessimistic view regarding the potential for democracy successfully to be used as a form of conflict management in plural societies. Several scholars who sought to understand the possibilities for stable and effective governance to take hold within deeply divided societies, particularly those emerging from the waves of decolonization following the end of World War II, expressed skepticism regarding the use of democracy as a form of conflict management in plural societies (e.g., Almond, 1956). Representative of this line of thought are Rabushka and Shepsle, who observe:

"Democracy, at least as it is known in the West, cannot be sustained under conditions of salient preferences because outcomes are valued more than procedural norms. The plural society, constrained by the preferences of its citizens, does not provide fertile soil for democratic values of stability" (2009: 92).

Scholars who sought to respond to pessimistic claims regarding democracy as a set of institutions for the management of conflict noted that, in the context of divided societies, it was majoritarian democracy that was potentially problematic as, in this system, government institutions do not share political power with groups outside the majority. Critics of majoritarian democracy observed that this system of rule could be expected to prove fragile in deeply divided societies, with groups that are denied meaningful participation in the institutions of government potentially withdrawing their support from the regime or employing violence to register their opposition (Lijphart, 1999; Nordlinger, 1972).

Seeking an alternative to the potentially permanent marginalization of the interests of minority communities by the institutions of majoritarian democracy, Arend Lijphart proposed the concepts of "consociationalism" and "consensus democracy." Conceived as a means of providing minority communities with greater opportunities to participate in governance than is the case in majoritarian democracy, each of these forms of democracy calls for sharing or dividing elements of political power among identity-based groups in divided societies. In the case of consociational democracy, Lijphart (1969, 1975, 1977) identified four defining features—the grand coalition, mutual veto, the principle of proportionality, and segmental autonomy—that he describes as the "pillars" of the system. Each of these elements is designed to enhance the ability of minority groups to express their political interests and potentially to achieve their preferences through policy outcomes. Mechanisms associated with the pillars also function by providing means for minority groups to hinder the majority will. Consensus democracy, a more flexible and encompassing concept than consociational democracy, saw Lijphart (1999) identify additional options along two dimensions—an executive-parties dimension and a federal-unitary dimension—that states might use to accommodate minority interests. These include executive power-sharing in multiparty coalitions and the use of proportional representation electoral systems as part of the first dimension, and a federal and decentralized government as part of the second dimension (Hartzell & Hoddie, 2020).

As the preceding summary makes clear, power-sharing mechanisms were initially identified as a means of ensuring the successful operation of democracy as a tool of conflict management in plural societies. More recently, however, scholars and policy-makers have moved to adapt the structures and processes identified by Lijphart as tools for managing conflict in a different setting, that of states emerging from civil war. This repurposing of power-sharing, from a focus on strategies seen as applying to several small European democracies to an approach for managing conflict in a broader range of countries experiencing armed intrastate conflict, was not without precedent. Lijphart's own work, *Power-sharing in South Africa* (1985), sought to highlight the utility of consociationalism and power-sharing as tools for managing conflict in a state experiencing civil war.[1] Nevertheless, it bears noting that the thrust of the scholarly work on power-sharing as a strategy for ending civil wars differs significantly from earlier research on power-sharing, in that its focus is on ending armed conflict rather than on promoting democracy in plural societies.

Where newer research on power-sharing as a strategy for ending civil wars intersects with the previous corpus of work on power-sharing and democracy is via the proposition that, by providing competing groups with a share of government power, power-sharing measures ensure that they will have the political voice and sense of security necessary for them to peacefully manage future conflict. By providing rival groups with tools that give them access to state power, power-sharing institutions help to prevent any one group from becoming dominant. This serves to reassure adversaries that no single group will be able to use the power of the state to promote its interests at the expense of others. In keeping with Lijphart's original perspective, power-sharing measures are thus hypothesized to increase the likelihood that contending groups will remain committed to the peace by addressing their security concerns and providing them with a stake in the government (Hartzell & Hoddie, 2003, 2007).

---

[1] Lijphart also included analyses of cases from the Global South, some of which are the subject of chapters in this book, in an earlier work, *Democracy in Plural Societies: A Comparative Exploration* (1977).

Power-Sharing Institutions in the Global South

The growth in research by scholars on power-sharing as a means of managing conflict in countries emerging from civil wars has seen a corresponding rise in interest on the part of the international community in its use for the same end (McCulloch & McEvoy, 2018). Because most intrastate conflicts in the post-World War II period have taken place in regions of the world considered to constitute the Global South, this has led to an increased emphasis on identifying the nature of the power-sharing measures that have proliferated in the Global South and the forces that have given rise to them. Accordingly, we focus on these two issues below.

As noted above, power-sharing institutions in the Global South by and large have been adopted to end civil wars and to prevent them from recurring. Power-sharing institutions of this nature have been defined as consisting of "rules that, in addition to defining how decisions will be made by groups within the polity, allocate decision-making rights, including access to state resources, among collectivities competing for power" (Hartzell & Hoddie, 2003: 320). Four different types of power-sharing have been identified, each of which is associated with a distinct dimension of state power: political, military, territorial, and economic.[2] Power-sharing arrangements used to end civil wars call for the sharing or dividing of power among two or more rival groups across one or more of these dimensions of state power.[3]

Political power-sharing measures emphasize proportionality in the distribution of central state authority among contending groups. Rival actors may be called upon to share power based on a political (e.g., ideology) or demographic (e.g., ethnic) element of their identity. State power in this instance may be distributed based on electoral proportional representation, administrative proportional representation, or proportional representation within the executive branch of the national government. Electoral proportional representation systems seek to ensure that

---

[2] The description of the different power-sharing mechanisms that follows is drawn from Hartzell and Hoddie (2007, 2020).

[3] Power-sharing institutions are generally agreed to as part of negotiated settlements of civil war such as Burundi (see Chapter 13 on Burundi in this volume), although there do exist a few instances of civil wars ended via military victory whose settlements have provided for power-sharing between the government and the defeated party as was the case in South Africa (see Chapter 3 on South Africa on this issue).

each group that secures electoral support will have a voice in the policy-making process by limiting the disparity between a party's share of the vote in the national election and the number of seats it holds in the legislature. Administrative proportional representation guarantees groups included in the power-sharing arrangement a predetermined number of positions on courts, commissions, the civil service, and other offices, and thus serves to increase the participation of diverse interests in the policy-making and implementation processes. Proportional representation in the executive branch requires cooperation among former rivals at the center of political authority, with representatives of groups taking on positions at the ministerial, sub-ministerial, and cabinet levels. As such, this form of power-sharing has the potential to be among the most significant types within the national government.

A variety of the foregoing elements of political power-sharing were present in Colombia's National Front, a power-sharing arrangement agreed to by the country's Conservative and Liberal parties to end a civil war that broke out in 1948.[4] A central component of the National Front agreement was political parity, with equal shares of political power allocated to the two parties, while all other political parties were excluded from power. Elected and non-elected positions ranging from the national to municipal levels were divided equally between the two parties. Additionally, the presidency alternated between the Conservative and Liberal parties every four years for a period of sixteen years, from 1958 until 1974, when the country returned to free elections. Once the National Front formally ended, power continued to be shared informally as elected presidents invited members of the defeated party to participate in the central government, an arrangement that finally came to an end in 1986.

Military power-sharing calls for the distribution of authority among rival groups within the coercive apparatus of the state. The goal in this instance is to ensure that the armed forces cannot be used to threaten the security of groups that have disarmed at the end of the civil war. Military power-sharing can be accomplished by integrating non-state actors' armed forces into a unified state security force; mandating the appointment of members of the subordinate group(s) to key leadership positions within the state's security forces; and, on rare occasions, allowing rival groups to

---

[4] For further information, see Chapter 4 on Colombia in this volume.

remain armed or to retain their own security forces as is the case in Iraq's Northern Kurdish region.[5]

Military power-sharing featured as a central component of the 1996 Final Peace Agreement in the Philippines. The agreement, signed by the Government of the Philippines and the Moro National Liberation Front (MNLF), called for qualified MNLF members to be integrated into the Armed Forces of the Philippines and the Philippine National Police. Notably, the peace agreement did not include a requirement that the MNLF disarm and demobilize. Burundi, one of the cases examined in this book, constitutes another example of military power-sharing. Considering the deep mistrust that the Hutu majority had of the country's armed forces, which had previously been controlled by the Tutsi minority, Burundi's peace agreement called for the integration of government and rebel forces in the new military, with no single ethnic group constituting more than 50% of the country's defense and security forces. In addition, 60% of the military's officers were to be drawn from the government army and 40% from the rebel Forces for the Defense of Democracy (FDD) (Nantulya, 2015).

Territorial power-sharing seeks to distribute political influence among different levels of government by creating forms of decentralized government that are territorially based. Agreements to structure post-war states to include provisions for regional autonomy offer regionally concentrated groups a degree of independent power from the central government. Regions within a federal system may secure representation within the institutions of the federal government, thus providing regional representatives with policy-making influence at the political center as well as a means of preventing other groups from potentially capturing the state.

Following years of armed violence, elites in South Africa negotiated a transition from the system of apartheid to democracy.[6] As part of the agreement, federal institutions in South Africa were crafted to accommodate the competing interests of the majority African National Congress (ANC), which sought to put in place a system of centralized government, and the minority National Party (NP), which opposed a strong central government that it would not control. The compromise that was agreed to by the two groups called for a strong central government that

---

[5] See Chapter 12 on Iraq in this volume.

[6] See Chapter 3 on South Africa in this volume.

granted the provinces "exclusive" or "concurrent" power with respect to planning, development, and services, as well as the "specific socio-economic and cultural needs" and "general well-being" of the inhabitants. In addition, the ANC, NP, and the Zulu Inkata Freedom Party (IFP) were guaranteed political control over at least one province, with borders drawn explicitly to produce political majorities in two NP provinces and one IFP province (Inman & Rubinfeld, 2008).

Economic power-sharing provides groups in divided societies access to or control of state resources using rules that mandate the distribution of wealth, income, natural resources, or production facilities based on group identity. Although economic power-sharing rules are generally not structured to achieve a balance in the distribution of wealth and income among groups, they do aim to at least prevent any one community from completely dominating access to or control of state-controlled economic resources.

Economic power-sharing was a central component of the Comprehensive Peace Agreement (CPA) that was signed by the Government of Sudan and the Sudan People's Liberation Movement (SPLM) in 2005 to end a civil war that had been ongoing for twenty-two years. The SPLM attached so much importance to gaining control of resources located in its home region that it negotiated a protocol on wealth sharing fully one year before signing the CPA. A central component of this protocol focused on principles for sharing oil revenue, with 50% of revenues allocated to the Government of Sudan and 50% to the government of Southern Sudan, with producing regions each first receiving a 2% share.

The four types of power-sharing institutions noted above have become an increasingly prominent feature of civil war settlements negotiated in countries of the Global South during the post-World War II period. Interestingly, however, the four types of power-sharing measures have not been evenly distributed among civil war settlements. During the years between 1945 and 2006, political power-sharing was the measure to be included most frequently in civil war settlements, accounting for 34% of total power-sharing measures. Military power-sharing accounted for 30%

of the power-sharing measures appearing in settlements, while territorial and economic types of power-sharing each accounted for 18% of the power-sharing measures agreed to by rival groups.[7]

This distribution of the different types of power-sharing institutions across power-sharing settlements raises the interesting question of why contending groups design such settlements in the manner they do. To some extent, the answer to this question is likely to depend on the particularities of the conflict that the adversaries are seeking to end. For example, not all conflicts lend themselves to the use of territorial power-sharing,[8] a factor that may account, at least in part, for why one sees this form of power-sharing appear less frequently in settlements. Additionally, it has been suggested that economic power-sharing measures see lower rates of implementation than other types of power-sharing, which may explain why one sees fewer such measures included in civil war settlements and why, among all the forms of power-sharing, this is the only one that has always been used in conjunction with at least one other form of power-sharing (Hartzell, 2019).

Although these observations may shed light on some of the variation we see in power-sharing settlements, they do not explain why civil war adversaries seek to include power-sharing measures among the numerous features of war-ending agreements. While scholars have offered a variety of responses to this question, there is general agreement that, in the context of civil wars, rivals seek to adopt power-sharing institutions as a means of providing for their security (Hartzell & Hoddie, 2007; Mattes & Savun, 2009). Groups in countries emerging from civil war have been found to suffer from threats to their physical, political, economic, and cultural/social security (Smith, 2006). These insecurities are often exacerbated by concerns regarding the role that the post-civil war state will play "in mediating or influencing the competition by... groups for security" (Saideman, 1998: 135). Power-sharing institutions can help to mitigate this insecurity by ensuring that no single collectivity controls

---

[7] This distribution of power-sharing occurred across a total of 127 civil war settlements, represented by a total of 53 instances of political power-sharing, 47 of military power-sharing, and 29 each of territorial and economic power-sharing (Hartzell & Hoddie, 2020: 59).

[8] Relevant examples of conflicts that did not lend themselves to territorial power-sharing include Burundi (see Chapter 13 in this volume) and Lebanon (see Chapter 10 in this volume).

all the levers of state power. Power-sharing also enhances the security of weaker groups or those formerly excluded from power by setting limits on the exercise of power and producing a rough balance among groups' access to power.

Empirical evidence in support of the role that insecurity plays in motivating the adoption of settlements that include the types of power-sharing measures noted above comes in the form of studies that find that civil war adversaries are most likely to agree to power-sharing arrangements when seeking to end particularly difficult conflicts (Hartzell & Hoddie, 2015, 2020; Wucherpfennig, 2021). Conflicts that are prolonged, produce large numbers of casualties, and that involve repeated cycles of violence among the parties are likely to produce more acute feelings of insecurity. These feelings of insecurity, Hartzell and Hoddie observe, are "a function of the higher costs associated with such conflicts as well as the realization that, if not checked in some fashion, a rival with sufficient power to engage and match one's forces in a protracted conflict may well be able to inflict further harm once a war is over" (2020: 88–89).

Power-Sharing in Practice

As the preceding discussion makes clear, in contrast to Europe, where the motivation for the practice of power-sharing has been to bolster democracy as a form of conflict management, elites associated with the contending groups that have entered power-sharing arrangements in the Global South generally have not agreed to do so with the goal of establishing democracy. Rather, since most power-sharing agreements in the Global South have been constructed as a means of ending intrastate conflicts, the architects of power-sharing have been motivated by a desire to produce stability and to provide for their security and that of their followers.[9] Accordingly, although some of the power-sharing institutions that have been employed in the Global South—particularly political power-sharing institutions—have roots in the consociational

---

[9] There are a few instances of power-sharing arrangements in the Global South in which measures for sharing power were agreed to not for the purpose of ending armed intrastate conflict but to enable elite cooperation and/or establish or reinvigorate democracy. Relevant examples of such cases include Fiji, Malaysia, and Mauritius. Because the bulk of power-sharing agreements in the Global South have been designed to end armed intrastate conflict, we focus on those in what follows.

and consensus power-sharing measures that have been used in Europe, because the motives for agreeing to power-sharing, as well as the contexts in which it has been implemented in the Global South, are so different, we should expect to see distinctive features where the practice of power-sharing in the Global South is concerned.

Drawing primarily on cross-national studies, we attempt to provide a picture of the practice of power-sharing in the Global South, including some of the post-conflict results or outcomes that have been shaped or produced by power-sharing institutions. We begin by focusing on the question of who has power under power-sharing arrangements.

Who Has Power?

Power-sharing agreements can be conceived of as pacts agreed to by elites. These agreements provide elites with a means of controlling social violence in an effort to protect elite interests. Power-sharing settlements give elites access to some element(s) of state power, thus giving them a means to check each other's ability to use violence against the other as well as a source of patronage they can use to ensure their followers' loyalty (Hartzell & Hoddie, 2020).

The process by which elites construct power-sharing settlements has been described as one that is exclusionary in nature. In one view, power-sharing settlements are made up of the elites who neither represent the views of civilian political parties nor those of the civil society groups. By implication, the concerns and ideas of most ordinary citizens (hence the voices of the marginalized groups) are not considered at the negotiating table, thus disregarding an important political imperative in conflict management (Simuziya, 2021: 58).

Although it is true that citizens and civil society organizations have seldom been represented at the negotiation table, the effects that elite-constructed power-sharing arrangements have on non-elite actors' ability to secure representation of at least some of their interests, and to participate in the political life of their countries, may not be as exclusionary as the process by which such arrangements are reached. One reason for this is, as Hartzell and Hoddie (2020) observe, power-sharing settlements are designed to include elite representatives of groups formerly excluded from power within one or more of the domains of state power. This serves to broaden elite coalitions, making them more representative. This suggests that a greater diversity of group interests should be represented than had previously been the case.

While power-sharing settlements may provide formerly marginalized or excluded groups access to political power, such arrangements generally suffer from what Agarin and McCulloch refer to as the "'exclusion amid inclusion' dilemma" (2020: 4). As they note, settlements constructed to foster stability by including certain groups in the power structure of a country have been predicated on the exclusion of non-dominant groups, including those constructed on the basis of gender, sexuality, and class identities. Power-sharing settlements constructed to be explicitly exclusionary in nature certainly pose a problem. The explicit exclusion from political competition of any political party representing interests other than those embodied in the Conservative and Liberal parties by Colombia's National Front agreement eventually led to armed challenges to the power-sharing arrangement and the emergence of a new civil war. However, in those cases in which power-sharing settlements do not explicitly rule out participation by certain groups, power-sharing institutions may be less inimical to, and may even present opportunities for, the exercise of power by individuals and groups (McCulloch, 2020).

Less explored is the possibility that, over time, power-sharing arrangements may serve to empower citizens and groups to participate in the political arena by enhancing their ability to engage with the political process. This may occur via the inclusion of formerly excluded actors in one or more domains of state power, which promotes more equal access to power among groups, as well as through the potential that the redistribution of state power via power-sharing has to reduce horizontal inequalities in such a way as to enhance individuals' and groups' ability to participate in the political process. Using data from the V-dem project (i.e., the Equal Access to Power Index and the Equal Distribution of Resources Index indicators), Hartzell and Hoddie (2020) find support for these propositions in tests for civil wars fought and ended between 1945 and 2006. Although the effects are not large, inclusion of a wider variety of power-sharing measures in civil war settlements was found to enhance the likelihood that diverse groups would have a greater de facto capacity to participate in politics. Additionally, political, military, and economic power-sharing measures were found to have a positive effect on the equal distribution of resources in post-civil war states, while territorial power-sharing exercised a significant and negative effect.

The potentially empowering effects of power-sharing noted above are not likely to be of such a magnitude as to alter the fundamental nature of power-sharing settlements as arrangements designed to protect elite interests. However, they do suggest that there is a need to focus further on the mechanisms by which power-sharing measures exercise an influence on society. Doing so may help improve our understanding of how to amplify the positive effects that power-sharing institutions produce as well as identify means for societies to minimize or cope with the deleterious effects of power-sharing (Bell, 2018). To that end, in what follows we briefly focus on some examples of how power-sharing institutions influence the exercise of power, providing examples of some of the effects that this has produced.

Effects Stemming from the Exercise of Power Via Power-Sharing Institutions

A growing body of research on power-sharing has sought to move beyond an examination of power-sharing's effects on the durability of peace to understanding how power-sharing measures shape a variety of post-conflict outcomes. Perhaps one of the most contested of these areas of study has been the effects of power-sharing on post-conflict democracy. Critics of power-sharing contend that power-sharing settlements stifle efforts to promote democracy in post-civil war states. Among the central arguments that have been advanced in support of this claim are that allocating positions in government to the leaders of minority groups hinders the ability of voters to use elections to hold politicians accountable (Jarstad, 2008); that apportioning state resources among groups on the basis of a set formula removes issues that should be the stuff of political debates from the political decision-making process (Roeder & Rothchild, 2005a); and that power-sharing arrangements allocate power to violent and often unsavory actors while excluding others from participating in government (Sriram & Zahar, 2010). There is merit to these criticisms of power-sharing. It is certainly the case that, in an effort to end armed conflict and to secure a stable peace, many power-sharing measures impose constraints on competition. However, as noted above, they also promote some degree of inclusion and empowerment, which are also values that many associate with democracy.

Efforts to identify the effects that power-sharing has on democracy in post-conflict states have taken as their starting point the premise that power-sharing settlements are not randomly assigned; rather, they are agreed to as a means of ending or managing particularly challenging conflicts, which often occur in countries with little to no history of democracy. Under such circumstances, argue Hartzell and Hoddie (2020), it is more reasonable to ask whether power-sharing can help facilitate a transition to a minimalist form of democracy rather than the form of liberal democracy that most critics of power-sharing appear to have in mind. Using cross-national data, Hartzell and Hoddie (2020) find support for this proposition: settlements that call for a range of power-sharing measures help to facilitate a transition to minimalist democracy. Additionally, and somewhat unexpectedly, they also find that settlements that include multiple forms of power-sharing have a positive effect on the development of electoral, liberal, and egalitarian democracy in the years following the end of a civil war.

Another criticism that has been made of power-sharing relevant to the exercise of power in the political realm is that it promotes stalemate at the political center, thereby leading to poor governance outcomes (Roeder & Rothchild, 2005b). Lebanon[10] and Iraq[11] are often cited as prominent examples of immobilism induced by power-sharing, resulting in weakened states unable to deliver security and governance. Cammett and Malesky (2012) engage with this issue by investigating the effects of power-sharing institutions on governance five years after the end of civil war. Disaggregating political power-sharing, they posit that executive power-sharing, administrative power-sharing, and the mutual veto are mechanisms likely to promote stalemate and inefficiency, thus producing poor governance outcomes. On the other hand, Cammett and Malesky argue that closed-list proportional representation electoral systems should result in better governance by providing a more institutionalized division of outcomes and thus more checks and balances, as well as "more programmatic party politics and consequently a higher likelihood of public goods expenditures over particularistic benefits" (2012: 988). Employing cross-national data, they find evidence that closed-list proportional representation is associated with improved governance on a range of measures.

Turning to the economic domain of power, Haass and Ottmann (2021) examine the redistributive effects of power-sharing. Noting that

---

[10] See Chapter 10 in this volume.

[11] See Chapter 12 in this volume.

participation in a power-sharing cabinet should provide the elite representatives of rebel organizations with access to state resources, Haass and Ottmann posit that rebel elites will direct resources to their constituencies in an effort to secure their political support. Focusing on subnational development in seven post-conflict countries in Africa, Haass and Ottmann link information regarding ethnic support for rebel organizations with subnational data on ethnic groups' settlement areas and data on night light emissions to test their hypothesis. Their findings indicate that ethnic groups represented by rebels in a power-sharing government manifest higher levels of night light emissions (their indicator for local economic development) than regions lacking such representation. These results, suggest Haass and Ottmann, indicate that post-conflict power-sharing arrangements can be conceived of as rent-generating and redistributive institutions, although whether they serve to alter objective and/or perceived group grievances remains an open question.

Trends in the Adoption and Evolution of Power-Sharing in the Global South: Past, Present... and Future?

Power-sharing arrangements have been adopted by countries in the Global South predominantly to end internal armed conflict and to help secure peace and stability. The political, social, and economic effects engendered by power-sharing institutions should be understood as being conditioned, in no small measure, by the challenging conditions under which actors agree to power-sharing settlements. However, domestic (and regional) conditions are not the only factors that have shaped the adoption—and outcomes—of power-sharing measures in the Global South. As becomes clear if we look at trends in the adoption of such power-sharing measures over time, the international community has also played a significant role in facilitating and implementing war-ending agreements that contain such measures.

The Cold War period following the end of World War II saw a limited number of settlements of civil wars in the Global South. Although some of these settlements contained power-sharing measures, most did not. This is not surprising given that the bulk of the intrastate conflicts ending during this period were terminated via military victory by one party. This pattern changed dramatically with the end of the Cold War, which proved to be a major breakpoint regarding the settlement of civil wars. The end of the Cold War saw a surge in civil war terminations as the superpowers ended their support for proxy wars in the Global South. Additionally, the two decades following the end of the Cold War saw a shift to the use of negotiated peace agreements, the majority of which called for some form of power-sharing, as a means of ending civil wars.

Two factors have been identified as central to the uptake of negotiated settlements as a means of ending civil wars. One of these is the role of mediators, who, by facilitating an exchange of information among conflict parties, can help adversaries reach a war-ending bargain, a role currently taken by the United Nations (UN) in the peace talks for the future of Syria.[12] The dramatic leap in mediation activity following the end of the Cold War, with increased numbers of actors involved in mediation and resources committed to attempting to end civil wars through diplomatic channels, is thought to have influenced the number of negotiated settlements as well as the inclusion of power-sharing measures as part of those settlements (Sisk, 1996). The wider deployment of international peace-keeping forces has also been identified as contributing to the surge in civil wars ending via negotiated settlements (Fortna, 2008), as well as the use of power-sharing (Sambanis, 2020), by acting as a guarantee of the safety of parties to the conflict.

Although several criticisms have been leveled at the use of power-sharing arrangements as a means of ending civil wars, in the absence of viable alternative means of terminating armed conflicts and providing a degree of protection and inclusion for minority groups, power-sharing has remained the default response of the international community where conflict resolution is concerned (Finlay, 2011). Nevertheless, it is the case that the past several years has seen a marked decline in the use of power-sharing agreements as a means of ending civil wars. Once again, factors operating at the level of the international system appear to be contributing to this new trend. Writing nearly a decade ago, Söderberg Kovacs and Svensson (2013) observed that a sharp decline in negotiated agreements had occurred since 2009. They attributed this decline to the re-emergence of the major power rivalry between the US and Russia, a growing disenchantment on the part of the international community with the results of some negotiated peace agreements, and fluctuating funding

---

[12] See Chapter 14 in this volume.

for peacemaking and peacekeeping in the wake of global economic crises. None of these factors, it should be noted, has abated in significance in the years since Söderberg Kovacs and Svensson undertook their analysis. Additionally, the emergence of new trends in armed conflict, including the growing number of non-state armed conflicts and the growing presence of jihadist groups that tend to pursue maximalist demands, raises questions regarding the relevance of power-sharing settlements as a means of ending such conflicts (Pettersson et al., 2021; von Einsiedel, 2017).

Have power-sharing settlements seen their heyday in the Global South? While the answer to that question may depend in no small measure on the willingness of the Global North to advocate for and support the use of power-sharing as a means of ending intrastate conflicts, the behavior of the Global North need not be determinative. High-profile power-sharing agreements have been struck in recent years in Colombia and South Sudan. And the use of power-sharing measures at the local level, a form of conflict resolution that merits further study, is ongoing in parts of the Global South (Mehler et al., 2019).[13] In the interim, efforts to learn more about the nature of power-sharing in the Global South, including those made by the contributors to this book, may help to ensure that power-sharing can be designed and implemented in such a way as to enhance its positive features while minimizing the problematic aspects associated with this form of conflict resolution.

REFERENCES

Agarin, T., & McCulloch, A. (2020). How Power-Sharing Includes and Excludes Non-dominant Communities: Introduction to the Special Issue. *International Political Science Review, 41*(1), 3–14.

Almond, G. (1956). Comparative Political Systems. *The Journal of Politics, 18*(3), 391–409.

Bell, C. (2018). *Political Power-Sharing and Inclusion: Peace and Transition Processes.* Political Settlements Research Program, University of Edinburgh.

---

[13] Heitz (2009) provides several examples of power-sharing at the local level in Man, a city in western Côte d'Ivoire, within the context of the armed conflict that began in that country in 2002. Man has seen the evolution of power-sharing measures between rebels and local community leaders and corporations. Among these measures is a form of political power-sharing centering on a civil society organization. This can be contrasted with power-sharing deals between the government and rebels that have been struck at the national level in an effort to end civil war.

34   C. A. HARTZELL

https://www.politicalsettlements.org/wp-content/uploads/2018/07/2018_
Bell_PA-X-Political-Power-Sharing-Report.pdf

Cammett, M., & Malesky, E. (2012). Power-Sharing in Postconflict Societies: Implications for Peace and Governance. *Journal of Conflict Resolution, 56*(6), 982–1016.

Finlay, A. (2011). *Governing Ethnic Conflict: Consociation, Identity and the Price of Peace.* Routledge.

Fortna, V. P. (2008). *Does Peacekeeping Work? Shaping Belligerents' Choices After Civil War.* Princeton University Press.

Haass, F., & Ottmann, M. (2021). Rebels, Revenue, and Redistribution: The Political Geography of Post-Conflict Power-Sharing in Africa. *British Journal of Political Science, 51*(3), 981–1001.

Hartzell, C. (2019). Economic Power-Sharing: Potentially Potent... but Likely Limited. In C. A. Hartzell & A. Mehler (Eds.), *Power-Sharing and Power Relations After Civil War* (pp. 125–146). Lynne Rienner.

Hartzell, C., & Hoddie, M. (2003). Institutionalizing Peace: Power-Sharing and Post-Civil War Conflict Management. *American Journal of Political Science, 47*(2), 318–332.

Hartzell, C., & Hoddie, M. (2007). *Crafting Peace: Power-Sharing Institutions and the Negotiated Settlement of Civil Wars.* Pennsylvania State University Press.

Hartzell, C., & Hoddie, M. (2015). The Art of the Possible: Power-Sharing and Post-Civil War Democracy. *World Politics, 67*(1), 37–71.

Hartzell, C., & Hoddie, M. (2020). *Power-Sharing and Democracy in Post-Civil War States: The Art of the Possible.* Cambridge University Press.

Heitz, K. (2009). Power-Sharing in the Local Arena: Man—A Rebel-Held Town in Western Côte d'Ivoire. *Africa Spectrum, 44*(3), 109–131.

Inman, R., & Rubinfeld, D. (2008). *Federal Institutions and the Democratic Transition: Learning from South Africa* (NBER Working Paper Series, Working Paper 13733). National Bureau of Economic Research. https://www.nber.org/system/files/working_papers/w13733/w13733.pdf

Jarstad, A. (2008). Dilemmas of War-to-Democracy Transitions: Theories and Concepts. In A. K. Jarstad & T. D. Sisk (Eds.), *From War to Democracy: Dilemmas of Peacebuilding* (pp. 17–36). Cambridge University Press.

Lijphart, A. (1969). Consociational Democracy. *World Politics, 21*(2), 207–225.

Lijphart, A. (1975). *The Politics of Accommodation: Pluralism and Democracy in The Netherlands* (rev. 2nd ed.). University of California Press.

Lijphart, A. (1977). *Democracy in Plural Societies: A Comparative Exploration.* Yale University Press.

Lijphart, A. (1985). *Power-Sharing in South Africa.* Institute of International Studies, University of California.

Lijphart, A. (1999). *Patterns of Democracy: Government Forms and Performance in Thirty-Six Countries.* Yale University Press.

Mattes, M., & Savun, B. (2009). Fostering Peace After Civil War: Commitment Problems and Agreement Design. *International Studies Quarterly, 53*(3), 737–759.

McCulloch, A. (2020). Power-Sharing: A Gender Intervention. *International Political Science Review, 41*(1), 44–57.

McCulloch, A., & McEvoy, J. (2018). The International Mediation of Power-Sharing Settlements. *Cooperation and Conflict, 53*(4), 467–485.

Mehler, A., et al. (2019). The Consequences of Power-Sharing at the Local Level. In C. A. Hartzell & A. Mehler (Eds.), *Power-Sharing and Power Relations After Civil War* (pp. 67–86). Lynne Rienner.

Nantulya, P. (2015, August 5). *Burundi: Why the Arusha Accords Are Central.* Africa Center for Strategic Studies. africacenter.org/spotlight/Burundi-why-the-arusha-accords-are-central/

Nordlinger, E. (1972). *Conflict Regulation in Divided Societies* (Paper No. 29). Center for International Affairs, Harvard University.

Pettersson, T., et al. (2021). Organized Violence 1989–2020, with a Special Emphasis on Syria. *Journal of Peace Research, 58*(4), 809–825.

Rabushka, A., & Shepsle, K. (2009). *Politics in Plural Societies: A Theory of Democratic Instability* (Longman Classics ed.). Pearson Longman.

Roeder, P., & Rothchild, D. (2005a). Power-Sharing as an Impediment to Peace and Democracy. In P. G. Roeder & D. Rothchild (Eds.), *Sustainable Peace: Power and Democracy After Civil Wars* (pp. 51–82). Cornell University Press.

Roeder, P., & Rothchild, D. (2005b). *Sustainable Peace: Power and Democracy After Civil Wars.* Cornell University Press.

Saideman, S. (1998). Is Pandora's Box Half Empty or Half Full? The Limited Virulence of Secessionism and the Domestic Sources of Disintegration. In D. A. Lake & D. Rothchild (Eds.), *The International Spread of Conflict: Fear, Diffusion, and Escalation* (pp. 127–150). Princeton University Press.

Sambanis, N. (2020). *Power-Sharing and Peace-Building* (Working Paper No. 1396). Economic Research Forum. https://erf.org.eg/app/uploads/2020/08/1598532147_921_579348_1396.pdf

Simuziya, N. (2021). Why Power-Sharing Pacts Fail to Hold in Africa: The Case of Somalia and the Paucity of the African Union. *Journal of Somali Studies: Research on Somalia and the Greater Horn of African Countries, 8*(2), 53–72.

Sisk, T. (1996). *Power-Sharing and International Mediation in Ethnic Conflicts.* US Institute of Peace Press.

Smith, J. (2006). Fighting Fear: Exploring the Dynamic Between Security Concerns and Elite Manipulation in Internal Conflict. *Peace, Conflict, and Development, 8.* https://www.bradford.ac.uk/library/find-materials/journal-of-peace-conflict-and-development/Fighting-fear.pdf

Söderberg Kovacs, M., & Svensson, I. (2013). *The Return of Victories: The Growing Trend of Militancy in Ending Armed Conflicts* (Unpublished manuscript). https://paperzz.com/doc/7794997/the-growing-trend-of-militancy-in-ending-armed-conflicts

Sriram, C., & Zahar, M. J. (2010). The Perils of Power-Sharing: Africa and Beyond. *Africa Spectrum, 44*(3), 11–39.

Von Einsiedel, S. (2017). *Civil War Trends and the Changing Nature of Armed Conflict* (Occasional Paper 10). United Nations University Centre for Policy Research. https://i.unu.edu/media/cpr.unu.edu/attachment/1558/OC_01-MajorRecentTrendsinViolentConflict.pdf

Wucherpfennig, J. (2021). Executive Power-Sharing in the Face of Civil War. *International Studies Quarterly, 65*(4), 1027–1039.

CHAPTER 3

The Idea of Power-Sharing in South Africa's Transition from Apartheid to Constitutional Democracy (1983–1993)

Derek M. Powell

POWER-SHARING AND CONSTITUTIONAL CHANGE IN SOUTH AFRICA

Was South Africa's five-year government of national unity (GNU) (1994–1999) an example of successful conflict-resolution through power-sharing, in more limited form than true consociation? Or was the GNU a pragmatic and makeshift transitional arrangement necessitated by the instability and escalating violence in the country after the first attempt at negotiations had failed (1991–1992)? In the literature both explanations can be found, that the GNU represented "success" for power-sharing (Southern, 2020: 282) and that it reflected a "principle born of pragmatism" (Atkinson, 1994b). This contribution examines the idea of power-sharing from a somewhat different angle: as an idea with a constitutional and intellectual history of its own, which must be understood

---

D. M. Powell (✉)
University of the Western Cape, Cape Town, South Africa

© The Author(s), under exclusive license to Springer Nature
Switzerland AG 2024
E. Wassim Aboultaif et al. (eds.), *Power-Sharing in the Global South*,
Federalism and Internal Conflicts,
https://doi.org/10.1007/978-3-031-45721-0_3

37

38   D. M. POWELL

within the historical context in which it had currency, as an argument for fundamental constitutional change in South Africa through consociational power-sharing between groups rather than majoritarian democracy. It focuses on the leading version of that idea, the consociational model proposed by Arend Lijphart, in seeking to understand how plausible South African scholars thought that model was, as an explanation of the conflict and an option for constitutional change. The context for this inquiry is the decisive last decade of political crisis and constitutional change that began with the constitutional reforms of apartheid in 1983 and concluded with the political and constitutional settlement that abolished apartheid and introduced constitutional democracy in 1993/1994, and a new constitution in 1997.

South Africa's political transition was a hard fought for process of political negotiations, conventionally understood to have started with President F. W. De Klerk's "bombshell" speech to parliament in February 1990, "a decisive turning point" in which he unbanned the liberation movements and announced the release of Nelson Mandela and the start of political negotiations (Lawrence, 1994: 7). The transition had two main phases (see generally Atkinson, 1994a; Friedman, 1993; Lawrence, 1994): The first phase of undemocratic multi-party political negotiations (1991–1993) culminated in the interim constitution (Act 200 of 1993) and the first democratic elections, the five-year GNU and the elected Constitutional Assembly/Parliament. In the second phase of democratic constitution-making, the Constitutional Assembly would draft the country's constitution over a period of two years, subject to thirty-four constitutional principles and the procedures for constitution-making and certification that the parties had agreed to in the interim constitution. Following the breakdown of negotiations, which led to an escalation of violence in 1992, the ANC and NP agreed to the GNU, as part of a package of transitional measures, commonly known as the "sunset clauses" (Friedman, 1993: 161). The second phase of democratic constitutional negotiations began after the elections in 1994 and concluded with the promulgation of the final constitution in 1997 after the constitutional court had certified that the revised text (the first version adopted by the Constitutional Assembly failed certification) conformed to the constitutional principles. The GNU was unquestionably one of the crucial compromises in the multi-party political negotiations (1992/1993) and a turning point in South Africa's hard-won transition from apartheid to constitutional democracy. At the time, the GNU was frequently referred to as an interim power-sharing arrangement, even by the ANC, which had previously shunned the idea (Friedman, 1993: 184). It succeeded in bringing the main protagonists in the conflict, namely the African National Congress, the National Party and the Inkhata Freedom Party, into government as partners in cooperative governance, peace-making and constitution-making, after the first democratic elections in 1994. A similar arrangement would also apply to provincial and local governments, though the transition path for local government was somewhat different to that of the national and provincial levels (see Powell, 2017). The GNU was thus a pivotal transitional arrangement that made an orderly and managed transition from the undemocratic political negotiations to the democratic constitutional negotiations possible.

South Africa's conflict over apartheid had long drawn the interest of international scholars of power-sharing, among them Arend Lijphart, a central figure in the country's political debates about constitutional change who wrote extensively about South Africa during this period (see Lijphart, 1980, 1982, 1985, 1989, 1998). For Lijphart, the plausible solution to the conflict lay with a model of consociation or power-sharing that he had developed based on ostensibly similar experience in Europe and elsewhere. His model was founded on three main propositions: South Africa was a plural society that was deeply divided on ethnic group (not racial) lines (1985: 19–36), majoritarian democracy would exacerbate not resolve the conflict and lead to one group dominating others (1985: 19), and the likeliest way out was through a consociational power-sharing model founded on group autonomy, proportional representation, a grand coalition on common affairs and a mutual group veto (1980: 60).

Throughout this period, Lijphart's model was a central point of reference and debate for scholars who supported and rejected power-sharing alike (Murray & Simeon, 2008: 419). Lijphart held up one end of a prominent debate with Donald Horowitz over whether "ethnic particularism" was best achieved through "consociational power-sharing" or a "single-transferable vote" (MacDonald, 1992: 710). It remains so today for scholars who have sought to explain apparent "consociational elements" in the 1993 constitution (Dlamini, 2017) or draw broader lessons about what makes for a "credible power-sharing agreement" (Wantchekon, 2000) or "the pitfalls of power-sharing for minority parties in a new democracy" based on the fate of the National Party (Southern, 2020). In the international scholarly literature, Lijphart's power-sharing theory connects the fields of comparative politics and comparative constitutional law to the ongoing debate about the conditions in which "integration" or "accommodation" become plausible strategies for constitutional design in divided societies (Choudhry, 2008). Lijphart's ideas about consociation were seemingly endorsed by the National Party, which "broadly" based its constitutional reforms in 1983 on principles drawn from the consociational model (Carpenter, 1987: 278). Lijphart himself was critical of "the exclusion of the majority" in the National Party's constitutional proposals, which for him were "a deviation from the principle of consociationalism" (SAIRR, 1982: 4). As late as 1990, some local academics still believed that a variant of the model addressed the reality of the country's communal conflict and offered a plausible third option to the dominance of Afrikaner and African nationalism, a way out of the country's impasse (Giliomee & Schlemmer, 1989, 1989/1990). Critics have attacked the coherence of the consociational model from several different angles, its workability in practice, its over-emphasis on ethnic group identity as the causal explanation of the conflict, and its disregard of the overlap between class and systematic racial engineering (Adam, 1982; Connors, 1996; Macdonald, 1992; Taylor, 1992).

To be sure, like the tricameral parliament introduced by the 1983 reforms before it, the GNU did not strictly conform to Lijphart's model. Communal or ethnic group identity was not the formal basis of constitutional design, not even in the case of the nine new provinces, into which the defunct ethnic homelands were to be incorporated. Cultural and ethnic group identity was "recognized but not empowered" as a fighting political faith (Murray & Simeon, 2008: 409). By 1993, the democratic principle was too firmly entrenched to be displaced by any model of unelected or permanent coalition government of pre-defined groups, and simple majority and ANC control would become the basis of decision-making in the GNU (Atkinson, 1994b: 106). In the interim constitution (see Act 200 of 1993: ss 75–95), there was no grand coalition of leaders representing the major ethnic groups or national communities, no veto for minority parties, not even a formula for consensus-seeking decision-making beyond the constitutional injunction on the President to consult the two Deputy Presidents (from the main opposition parties) on major issues and for decision-making in cabinet to seek consensus (Atkinson, 1994b: 106). Indeed, by 1992/1993 the NP itself had undergone "a paradigm shift," according to its chief negotiator, Roelf Meyer (2001: 58), which saw it moving away from group rights altogether and arguing for "individual rights." Two years later the National Party would leave the GNU; ten years thereafter (2004) the behemoth was gone from national politics altogether. These facts must be given their due weight whenever the "success" or "credibility" of the GNU as a "limited" form of "power-sharing" is chalked up to a theory of power-sharing theory. Writing in 1998, Lijphart (1998: 146) certainly believed that the interim constitution met his four criteria and "was a perfectly consociational constitution." The decade's unity as a specific period of South African constitutional, political and intellectual history subsists in the structural interlinkages that connect these two constitutional episodes to the politics of apartheid and national liberation and the contemporary battle of ideas over whether peaceful coexistence was to be found in group-based power-sharing, majoritarian democracy or constitutionalism.

The integrity and plausibility of the consociational model as explanation of the origin and function of the GNU and which international scholar's theory was the more persuasive are well-treated in the literature and not my concern in this essay. The research question that interests me here is specifically concerned with how Lijphart's theory was received by prominent local scholars in South Africa during this period. How plausible did South African scholars think the model was in that period, as an argument for the political and constitutional changes that took form in 1983 and 1993? To be plausible (as an analytical model and a political project), consociation had to make a winning case around its two main claims, which were that the true nature of the conflict was group-based and ethnic, and that the best constitutional model to resolve the conflict was consociation not majoritarian democracy. Fail on the first and consociation was not a plausible explanation of the conflict in the country; fail on the second and it was not a plausible way to resolve the conflict.

The essay is no more than a foray into this issue and my focus is restricted to two sets of texts published at either end of that historical period. *Constitutional Change in South Africa* (edited by John Benyon) published in 1978 was a verbatim record of the proceedings of a conference that discussed the National Party's initial proposals for what became the 1983 constitutional reforms. *From Apartheid to Nation-Building* (Giliomee and Schlemmer) published in 1989 (with a postscript in 1990) was their contribution to the national debate that preceded and would inform the multi-party negotiations from which the 1993 constitution emerged. Why make these two texts the object of this essay? In the first place, because both texts reflect the contemporary thought of local scholars who were prominent participants in the intellectual and political debates about constitutional change during the period, they offer a snapshot of how a broad cross-section of the local academy understood the power-sharing argument in its political context at that time. Second, because both texts were published slightly before the constitutional changes were introduced, we get some idea about how plausible the argument for power-sharing was when judged against those constitutions, the extent to which ideas about power-sharing were implicated in and discredited by the events they sought to explain and influence 1983, and the limits of power-sharing theory in predicting plausible constitutional change in the country. The third reason is that consociationalism and Lijphart's model were focal points of the debate in both texts.

My method of examination is borrowed from a historian of ideas, Professor Quinton Skinner (1969), which is to read these two texts as specific performative interventions that sought to frame and influence unfolding political events, as situated arguments for or against consociation as a feasible course for change whose explanatory force must be assessed in that context. What we see is that as far back as the late 1970s, many of South Africa's leading scholars were less than sanguine about the workability of consociational power-sharing, in the form that Lijphart or the National Party had proposed, and enthusiasts tended to see the model as either a step towards a constitutional solution in future or one that should be adapted in line with their understanding of the communal nature of the conflict or the process of constitutional change the country needed. Reading these texts as interventions in the political context of that period, one is left with two sharp impressions. One is that consociation was always a theory searching for and not finding a plausible concept of the group upon which to build a broad consensus on power-sharing as an alternative to majoritarian democracy. The other is discredited by the failed reforms of 1983 that took its name without any genuine commitment to its ideas that the consociational model could not gather a national consensus for its aims in 1993 and, in the end, had no major political constituency backing it, not even the National Party.

The first section examines the idea of power-sharing in the context of the reform of apartheid (the 1983 constitution); the second section examines the idea in the context of the transition to democracy (the 1993 interim constitution). The final section relates the South African experience to the wider development of power-sharing theory as a social science.

Power-Sharing and the Reform of Apartheid

Constitutional Change in South Africa collected and published the papers and proceedings of a conference on "the pressing problems of constitutional change" and "constitutional models" for "the desired solution of a more harmonious life for all in the country" that took place in February 1978 at the University of Natal (Benyon, 1978: Inside cover). The political context for that conference on constitutional change mattered because the external context determined and narrowed the field of argument about what ideas for constitutional change were feasible and how so. Three key events defined the immediate political climate in the country in general and the National Party's posture on constitutional reform more specifically. These events anchored and contextualized the academic discussions at the conference.

The first event occurred in 1976, when a part of the country which now forms part of the Eastern Cape Province (then known as the Transkei) became "a state," the first of the so-called TBVC "independent states." Bophutaswana (1977), Venda (1979) and Ciskei (1981) would follow the Transkei to become independent ethnic states (Welsh, 2009: 70). None of these so-called independent states were recognized as such by either the international community, the majority of black South Africans, or the majority of the "citizens" of these states themselves. Thus the conference took place just as apartheid was entering into its so-called high or grand phase, the territorial and political separation of the African population into various independent ethnic states, without their consent, despite their resistance, as deliberate government racial policy. There could be no uncertainty at all about the aim of the government's constitutional policy towards the African population, which the responsible minister had explained to parliament a few days before the conference took place:

> If our policy is taken to its logical conclusion as far as black [African] people are concerned there will not be one black man with South African citizenship...Every black man will eventually be accommodated in some independent new state in this honourable way and there will no longer be an obligation on this parliament to accommodate those people politically. (quoted in Welsh, 2009: 70)

44   D. M. POWELL

The political and legal effect of this policy was that Africans ceased to be citizens of South Africa. They became foreigners with no civic or political rights in their own country who were permitted to stay in white areas only under the most stringent legal restrictions and for as long as they were useful as labor, and they were repatriated to the homelands once they became surplus to economic requirements or were unable to work (Welsh, 2009: 70). Administration of black local affairs was placed under the control of central government appointed boards that were responsible for regulating the lives of black urban residents, which received no funding from the fiscus, and which provided only the most basic services (Brooks & Brickhill, 1980: 318). This was the start of apartheid as a separate development, of systematic racial discrimination that served the economic exploitation of cheap black labour while denying black people any political or civic rights in South Africa (Welsh, 2009: 326). Almost 8 million people were affected (Welsh, 2009: 71). In 1978, this was the constitutional future that awaited all black South Africans.

The second event occurred just two years before the conference, the Soweto uprising of June to December 1976, according to historian David Welsh (who was at the 1978 conference), "a seminal event in the decline of apartheid" (Welsh, 2009: 101). The police used live fire on a peaceful protest by students over the government's decision to make Afrikaans (instead of English) the language of instruction for black education, unleashing a revolt by black youth in Soweto, a township of Johannesburg, that soon spread rapidly to other areas and resulted in the deaths of around 500 people (Brooks & Brickhill, 1980). Widely condemned internationally and locally in the liberal press and by opposition parties and the liberal and radical strata of the English and Afrikaans communities, the police actions demonstrated two things about apartheid. One was the deadly seriousness of the National Party government's intention to enforce its apartheid policy, if necessary, by using state violence (Brooks & Brickhill, 1980:168). The other was that cities were without doubt the "storm centres of today and tomorrow" (Brooks & Brickhill, 305). Why so? Because none of the homelands were economically viable, and a supply of cheap and increasingly also skilled black labour was the very lifeblood of the entire economic and social system in "white" South Africa. The trend in African urbanization was unstoppable and that fact was well-known to apartheid's planners. In 1948, the government appointed Fagan Commission on Native Laws had said in its report that "the idea of total segregation is utterly impracticable...the movement from country to town has a background of economic necessity...[and] cannot be stopped or turned in the opposite direction...[and] that in our urban areas there are not only Native migrant labourers, but there is also a settled, permanent Native population" (Welsh, 2009: 19, author's inserts in brackets). What Transkei and Soweto demonstrated in practice was that the National Party government was doggedly prepared to force an irrational programme of racial engineering on the country which they knew could not work, no matter the cost. The form it took may change but the fact of imposed racial discrimination was not negotiable.

The third development was the reason and immediate context for this conference, the government's proposals to change the Union constitution of 1910 in order to introduce a new three-chamber parliamentary system for white, Indian and coloured racial groups. These proposals were the precursor to what would become the 1983 constitution and ostensibly based on a Lijphartian idea of consociational power-sharing. In his forward, the conference organizer and Vice-Principal of the University, Professor Schreiner, carefully and explicitly linked the purpose of the conference to the proposed constitutional changes as well as the wider political context in South Africa and on the continent. He began by pointing to the paradox (xi) of the political context, which was "a new national consensus "amongst South Africans of all racial groups and of all political persuasions" on the necessity of political change "to extend...those political powers reserved for whites to other South Africans...excluded from the political processes" without there being an agreement on the form of constitutional change that was needed. Three factors obstructed agreement, said Schreiner (xi): first, there was "minimal discussion" and thus no possibility of national consensus among "white and black South Africans"; second, several constitutional models were not only on the table, but constitutional reform was being pushed through "party-political caucuses" without "wide and necessary public debate," and "irreversible steps were being taken" that made national consensus impossible; and third "a new language" of "plural societies" and "consociational government" was being used "by political scientists" to talk about these reforms that was not only unfamiliar to people, but likely to raise suspicion and mistrust that these "were merely methods of excluding from real political power those who were now theoretically to be newly admitted to such power."

The conference was to be "a guide to those who would, in the immediate future, be involved in further debate, negotiation and, ultimately, in the decisions about our future constitution" (Schreiner, 1978: xii–xiii). The participants at the conference, who came from "a wide-spectrum" of society (social groups, business, political parties, homeland administrations) would discuss papers presented by "specialist academic experts from all South African universities." Inclusiveness was clearly intended to be a signature of the conference, notwithstanding the absence of the liberation movements (notably the ANC, whose leadership was in exile, prison or under house arrest after its banning in 1960). According to that list, representatives from the apartheid government and the National Party were not present either. Neither side of the negotiating table that would produce the interim constitution in 1993 were thus in the room. Among the academics who were in the room were some of the most prominent and respected legal scholars and social scientists from the country's white, black, conservative, liberal, radical, English-speaking and Afrikaans-speaking universities, as the case may be. Some of these scholars would later achieve renown as scholars in their field, struggle activists, constitutional advisors during the political transition and even senior officials in the first democratic government of 1994.

The conference's credentials as a guide to South Africa would be its own example—inclusive and representative participation (a microcosm of what national debate should be) in a process of "cooperative discovery of both common purpose and disagreement, of adjustment of views and attempted understanding between South Africans." Schreiner noted one striking absence from the conference, and his words appeared to be carefully chosen. "It must be remembered that, *by virtue of past action* against *individuals and organizations, some views*, which may later prove important in any settlement, could not be represented at the Conference" (xiii) (my italics). The missing views alluded to were those of the liberation organizations (such as the ANC), which the government had banned (the past actions), and their leaders (such as Nelson Mandela), who were in prison for their resistance to apartheid and advocacy of majority rule or in exile. It was the viewpoint of the excluded black majority population that was missing from the programme. It is necessary to keep this context in mind when we look at the discussion of the idea of power-sharing at the conference because it shows the political mountain genuine enthusiasts of consociation would have to climb to make a plausible case for power-sharing arrangements that left white control and racial domination

3 THE IDEA OF POWER-SHARING IN SOUTH AFRICA'S ... 47

intact and excluded the majority of the population whose leadership was committed to liberation struggle and majoritarian democracy. Let us turn our attention to how some of the key experts at the conference viewed the road towards a consociational future.

The discussion on the government's proposals was the centrepiece of the conference, and the structure of that particular panel appears to have been a deliberate attempt to widen the intellectual debate to make it both more inclusive and more critical. First came two papers by constitutional experts, one the leading Afrikaans professor of constitutional law, the other a leading English liberal professor. Then came the presentation of the proposals themselves by a serving MP. The discussant panel that would respond to the presentation comprised one African, Indian and Coloured government official. Finally came a broader discussion chaired by a Professor from one of the historically black universities. The structure and mix of the panels seem too deliberately symbolic not to have been intended to be a message to the government and country about what a rational and inclusive constitutional discussion was. We will begin with a brief snapshot of the proposals, go to the experts, next for their views on the workability of consociation, and then to the discussants to show how the consociational model was received.

The proposals were complex, opaque, still incomplete, but the basic idea, presented by Dr Worrall, was this (Worrall, 1978: 127–135): A new parliament with three chambers would be established, one each for the white, coloured and Indian communities. Each community would have legislative autonomy over and govern its own affairs through its own chamber and executive. All three would co-govern on matters of general and common concern through joint structures, notably a super council of cabinets chaired by an executive president (a new institution) and an advisory president's council that would play a role in law-making, policy and constitutional development. Representation in all these organs would be on the basis of proportionality (4:2:1—white, coloured, Indian), but decision-making would be consensus-seeking, with the president set up as the mediator between groups and conflict-resolution in the legislative process taking place through a variety of interlocking procedure and committees. The ideological and operational logic were to be found in the crucial foundational distinction between own (or group) affairs and general (or common) affairs, which set up the institutional framework for segmental autonomy (separate legislative chambers) and consociation (joint structures for common affairs). Worrall (1978: 130) was explicit about what that logic was, "[t]he main assumptions underlying these proposals are that South Africa is a multi-ethnic society and that in order to achieve democracy in such a society, it is essential, first to acknowledge that diversity and, second, to decentralize or devolve political power to the maximum." International research, he went on to point out, showed that in deeply divided societies, democracy would produce conflict because one group would end up dominating the rest, whereas the successful regulation of "intense conflict" has always involved "conflict-regulating practices: stable governing coalitions, the principle of proportionality, the mutual veto, purposive depoliticization, compromise and concession" (Worrall, 1978: 132). It seemed to be something like what Lijphart had in mind, even though he was not among the references cited: group autonomy and grand coalition, minus the mutual veto, except for the white community that is (because of the 4:2:1 ratio). Much would change in the 1983 constitution, but this distinction between group affairs and common affairs and the consociational tag would remain the axis of the entire scheme.

To meet its own selection criteria and rationale as the only plausible model for the country, this constitutional scheme would have to cross several political–analytical thresholds. First, where precisely did these groups that made up this deeply divided society come from, and who decided that the population, conflict and resolution had to fit precisely those categories? Without a broad consensus on the primacy of the very group categories that were necessary to define and also resolve the conflict, the broad national agreement that Schreiner viewed as essential for successful constitutional change would be absent and, as some participants foresaw, the model would fail. Second, where did the excluded African majority, three-quarters of the population, fit into the scheme for constitutional change? The central conflict in the country was about the political exclusion and economic exploitation of the African population. Third, what about the democracy principle—in terms of how constitutional change was to be undertaken in the society (process) and in terms of the place to be given to majority rule based on universal suffrage as a foundational constitutional principle (substance). Democracy had such high standing in the Western constitutional tradition generally and (Seekings, 2000: 2) in the freedom struggle in South Africa specifically, no alternative model could work that ignored the political ground it claimed and occupied. Should it fail at any of these turns, the consociational idea would be a dead end.

The first of the expert presentations, by Professor Irvine, a leading scholar of liberalism and an active member of the Liberal Party, focused on the core concept of pluralism, which he thought "somewhat elusive" (Irvine, 1978: 94). In essence, Irvine posed two basic questions (1978: 96 onwards) about this ground concept. First of all, what was the fundamental a priori set of facts of the cleavages in this "plural" society that made group-based (non-democratic) power-sharing the only solution to the conflict in this type of society (instead of democratic liberalism)? Why should political interaction in society only occur through groups, and how were those groups to be determined? He found no answer to this question in the literature. He also thought that the science on pluralism was vague and at best inconclusive. As applied in South Africa, he thought that the concept also suffered from analytical incoherence—for example, it ignored the common language that united white and coloured Afrikaners in dividing these two groups on racial lines, disregarded the strong correlation between race and class in South Africa and failed to explain the fact that "even among many blacks who support homeland independence this is regarded as a means towards the end of reunification on a more equitable basis" (Irvine, 1978: 95–99). Secondly, how should those cleavages inform constitutional design? How were these groups to be brought into a common political life and on what terms, differentially or on the basis of equal rights and citizenship? The signs of differential incorporation were obvious, he thought, because neither Indians nor coloureds would enjoy equal rights of citizenship with whites, Africans inside South Africa would have no rights at all and Africans who were citizens of homelands that would remain "enmeshed in the common economy" would be "incorporated into South African society on a differential basis" (Irvine, 1978: 101). Irvine effectively dismissed Lijphart's model and the government's constitutional proposals based on consociation, neither of which, he thought, could ever be taken seriously and accepted "at both the mass and leadership levels" when nothing more than a "more sophisticated form of differential incorporation" (Irvine, 1978: 101).

The second presentation was by Professor Marinus Wiechers. One of the foremost constitutional experts in the country, Wiechers was engaged in constitution-making in what was then South West Africa (Namibia) and would play a key role as advisor in the Namibian constitutional process in the late 80s and later in the multi-party negotiations in South Africa during the 1990s. Wiechers was candid about what he thought

50   D. M. POWELL

were the chief weaknesses of the consociational model and the government's proposals and the better course for constitutional change to take. He thought that the preconditions for consociation to work were both onerous and absent in present-day South Africa, and those were "political maturity and stability," greater social and economic equality and "a deep sense of constitutionalism" (Wiechers, 1978: 112). He criticized the government for failing to act on the Tomlinson Commission's report (1955) that had proposed incorporation of the homelands into the provinces on federal lines, and the Theron Commission report (1976), which favoured direct representation for coloureds and Indians in parliament and joint decision-making (Wiechers, 1978: 114). Instead of going these routes, the government had opted to create "independent states" in "scattered pieces" and "assign citizenship" to "more than half of the South African blacks" in a "country" "in which they do not live and most probably never will regard as theirs" (Wiechers, 1978: 114). Perhaps his most telling criticism was reserved for the category "white group." Of all the groups, the identity of the white group ought to have been the easiest to establish and justify in fact. After all the constitutional proposals were predicated on the idea of the unity of the white community and its fundamentally different group identity to that of the Indian and coloured groups. The distinction between own and general affairs was intended to map onto group boundaries. The white group was to be the fulcrum of the entire constitutional scheme. But what was that white group identity based on, he wanted to know? A common culture and European descent, said Worrall, which he equated to ethnicity, a correspondence he thought "perfectly appropriate" (Worrall, 1978: 131). For Wiechers (1978: 109) the white group itself was a plural society:

> But, for most of the time, the fact that in the white population group South Africa has, in the true continental sense of the word, a truly plural society is totally ignored. The cultural, language and political differences which divide the white people in our country are still very real. It is only when the broader differences based on colour are often conveniently pushed into the background...There is, logically, no reason why there should not be separate Afrikaner and English homelands in South Africa, if provision is made for such territorial units for the different Sotho or Nguni peoples.

3 THE IDEA OF POWER-SHARING IN SOUTH AFRICA'S ...

A similar argument was later raised by Adam (1982: 40–42) and by Gretchen Carpenter (1987: 285), who, writing about the distinction between own and general affairs in the 1983 constitution, observed that "the English- and Afrikaans-speaking sectors of the white group, the two main sub-groups, do not share a common cultural heritage." For leading scholars the group identity that was supposed to be the fulcrum of the consociational scheme was incoherent and implausible. Where did the definition of groups come from? According to Carpenter (1987: 285), the concept of group used in the constitutional proposals was racially defined, taken directly from the Population Registration Act of 1950, the legislated system of racial classification upon which the government's apartheid machinery was built.

What Wiechers had in mind, it seems, was neither a rejection of consociation or a final decision for either consociation or democracy, but rather a "series of progressive settlements" to incorporate other groups, including Africans, into existing structures at provincial and local levels (Wiechers, 1978: 116). Like Lijphart (1980: 67), Wiechers (1978: 116) too thought the failure to incorporate urban Africans into the constitution a major failing, but incorporation was to be a progressive process that started at subnational level, not a sudden and comprehensive change. Stepped stage, he believed, would allow time to experiment with possibilities for "joint representation and power-sharing on these levels before the ultimate task of creating institutions for a central government can be undertaken" (Wiechers, 1978: 116). What he had in mind, it seems, was a process of constitutional development which would allow a broad national consensus to develop over time that one day might lead towards federalism or even towards unitary government on majority lines. For Wiechers (1978: 117), consensus had to be built in this way, constitutional change for the country could not be "simply decided by one political party's ideology," without being perceived as a fraud. Precisely how this stepped process would unfold over time and under whose authority, how long constitutional development should take, how the process would be managed and on what terms, and how the staggered reforms would contain the pressures that were building in and on the country, particularly in the cities, Wiechers did not say.

If the experts were less than sanguine about the prospects for consociationalism, the three panel discussants (ostensibly chosen to "represent" African, Coloured and Indian communities) were of one mind in rejecting the government's proposals as a solution. Faint praise, such as there was, went something like this: at least the reforms were movement towards unification of some kind, after three decades of no movement other than towards outright racial domination and separate development (Rajah et al., 1978: 139). It was a refrain that reformers and apologists for the 1983 constitution would take up throughout the 1980s—however imperfect these steps were they were the start of a process towards the abolition of apartheid that should be given a chance. How the government's virtue signalling action in deciding upon these proposals was to be squared with its practices of actual and continued racial domination and exclusion and its use of deadly force against schoolchildren in Soweto, was not explained. The panellist's lines and methods of attacks were more or less identical, they related the constitutional proposals to the political crisis in the country and found them to be deeply flawed. One panellist, Professor Ngcobo, a serving official in a homeland administration, began by noting the "very awkward position" which he found himself in, on the one hand, expected to respond to constitutional proposals touted for their inclusive aims, on the other hand, excluded from common political life by virtue of racial categories imposed on him by apartheid (Rajah et al., 1978: 144). His own exclusion merely represented the total exclusion of Africans, who (he said) only wanted inclusion in a common society and government based on equal rights, not the independent statehood and nationhood in a racial society that "the white governing party has given them" (Rajah et al., 1978: 146–147). Instead of constitution-making involving "all the population groups," the coloured and Indian communities were being "coerce[d] into accepting this constitution" whether they agreed with it or not, and even if they rejected it (Rajah et al., 1978: 146). The panellists saw the government's failure to address the real issues, as well as its willingness to impose constitutional change unilaterally, as signalling its true motives, which were to perpetuate and entrench National Party control and racism in a modified form (Rajah et al., 1978: 146). Furthermore, the panellists foresaw that this constitutional fraud would have dangerous consequences for the country, "the coloured and Indians are to be assimilated into the white bloc against African people, thereby intensifying racial conflict and group conflict" (Rajah et al., 1978: 140).

In 1983, the government would push these constitutional reforms through parliament over the objection of political parties inside parliament, political organizations outside of parliament, and the scepticism of many leading constitutional experts. The popular rejection of those reforms would confirm the warnings of the conference in unexpected ways and at enormous cost in human life, in the ferocious conflict that ensued in the 1980s to plunge the country into crisis. Inspired by Lijphart's idea of consociationalism, if not fully faithful to them, rather than resolve the conflict in this "deeply divided society," as consociationalists believed, rather than entrench the dominance of National Party and racial rule, as the sceptics argued and the government had ostensibly sought to do, the introduction of the 1983 constitution proved to be the denouement of the entire apartheid system.

Power-Sharing in the Transition to Democracy

"If Adam and other critics were right, one wonders what the decades of conflict in modern South Africa have been all about. The optimistic claims of these critics conflict with the available empirical evidence. As far as we are aware, no single representative political opinion poll conducted among whites has shown that more than 10 to 15 percent of whites are prepared to entertain an undifferentiated mass-based political system" (Giliomee & Schlemmer, 1989/1990: 243). These words appeared in February 1990 in a postscript to a book that Professors Gilliomee and Schlemmer had published just 7 months earlier, in August 1989. The Adam to whom the question was directed was Heribert Adam, who had published a paper in October 1989 in which he had not only rejected the weight [Gilliomee and Schlemmer] gave "to ethnic minority agendas" but thought it highly doubtful "that the majority of whites would want to defend their position as if they were a national identity under threat" (Giliomee & Schlemmer, 1989/1990: 242).

Postscript and date were hugely significant, because the book had been published on the eve of the unexpected and sweeping political changes that President De Klerk would announce in 1990, changes that would culminate a mere four years later in precisely the outcome which the data cited by the authors ruled out and Adam had predicted. Full of interesting observations that are worth much closer study than is possible in this essay, but wrong on the main point, this book was neither a plaintiff cry for the retention of apartheid's racial and ethnic group categories nor a wholesale resurrection of the Lijphart model per se. Before we come to their approach, however, we must briefly consider the very different context in which their proposals were made.

Three domestic political trends were strengthening or well-established at this end of our historical period, and any model of power-sharing would have to respond to these developments to be credible. First, the 1983 constitution had failed. Election results showed little or no support from the coloured and Indian communities. What the attempt to exclude Africans and divide communities racially and constitutionally had done however was to inspire the rise of a non-racial, multi-class, multi-sector mass democratic movement that would have a formidable influence on the course of constitutional and political change, the ANC-aligned United Democratic Front (Seekings, 2000: 2). Reforms to black urban local authorities that were introduced in 1985, for reasons much like those that Marinus Wiechers had suggested in 1978, to integrate urban blacks politically at local (but not national) levels had also failed. Rather than stepped inclusion, the local government reforms inspired massive urban unrest that led to the imposition of several states of emergency, and the rise of civic structures and tactics of resistance in townships that would profoundly influence the negotiations on democratic local government in the 1990s (Seekings, 2000; Powell, 2017). Second, the other side of the negotiating table was beyond doubt. Meaningful political negotiations could not occur or succeed without the committed participation of the ANC, which enjoyed massive popular as well as international support. The era of unilateral constitutional change at the behest of the government or negotiations only with puppet regimes were past (a last attempt at which had failed in 1988). Third, the principle of majoritarian democracy under universal common suffrage was firmly established as the driving principle of the anti-apartheid freedom struggle and there was little doubt that democracy would determine the legitimacy of any constitution-making process and future government.

With the failure of the first round of negotiations came a massive escalation of violence in the country and enormous pressure on the major parties, the National Party especially, to agree on a firm date for democratic elections to instal a legitimate government and constitution-making process (Friedman, 1993: 139). None of these conditions had existed ten years earlier. These shifts in the political context meant that high as it had been in 1983 the political bar for any theory of power-sharing between groups to pass would be that much higher once negotiations got underway. The majority of the population, its leaders (such as Nelson Mandela) and democracy were unquestionably at the high table, and in the ascent, unlike in 1983. Any credible theory of power-sharing would have to confront this new reality even as it sought to rescue the idea of protected group rights and a constitutional pact on a power-sharing consociation from the wreckage of the failed 1983 constitution project. By 1992, group rights would have no committed political champions and remain a rallying point only among fringe right-wing parties, because the National Party itself underwent what Roelf Meyer, its chief negotiator, would later call a "paradigm shift," and it too let go of the idea of group rights for whites or minorities (Meyer, 2001: 56).

What Schlemmer and Gilliomee (1989/1990: 222ff) were proposing was a modified theory of the "bi-communal" nature of the conflict and a variant of the consociation idea, more than an entirely new theory. How were their ideas on this central issue of group identity different from those that had given ballast to the original version that had taken root in 1983? Let's begin with what was gone from the variant compared to the original model: the ethnic group categories used by apartheid, ascribed and enforced group classification, explanations of the conflict that were based purely on race and class, hostility to democracy, even in its majoritarian form, imposed constitution-making, non-recognition of the ANC and liberation movements and the mutual group veto. Apartheid, they discovered, was not an ethnic or racial conflict but rather a communal conflict, or rather a bi-communal conflict, between the two main groups, which they variously called African and Afrikaner nationalism, African and Afrikaner (white) groups or majority and minority blocs.

As before, if the case could not be made on the basis of the unity of the Afrikaner (white) group/bloc/nationalism, there was no case to be made for special recognition of and protection for this group outside of the normal protections for multi-party democracy, the rule of law, constitutionalism and human rights that constitutional democracy ordinarily offered minorities. Weichers, Adam and Carpenter had dismissed the idea that the English and Afrikaners were a unified white group with its own national identity. After 1983 and with the rise of the mass democratic movement, the cleavages within and between English and Afrikaner communities had become even more varied and complex for simple explanations based on racial group demarcations. Whites generally would overwhelmingly vote for constitutional change in 1992 and for constitutional democracy in 1994. Even if the latter events were not yet in sight, the idea that group rights was anything more than a rearguard reaction to obstruct freedom and democracy for the black majority was already drifting from the mainstream of Afrikaner nationalism towards the extreme right-wing fringe of Afrikaner politics.

56   D. M. POWELL

In places opaque or too general and hedged with qualifications, the argument for why this was a communal conflict went like this (Giliomee & Schlemmer, 1993: 222ff): There was no common sense of nationhood. What social data showed instead was that there were two very different ways of life (that of "the majority" bloc and that of "the minority" bloc—primarily but not exclusively black and white blocs). Each of these groups had been socialized into a political culture that was opposed to the other (majoritarian democracy and individual rights v. ethnic self-determination and group rights). The aspirations of the two groups were incompatible (majority rule and socio-economic transformation v. retaining material and symbolic power) and, if there was sudden and comprehensive constitutional change, conflict would ensue between the two blocs. It may be that constitutional democracy would protect minority interests from majority excesses, but constitutional politics would need time to take root and mature, and for the minority there was no safe bet that it would. Because of these risks, change must be managed. A transition period of ten years was necessary for politics to settle into more normalized patterns (presumably before general elections could take place). In that transition, a government of national unity comprised of voluntary alliances between political parties representing the majority and minority blocs (not ethnic groups) would be established. Each bloc would elect its own side and both sides would form a grand coalition on general matters. Parties could also choose to be in a non-aligned bloc. Socio-economic measures would be introduced to lessen inequality between majority and minority. After ten years, a commission (whether it was to be political/elected or technical/appointed was unclear) would take stock of the state of constitutional development and propose an extension of the transition or further constitutional changes. What their idea offered, they argued, was a realpolitik approach that explicitly acknowledged this basic fact about the bi-communal South African conflict and made it the point of departure for theoretical analysis and advocacy.

What criteria would define and distinguish the majority and minority blocs and fix them in place as a grand coalition of autonomous alliances for ten years, how would those alliances be set in place as constitutional forms and by whom? How would the conflict over the NP government's lack of democratic legitimacy be defused by a government of unity that would have to reconcile and address the expectations of the two groups without itself having popular or constitutional legitimacy? These were only some of the blind spots. Moreover the central assumption upon which the whole idea turned was itself unstable, as Adam and Wiechers before, among others, had already pointed out. Their assumption was that without this kind of minimum guarantee for their established interests and way of life, the white minority (and the National Party in particular) would not negotiate itself out of power into "second class citizenship." What exactly the unifying factor was that gave whites as a group that common national identity, such that the communal nature of the conflict must take pride of place as the axis of any negotiated settlement, and general elections and constitutional democracy must be delayed for at least ten years, if not longer, was never convincingly explained, as Adam and others argued, and subsequent events would confirm.

South African Constitutional History and the Idea of Power-Sharing: Concluding Observations

Power-sharing, understood as a constitutional model based on group autonomy and consociation, was an idea that had airtime during the constitutional changes of 1983 and 1993, even though the classical form never had the traction its proponents wanted. These two very different constitutional episodes bracketed a period in the country's political and constitutional history that began with the failed and discredited constitutional reforms which the National Party introduced in 1983 to reform apartheid and drew to a close with the country's transition to democracy under the interim constitution in 1993/1994. I have argued that the significance, influence and limits of the classical Lijphartian idea of power-sharing must be understood in the political context delimited by these constitutional episodes, and understood for what they were, as arguments that were implicated in the political events whose course they sought to explain and influence. I focused on particular prominent local scholars in that period and the conditions in which they thought consociation could inspire broad agreement and be a plausible solution in both constitutional contexts. We saw that the idea would have to cross certain thresholds to be plausible. First it had to explain South Africa's conflict as one between primordial ethnic groups, and in so doing convince the major political parties locked into the conflict and the majority of the population locked out of common political life and seeking inclusion. Second, it must justify consociation as preferable to majoritarian or constitutional democracy that the conflict was ethnic group-based. No ethnic group conflict, no protected constitutional status for groups, no plausible case to make against constitutional democracy.

The first, more general observation I would like to make is that in South Africa at that time these were un-crossable thresholds for power-sharing theory, moreover, the failure to make the case for consociation in 1983 undermined that possibility in 1993. Ironically, the political consequences of that failure contributed to the downfall of the apartheid system which the National Party's version of power-sharing theory had sought to reform, and opened the way for the principle of democracy, which it had sought to thwart. The fact is that the National Party was never in a position to offer a progressive idea of constitutional power-sharing to unite Afrikaners, let alone to rally the English around a unified national identity. Indeed, the constitutional reforms of 1983 had the opposite effect of further dividing Afrikaners (the conservative wing of the NP split) and the white group. Furthermore, the leading establishment scholars thought that the reforms were flawed or deception. Attempts to re-theorize groups along new lines of ethnicity proved to be equally fruitless. As early as 1990, as Giliomee and Schlemmer had observed, there were already signs that the National Party would abandon the concept of ethnic groups in favour of the concepts of majority and minority. When it abandoned group rights in 1992, there was no longer any political champion for the consociational model at the centre of white politics and the idea of group autonomy passed to the fringes of right-wing political parties that were intent on creating an Afrikaner homeland. Nor did the power-sharing proposals in 1983 convince the Indian and coloured communities to support the reforms or seek to include the African majority. Power-sharing had the opposite effect, which was to exclude the black majority from any genuine power-sharing. Thereafter, any attempt to include blacks at lower levels of government through local authorities, devolution and consociation was seen to be a fraud, not genuine inclusion. The power-sharing reforms had unintended consequences that would be their undoing, they inspired the rise of a mass democratic movement, reinforced the ideal of majority rule and democracy and provoked the violent urban unrest that would cause thousands of deaths throughout the transition period and render many urban areas ungovernable. When 1983 and 1993 are understood as connected political events as well as the hermeneutic context in which the case for consociation had to be made and won, we see that the conditions for power-sharing to have any effect on constitutional change no longer existed in 1993. Discredited by major local scholars and all major political parties in the liberation camp, finally, the idea was abandoned even by the National Party itself.

The second observation concerns the relationship between the theory of power-sharing and the political context which that theory sought to explain or influence. Looking forward from 1983 to 1993, the idea that power-sharing could work in South Africa was always a kind of prophecy addressed to the unknown, an idea looking for a reality that conformed. The failure and unintended consequences of that idea in the South African context showed the limitations of prophecy. Looking at that entire period through the lens of historical analysis, we can see why the GNU cannot be convincingly explained in terms of the classical idea of power-sharing, even if only as a deviation from the ideal. To do so we must ignore the historical fact that the idea itself was deeply implicated in the politics of reforming apartheid in 1983, that it was discredited by its association with the exclusion of the majority and political deception, and that it was never able to offer a plausible model of group-based power-sharing that could convince a political majority committed to constitutional democracy to abandon majoritarian democracy under universal suffrage as the legitimating idea of government and constitution-making in the country. We must look rather to the structure of the negotiations as a whole and the terms of the comprehensive pragmatic package-deal that the two main parties, the ANC and the NP, struck in 1992/1993, rather than to a single theory, for a theory that explains the form of the political settlement. But that is a larger project for a book, not for this essay.

References

Adam, H. (1982). Possibilities and Limits of Ethnic Conflict Resolution: South Africa in Comparative Perspective. In Buthelezi Commission, *The Requirements for Stability and Development in Kwazulu and Natal* (Vol. II, pp. 23–40).

Atkinson, D. (1994a). Brokering a Miracle? The Multiparty Negotiating Forum. In S. Friedman & D. Atkinson (Eds.), *The Small Miracle: South Africa's Negotiated Miracle* (pp. 13–43). Ravan Press.

Atkinson, D. (1994b). Principle Born of Pragmatism? Central Government in the Constitution. In S. Friedman & D. Atkinson (Eds.), *The Small Miracle: South Africa's Negotiated Miracle* (pp. 92–120). Ravan Press.

Benyon, J. A. (Ed.). (1978). *Constitutional Change in South Africa*. University of Natal Press.

60   D. M. POWELL

Brooks, A., & Brickhill, J. (1980). *Whirlwind Before the Storm*. International Defence and Aid Fund for Southern Africa.

Carpenter, G. (1987). *Introduction to South African Constitutional Law*. Butterworths.

Choudhry, S. (2008). Bridging Comparative Politics and Comparative Constitutional Law: Constitutional Design in Divided Societies. In S. Choudhry (Ed.), *Constitutional Design for Divided Societies: Integration or Accommodation?* (pp. 3–40). Oxford University Press.

Connors, M. K. (1996). The Eclipse of Consociationalism in South Africa's Democratic Transition. *Democratization, 3*(4), 420–434.

Dlamini, S. (2017). Historical Analysis of Power-Sharing and Consociational Democratic Practice in South Africa. *Ubuntu: Journal of Conflict and Social Transformation, 6*(1), 7–35.

Friedman, S. (Ed.). (1993). *The Long Journey. South Africa's Quest for a Negotiated Settlement*. Raven Press.

Giliomee, H., & Schlemmer, L. (1989). Review: Guidelines and Goals for Resolution. In H. Giliomee & L. Schlemmer (Eds.), *Negotiating South Africa's Future*. Southern Book Publishers.

Giliomee, H., & Schlemmer, L. (1989/1990). *From Apartheid to Nation-Building*. Oxford University Press.

Giliomee, H., & Schlemmer, L. (1993). *From Apartheid to Nation-building: Contemporary South African Debates*. Oxford University Press.

Irvine, D. McK. (1978). Plural Societies and Constitution-Making. In J. A. Benyon (Ed.), *Constitutional Change in South Africa* (pp. 94–106). University of Natal Press.

Lawrence, R. (1994). From Soweto to Codesa. In S. Friedman & D. Atkinson (Eds.), *The Small Miracle: South Africa's Negotiated Miracle* (pp. 1–12). Ravan Press.

Lijphart, A. (1980). Federal, Confederal, and Consociational Options for the South African Plural Society. In R. I. Rotberg & J. Barratt (Eds.), *Conflict and Compromise in South Africa*. David Philip.

Lijphart, A. (1982). Governing Natal-KwaZulu: Some Suggestions. In Buthelezi Commission, *The Requirements for Stability and Development in Kwazulu and Natal* (Vol. II, pp. 76–82).

Lijphart, A. (1985). *Power-Sharing in South Africa*. Institute of International Affairs.

Lijphart, A. (1989). The Ethnic Factor and Democratic Constitution-Making in South Africa. In E. J. Keller & L. Picard (Eds.), *South Africa in Southern Africa: Domestic Change and International Conflict*. Lynne Rienner.

Lijphart, A. (1998). South African Democracy: Majoritarian or Consociational? *Democratization, 5*(4), 144–150.

Macdonald, M. (1992). The Siren's Song: The Political Logic of Power-Sharing in South Africa. *Journal of Southern African Studies, 18*(4), 709–725.

Meyer, R. (as told to H. Marais). (2001). From Parliamentary Sovereignty to Constitutionality: The Democratization of South Africa, 1990–1994. In P. Andrews & S. Ellmann (Eds.), *The Post-Apartheid Constitutions: Perspectives on South Africa's Basic Law* (pp. 48–70). Witwatersrand University Press.

Murray, C., & Simeon, R. (2008). Recognition Without Empowerment: Minorities in a Democratic South Africa. In S. Choudhry (Ed.), *Constitutional Design for Divided Societies: Integration or Accommodation?* (pp. 281–299). Oxford University Press.

Powell, D. M. (2017). *State Formation After Civil War: Local Government in National Peace Transitions.* Routledge.

Rajah, D. S., Curry, D. M. G., & Ngcobo, S. B. (1978). Constitutional Proposals: Panel Discussion. In J. A. Benyon (Ed.), *Constitutional Change in South Africa* (pp. 136–148). University of Natal Press.

Schreiner, G. D. L. (1978). Foreword. In J. A. Benyon (Ed.), *Constitutional Change in South Africa* (pp. xi–xiii). University of Natal Press.

Seekings, J. (2000). *The UDF: A History of the United Democratic Front in South Africa 1983–1991.* David Philip. James Currey. Ohio University Press.

Skinner, Q. (1969). Meaning and Understanding in the History of Ideas. *History and Theory, 8*(1), 3–53.

South African Institute of Race Relations. (1982). *Survey of Race Relations in South Africa.* SAIRR.

Southern, N. (2020). The Pitfalls of Power Sharing in a New Democracy: The Case of the National Party in South Africa. *Journal of Modern African Studies, 58*(2), 281–299.

Taylor, R. (1992). South Africa: A Consociational Path to Peace. *Transformation, 17*, 1–11.

Wantchekon, L. (2000). Credible Power-Sharing Agreements: Theory with Evidence from South Africa and Lebanon. *Constitutional Political Economy, 11*, 339–352.

Welsh, D. (2009). *The Rise and Fall of Apartheid.* Jonathan Ball.

Wiechers, M. (1978). Possible Structural Divisions of Power in South Africa. In J. A. Benyon (Ed.), *Constitutional Change in South Africa* (pp. 107–118). University of Natal Press.

Worrall, D. (1978). The South African Government's Constitutional Proposals. In J. A. Benyon (Ed.), *Constitutional Change in South Africa* (pp. 127–135). University of Natal Press.

CHAPTER 4

Power-Sharing in Colombia: Bipartisanship, Leftist Insurgencies, and Beyond

Ana Sánchez Ramírez and Madhav Joshi

INTRODUCTION

In comparative politics, the form of government is often understood as either power-sharing or power-concentrating. It manifests in the form of the electoral system (majoritarian vs. proportional), the way the government is composed (parliamentary vs. presidential), and the exercise of state sovereignty (unitary vs. federal system) (Cheibub, 2007; Keil et al., 2021; Lijphart, 1999; Norris, 2008). In the civil war termination literature, power-sharing is conceptualized as a way of ending war and political instability to institutionalizing peace by addressing the issues specific to the rebel group's legitimate claim to participate in the government,

---

Present Address:
A. S. Ramírez (✉) · M. Joshi
University of Notre Dame, Notre Dame, IN, USA
e-mail: asanch14@nd.edu

M. Joshi
e-mail: Madhav.R.Joshi.6@nd.edu

© The Author(s), under exclusive license to Springer Nature Switzerland AG 2024
E. Wassim Aboultaif et al. (eds.), *Power-Sharing in the Global South*, Federalism and Internal Conflicts,
https://doi.org/10.1007/978-3-031-45721-0_4

63

their security concerns, and access to economic and territorial power (Hartzell & Hoddie, 2003, 2007).

Informed both by the comparative politics and civil war termination literature, this chapter conceptualizes power-sharing as institutional arrangements designed for broad participation in government that include mechanisms to safeguard political participation and access to economic resources (e.g., land reform and land title). We explore and discuss the case of Colombia, which has a history of sharing power with political oppositions through institutional arrangements. As such, this chapter will provide a general overview of the evolution and institutionalization of power-sharing that dominated Colombian politics for over a century.

The first part of the chapter explains the early practice of sharing power as a way of managing contestation of access to political power between conservatives and liberals. The second part of the chapter discusses the emergence of the leftist insurgency and how the historical practice of sharing power with other political forces has uniquely influenced the power-sharing arrangements negotiated in peace agreements with various insurgent movements between 1984 and 2010. The third part presents the power-sharing elements in the 2016 peace agreement negotiated with FARC and offers a glimpse of the implementation of those power-sharing elements. The conclusion section provides key insights and the significance of power-sharing in Colombia.

POWER-SHARING IN THE BIPARTISAN SYSTEM (1905–1974)

The history of power-sharing in Colombia reaches back to the mid-nineteenth century when the cleavages between the liberal and conservative parties first came to the center of national politics. Following independence from Spain in 1819, the novel republic faced numerous civil wars motivated by a complex combination of local, regional, and national disputes (González, 2014: 186). The War of the Supremes from 1839 to 1841, initially prompted by local disputes in the Colombian south, is considered to have first outlined the differences between the incipient parties (Bushnell, 2009: 76). Five subsequent armed conflicts (in 1851, 1854, 1861, 1876, and 1885) consolidated the liberal and conservative partisan identities around questions of economic modernization, education, federalism versus centralism, and the relationship of the Catholic Church with the state (González, 2014: 192–195; Moreno et al., 2010:

187–205). Liberals sought electoral reforms in 1898 to ensure participation in the government. The failure of this initiative resulted in a new armed confrontation known as the Thousand Days' War (1899–1902). Since 1880, and for half a century, the Conservative Party would preserve power in open alliance with the Catholic Church.

Mazzuca and Robinson contend that the introduction of power-sharing mechanisms in the early twentieth century was the determining factor of social order between 1905 and 1948 in Colombia (2009: 285–321). They suggest that the 50 years of the "Conservative Hegemony" from 1880 to 1930 can be divided into two periods. The years preceding 1905 were marked by violent bipartisan confrontations. That year, moderate factions of both parties successfully passed the incomplete vote reform to halt violence. This passage led to a period of peace that extended until the late 1940s because the incomplete vote, which allocated 2/3 of Congress seats to the winning party and 1/3 to the runner-up, successfully prevented armed rebellion from the Liberal Party in this period. This was true even in the face of increasing presidentialism in the immediate passage of the reform and later indications of electoral fraud in 1922. The period also signified a visible reduction of state repression in the hands of the conservative government. In 1929, liberals and a faction of conservatives passed the quotient rule electoral reform that allowed for proportional representation of parties in Congress. The arguments in favor of the reform often invoked the need to include third forces in the government. Despite this new power-sharing institutional design, the end of the Conservative Hegemony in the 1930 election led to an outburst of armed confrontations in the departments of Santander and Boyacá that left around 10,000 casualties (Guerrero, 1991; Guzmán et al., 1962: 24–33).

Tensions continued in the 1930s and 1940s, with violence escalating significantly after 1946. After the assassination of the liberal presidential candidate Jorge Eliécer Gaitán on April 9, 1948, the country entered a period of large-scale bipartisan confrontations. Liberals and conservatives throughout Colombia, especially in the rural areas, engaged in extermination campaigns of their political opponents. The death toll was such that the period became known simply as *La Violencia* (The Violence). Mazzuca and Robinson attribute this outcome to the fact that the incomplete vote is better suited for "oligarchic governments" (2009: 316). Once economic modernization took hold in the early decades of the twentieth century, the authors argue, the institutional form of bipartisan power-sharing proved unable to address any democratic demands from emerging political actors. Simultaneously, the authors contend that since the 1920s the parties became more invested in the profits of the presidential office rather than the legislature, which transferred the bulk of partisan rivalry to controlling the executive branch. The 1929 reform, therefore, had been unsuccessful in preventing partisan cleavages and popular demands for democratization from resulting in violence once again.

As the civil war escalated, internal fractures in the Conservative Party led to a military coup in 1953 that deposed the government of Laureano Gómez and appointed General Gustavo Rojas Pinilla as president (González, 2014: 275). Seeking to pacify the country, Rojas issued amnesty and pardon laws and negotiated peace agreements with armed groups in the Colombian plains. Despite these efforts, violence continued for the rest of his period. Rojas' government soon proved authoritarian by censoring the press, repressing social protest, and creating intelligence agencies with a distinct anticommunist purpose (Beltrán, 2019: 20–47). Although the elites had initially supported the military government, by 1957, sectors from both parties became increasingly concerned with the onslaught of violence in the Colombian countryside and with Rojas' intentions to stay in power for another four years. General opposition to the government soared and Rojas retired in May, leaving a military *junta* in the presidential post. Simultaneously, the conservative Laureano Gómez and the liberal Alberto Lleras had begun working on a new power-sharing agreement that could put an end to both the dictatorship and the civil war.

The focus on the presidency that had grown in the years before "The Violence" was at the center of the consociational pact between liberals and conservatives in 1958. Gómez and Lleras issued the Sitges Declaration in July 1957 and set in motion the agreement known as the *Frente Nacional* (National Front). The agreement included parity for twelve years in Congress, the cabinet, and other public administration posts. Furthermore, it required 2/3 votes for decisions in Congress until 1968; allocated veto power to both parties over government expenses; and most significantly, established alternance in the presidency between the parties for twelve years (Daly, 2014: 335; Hartlyn, 1988). In December 1957, the military *junta* called for a plebiscite to ratify the bipartisan agreement. Colombians voted over 90% in favor of the power-sharing measures and in 1958 Alberto Lleras took office as the first president of the National Front (Daly, 2014: 335). In 1959 the alternance in the presidency was extended until 1974, and in 1968 Congress decided that there would be parity in public administration until 1978. The agreement had therefore established clear deadlines for the mechanisms expected to provide government stabilization and national pacification. Throughout the 1960s, however, the first leftist insurgencies of FARC, ELN, and EPL emerged in the country. Amid the escalating armed conflict, some scholars contend that there was a de facto National Front until the 1991 Constitutional Assembly derogated Article 120 of the Colombian Constitution, which required adequate and equal participation in public administration for the runner-up party (Archila, 2003: 87).

From its beginning in 1958 to its formal ending in 1974, the National Front was upheld by both parties, albeit with some internal factionalism. The distribution of public posts configurated what has been called a "limited democracy" in Colombia (Dávila, 2002: 48–97). Some scholars have underscored that the power-sharing agreement was slightly flexible, allowing the inclusion of a few other political forces within the electoral lists of the traditional parties (Daly, 2014: 347). Yet others have challenged this reading of flexibility, arguing that the factions in the Liberal Party for instance, could not sufficiently incorporate the more radical movements and organizations that consolidated in Colombia at the time (Archila, 2003: 90). Electoral competition was thus heavily restricted to intra-party disputes. The National Front period was also characterized as one of high concentration of power in the executive branch as the Doctrine of National Security and the "internal enemy" ideology took hold in Colombian politics (Archila, 1997: 89–22). During the 16 years of presidential alternance, liberal and conservative governments alike used the legal figure of the state when under allegations of coup threats and when threatened by the existence of subversive forces.

With the National Front in place, the bipartisan divide subsided from the motivations for political violence (Hurtado, 2006: 100). However, this failed to prevent armed confrontations from continuing as the first communist guerrillas emerged in Colombia since the mid-1960s. The scholarly debate is still open on the reasons behind this reappearance of violence in the country. Historical partisan hatreds, underlying grievances, political exclusion outside the bipartisan divide, and internal party fractures between elites and middle managements are among the proposed causal mechanisms behind the cycle of armed confrontations that the National Front was unable to contain (Daly, 2014: 341). For the purposes of this chapter, however, it is not necessary to arbitrate this debate. Instead, the qualitative differences between The Violence (a bipartisan confrontation) and the internal armed conflict (multiple rebel forces seeking to overthrow the Colombian government) suffice to argue that the consociational system between the Liberal and Conservative parties was successful mostly at the elite level of the traditional parties (Hurtado, 2006: 100). The National Front left numerous popular demands unattended, some of which found expression in the guerrilla organizations that took central stage in the political struggle for the remainder of the twentieth century. Furthermore, the National Front configured a new cleavage in Colombian politics between the supporters and critics of the 1958 consociational agreement (Gutierrez & Ramirez, 2004: 231). This new scenario posed additional challenges for the power-sharing agreements advanced during the late 1980s and early 1990s in Colombia.

Leftist Insurgency, Partial Peace Agreements, and Power-Sharing

After its formal ending, the National Front left an imprint in the Colombian political system and its institutional outlook. These legacies were visible, for instance, in the recurrent use of the state of siege by the liberal and conservative governments from 1974 onward. Under the state of siege the executive branch allocated itself extra-constitutional powers meant to quell the multiplying insurgent armies in the country. This legal figure also allowed for repressive policies against non-violent social protest and the political persecution of leftist organizations. For example, in 1978, the liberal government of Julio Cesar Turbay issued Decree 1923, also known as the Security Statute. Among other dispositions, the Statute granted special faculties to the military to apprehend, interrogate, and prosecute civilians suspected of crimes of rebellion (Jiménez, 2017: 83). This and other measures signified an effective constraint for third party forces to enter the electoral scene in Colombia. Furthermore, although factionalism increased within the traditional parties, once electoral competition between them was reinstated, electoral preferences continued to indicate their predominance in public posts (Gutierrez & Ramirez, 2004: 237).

By accommodating ideological differences in the government, the Conservative and Liberal parties managed to alleviate political instability at the political center. However, this failed to alleviate the staggering levels of economic inequality and grievances of Colombia's rural and marginalized communities. In fact, the political elites agreed on exclusionary bargaining over land rights in the early part of the twentieth century that institutionalized this inequality (Flores, 2014: 7). The elite power-sharing that dominated the second half of the twentieth century deepened the vertical inequality further. The Colombian countryside became fertile grounds for the onset and persistence of leftist insurgencies.[1]

Figure 4.1 provides an overview of politically organized armed groups that existed or came into existence from the second part of the twentieth century until 2020. As seen in the figure, more and more politically organized armed groups emerged in the 1960s and 1970s. Within a few years of the onset of the Revolutionary Armed Forces of Colombia (FARC) insurgency, leftist groups like the National Liberation Army (ELN) and Popular Liberation Army (EPL) organized violence in the Colombian countryside. In the 1970s, groups emerged with increased support and a larger presence in urban centers, such as the Movement April 19 (M-19) and the Workers' Self-Defenses (ADO). In the early 1980s, the Revolutionary Workers' Party (PRT) and the Quintín Lame Armed Movement (MAQL) appeared. Internal divisions and fractionalization in many of these groups contributed to a further increase in the number of rebel forces in this period. The diversification of the guerrillas in Colombia responded to their various ideological leanings, social composition, and territorial incidence (Pizarro, 1991: 8).

By 1984, there were at least seven active guerrilla groups in Colombia. It was also in 1984 that the government started negotiating with these groups in an effort to achieve their demobilization. The Colombian government negotiated the Uribe Agreement with FARC in March 1984 and the Corinto Accords with EPL and M-19 in August 1984. ADO adhered to these two agreements in a separate ceasefire accord later that month. Although the agreements did not terminate these conflicts, they can be seen as a prelude to sustained negotiations with various armed groups that marked a decline in the number of insurgent groups in Colombia. The sustained dialogues resulted in at least 20 peace agreements negotiated between 1984 and 1994 with all significant insurgency movements, including FARC, ELN, EPL, M-19, and the breakaway

---

[1] One of the key factors for the sustenance of the insurgency is illicit drugs, which is not the focus of this chapter. For more on the significance of illicit drugs, see Rabasa and Chalk (2001) and Holmes et al. (2006).

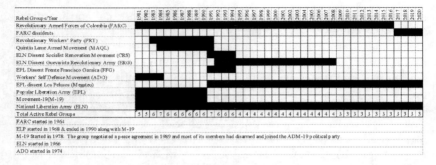

Fig. 4.1 Number of active armed groups with stated political incompatibility

factions of these groups.[2] While the peace agreements negotiated with these groups were not comprehensive enough as defined in comparative peace process literature (Joshi & Darby, 2013), the EPL and M-19 stopped fighting in 1990. Two other groups, the PRT and MAQL, stopped fighting in 1991. The negotiations processes also contributed to fractionalization within the ELN and EPL, and three different splinter groups emerged. Two of these three groups negotiated peace agreements and stopped fighting in 1994. As shown in Fig. 4.1, the number of active rebel groups declined significantly, although the two major groups, FARC and ELN, continued fighting. Since 1994, negotiations persisted with FARC, ELN, and the Guevarista Revolutionary Army (ERG). The ERG stopped fighting in 2008 after a demobilization agreement. The peace agreements negotiated with these groups contained some elements of power-sharing that have been found to be essential for securing peace in the post-accord period.

Scholars of civil war termination have identified that power-sharing mechanisms incentivizes armed rebel movements to negotiate a peace agreement (Hartzell & Hoddie, 2003, 2007). Such provisions address uncertainties related to their future and the cause they were fighting for. In advancing this line of research, Hartzell and Hoddie outline four types of power-sharing arrangements in civil war peace agreements: political power-sharing, military power-sharing, economic power-sharing, and territorial power-sharing. Their research suggests that power-sharing has a

---

[2] Table 4.1 provides a list of peace agreements.

4 POWER-SHARING IN COLOMBIA: BIPARTISANSHIP, LEFTIST ...   71

cumulative effect on durable post-war peace (Hartzell & Hoddie, 2003, 2007: 318–332). Not all elements of power-sharing are present in the peace agreements negotiated in Colombia until 2008. Nevertheless, an in-depth study of 35 peace agreements that were negotiated between 1984 and 2008 reveals that the signatories attempted to address two underlying causes of the conflict: political exclusion and economic marginalization. These agreements are presented in Table 4.1.

With respect to the issue of political exclusion, the Colombian state and the armed rebel groups negotiated provisions specific to amnesty and electoral reforms. Among 35 peace agreements negotiated with various groups between 1984 and 2008, eleven peace agreements had amnesty provisions and 13 had electoral reform provisions with six agreements having both. While amnesty in a war-to-peace transition can be interpreted as a strategic option for the government (Daniels, 2021: 401–408), it is a key factor that also enables former rebel leaders to compete for political office.[3] Without amnesty, rebel combatants would not be able to return to their civilian lives and aspirant leaders would not be able to compete in elections.

Amnesty and electoral reforms applied to members of FARC under the Uribe Agreement. As preconditions for the full demobilization of the group, the accord allowed for a period of verification of the ceasefire in which FARC could create a formal political party and participate in elections, which culminated in the creation of the Patriotic Union (UP) in 1985. The emergence of the UP coincided with a process of decentralization that had allowed for popular elections of mayors in Colombia since 1986. This opportunity to partake in local electoral competition made evident the growing support to the UP throughout the country, which in turn made UP militants the targets of a violent reaction (Sánchez, 2018: 169). Between 1986 and 1987, the assassination of UP members represented 60% of the political violence in the country. During the first five years, this violence was "selective[ly] being deployed, mainly, in the territories in which the group had receive[d] greater popular support and positive electoral results" (Vargas, 2021: 1359). What became known as the "UP genocide" (Sánchez, 2018: 19) negatively impacted the peace process between the government and FARC, eventually resulting

---

[3] The practice of amnesty, however, is not new in Colombian politics. The liberals and conservative parties frequently used pardons and amnesty to resolve their conflicts in the late and early parts of the 20 century (González, 2014).

72   A. S. RAMÍREZ AND M. JOSHI

Table 4.1 List of Peace Agreements negotiated with armed insurgent groups in Colombia

Rebel groups	Date	Agreement name (short)
FARC-EP	3/28/ 1984	Uribe Agreements
M-19, M-L, EPL	8/24/ 1984	Corinto Accords
ELN	12/9/ 1985	Accord Between the Commission of Peace and National Liberation Army
FARC-EP, ADO, ELN	3/2/ 1986	Agreement on the Extension of the Truce
M-19	11/2/ 1989	Political Pact for Peace and Democracy (Government, m-19, Liberal Party, Legislative Chambers, Catholic Church)
M-19	3/9/ 1990	Political Agreement Between the National Government, Political Parties, and the m-19
PRT	1/25/ 1991	Final Agreement Between the National Government and the PRT
EPL	2/15/ 1991	Agreement on E.p.l. Camps – National Government
EPL	2/15/ 1991	Final Agreement Between the National Government and the Epl
MAQL	3/6/ 1991	Agreement Between the National Government and Maql
FARC & ELN	5/15/ 1991	Cravo Norte Agreement
MAQL	5/27/ 1991	Final Agreement Between the National Government and the Maql
FARC, ELN, EPL	6/6/ 1991	General Agenda and Calendar of the Complete Negotiation Process
CRS, EPL	3/20/ 1992	Agreement Between Commands Ernesto Rojas and National Government
EPL	2/15/ 1994	Agreement Between the Government and the EPL
CRS	4/9/ 1994	Current of Socialist Renewal (Crs)
Various Militias	5/26/ 1994	Final Agreement for Peace and Conviviality, National, Departmental, and Municipal Government and the Militias of Medellín
FFG - Dissent of EPL	6/14/ 1994	Francisco Garnica Front
FFG - Dissent of EPL	6/30/ 1994	Final Agreement National Government Francisco Garnica Guerrilla Coordination Front

(continued)

Table 4.1 (continued)

Rebel groups	Date	Agreement name (short)
ELN	11/1/1997	Agreement for the Liberation of the Oea Delegates
ELN	2/9/1998	Declaration of Viana
ELN	7/15/1998	Puerta Del Cielo Agreement
MIR-COAR	7/29/1998	Final Agreement Independent Revolutionary Movement-Armed Commandos
FARC	5/2/1999	Caquetania Agreement
FARC	5/6/1999	Common Agenda for the Path to a New Colombia
ELN	10/30/2000	Agreement Between the Government and the National Liberation Army (Eln)
FARC	2/9/2001	Los Pozos Agreement Between the Government of Colombia and Farc
FARC	10/5/2001	San Francisco De La Sombra Agreement to Define and Consolidate the Peace Process
ELN	11/24/2001	Accord for Colombia Between Colombian Government and Eln
FARC	1/20/2002	Accord for a Timetable for the Future of the Peace Process
FARC	2/7/2002	Agreement on the National and International Involvement at the Table of Dialogue and Negotiation
AUC[a]	7/15/2003	Santa Fe De Ralito Agreement to Contribute to the Peace of Colombia
AUC	5/13/2004	Fátima Agreement with AUC
ERG	8/2/2008	Agreement with the Guevarista Revolutionary Army
FARC	8/26/2012	General Agreement for the Termination of the Conflict
FARC	11/24/2016	Colombian Final Agreement

[a]The AUC was a confederation of paramilitary groups formed in 1997. The agreements signed with the AUC were strictly circumscribed to DDR provisions, excluding amnesty or power-sharing mechanisms. Given the distinct character of these paramilitary organizations and the lack of power-sharing provisions in these agreements, in this chapter we focus on agreements signed with the insurgent guerrillas.

in the breakdown of the ceasefire agreement between the parties in 1987 (Villarraga, 2009: 447).

Comprehensive partial peace accords followed a different trajectory than the Uribe Agreement. All four rebel groups that ceased fighting between 1990 and 1994 negotiated amnesty and electoral reform provisions with some power-sharing elements. Unlike power-sharing in a transitional government as commonly negotiated in civil war peace agreements (Ottmann & Vüllers, 2015: 327–350), parties in Colombia seemed to favor electoral reforms and special representation of the insurgent groups through special districts. For example, the 1990 Political Agreement with Movement-19 has the following specific provision with respect to power-sharing:

> 2. To promote the incorporation of guerrillas into civilian life and their transfer from the armed struggle to political life, they pledge to support the establishment, only once, of a Special Peace District for political parties emerging from insurgent movements that are demobilized and reincorporated into civilian life. This District for the Senate of the Republic and the House of Representatives will apply no later than the 1992 elections, and its features will be defined among the signatories in the posterior Agreement.

The peace negotiation processes of the 1980s, along with popular demands for democratization, coalesced in the 1991 National Constituent Assembly (ANC) that proclaimed a new Colombian constitution. The recently demobilized M-19, constituted in the Democratic Alliance M-19 (AD M-19) party, was able to capitalize on its urban presence and achieve significant representation in the ANC (Hurtado, 2006: 100). The 1991 agreement with the EPL allowed two spokespersons in the ANC with the possibility of them moving up to become permanent delegates with full rights in the same assembly after the surrendering of weapons took place. MAQL and PRT, which both also demobilized that year, were able to have representatives in the ANC. FARC, ELN, and an EPL dissidence, grouped under the Guerrilla Coordination Simón Bolívar, proposed to the government to allocate their group 20 seats in the ANC without disarming their members (ibid.). The government's denial of this proposal demonstrated how the provisions of power-sharing were a central bargaining point in the negotiations. The 1991 constitution condensed hopes that with more participation violence would decrease. However, the persistence of the major insurgent groups and the escalation of paramilitary violence curtailed these expectations (ibid.: 102). Among its progressive measures in terms of power-sharing, the ANC established a pluri-partisan system, created the Special Indigenous Circumscription, and disrupted the disproportionate concentration of power in the executive (Gutierrez & Ramirez, 2004: 229).

Economic power-sharing, as commonly understood in civil war peace agreements, involves sharing revenue from extractive resources (Hartzell & Hoddie, 2003: 318–322). While illicit mining was a key driver for conflict in rural Colombia and indigenous communities were disproportionally affected (Idrobo et al., 2014: 83–111; Rettberg & Ortiz-Riomalo, 2016: 86–96), revenue sharing was not negotiated in peace agreements. The economic marginalization issue was addressed through agrarian reforms initiatives, with elements of land redistribution in some instances. Out of 35 peace agreements, however, only seven contained provisions specific to land reform or agrarian reform. Three out of four rebel movements that were terminated between 1990 and 1994 negotiated land or agrarian reform provisions. Although a previous partial agreement included mention of economic inequality issues, the final peace agreement with M-19 did not include agrarian or land reform provisions. Furthermore, the low levels of implementation of these provisions showed the general reluctance of the Colombian elites to advance significant economic reforms to reduce inequality; a situation only reinforced by the "economic opening" of the 1990s (Álvarez, 2006: 256–272).

Power-sharing mechanisms in the 1980s and 1990s established through partial peace agreements between the government and the guerrillas constituted substantial incentives for the disarmament of some of these groups. The timeline established for these mechanisms, however, was significantly shorter than the provisions of the National Front and therefore offered no guarantees that the democratic opening represented in the ANC and other participation benefits would extend into the future. For instance, after the ending of the Special Peace District and the Special Territorial Circumscription for Peace, the AD M-19 party quickly faded from electoral politics by the late 1990s (Patiño et al., 2009: 83–88).[4] The experience of the UP offers a further cautionary tale about the dire

---

[4] The Special Peace District was ratified in Transitory Article 12 of the 1991 Constitution as a one-time measure in the 1991 Congress elections. The Special Territorial Circumscription for Peace was part of the government's strategies to strengthen the

consequences that can follow from the stagnation of peace negotiation processes. Having endured a violent reaction to its legal political party, FARC would remain an active guerrilla group for almost three more decades. Economic power-sharing failed to materialize in the accords of this period and the lack of comprehensive reforms in this realm continued to be invoked by the guerrillas as motivations for the armed struggle. The issues of political exclusion and economic inequality lingered in the peace negotiation agenda in the 1990s and reemerged in the peace process with FARC in Havana, Cuba that began in 2012.

POWER-SHARING IN CONTEMPORARY COLOMBIA: THE 2016 PEACE AGREEMENT

Over the decades preceding the 2016 agreement between FARC and the Colombian government, the parties made several attempts to advance peace negotiations. Dialogues with the CGSB resumed even before the passage of the 1991 Constitution, first in Caracas, Venezuela and later in Tlaxcala, Mexico. The parties initially achieved an agenda agreement in this cycle of negotiations including the issue of political participation of armed groups.[5] However, the process quickly deteriorated given the lack of consensus on the priorities of the agenda, and the peace talks ended by June 1992 (García-Durán, 1992: 499–572). Following a period of escalation of the armed conflict in the mid-1990s, FARC and the government initiated formal negotiations once more in 1998.[6] The parties decided on a negotiation agenda that considered electoral and political reform, with a special focus on equal participation of the opposition and minority groups in elected posts.[7] As part of the peace process, the Colombian government agreed to demilitarize a zone in the Meta department; however, this condition was not formalized as a provisional territorial power-sharing agreement. Instead, the "distension zone"

---

implementation of the accords in 1994 and guaranteed seats at Municipal Councils of 199 towns and cities for members of the demobilized guerrillas.

[5] See: Caracas Agenda, 1991.

[6] After the dissolution of the CGSB the government and the ELN also attempted negotiations without arriving at a comprehensive peace agreement by 2021.

[7] See: Common Agenda for the Path to a New Colombia, 1999.

4 POWER-SHARING IN COLOMBIA: BIPARTISANSHIP, LEFTIST ... 77

was the subject of much controversy and contributed to the deterioration of the negotiations. Allegations that FARC was using the zone to reinforce its military strength and the parties' inability to agree on prisoner exchange resulted in the end of these negotiations (Villarraga, 2015: 139–179). Starting in 2002, the incoming government adopted a distinct approach to the armed conflict, focusing on military strategy rather than peace dialogues. During this period, armed confrontations between the government and FARC continued.

The parties began a rapprochement first made public in 2012. The government had initiated the process since 2010 through the opening of communication channels with the FARC secretariat (Oficina del Alto Comisionado para la Paz, 2018: 34). In 2012, the parties held eight rounds of private exploratory meetings developing an agenda for the peace negotiations. On August 28, 2012, they signed the "General Agreement for the Termination of the Conflict and the Construction of a Stable and Lasting Peace" and agreed that on 12 October of that year, they would begin formal peace talks. The second point of the agenda was political reform. In 2013, after completing discussions on the rural development item of the agenda, the parties began negotiations on political participation. On 6 November, the parties announced they had arrived at an agreement on the subject, entitled "Political Participation: Democratic Opening to Build Peace." The agreement on political participation included provisions for the free exercise of political opposition, democratic mechanisms for citizen participation at various scales, and effective measures for promoting larger participation of vulnerable populations with equal opportunities and security guarantees. This preliminary agreement was later ratified in the 2016 final accord. The agreement includes far-reaching reform initiatives in terms of agrarian reforms and rural development never seen in modern times in civil war settlements. From a power-sharing perspective, the 2016 Colombian Peace Agreement is also unique in a number of dimensions.

First, unlike in other peace agreements with power-sharing arrangements, such as in Nepal, FARC did not receive direct access to the executive branch of the government. Instead, they shared political power in the form of political representatives in the Colombian Congress. After completing the demobilization process and transitioning into a political party, the Revolutionary Alternative Common Force (FARC party), the FARC party received five seats in the 108-member Senate and five seats in the 178-member House of Representatives in July 2018. As provided in the agreement, the Colombian Congress passed an amnesty law in December 2016 granting amnesty to FARC members and state armed forces eligible for general amnesty or pardon and were not required to go through the Special Jurisdiction Peace (JEP) process. Accordingly, 80% of FARC and armed force members qualified for general amnesty (Peace Accords Matrix Barometer Initiative, 2019, 2021). Based on this law, the qualified FARC prisoners were pardoned and released.

Second, the agreement also created 16 Special Transitory Peace Electoral Districts for two electoral periods, meant to encourage conflict victims themselves to represent their conflict-affected communities. As such, the legislative power was shared both with the FARC party and the victims of the conflict. Although not implemented as of November 2020, as noted in the Peace Accords Matrix Barometer Initiative report on the implementation of the 2016 Colombian Peace Agreement, this is the first time a peace agreement provides political space for the victims in the legislative branch of the government.

Third, the signatories of the 2016 Peace Agreement in Colombia agreed to create a Security and Protection Corps to protect the legal activities of the new political party emerging out of the FARC rebel movements and its combatants. In a war-to-peace transition, military power-sharing with the rebel groups provides assurance of safety and security for rebel leaders and combatants (Hartzell & Hoddie, 2003). But the 2016 Colombian peace agreement, instead of incorporating FARC combatants into the existing security agencies, creates a new body:

> The National Government shall create a Security and Protection Corps, in accordance with what is established in this agreement, with a mixed composition, consisting of trusted personnel from the new political movement or party that emerges from the transition of the FARC-EP to legal activity, which shall coordinate and have a direct contact with the National Police, which shall in turn appoint contacts for each security and protection scheme, at national, departmental and municipal level according to the operating scheme established.[8]

As of 2019, this form of power-sharing is fully completed, with over 80% FARC ex-combatants holding guard positions out of the 1129 total guards (Iniciativa Barómetro Matriz de Acuerdos de Paz, 2019).

---

[8] See: Colombian Final Agreement, 2016.

Fourth and finally, the agreement has elements of economic power-sharing that include provisions specific to land title distribution, totaling 3 million hectares over the next 10 years. According to the latest Peace Accords Matrix Barometer Initiative report, the land fund is established and operational. Although the 2016 Colombian Agreement does not have provisions specific to territorial power-sharing, it includes a significant number of local-level initiatives intended to implement programs specific to territorial development plans (PDET), crops substitution, and its alternatives (PNIS and PISDA).

The power-sharing mechanism in the 2016 Colombian peace agreement devises institutional mechanisms for FARC to share legislative power for two electoral cycles while it transitions to a political party. The qualified FARC combatants and prisoners also received amnesty and the pardons necessary for the FARC party to organize and participate freely in the democratic process. The agreement guarantees the exercise of political opposition and provides safeguards for political participation. The creation of the Security and Protection Corps can be viewed as a security guarantee necessary for the political participation of the opposition in the democratic process. The land distribution and territorial development initiatives involving the bottom-up processes can be viewed as economic and territorial power-sharing. FARC does not have access to economic resources or power at the local level. But these two dimensions of power-sharing address the underlying grievances of economic inequality and underdevelopment of the Colombian countryside. Except for the political and military power-sharing arrangements, the implementation of economic and territorial power-sharing arrangements remains a long-term priority.

CONCLUSION

The history of power-sharing in Colombia offers insights about these mechanisms' effect in political stability and armed conflict prevention. In the Colombian case, consociational pacts have been historically focused on political power-sharing rather than military, economic, or territorial. First, we observe how bipartisan cleavages between liberals and conservatives led to cycles of violence for over a century, which only subsided with a two decade-long enduring power-sharing agreement. The National Front, however, has been long criticized for excluding third party forces from electoral participation. Thus, restricting democracy for the benefit of two majority parties incited other forms of contentious politics in the 1960s.

Second, the partial peace agreements of the 1980s and 1990s demonstrate that the insurgent guerrillas pursued power-sharing mechanisms in these accords to address the underlying causes of the conflict. The National Constitutional Assembly of 1991 served as an incentive in the negotiations and led to the definitive demobilization of four guerrillas. Nonetheless, the short durability of these provisions was an obstacle to sustain political inclusion and democratic opening into the future. After the special jurisdiction provisions expired, the political parties that had emerged from the demobilized guerrilla organizations tended to disappear from electoral participation. Furthermore, the continuation of the armed conflict with the two largest groups (FARC and ELN), in addition to the paramilitary escalate of the 1990s, reinforced violent political exclusion, as exemplified in the UP genocide. Power-sharing mechanisms with rebel groups therefore demand a significant commitment with security provisions for former combatants or they can produce the opposite effect and heighten violent confrontations.

Third, the 2016 comprehensive peace agreement between the government and FARC included provisions that can configure power-sharing at the political, military, economic, and territorial level. These provisions have a longer temporal horizon than those envisioned in the partial peace accords of the previous decades. As one of the innovative features of the 2016 agreement, these power-sharing mechanisms go beyond the signatory parties to include victims of armed conflict. The Peace Accord Matrix Barometer Initiative has found more progress on political and military power-sharing mechanisms than economic and territorial ones. Looking back at Colombia's experiences with power-sharing in the twentieth century indicates that the comprehensive implementation of these provisions has the potential to address the underlying causes of the armed conflict and assist in political stability and sustainable peacebuilding in the country.

REFERENCES

Álvarez, J. (2006). Las reformas estructurales y la construcción del orden neoliberal en Colombia. In A. Ceceña (Ed.), *Los desafíos de las emancipaciones en un contexto militarizado* (pp. 247–284). Consejo Latinoamericano de Ciencias Sociales (CLACSO).

Archila, M. (1997). El Frente Nacional: una historia de enemistad social. *Anuario Colombiano de historia social y de la cultura, 24*, 189–215.

Archila, M. (2003). *Idas y venidas, vueltas y revueltas. Protestas sociales en Colombia 1958–1990.* Instituto Colombiano de Antropología e Historia (ICANH) and Centro de Investigación y Educación Popular (CINEP).

Beltrán, M. (2019). La dictadura de Rojas Pinilla (1953–1957) y la construcción del "enemigo interno" en Colombia: El caso de los estudiantes y campesinos. *Revista Universitaria De Historia Militar, 8*(17), 20–47.

Bushnell, D. (2009). Política y partidos en el siglo XIX. In G. Sánchez & R. Peñaranda (Eds.), *Pasado y presente de la violencia en Colombia* (pp. 73–80). La carreta editores.

Cheibub, J. A. (2007). *Presidentialism, Parliamentarism, and Democracy.* Cambridge University Press.

Daly, S. (2014). The Dark Side of Power-sharing: Middle Managers and Civil War Recurrence. *Comparative Politics, 46*(3), 333–353.

Daniels, L. (2021). Stick Then Carrot: When Do Governments Give Amnesty During Civil War? *International Studies Quarterly, 65*(2), 401–408.

Dávila, A. (2002). *Democracia pactada: el Frente Nacional y el proceso constituyente de 1991 en Colombia.* Lima: Institut Français d'Études Andines.

Flores, T. (2014). Vertical Inequality, Land Reform, and Insurgency in Colombia. *Peace Economics, Peace Science and Public Policy, 20*(1), 5–31.

García-Durán, M. (1992). *De La Uribe a Tlaxcala. Procesos de Paz.* CINEP.

González, F. (2014). *Poder y violencia en Colombia.* Editorial Pontificia Universidad Javeriana.

Guerrero, J. (1991). *Los años del olvido. Boyacá y los orígenes de la Violencia.* Tercer Mundo Editores and Instituto de Estudios Políticos y Relaciones Internacionales (IEPRI) Universidad Nacional de Colombia.

Gutierrez, F., & Ramirez, L. (2004). The Tense Relationship Between Democracy and Violence in Colombia, 1974–2001. In J. Burt & P. Mauceri (Eds.), *Politics in the Andes: Identity, Conflict, Reform* (pp. 228–246). University of Pittsburgh Press.

Guzmán, G., Fals, O., & Umaña, E. (1962). *La violencia en Colombia: estudio de un proceso social Tomo 1.* Ediciones Tercer Mundo.

Hartlyn, J. (1988). *The Politics of Coalition Rule in Colombia.* Cambridge University Press.

Hartzell, C., & Hoddie, M. (2003). Institutionalizing Peace: Power Sharing and Post-Civil War Conflict Management. *American Journal of Political Science, 47*(2), 318–332.

Hartzell, C., & Hoddie, M. (2007). *Crafting Peace: Power-Sharing Institutions and the Negotiated Settlement of Civil Wars.* Pennsylvania State University Press.

Holmes, J. S., De Pineres, S. A. G., & Curtin, K. M. (2006). Drugs, Violence, and Development in Colombia: A Department-Level Analysis. *Latin American Politics and Society, 48*(3), 157–184.

Hurtado, M. (2006). Proceso de reforma constitucional y resolución de conflictos en Colombia: El Frente Nacional de 1957 y la Constituyente de 1991. *Revista de Estudios Sociales, 23*, 97–104.

Idrobo, N., Mejía, D., & Tribin, A. (2014). Illegal Gold Mining and Violence in Colombia. *Peace Economics, Peace Science and Public Policy, 20*(1), 83–111.

Iniciativa Barómetro Matriz de Acuerdos de Paz. (2019). *Tercer Informe sobre el Estado de Implementación del Acuerdo de Paz de Colombia*. Universidad de Notre Dame, Notre Dame, IN. https://peaceaccords.nd.edu/wp-content/uploads/2020/09/090919-Informe-3-1.pdf

Jiménez, C. (2017). El Estatuto de Seguridad, la aplicabilidad de la doctrina de la Seguridad Nacional en Colombia. *Colección, 20*, 75–105.

Joshi, M., & Darby, J. (2013). Introducing the Peace Accords Matrix (PAM): A Database of Comprehensive Peace Agreements and their Implementation, 1989–2007. *Peacebuilding, 1*(2), 256–274.

Keil, S., & McCulloch, A. (Eds.). (2021). *Power-Sharing in Europe: Past Practice, Present Cases, and Future Directions*. Palgrave Macmillan.

Lijphart, A. (1999). *Patterns of Democracy: Government Forms and Performance in Thirty-Six Countries*. Yale University Press.

Mazzuca, S., & Robinson, J. (2009). Political Conflict and Power Sharing in the Origins of Modern Colombia. *Hispanic American Historical Review, 89*(2), 285–321.

Moreno, O., García, L., & Clavijo, J. (2010). Nacimiento del bipartidismo colombiano: pasos desde la Independencia hasta mediados del siglo XIX. *Estudios Políticos, 37*, 187–205.

Norris, P. (2008). *Driving Democracy: Do Power-Sharing Institutions Work?* Cambridge University Press.

Oficina del Alto Comisionado para la Paz. (2018). *Biblioteca del proceso de paz con las FARC-EP. Tomo I. El inicio del proceso de paz: la fase exploratoria y el camino hacia el acuerdo general*. Presidencia de la República, Oficina del Alto Comisionado para la Paz.

Ottmann, M., & Vüllers, J. (2015). The Power-Sharing Event Dataset (PSED): A New Dataset on the Promises and Practices of Power-Sharing in Post-Conflict Countries. *Conflict Management and Peace Science, 32*(3), 327–350.

Patiño, O., Grabe, V., & García-Durán, M. (2009). El camino del M-19 de la lucha armada a la democracia: una búsqueda de cómo hacer política en sintonía con el país. In M. García-Durán (Ed.), *De la insurgencia a la democracia. Estudios de caso*. CINEP.

Peace Accords Matrix Barometer Initiative. (2019). *Implementation of the Colombia Peace Accord: A Comprehensive Report after Two Years Executive*

Summary. University of Notre Dame, Notre Dame, IN. https://peaceacco
rds.nd.edu/wpcontent/uploads/2021/12/190418-Executive-Summary-of-
the-Kroc-Institute-Barometer-Report-3.pdf

Peace Accords Matrix Barometer Initiative. (2021). *The Colombian Final Agreement in the Era of COVID-19: Institutional and Citizen Ownership is Key to Implementation*. University of Notre Dame, Notre Dame, IN. https://peaceaccords.nd.edu/wp-content/uploads/2020/09/091620-Reporte-4-Digital-.pdf

Pizarro, E. (1991). Elementos para una sociología de la guerrilla colombiana. *Análisis Político, 12*, 7–22.

Rabasa, A., & Chalk, P. (2001). *Colombian Labyrinth: The Synergy of Drugs and Insurgency and Its Implications for Regional Stability*. Rand Corporation.

Rettberg, A., & Ortiz-Riomalo, J. (2016). Golden Opportunity, or a New Twist on the Resource-Conflict Relationship: Links Between the Drug Trade and Illegal Gold Mining in Colombia. *World Development, 84*, 82–96.

Sánchez, G. (2018). *Todo pasó frente a nuestros ojos: El genocidio de la unión patriótica 1984–2002*. Centro Nacional de Memoria Histórica.

Vargas, A. (2021). *Acción para la conciencia colectiva: La defensa de los derechos humanos y las luchas por la configuración de la justicia en Colombia, 1970–1991*. Editorial Universidad del Rosario.

Villarraga, A. (2009). *Biblioteca de la Paz-1986–1990. Se inician acuerdos parciales. Pacto Político con el M-19*. Fundación Cultura Democrática.

Villarraga, A. (2015). *Biblioteca de la Paz-1980–2013. Los procesos de paz en Colombia, 1982–2012. Documento Resumen*. Fundación Cultura Democrática.

CHAPTER 5

Power-Sharing Processes in Post-Arab Spring Tunisia: From Elite Compromise to Presidential Monopolization

Julius Dihstelhoff and Moritz Simon

INTRODUCTION

In the context of the so-called Arab Spring, Tunisia is considered the only country in the Middle East that has experienced a relatively successful formal democratic transition since 2010/2011, managing not only to initialize it, but also to consolidate it. Such consolidation can largely be traced back to an elite compromise (*Itifaq al nukhba*), which began during the power vacuum that occurred in the immediate wake of the 2010/2011 transformation process to facilitate power-sharing.

J. Dihstelhoff (✉)
Philipps-Universität Marburg, Marburg, Germany
e-mail: julius.dihstelhoff@uni-marburg.de

Merian Centre for Advanced Studies in the Maghreb, Tunis, Tunisia

M. Simon
Goethe Universität Frankfurt Am Main, Frankfurt Am Main, Germany

© The Author(s), under exclusive license to Springer Nature
Switzerland AG 2024
E. Wassim Aboultaif et al. (eds.), *Power-Sharing in the Global South*,
Federalism and Internal Conflicts,
https://doi.org/10.1007/978-3-031-45721-0_5

This specific format of power-sharing in the "democratic lighthouse of the Arab world," which was especially prominent between 2011 and 2018, was largely shaped by a rapprochement between the two separate party structures and officials of the secular-laicist bloc around the Nidaa Tounes party and the Islamist Ennahda party. This format of power negotiation between different segments of the political elite can be linked to various works from the literature. As the "father of the power-sharing concept" Arend Lijphart has pointed out, "[C]ooperation at the elite level could overcome the conflict potential inherent in [...] deep cleavages" (Lijphart 2008: 2). *Compromise* is first understood in very general terms as a feature of human relationships and interactions, a practical activity that is essential for maintaining social ties and the flow of exchanges and transactions (cf. Chérif, 2016; M'rad, 2016, 2018; Nachi, 2017; Netterstrøm, 2015; Zghal et al., 2016). In politics, this is translated into a form of agreement and regulation among elites that presupposes mutual action, negotiation, cooperation, and concessions. Ideally, this aims to contribute to social regulation and conflict resolution while asserting principles of pluralism—the coexistence of sociopolitical forces with conflicting interests and goals (ibid.). Looking at Tunisian governance in the post-Arab Spring period, political scientist Amel Boubekeur, for example, refers to it as "bargained competition" (Boubakeur, 2016: 124). Thierry Brésillon, an independent French journalist living in Tunisia, uses the term "pacted transition" (Brésillon & Meddeb, 2020; Brésillon, 2018) to make a similar point: Specific deals, i.e., personal negotiation processes of decisions that take place inside and outside formalized structures. Inherent in both concepts is that they describe a political system in a Tunisia-in-transition that, after the adoption of the constitution in 2014, corresponded, at least formally, to an institutional democracy over the past decade.

However, since 2018, the decline of the Tunisian post-Arab Spring elite compromise as a power-sharing system could be observed. This began with an increasing fragmentation of the centers of power and culminated in the abolition of the previous division of powers in favor of a presidential monopoly on power.[1]

---

[1] For a simplified illustration, a table showing the main milestones of the power-sharing processes in post-Arab Spring Tunisia is provided as Appendix to this chapter.

By means of sociohistorical reflection, the characteristics of the Tunisian format of *power-sharing*, i.e., the elite compromise, will be specified in terms of its (1) "adoptability" (*"How power-sharing has been adopted?"*), (2) "functionality" (*"How has it been functioned?"*), and (3) "end-ability" (*"How has it ended?"*) (McCulloch, 2021) in a three-step process: First, following "adoptability," an overview of the formation of the elite compromise in post-Arab Spring Tunisia is provided. In this context, the specific conditions under which power-sharing was agreed to, particularly in the early phase of Tunisia's transformation process, and the political actors involved in it, form the core of the analysis. This is followed by an examination of "functionality"—the functional implementation in the sense of the development and adaptation of the elite compromise over time regarding the institutional structure. Here, we will focus on the design of the elite compromise based on and in interaction with the constitution. Finally, we will focus on the Tunisian-specific "end-ability" of the power-sharing system, mainly the central problematics and challenges that led first to the decline and then to the dissolution of the elite compromise. From there, we both conjecture about the Tunisian state's ability to reform its power-sharing rules and assess the longevity of the elite compromise.

How Has It Been Adopted?—Establishing the Elite Compromise in Post-Arab Spring Tunisia

The central challenge in post-Arab Spring Tunisia was finding a *generally accepted* political arrangement to fill the power vacuum created by the fall of Ben Ali. This was addressed by creating a compromise between different segments of the political elite. The convergence between opposing party structures and officials, the secular-laicist Nidaa Tounes and the islamist Ennahda, made this "elite compromise" (*Itifaq al nukhba*) possible *as a specific format of power-sharing* (Dihstelhoff, 2019). In this context, Dihstelhoff (2019) specifies that the political actors involved developed overarching narratives shaped by three metaphorical leitmotifs: "national unity" (Wahda wataniya), "national consensus" (Ijmaa' watani), and "national reconciliation" (Al Mussalaha al wataniya). In addition, the descriptions of this compromise mentioned at the beginning as "bargained competition" (Boubakeur, 2016) and "pacted transition" (Bras & Gobe, 2017; Brésillon, 2018) have a long tradition at the democratic-theoretical level. Here, "pacted transition" was defined, for example, by O'Donnell and Schmitter (1986) as an "[...] explicit, but not always publicly explicated or justified, agreement among a select set of actors which seeks to define (or better, to redefine) rules governing the exercise of power on the basis of mutual guarantees for the 'vital interests' of those entering into it" (cited in: Hamann, 1997: 111). The basic reasoning is that elite compromise increases the chances of establishing and consolidating a democracy because "[...] elites from the previous autocracy and its opposition reach a stalemate and find themselves compelled to respect each other's interests" (Schmitter 1994 in: Hamann, 1997). Following this view that compromise can be counted as constitutive of the functional logic of any democratic experience, Nachi (2017) understands elite compromise to be simultaneously a promise to lay the foundations for a rule of law based on pluralism and democracy. Hamann (1997) sees the most important function of "pacted transitions" in the reduction of uncertainties she diagnoses in transition processes from three different sources, which in turn can be conflated with the conceptual three-steps from the power-sharing literature: (1) uncertainty regarding political actors, their strategies and preferences with regard to the emergence of a particular power-sharing format; (2) uncertainty regarding rules and institutions following the functional implementation of the established power-sharing system; and (3) uncertainty regarding political "outcomes," taking into account the longevity and the capacity of the power-sharing system to be incorporated and delimited in the sense of a reform capacity of the state together with its actors.

In order to outline the different actors and camps in the Tunisian power-sharing process, the following section first examines the early phase of the transformation process, which is characterized by the efforts of Tunisian party leaders to reintegrate themselves into a future political order.

Power-Sharing in Direct Response to the Fall of Ben Ali

To examine the initial distribution of power in post-Arab Spring Tunisia, we must first, following Hamann's (1997) assumption that systemic transition processes are accompanied by uncertainty, consider two central contexts of this early phase of Tunisia's transformation process:

1. The "ancien régime politique" attempted to regain hegemony over the very young revolutionary process in the first two months

between January 14 and March 15, 2011, in response to the fall of long-term ruler Ben Ali. Thus, the transitional government under the provisional leadership of the new prime minister and interim president, Mohammed Ghannouchi, attempted to provide supposed state security and preserve the existing state order while allowing state institutions to continue to function. Using tactical compromises, Ghannouchi attempted to gain the necessary legitimacy as Ben Ali's successor (Nachi, 2017: 78). However, the population mobilized in counter-protest during the sit-ins known as "Kasbah I" and "Kasbah II." The following seven months (March 15–October 23, 2011) saw the development of essential foundations for democratization, such as principles, norms, and practices (cf. Chouika & Gobe, 2015, 82). In response to the protestors' central demand and with the assumption of office by the new interim president, Fouad Mbazaa, free elections were announced on March 3, 2011, with the goal of electing a Constituent Assembly. To prepare for these elections, a new technocrat government was to be named, which began its work under Béji Caiid Essebsi on March 7, 2011. In a very short time and in a consensual manner, this new government drafted a decree to regulate the provisional organization of public institutions on March 23, 2011, pending the establishment of a Constituent Assembly. This replaced the constitutional order based on the 1959 constitutional text with a new legal order endowed with revolutionary legitimacy (Nachi, 2017: 79). However, the first compromises among the transitional elite did not occur until March 15, 2011, with the establishment of the Haute Instance pour la Réalisation des Objectifs de la Révolution (HIROR), an informal, temporary, and unelected advisory body. The HIROR consisted of two sections—a council of more than 150 representatives from different sectors of Tunisian society and a council of experts consisting of 21 lawyers (*Le Monde Afrique*, 2011). Despite its focus on deliberation, this proto-parliamentary body was subsequently also responsible for controlling the government and electing the members of the electoral authority, the Instance supérieure indépendeante pour les éléctions (ISIE). In addition, proposals for legal foundations for the organization of the transition process were among its core tasks (Nachi, 2017: 79ff.). On this basis, the initial political formulation after Ben Ali's fall can be seen as the result of a broad public sociopolitical discourse, while witnessing polarization between supposedly "revolutionary" and "anti-revolutionary" attitudes (M'rad, 2015).

2. The elections to the Constituent Assembly (ANC) on October 23, 2011, can be seen as a first litmus test for all parties in post-Arab spring Tunisia. The islamist Ennahda party won, which then went in search of political partners to form a future government. However, the ideological and political polarization between "secular-laicist or anti-Islamic" and "pro-Islamic" elements overlapped the sociopolitical dividing lines between supposedly "revolutionary" and "anti-revolutionary" values (Boubakeur, 2016: 110ff.; Netterstrøm, 2015), making the search difficult. After no party achieved an absolute majority following the ANC elections, a so-called troika government was formed, with the three presidents divided among the coalition members. The prime minister for the islamist Ennahda, the president of the state for the secular Congrès pour la République, and the speaker of parliament for the secular Ettakatol party (Nachi, 2017: 80). The troika can be seen as a first attempt to unite the conservative bourgeoisie, which represents Ennahda's social base, and part of the secularized "modernizing" elite (Dihstelhoff, 2019: 240).

Power-Sharing Through a "Historic Compromise"

After the elections to the Constituent Assembly, the process of negotiating individual constitutional articles between October 2011 and January 2014 proved controversial and protracted. With the overarching goal of achieving greater balance in Tunisia's political field, Béji Caiid Essebsi founded Nidaa Tounes in June 2012 because he (1) anticipated the danger of fragmentation in the secular-islamist party spectrum due to too many micro-parties and (2) feared that Ennahda would become too dominant in the party structure (Essebsi & Chablot, 2016: 46). The challenges and problems in the constitution-making process raised awareness among members of the secular modernizing elite and the Ennahda party that only significant concessions could establish a lasting climate of consensus. This awareness made a "historical compromise" (Merone & Cavatorta, 2013: 311 f.; Nachi, 2017: 30; Zghal et al., 2016) between two societal projects that went beyond temporary alliances possible. Its basis was a dialectical approach (Dihstelhoff, 2019: 239ff.):

1. The historical compromise involved Ennahda recognizing the Bourguibist discourse of "Tunisité." In Bourguiba's understanding, the discourse of "Tunisité" served to establish secularism as an undisputed, hegemonic national reference (Chérif, 2016). This privileged the predominantly francophone social groups engaged in the colonial economy, while devaluing and excluding religious actors, and the arabophone, more conservative elites, the large landowners, and the southern tribes from the discourse.[2] Essebsi expanded the idea of "Tunsité" to be understood as a culture of modernity and consensus in the sense of a "vertu médiane" (Essebsi & Chablot, 2016: 29), a non-negotiable republican political model that, according to its own statements, rejects political, ideological, and religious extremism.

2. Furthermore, the elite compromise is based on the willingness of the secular modernizing elite to retain Article 1 of the constitution from Tunisia's first constitutional text of 1959, while the rest of the constitutional text completely dispenses with references to Islam (Dihstelhoff, 2019: 240). For example, the January 26, 2014, constitution states, "Article 1: Tunisia is a free, independent, and sovereign state; its religion is Islam, its language is Arabic, and its order is the republic" (Constitute, 2017). On this basis, Essebsi makes the outcome of the negotiations clear: "*Nous avons ouvert la voie de la démocratie en terre d'Islam. Il n'y aura pas de retour en arrière*" (Essebsi & Chablot, 2016: 211).

The core concern of the Tunisian elite compromise is twofold: On the one hand, it is about reestablishing a political order that unifies Tunisia's political field in the national interest (Essebsi & Chablot, 2016: 37, 53). On the other hand, reconciliation between democracy and Islam plays an elementary role (ibid.: 9). Overall, the dialectical core of this compromise

---

[2] Similar social structural patterns already characterized the history of Tunisia, around the time of the French withdrawal and thus in the context of Tunisian independence in the 1950s, in which the disputes over the positions and decisions of the Bourguibists and Youssefists, determined the Tunisian liberation movement (Lübben, 2017).

in Tunisia is made up of both the mutual recognition of historical analogies, especially the achievements of Habib Bourguiba, and the connection of the secularly connoted bourguibist discourse of "Tunisité" with Islam.

Arguably the most important key initiative in forging and sealing the elite compromise and paving the way for the adoption of a consensual constitutional text on January 26, 2014, was the first secret meeting between the main political players—the "two sheikhs" (Abderrahmen, 2018)—Essebsi and Ghannouchi on August 14, 2013, in Paris. This set the central starting point for the reconciliation of two historical rivals and for the creation of informal communication structures between parts of the party elites. In terms of content, a national dialogue was initialized by the adoption of a political road map, which focused primarily on the continuation of the constitutional process and the nature of the transition period following the adoption of the constitution (Essebsi & Chablot, 2016: 41, 44). These agreements, which were ultimately largely honored, included: (1) Ennahda's willingness to compromise and resign as a government cabinet legitimized by elections before the constitution was adopted in order to form a technocratic government led by Mehdi Jômma as a transitional solution; (2) the timely adoption of the constitution as a top priority, which was then adopted on January 26, 2014, with overwhelming approval by the deputies and subsequently proclaimed by a majority of the party elite as a symbol of national unity, consensus, and reconciliation; (3) the holding of parliamentary and presidential elections based on the new constitution in November 2014; (4) the idea of forming a quartet for national dialogue (*al-ḥiwār al-waṭanī*) (Dihstelhoff & Sold, 2016) was negotiated between Ghannouchi and Essebsi along with all "concessions nécessaires" (Essebsi & Chablot, 2016: 45). This quartet, consisting of the Tunisian Trade Union Confederation (UGTT), the Employers' Association (UTICA), the Human Rights League (LTDH), and the Lawyers' Association, was a key initiative of the elite compromise to reduce sociopolitical tensions, avoid further political deadlocks, and facilitate mediation between party leaders and civilians (ibid.: 39). This format—the elite compromise—thus contributed to the consensus orientation of numerous actors in Tunisia's transformation process. Not least for this reason, the coalition was awarded the Nobel Peace Prize in 2015 (Dihstelhoff & Sold, 2016).

How Has It Been Functioning?—Implementing the Power-Sharing System in the Tunisian Post-Arab Spring Transformation Process

A consensual milestone was achieved following the fall of Ben Ali when the Tunisian elite compromise was formalized or institutionalized with the constitution of January 26, 2014,[3] which can be understood as a consensual milestone in Tunisia's young history of transformation (Dihstelhoff, 2019; Netterstrøm, 2015). Moreover, it can be interpreted as an outcome of sociopolitical negotiations between the largest ruling party, the islamist Ennahda Party, and the largely secular-laicist opposition forces (cf. M'rad, 2016). The organization of powers, based on the constitutional text, contains peculiarities: Although it is (1) commonly described as a "half-parliamentary, half-presidential political system," or a "semi-presidential system" with checks and balances, in which the legislature predominates over the executive, there is no specific article in the constitution that specifies whether the political system should be parliamentary, presidential, or a combination. Moreover, (2) as explained later, there is a risk of crisis regarding specific jurisdictional arrangements between individual state offices (Brésillon, 2021). The roles of the "three presidents"—the republic, the government (prime minister), and the parliament—can be cited (cf. ibid.). On the one hand, the constitution explicitly avoids a concentration of power and thus simultaneously lays a potential basis for institutional "compromise"; on the other hand, the problem arises, that the functions, powers, and rights, as well as roles and responsibilities, of the presidents are not clearly described and demarcated from one another. Likewise, the implementation of constitutional law in many areas of society was lacking, creating ambiguity and power vacuums. The most

---

[3] This constitution represents the "fourth" constitutional text in the country's history, after the 1861 constitution, the 1959 constitution (First Republic), and the 2011 law on the provisional organization of public authority (cf. Gaddes, 2014). The following can be highlighted as particular peculiarities of the 2014 constitutional text: (1) the enshrinement of individual freedoms, fundamental freedoms, as well as equality (Arts. 20, 23, 30, 31, 35–37, 46); (2) social and economic rights of citoyeneté (Arts. 12, 38–40), which are the cornerstones for a welfare state with rights and duties; (3) decentralization as the realization of citoyeneté through the establishment of local democracy (Arts. 131–139); (4) Establishment of gender parity in the allocation of public offices and in elections (a first in the Arab world); (5) No references to an Islamic jurisprudence (see *Le Monde* 2014; *Le Point* 2014; Netterstrøm, 2015; Yared, 2021: 24).

salient example of tension between the law and its implementation lies in the ability of the system of independent judicial authorities to function, including five constitutional bodies, the Constitutional Court, and the Supreme Judicial Council. The Constitutional Court has been discussed in parliament over the past 10 years but has repeatedly failed to obtain the necessary two-thirds parliamentary majority to elect some of the constitutional judges, although it should have been established by the end of 2015 (Attia, 2018; Blaise, 2019a, 2019b; Nafti, 2021).

Elections and Coalitions Based on the Constitution: The Elite Compromise in Practice

An integral part of both the elite compromise and the constitution was the promise of free and fair elections. The first parliamentary elections explicitly based on the new constitution were won in 2014 by the secular party Nidaa Tounes, whose leader Beji Caid Essebsi won the presidency in the subsequent presidential elections that same year. By guaranteeing their security and thus turning away from the repressive policies of the old regime against Ennahda, Essebsi was already discursively preparing the ground for Ennahda's integration into the Tunisian state between the two presidential elections (Brésillon, 2014). He also claimed to present himself to the Tunisian people as the self-declared president of all Tunisians (Dihstelhoff, 2019: 242). Accordingly, Essebsi argued also at the legislative level, for a majority government, based on consensus with Ennahda. This was more of an alliance of convenience since, in his estimation, a strong islamist actor in opposition was more dangerous than in government and Tunisia needed a leadership with a legitimate base to avoid polarization (Brésillon & Meddeb, 2020; Essebsi & Chablot, 2016: 48; Laurence, 2015). Thus, another important initiative of the elite compromise was a debate on the inclusion of Ennahda in the governing coalition (Dihstelhoff, 2019: 245f.). This period saw an increased number of secret meetings between Ghannouchi and Essebsi and the final integration of Ennahda as a junior partner in the government (De Grandi, 2015). Although underrepresented in the cabinet compared to its electoral results and compared to other governing parties, the party justified its symbolic participation as a contribution to supporting a "national consensus."[4] Even Prime Minister Essid (February 2015–August 2016) described Ennahda's involvement as an attempt to represent as many Tunisians as possible through a broad coalition government (Agence Ecofin, 2014). Nidaa Tounes, however, faced internal party tensions and a wave of resignations due to Ennahda's participation in a government, as well as the rise of Essebsi's son Hafedh and his nomination as Nidaa party leader (Essebsi & Chablot, 2016: 53). Against this backdrop, Ennahda henceforth found itself neither in true opposition nor in government according to the corresponding balance of power. But from then on until the suspension of parliament on July 25, 2021, Ennahda would constitute the largest faction in parliament. In doing so, it always supported the continuation of the governing coalition and exerted its influence through informal political channels. Moreover, an important argument for this consensual approach also seems to be the fear of possible repression as an opposition party, which Grewal and Hamid (2020), for example, interpret as postponing rather than overcoming the islamist-secular divide.

Carthage I: The Climax of Post-Arab Spring Elite Compromise

In response to three terrorist attacks that occurred in Tunisia in 2015 (March 18/June 26/November 24, 2015),[5] Essebsi and Ghannouchi focused on re-prioritizing the political agenda on security policy and the fight against terrorism, as well as explicitly promoting sociopolitical cohesion (cf. Dihstelhoff & Sold, 2016; Maghreb, 2015). As a possible way to address this crisis, Essebsi called for a change of government in favor of the historically innovative formation of a *government of national unity* (NUG—*Hukuma Wahda wataniya*), which was finally formalized in the first Carthage Agreement (*Itifaq Qartage*) on July 13, 2016 (Dihstelhoff, 2019: 248ff.; *Jeune Afrique*, 2016; M'rad, 2016). In the following government cabinet, nine political parties and three civil society actors participated in this compromise (Essebsi & Chablot, 2016: 200). The content of the "Carthage Agreement" was comparable to the program of the NUG and offered a roadmap with guidelines for problem solving

---

[4] Cf. background discussion with Meherzia Labidi and Mohamed Mahjoub at the event "The Role of the Nahda in the Transformation Process: Experiences and Perspectives," March 2–5, 2015, Federal Foreign Office, Berlin.

[5] Attacks on the Bardo National Museum, hotels in Sousse, and a Tunisian Presidential Guard bus in Tunis.

based on an outline of the national crisis (Dihstelhoff & Sold, 2016). However, discussions about the content of the agreement were overshadowed by the question of the personnel for the new government. Nonetheless, the first Carthage Pact constructed a renewed and broader bipartisan consensus whose specific format of a NUG can be described, for the time being, as the crowning achievement of the elite compromise (Dihstelhoff, 2019: 248). It symbolizes the elites' claim to elevate their compromise to the status of a permanently altered political foundation, based on a series of agreements and meetings between Ennahda and Nidaa Tounes in the months and years since August 2013 (M'rad, 2016). This expanded the existing elite compromise by including as many political and civil society actors as possible, while enabling increasing institutionalization of the elite compromise (Essebsi & Chablot, 2016: 198ff.).

How Has It Ended?—Evaluating the Longevity of the Elite Compromise and Its Functioning

The post-Arab spring elite compromise was dismantled as the decisive Tunisian power-sharing process in three successive time phases of the transformation process and then finally dissolved in a fourth phase through the president's monopolization of power. Accordingly, (1) the decline of the elite compromise began with the "second Carthage Accord," which (2) was cemented by the changing balance of power in the executive and legislative branches after the 2019 parliamentary and presidential elections. Then, (3) the COVID-19 pandemic exacerbated a governance crisis in which Tunisia's president cultivated an increasingly uncompromising and non-negotiating style of action. (4) Since the Tunisian president assumed sole power on July 25, 2021, the previously valid and practiced division of powers and authority has been abolished in favor of a presidential monopoly on power.

Carthage II: The Decline of the Elite Compromise

Based on the self-imposed goals, the track record after two years of NUG under Youssef Chahed's leadership was quite ambivalent (Dihstelhoff, 2018; M'rad, 2018). Although many economic and anti-corruption reform projects had been implemented, an increasingly large proportion of the civilian population complained that the country's greatest challenges had still not been resolved and that some had worsened. Moreover, the NUG had little impact on political polarization among coalition members, instead leading to reduced parliamentary activity by the two largest governing parties, Nidaa Tounes and Ennahda (Kubinec & Grewal, 2018). This was compounded by the government's failure to implement broader structural reforms to meet the demands of the 2011 uprisings or the agreed reforms of the Carthage Accord. No party wanted to take responsibility for lengthy and costly (structural) reforms (Boubakeur, 2016; Brésillon & Meddeb, 2020; Kubinec & Grewal, 2018). Instead, by incorporating all opposition parties into a single political entity, progressive reforms were largely postponed for the sake of consensus (Dihstelhoff, 2018, 2019: 248ff.; Yerkes & Yahmed, 2019). Further, without a Constitutional Court or a serious opposition, the NUG implemented several regressive laws, such as the 2017 Economic Reconciliation Law, which protects officials who engaged in corrupt practices during the Ben Ali era (Abderrahmen, 2018; Yerkes & Muasher, 2017). These developments contributed to the crumbling of the NUG's political base—in January 2018, two of the original signatories to the Carthage Agreement, Afek Tounes and Mashrou Tounes, publicly distanced themselves from the agreement, citing the apparent failure of consensus politics to pursue official legislative initiatives. In March 2018, President Essebsi convened a panel of experts composed of the eighteen members of the stakeholders who had signed the first agreement. After two months of work, this expert panel presented a new draft agreement on May 28, 2018, shortly after the first free and fair municipal elections in Tunisia, which became known as the "*Second Carthage Agreement*" (Dihstelhoff, 2018; Leaders, 2018; *L'Économiste Maghrebin*, 2018). This agreement was essentially an action plan that (1) proposed economic, social, political, and administrative reforms, (2) called for a major government reshuffle, and (3) envisioned a national unity government without Chahed as prime minister. However, the last point led to a dispute between President Essebsi and Ennahda (Dihstelhoff, 2018). As Ennahda continued to cling to Chahed, the dispute culminated in an interview with Essebsi on September 24, 2018, in which he announced the official end of consensus politics (ibid., 2018). This showed that the durability of consensus politics was closely linked to patronage-based personnel politics.

Parliamentary and Presidential Elections 2019: Turning Away from the Elite Compromise

The NUG crisis led to increasing popular dissatisfaction with the consensus model, which culminated with the 2019 parliamentary and presidential elections and the loss of power of the established parties, including Nidaa Tounes and Ennahda, in favor of political outsiders, such as Kais Saied, as well as new parties (cf. Grewal, 2019a; Grewal & Hamid, 2020). It became apparent that the election results led to a fragmented party system and were a clear vote against the previous elite compromise (Grewal, 2019b). However, this cannot be deduced from the election results alone, but can also be explained by the ailing party structures in Tunisia. While the parties that were most recently in government functioned primarily as amplifiers of the political aspirations of individuals, such as Essebsi, they failed, apart from Ennahda, to build a nationwide voter base. Grewal and Hamid (2020) see this as a weighty factor in the reestablishment of radical parties on both sides of the political spectrum. While Ennahda emerged victorious in the parliamentary elections, winning around 24% of the seats despite halving its 2014 result, Nidaa Tounes was no longer represented in parliament following divisions within the party (Brésillon & Meddeb, 2020). Instead, the secularist newcomer party *Qalb Tounes ("Heart of Tunisia")* led by its founding father, and the businessman notorious for money laundering and tax evasion, Nabil Karoui, became the second strongest party and won 18% of the seats. However, it was not enough for the two first-place finishers to form a governing coalition-especially since they fought a bitter election campaign beforehand. While Ennahda described Nabil Karoui's party as corrupt and populist (Bghouri, 2020; Gobe, 2020), Qalb Tounes accused Ennahdha of being religious extremists (Bghouri, 2020; Ghorbal, 2016). Since all possible political partners for Ennahda ruled out government cooperation in accordance with the new balance of power, no government could be formed for the time being (Brésillon & Meddeb, 2020; Grewal, 2019b).

In the 2019 presidential election, academic Kais Saied, a political outsider with no formal party affiliation, but with strong grassroots support, won by a landslide of 72.71% of the vote (BBC, 2019; Brésillon, 2019; Grewal, 2019a; Safi, 2019). Saied, a conservative constitutionalist who had previously been unknown to the broader public as well as politically, was seen as a candidate of the anti-establishment and the youth, and without an obvious power base in the form of his own party, lobby, or other support groups (Boukhras, 2019; Gobe, 2020). His election campaign envisioned a complete reorganization of power in Tunisia. According to Saied, this involves an alternative concept for a democratic process without parties, based on the principles of direct democracy from below—an "inverted pyramid"[6] (Brésillon, 2019; Mornagui, 2021).

After months of political negotiations and disputes between President Saied and Ennahda, whose candidate, Habib Jemli,[7] for prime minister failed to form a government two months after the election (Dahmani, 2019b; *Le Monde*, 2020), Saied finally appointed Elyes Fakhfakh as the new prime minister on February 27, 2020, a consensus candidate who had no party affiliation at the time of his appointment (Boussen, 2020; Serrano, 2020). Fakhfakh's government represented a clear break with the old paradigm of national consensus, as it awarded a majority of ministerial posts to individuals with no party affiliation or experience in office and granted parliament a strong opposition capable of taking action (cf. Safi, 2019). Prior to forming a government, Ennahda sought to have its chairman elected speaker of parliament, thus "[…] *se positionnerait ainsi, à la fois comme le deuxième personnage de l'État, et comme l'interlocuteur privilégié du gouvernement*"[8] (Gobe, 2020). This led to talks and a deal[9] between Ennahda and Qalb Tounes, after which Qalb Tounes made a positional U-turn and elected Rached Ghannouchi as parliamentary speaker, even though the party had vowed never to vote for Ennahda while in the election campaign (Dahmani, 2019a).

Overall, the political context during this period was characterized by a president without parliamentary but popular support and a fragmented party system. Consequently, two competing sources of legitimacy

---

[6] In Saied's concept, which is also referred to as the "inverted pyramid," there would be 264 local councils at the top level, corresponding to the number of delegations in Tunisia, whose representatives would be directly elected. This in turn gives rise to the regional councils, which represent the 24 governorates and each contain one member representing each delegation within the governorate. Finally, a parliament with members from the local councils is at the lowest level of the power pyramid.

[7] Agricultural engineer Habib Jemli already had government experience between 2011 and 2014 as undersecretary at the Ministry of Agriculture (see Dahmani, 2019b).

[8] "[…] would thus position itself as the second most important person in the state, and as the privileged interlocutor of the government" (Translation of the authors).

[9] This deal stipulated that Qalb Tounes agreed to elect Rached Ghannouchi as speaker of parliament in exchange for the vice chairmanship of the assembly falling to a Qalb Tounes deputy, Samira Chaouachi (see Blaise, 2019a, 2019b).

emerged on the basis of this executive and legislative branch, vying for influence over the governing coalition and thus over the parliamentary (reform) agenda (cf. Brésillon & Meddeb, 2020). In this scenario, Ennahda was caught between its role as a minor player in the coalition, on the one hand, and as a partner in the strategic consensus with Qalb Tounes in the election of Rachid Ghannouchi as parliamentary speaker, on the other hand (ibid.).

COVID-19 Pandemic Meets Government Crises and Intra-Party Fragmentation

In the spring of 2020, the COVID-19 pandemic hit Tunisia at a difficult time marked by political struggles and economic uncertainty (Brésillon & Meddeb, 2020; Makni, 2020; Otay, 2020). After initial denial of the pandemic, the ruling coalition responded with a series of strict measures to combat its spread—including a national "confinement général" (BBC, 2020; Hizaoui, 2020) (March 22–May 4, 2020), varying curfews, closing land, air, and sea borders, banning gatherings, markets, and non-emergency domestic travel (ACLED, 2020; Mezran et al., 2020). The onset of the pandemic appeared to at least temporarily consensualize the political parties. For example, the Fakhfakh government was granted special powers that were supported by all parties. These included both the right of the government to issue decrees, conclude purchase contracts, and raise funds without having to consult parliament in order to effectively combat the pandemic (Reuters, 2020).

However, party dissent became increasingly evident again from the summer of 2020, when the first lockdown measures were relaxed and party rivalries reclaimed the political discourse (Brésillon & Meddeb, 2020). One important factor in this discourse was an application on June 3, 2020, condemning Turkish intervention in Libya and rejecting foreign intervention in Libya in general, which was supported by both opposition parties and members of the governing coalition, while Ennahda officially opposed (Brésillon & Meddeb, 2020; Guerraoui, 2020). This conversation sparked a social discourse about the appropriate scope of parliamentary diplomacy, as well as Ennahda's perceived entanglement of international party interests, along the lines of attitudes of international Muslim Brotherhood organizations, with international affairs of state, which, according to the design of the separation of powers, are more properly the preserve of the president and other members of the executive branch (cf. Siebert, 2020). Due to the discursive pressure and lack of elite compromise that weighed on Ennahda after the request, the party sought ways to strengthen its political position and therefore immediately demanded an investigation into Fakhfakh's alleged conflicts of interest. The latter had been involved in private investments in companies that were awarded government contracts (Serrano, 2020). These circumstances ultimately led to Fakhfakh's sudden resignation on July 15, 2020.

As a result of the renewed power vacuum caused by Fakhfakh's resignation, President Kais Saied designated the nonpartisan Interior Minister Hichem Mechichi as head of the future government on July 25, 2020, but without having negotiated with the parties beforehand (Ben Salah, 2020). The latter has now been tasked with forming a government that should manage without nominating members from parties or parliamentary blocs in order to counter corruption as well as further polarization (Boudhrioua, 2021). However, the appointment of Mechichi can also be seen as an attempt by President Saied to ensure that Ennahda is sidelined (Serrano, 2020). Not least because Saied announced that new elections would be held if a government could not be formed by September 2020, all influential parties in parliament supported the Mechichi government (ibid.; Siebert, 2020).

However, as early as January 2021, the new government faced a major crisis when President Saied refused to invite the appointed ministers of the Mechichi government to take their constitutional oath, following a political reshuffle of eleven ministers at the request of the parties supporting the government (Al Jazeera, 2021; Boudhrioua, 2021; Kavaler, 2021). The president argued that he had reservations about individual appointments because of conflicts of interest and allegations of corruption (*Arab Weekly*, 2021). Nevertheless, since there was still no Constitutional Court, this step led to a political crisis over the interpretation of the constitution and the president's (overstepping of) authority. Experts interpret the real reason for the political conflict as Saied's accusation that Mechichi had breached his contract by forming a government in agreement with the political parties, especially Ennahda, instead of following Saied's desire to form a government without party influence (Boudhrioua, 2021; Guesmi, 2021; Sasmaz & Grubman, 2021). Even though the confrontation between the executive and legislative branches weakened in February 2021 (Middle East Monitor, 2021a), the government remained fragmented, with only one-third of cabinet members now in office and several

102   J. DIHSTELHOFF AND M. SIMON

ministerial posts remaining vacant because of the still unclear government reshuffle process (Boudhrioua, 2021). Tensions between Saied and Mechichi continued on the basis of disagreements in the following months (Grewal, 2021b; Kavaler, 2021; MENA Affairs, 2021; Middle East Monitor, 2021b).

Overall, this crisis, described as a "political stalemate" (Kadura & Jmour, 2021; Mersch, 2021), "political deadlock" (Aljazeera 2021), or "stalemate between presidency and parliament" (Kavaler, 2021), paralyzed the country. In the process, institutional deadlocks between the country's executive and legislative branches intensified, already absorbing much of the political energy that was needed to address Tunisia's pressing economic, health, and sociopolitical crises (Grewal, 2021a; Siebert & Abouaoun, 2021). (1) Tunisia was nearly bankrupt economically by early summer 2021 due to rapidly declining creditworthiness, and international donors could no longer find guarantees for their budget support (Blaise, 2021; Brésillon, 2021; Kapitalis, 2021). In addition, (2) the health system collapsed in the summer of 2021, during which time Tunisia had the highest corona-related mortality rate in Africa and the Arab world and also experienced a shortage of necessary oxygen cylinders and ventilators (Galtier, 2021; Khadraoui & Ben Hamadi, 2021). Simultaneously, (3) nationwide youth protests occurred in 2021 against the perceived inaction and corruption of elites and demanding political solutions to the economic and sanitation misery (Abdslem, 2021; Human Rights Watch, 2021a, 2021b).

The Presidential Sonderweg Instead of 'Paced Transition': Saied's Monopolization of Power

The context of the political stalemate changed drastically at the end of July 2021. On the evening of July 25, 2021—which is by all means considered historic[10]—Kais Saied, in the presence of representatives of

---

[10] July 25 is Republic Day in Tunisia; the two-year anniversary of the death of former President Essebsi; eight years after the murder of political opposition figure Mohamed Brahmi; as well as—not really mentioned in public discourse—the day of Ennahda's ultimatum to the president for reparations, which in turn stem from political deals made in 2017. These included demands for reparation payments amounting to several million dinars—this brought quite a lot of people to the streets for mass protests on July 25, 2021, despite the curfew.

all security forces, invoked Article 80 of the 2014 Tunisian constitution (Constitute, 2017), which allows for the declaration of a state of emergency by the president of the republic in the face of an "imminent threat" (Ben Hamadi, 2021; International Crisis Group, 2022). This included (1) the freezing of parliament for 30 days, (2) the lifting of parliamentary immunity, and (3) the dismissal of Hichem Mechichi, the prime minister and interim interior minister (France24, 2021a). Saied also declared that he would henceforth assume leadership of the executive branch alongside a new prime minister under a state of emergency, whom he planned to appoint shortly. However, in comparison with Article 80, it was quite arguable whether there was an imminent danger threatening the nation's institutions and the security and independence of the country and impeding the proper functioning of the organs of state. In addition, neither the head of government nor parliament was informed, nor could a Constitutional Court be consulted. The measures were not in the context of the constitution's stated goal of a rapid return to the regular operation of the authorities through a permanent state of assembly of the people's representatives. Instead of ensuring a high level of activity of the legislature, although it was not dissolved at that time, any activity was frozen. Nor could a call for a review of the state of emergency be made by the Assembly of People's Deputies after the 30 days had expired to the Constitutional Court, as the latter simply did not exist. Even before the 30 days expired, ministers were dismissed, house arrests were imposed, and informal talks with social interest groups were held to the exclusion of the parties (France24, 2021c; *Jeune Afrique*, 2021).

As a result, a split could be observed regarding the evaluation of these measures, both among the elites and the population, which continues to this day. Regardless of whether this was a coup d'état, two conclusions can be drawn: First, it is no longer possible to speak of power-sharing in Tunisia. Second, in view of the disconnect between the procedural level of actors and the formal constitutional level, it seems necessary to revise the latter. Saied's decisions of July 25, 2021 can be interpreted as a sanctioning of the institutions created by the 2014 constitution, which, in Saied's view and in the view of many Tunisians—as opinion polls show—are responsible for the multidimensional health, financial, social, and political crisis (Brésillon, 2021).

After the 30-day period expired on August 23, 2021, and Saied extended the exemptions indefinitely without presenting a political road map or appointing a government or prime minister, he issued presidential *Decree 117* on September 22, 2021 (DCAF Tunisie, 2022), which had serious implications for Tunisia's political regime. This can be interpreted as a further presidentialization of the system (France24, 2021b; Werenfels, 2022). *Decree 117* consists of 23 articles in four chapters and includes: (1) the suspension of the constitution in force since 2014—including Article 80 as Saied's previous standard of justification—and thus of the political system implemented on its basis, along with the separation of powers and municipal structures; (2) presidential powers in all areas of public life instead of the separation of powers—i.e., it is a monopolization of powers, so that, for example, no presidential control body is provided; (3) the irrevocability of presidential decrees; (4) the abolition of the provisional body for reviewing the constitutionality of draft laws (Human Rights Watch, 2021a, 2021b; International Crisis Group, 2022). Only some elements were retained from the 2014 constitutional text: the preamble, fundamental freedoms and rights from the first and second chapters, and international conventions. Furthermore, on the basis of Article 22, the use of democratic and participatory mechanisms is still possible, if the president allows it. It is noticeable that the decree contains neither a time limit for the exceptions nor information on how they will be administered.

On December 13, 2021, the president published a meager road map for constitutional change, which is received, among other things, as a "fig leaf for the concentration of power" (Dworkin cited in Deutsche Welle, 2022) and which is to be accompanied by political-technical innovations: (1) January 15–March 20, 2022: Conduct a digital referendum on the subject of Tunisia's future political system; (2) March 20-22–July 20-22: Evaluation of the results of the referendum by a council of experts appointed by the president in order to submit a constitutional proposal on this basis; (3) July 25, 2022: Holding of a constitutional referendum; (4) December 2022: Holding of elections based on the new electoral system that will then come into force (Nadhif, 2021).

Overall, President Kais Saied appears to be further expanding his monopolistic grip on the country: (1) On February 6, 2022, Saied dissolved the Supreme Judicial Council—an independent post-Arab Spring body of judicial oversight to protect judges from government influence. According to various human rights organizations, this threatens the independence of the judiciary (Amnesty International,

2022; Euromed, 2022). Consequently, Saied replaced the Supreme Judicial Council with a *temporary* judicial council and empowered himself to dismiss judges and prohibit them from striking. (2) On February 24, 2022, Saied made the announcement to revise Decree 88 to prevent foreign donors from influencing civil society organizations. Until now, these would have acted as an extension of external powers and even political parties, thus harming Tunisia (Barisch, 2022; Mzalouat et al., 2022). (3) After 120 of the suspended parliament's 217 deputies participated in a virtual meeting on March 30, 2022, in which they called for an end to the special measures, Saied dissolved the parliament the same day in an announcement at the National Security Council meeting, accusing the deputies of an attempted coup and announcing criminal investigations against them (Euromedmonitor, 2022; Fischer, 2022). (4) On May 9, 2022, Saied appointed new members of the Instance supérieure indépendeante pour les éléctions (ISIE), having previously announced changes to its structure. Previously, ISIE members were elected by parliament after applying for the position. (5) On June 1, 2022, Saied issued a decree removing 57 judges from service, accusing them of corruption and protecting terrorists. According to a communiqué signed by ten human rights organizations, this was *"a serious blow to the independence of the judiciary"* (Human Rights Watch, 2022) and Kais Saied's actions *"[were] an attack on the rule of law"* (ibid., 2022).

In view of this monopolization of power and autocratic consolidation (Werenfels, 2022), democratization efforts are on the brink of collapse a little more than a decade after the so-called Arab Spring. Just as then, the military will play a decisive role.

CONCLUSION

The sociohistorical analysis of the Tunisian format of power-sharing, the elite compromise, evokes a number of peculiarities that are an integral part of Tunisian socialization. In the following, key findings from this analysis will be summarized by reflecting on the three core criteria from the power-sharing theory—"adoptability"/"functionality"/"endability"—based on the multitude of empirical findings and following Hamann (1997):

1. With regard to the "adoptability" of power-sharing, the analysis shows that the initialization of the elite compromise in post-Arab Spring Tunisia is related, on the one hand, to the early phase of Tunisia's transformation process (2011–2014) and the reduction of uncertainties among the political actors involved in it, especially Ennahda and Nidaa Tounes. Second, the post-2011 elite compromise is based on a "historical compromise" between the aforementioned actors around competing "secular-laicist" and "pro-islamic" social designs, the origins of which date back to the time of the national independence movement. The analysis makes clear that this period is marked primarily by political uncertainty and a lack of institutionalization and, secondly, by the protracted and complicated constitutional process in Tunisia. In the process, new sociocultural and political dynamics were evoked that led to a new process of negotiating collective identities, which in its course has repeatedly been linked to tendencies toward division within Tunisian society. In the context of the systemic processes of upheaval, these cleavages were able to reconfigure themselves anew, as they had been suppressed in their breadth by the authoritarian governments before the Arab Spring. Thus, their return was an expression of historically grown opposing and competing tendencies that defined the sociopolitical space and inevitably necessitated new processes of negotiation over the future division of power. Moreover, alluding to Nachi (2017), the emergence of the elite compromise in post-Arab Spring Tunisia can be seen as a constitutional and pluralistic promise for democratization.

2. Regarding "functionality," the analysis reveals insights into the development and adaptation of the elite compromise over time. However, it becomes apparent that between 2014 and 2018 there are uncertainties in the functional implementation of the consolidated power-sharing system. These, in turn, manifest themselves in the form of a discrepancy between the formalistic, institutional level, and the procedural actor level. For example, although the power-sharing system was formally placed on a constitutional footing in 2014, it was never fully exploited, particularly because of the lack of a judiciary, due to persistent differences at the actor level outside the elite compromise. Otherwise, the elite compromise became politically expedient and action-guiding in that it often preceded the decisions of democratic institutions. It advanced to become both

an essential power-sharing format and an ordering factor in official decision-making processes in Tunisia's democratization process during this period. The process reached its climax when compromise orientation was elevated to a genuine form of government ("Carthage I") and was recognized by much of the population and the actors of the sociopolitical establishment as the source of a new "compromise legitimacy." In summary, the Tunisian elite compromise succeeded primarily in the area of temporary conflict and violence prevention by weakening sociopolitical polarization and contributing to Tunisia's democratization. Consequently, the elite compromise formed a central structural element of post-Arab Spring coexistence, characterized by political pluralism and sociocultural diversity.

3. In terms of 'end-ability', the analysis highlights key problematics and challenges of the post-Arab Spring power-sharing system that led first to the successive decline by fragmentation processes since 2018 ("Carthage II"; parliamentary and presidential elections of 2019; government crisis in the context of the COVID-19 pandemic) and then to the unraveling of the elite compromise by the sole power of the Tunisian president on July 25, 2021. Thus, the elite compromise implied not only inclusive but also exclusive tendencies: Accordingly, this power-sharing format primarily involved either convergences between two party structures and their two founding fathers, or between the "three presidents," so that the Tunisia-specific 'pacted transition' was founded only on a narrow sociopolitical basis. Moreover, it represented exclusive individual interests of Nidaa Tounes and Ennahda in addition to collective national interests and was also organized top-down by means of "backroom diplomacy." In addition, the political outcomes of the unity government ("Carthage I") were perceived by the majority in Tunisia as ambivalent. Against this backdrop, the elite compromise fueled growing distrust of the political establishment among the population and consequently led to a major rejection of compromise as a viable organizational principle of political life among political decision-makers.

In evaluating the longevity of the elite compromise, it can be concluded that while the executive branch under Essebsi (2014–2018) was still an integral part of it; Saied increasingly freed himself from it between 2019 and 2021 and took a *Sonderweg*. He first devalued the previously valid power-sharing system through an uncompromising and non-negotiating style of action and then, since July 25, 2011, abolished the separation of power. Since then, an authoritarian culture and a monopolization of power with an unclear policy model and outcome has characterized the end of a decade of "pacted transition" in post-Arab Spring Tunisia. With the planned changes in Tunisia's superstructure, a hybrid model consisting of a strong presidentialization and some elements of direct democracy based on his concept of the "inverted pyramid" can currently be expected under Saied.

Appendix: Milestones of the Power-Sharing Processes in Post-Arab Spring Tunisia

Initialization	17 December 2010–14 January 2011	The revolutionary upheavals that led to the fall of Zine El Abidine Ben Ali
	14 January 14–15 March 2011	The "ancien régime" attempted to regain hegemony over the revolutionary process—"Kasbah I" and "Kasbah II"—Mobilization of counter-protests
	15 March–23 October 2011	Development of essential foundations for democratization (principles, norms, practices)
	3 March 2011	Announcement of free & fair elections with the goal of electing a Constituent Assembly
	7 March 2011	Installation of a technocrat government under Prime Minister Béji Caiid Essebsi
	15 March 2011	Establishment of the Haute Instance pour la Réalisation des Objectifs de la Révolution (HIROR)

(continued)

(continued)

	23 October 2011	Implementation of the elections to the Constituent Assembly (ANC) with Ennahda as election winner
	October 2011–January 2014	Contested constitutional process incl. negotiations of individual constitutional articles and two political assassinations
Elite compromise (*Itifaq al nukhba*)	13 August 2013	Meeting between the main political players, Essebsi and Ghannouchi, in Paris
	26 January 2014	End of the constitution-making process through the adoption of a consensual constitutional text
Consolidation	26 October/23 November/21 December 2014	First parliamentary and presidential elections (first & second round) based on the new constitution with Béji Caid Essebsi as newly elected president
	November 2014–January 2015	(Informal) Coalition building processes and President Essebsi's approach of a majority government based on consensus between Nidaa Tounes and Ennahda
	January 2015–July 2016	Habib Essid as new prime minister and the controversial inclusion of Ennahda as a junior partner in the governing coalition

(continued)

(continued)

	13 July 2016	Formation of a Government of National Unity (NUG), formalized as Carthage Agreement I
	August 2016–May 2018	NUG's ambivalent track record under the leadership of Prime Minister Youssef Chahed: Progressive reforms were largely postponed for the sake of consensus
Fragmentation	January 2018–May 2018	Crumbling of the NUG: Two of the original signatories publicly distanced themselves from the Carthage Agreement
	28 May 2018	An expert panel presented the Second Carthage Agreement, shortly after the first free and fair municipal elections
	24 September 2018	President Essebsi announced the official end of "consensus politics"
	15 September/6 October/13 October 2019	Parliamentary and presidential elections resulted in a fragmented party system with the loss of power of the established parties, in favor of political outsiders, such as Kais Saied, as well as new parties
	From Spring 2019	Covid-19 Pandemic exacerbates/ reinforces a governance crisis

(continued)

(continued)

	27 February 2020	Appointment of Elyes Fakhfakh as the new prime minister by President Kais Saied
	15 July 2020	Resignation of Elyes Fakhfakh as prime minister
	25 July 2020	Appointment of Hichem Mechichi as new prime minister
	January–July 2021	Worsening government crisis due to stalemate between presidency and parliament
Monopolization	25 July 2021	President Kais Saied assumes sole power: the beginning of a "Sonderweg" incl. the Monopolization of Power by implementing a declaration of a state of emergency under Article 80 of the 2014 Tunisian constitution
	23 August 2021	Extension of the state of emergency indefinitely
	22 September 2021	Saied issued presidential Decree 117—the suspension of the constitution in force since 2014 and thus of the political system with separated powers
	6 February 2022	Dissolution of the Supreme Judicial Council
	24 February 2022	Announcement to revise Decree 88 to prevent foreign donors from influencing civil society organizations

(continued)

(continued)

30 March 2022	Virtual Meeting of 120 of the suspended parliament's 217 deputies and dissolution of the parliament
9 May 2022	Appointment of new members for the Instance supérieure indépendeante pour les éléctions (ISIE)
1 June 2022	Decree dismissing 57 judges from service

REFERENCES

Abderrahmen, A. (2018). *How Tunisia's "Two Sheikhs" Sought to Halt Transitional Justice*. The Tahrir Institute for Middle East Policy. https://timep.org/commentary/analysis/how-tunisias-two-sheikhs-sought-to-halt-transitional-justice/

Abdslem, H. (2021). *The "Wrong Generation" Leads Tunisia's Protests*. https://carnegieendowment.org/sada/84596

ACLED. (2020). *Demonstrations Spike in Tunisia Despite COVID-19 Pandemic*. https://acleddata.com/2020/06/29/demonstrations-spike-in-tunisia-despite-covid-19-pandemic/

Agence Ecofin. (2014). *Tunisie: Habib Essid revoit sa copie et présente une nouvelle composition du gouvernement avec Ennahdha*. Agence Ecofin. http://www.agenceecofin.com/politique/0202-26269-tunisie-habib-essid-revoit-sa-copie-et-presente-une-nouvelle-composition-du-gouvernement-avec-ennahdha

Al Jazeera. (2021). *Tunisia: An Overlapping Political and Constitutional Crisis*. https://studies.aljazeera.net/en/policy-briefs/tunisia-overlapping-political-and-constitutional-crisis.

Amnesty International. (2022). *Tunisie. Les mesures prises par le président pour fermer le Conseil supérieur de la magistrature représentent une menace grave pour les droits humains*. Amnesty International. https://www.amnesty.org/fr/latest/news/2022/02/tunisia-presidents-moves-to-shut-down-high-judicial-council-poses-grave-threat-to-human-rights/

Arab Weekly. (2021). Constitutional Crisis Blocks New Tunisian Ministers from Oath of Office. https://thearabweekly.com/constitutional-crisis-blocks-new-tunisian-ministers-oath-office

Attia, S. (2018). Tunisie: pourquoi l'élection des membres de la Cour constitutionnelle patine. *Jeune Afrique*. https://www.jeuneafrique.com/542923/pol itique/tunisie-pourquoi-lelection-des-membres-de-la-cour-constitutionnelle-patine/

Background Discussion with Meherzia Labidi and Mohamed Mahjoub at the Event "The Role of Nahda in the Transformation Process: Experiences and Perspectives". (2015, March 2–5). Federal Foreign Office, Berlin.

Barisch, V. (2022). *Foreign Funds Cause Debate*. Disorient. https://www.disori ent.de/magazin/auslaendische-gelder-sorgen-fuer-diskussionen

BBC. (2019). *Qui est Kais Saied, le nouveau président tunisien?* https://www.bbc.com/afrique/region-50049161

BBC. (2020). *Levée progressive du confinement en Tunisie*. https://www.bbc.com/afrique/region-52525320

Ben Hamadi, M. (2021). *HowDdid Kaïs Saied Apply Article 80? Comparing the Legal Text to his Speech*. Inkyfada. https://inkyfada.com/en/2021/07/29/kais-saied-article-80-constitution-legal-text-speech-tunisia/

Ben Salah, N. (2020). *Portrait: Hichem Mechichi, l'ombre désignée de Kais Saied*. https://nawaat.org/2020/08/18/portrait-hichem-mechichi-lombre-designee-de-kais-saied/

Bghouri, N. (2020). *Qalb Tounes and Al-Karama Confess Their Love*. https://nawaat.org/2020/10/06/qalb-tounes-and-al-karama-confess-their-love/

Blaise L. (2019). *Au Parlement tunisien, une victoire en demi-teinte pour le parti islamo-conservateur Ennahda*. Le Monde Afrique. https://www.lemonde.fr/afrique/article/2019/11/14/au-parlement-tunisien-une-victoire-en-demi-tei nte-pour-le-parti-islamo-conservateur-ennahda_6019105_3212.html

Blaise, L. (2019). *Sana ben Achour: "L'absence de Cour constitutionnelle menace le devenir démocratique de la Tunisie."* Middle East Eye. https://www.mid dleeasteye.net/fr/entretiens/sana-ben-achour-labsence-de-cour-constitution nelle-menace-le-devenir-democratique-de-la

Blaise, L. (2021). *Pour échapper au piège de la dette, la Tunisie doit changer de moteur économique*. Le Monde Afrique. https://ecfr.eu/publication/reform_ from_crisis_how_tunisia_can_use_covid_19_as_an_opportunity/

Boubakeur, A. (2016). Islamists, Secularists and Old Regime Elites in Tunisia: Bargained Competition. *Mediterranean Politics, 21*(1), 107–127.

Boudhrioua, O. (2021). *The Roots of Tunisia's Current Political Crisis*. Fikra Forum. https://www.washingtoninstitute.org/policy-analysis/roots-tunisias-current-political-crisis

Boukhras, A. (2019). *Tunisia Crying out for Change, Carnegie Endowment for International Peace*. https://carnegieendowment.org/2019/09/27/tunisia-crying-out-for-change-pub-80008

Boussen, Z. (2020). *Tunisia: New Government, New Dynamics?* Centre for Euro-Mediterranean and African Studies. http://www.cemas.org.uk/index.php/north-africa/6449-tunisia-new-government-new-dynamics-2

Bras, J. P., & Gobe, É. (2017). Legitimacy and Revolution in Tunisia. The Tunisian Lessons of the High Authority for the Achievement of the Revolution Objectives. *Revue des mondes musulmans et de la Méditerranée*. https://doi.org/10.4000/remmm.957310.4000/remmm.9573.

Brésillon, T. (2014). Béji Caïd Essebsi affirme: "Je garantis personnellement la sécurité des islamistes." *La Tribune*. https://www.djazairess.com/fr/latribune/110627

Brésillon, T. (2018). *En Tunisie, une démocratie sans citoyens?* Orient XXI. https://orientxxi.info/magazine/en-tunisie-une-democratie-sans-citoyens,2484

Brésillon, T. (2019). *Kais Saied: un projet de démocratie radicale pour la Tunisie.* Middle East Eye. https://www.middleeasteye.net/fr/decryptages/kais-saied-un-projet-de-democratie-radicale-pour-la-tunisie?fbclid=IwAR2OdF1kLlMii b7o5jRrPaeUl5B8dj5-UONeJwqgiHHC_RwPV4klAztai5Q

Brésillon, T. (2021). *Faut-il changer la Constitution tunisienne?* Middle East Eye. https://www.middleeasteye.net/fr/opinion-fr/tunisie-constitution-democratie-kais-saied-ennahdha-nidaa-tounes-parlement-r%C3%A9volution

Brésillon, T., & Meddeb, H. (2020). *Reform from Crisis: How Tunisia Can Use Covid-19 as an Opportunity.* European Council on Foreign Relations. https://ecfr.eu/publication/reform_from_crisis_how_tunisia_can_use_covid_19_as_an_opportunity/

Chérif, Z. E. H. (2016). *L'islam politique face à la société tunisienne: du compromis politique au compromis historique?* Nirvana.

Chouika, L., & Gobe, E. (2015). *Histoire de la tunisie depuis l'indépendance.* La Découverte.

Constitute. (2017). *Tunisia's Constitution of 2014.* https://www.constituteproject.org/constitution/Tunisia_2014.pdf

Dahmani, F. (2019a). Tunisie: Jeux d'alliances et volte-faces, les dessous de l'élection de Rached Ghannouchi à la tête du Parlement. *Jeune Afrique*. https://www.jeuneafrique.com/856604/politique/tunisie-jeux-dalliances-et-volte-faces-les-dessous-de-lelection-de-rached-ghannouchi-a-la-tete-du-parlement/

Dahmani, F. (2019b). Tunisie: Habib Jemli, un chef du gouvernement "sans surprise et bon exécutant". *Jeune Afrique*. https://www.jeuneafrique.com/858079/politique/tunisie-habib-jemli-un-chef-du-gouvernement-sans-surprise-et-bon-executant/

DCAF Tunisie. (2022). *Décret Présidentiel n° 2021–117 du 22 septembre 2021, relatif aux mesures exceptionnelles.* https://legislation-securite.tn/law/105067

De Grandi, M. (2015). *Tunisie: des islamistes intègrent le gouvernement.* LesEchos.fr. http://www.lesechos.fr/02/02/2015/lesechos.fr/0204127714397_tunisie---des-islamistes-integrent-le-gouvernement.html

Deutsche Welle. (2022). *Tunisia's First Digital Political Consultation Divides Opinions.* https://www.dw.com/en/tunisias-first-digital-political-consultation-divides/a-60390183

Dihstelhoff, J. (2018). *Tunisian Politics Between Crisis and Normalization.* Sada Carnegie. https://carnegieendowment.org/sada/77582

Dihstelhoff, J. (2019). Unity-Consensus-Reconciliation: The Substance of Tunisia's Elite Compromise; an Analysis of Post-revolutionary Metaphors. In E. Mohamed & D. Fahmy (Eds.), *Arab Spring and the Quest for New Metaphors—Modernity, Identity and Change.* Palgrave Macmillan.

Dihstelhoff, J., & Sold, K. (2016). *Nobel Peace Prize for a Temporary Mediation Success in Tunisia.* DGAPStandpunkt. https://dgap.org/de/article/get FullPDF/27229

Essebsi, B. C., & Chablot, A. (2016). *Tunisie: la démocratie en terre d'Islam.* PLON.

Euromed. (2022). *Tunisie: un pas de plus vers la concentration des pouvoirs.* https://euromedrights.org/fr/publication/tunisie-un-pas-de-plus-vers-la-concentration-des-pouvoirs/

Euromedmonitor. (2022). *Tunisie: La dissolution du Parlement enfreint la constitution et complique davantage la crise.* https://euromedmonitor.org/fr/article/5015/Tunisie-:-La-dissolution-du-Parlement-enfreint-la-constitution-et-complique-davantage-la-crise

Fischer, K. (2022). *Un pas de plus, un pas de trop?* Deutsche Welle. https://www.dw.com/fr/tunisie-kais-saied-dissolution-du-parlement-fondation-friedrich-ebert-d%C3%A9rive-autoritaire/a-61322331

France 24. (2021a). *Kaïs Saïed suspend le Parlement et démet le Premier ministre Hichem Mechichi.* https://www.france24.com/fr/info-en-continu/20210725-tunisie-le-pr%C3%A9sident-ka%C3%AFs-sa%C3%AFed-suspend-le-parlement-et-d%C3%A9met-le-premier-ministre-hichem-mechichi

France 24. (2021b). *Nouvelles mesures d'exception en Tunisie: Kaïs Saïed renforce les pouvoirs de la présidence.* https://www.france24.com/fr/afrique/20210922-tunisie-le-pr%C3%A9sident-ka%C3%AFs-sa%C3%AFed-renforce-son-pouvoir-au-d%C3%A9triment-du-gouvernement

France 24. (2021c). *Le président Kaïs Saïed prolonge "jusqu'à nouvel ordre" le gel du Parlement.* https://www.france24.com/fr/info-en-continu/20210824-tunisie-le-pr%C3%A9sident-ka%C3%AFs-sa%C3%AFed-prolonge-jusqu-%C3%A0-nouvel-ordre-le-gel-du-parlement

Gaddes, C. (2014). *Le Régime Politique Tunisien dans la Constitution de 2014 et son fonctionnement après les Élections*. https://tn.boell.org/fr/2014/10/24/le-regime-politique-tunisien-dans-la-constitution-de-2014-et-son-foncti onnement-apres-les

Galtier, M. (2021). Covid: la Tunisie noyée par la pandémie. *Libération*. https://www.liberation.fr/international/europe/covid-la-tunisie-noyee-par-la-pandemie-20210710_GDRAWHNNHVEN3BR7A5XAXSDSX4/

Ghorbal, S. (2016). "La promesse du printemps," Aziz Krichen fait un rêve. *Jeune Afrique* https://www.jeuneafrique.com/mag/320440/politique/tun isie-aziz-krichen-reve/

Gobe, É. (2020). Tunisie 2019: Chronique d'une surprise électorale annoncée. *L'Année du Maghreb, 23*. http://journals.openedition.org/anneemaghreb/6811

Grewal, S. (2019a). *Political Outsiders Sweep Tunisia's Presidential Elections*. Brookings Institute. https://www.brookings.edu/blog/order-from-chaos/2019/09/16/political-outsiders-sweep-tunisias-presidential-elections/

Grewal, S. (2019b). Winners and Losers of Tunisia's Parliamentary Elections. Monkey Cage. *The Washington Post*. https://www.washingtonpost.com/pol itics/2019/10/08/winners-losers-tunisias-parliamentary-elections/

Grewal, S. (2021a). *Kais Saied's Power Grab in Tunisia*. Brookings Institute. https://www.brookings.edu/blog/order-from-chaos/2021/07/26/kais-sai eds-power-grab-in-tunisia/

Grewal, S. (2021b). *How COVID-19 Helped Legitimize the Tunisian President's Power Grab*. Pomed. https://pomed.org/how-covid-19-helped-legiti mate-the-tunisian-presidents-power-grab/

Grewal, S., & Hamid, S. (2020). *The Dark Side of Consensus in Tunisia. Lessons From 2015–2020*. Brookings Institute. https://www.brookings.edu/wp-con tent/uploads/2020/01/FP_20200131_tunisia_consensus_grewal_hamid.pdf

Guerraoui, S. (2020). *Ghannouchi Seeks to Dismiss Some Coalition Ministers from Cabinet*. Middle East Online. https://middle-east-online.com/en/gha nnouchi-seeks-dismiss-some-coalition-ministers-cabinet

Guesmi, J. (2021). Ghannouchi's Constitutional Spin Exacerbates Rift in Tunisia. *The Arab Weekly*. https://thearabweekly.com/ghannouchis-constitut ional-spin-exacerbates-rift-tunisia

Hamann, K. (1997). The Paced Transition to Democracy and Labor Politics in Spain. *South European Society and Politics, 2*(2), 110–138.

Hizaoui, N. (2020). *Entrée en vigueur aujourd'hui du déconfinement ciblé: relancer l'économie sans réveiller la pandémie*. LaPresse.tn. https://lapresse. tn/60832/entree-en-vigueur-aujourdhui-du-deconfinement-cible-relancer-lec onomie-sans-reveiller-la-pandemie/

Human Rights Watch. (2021a). *Tunisie: La police a violemment réprimé des manifestations.* https://www.hrw.org/fr/news/2021/02/05/tunisie-la-police-vio lemment-reprime-des-manifestations

Human Rights Watch. (2021b). *Tunisie: Confiscation sans précédent du pouvoir par la présidence: Déclaration commune de quatre organisations dont.* https://www.hrw.org/fr/news/2021/09/27/tunisie-confiscat ion-sans-precedent-du-pouvoir-par-la-presidence

Human Rights Watch. (2022). *Tunisia: Arbitrary Dismissals a Blow to Judicial Independence: Revoke Decree Granting President Power to Remove Judges.* https://www.hrw.org/news/2022/06/10/tunisia-arbitrary-dismissals-blow-judicial-independence

International Crisis Group. (2022). *La Tunisie de Saïed: privilégier le dialogue et redresser l'économie.* https://www.crisisgroup.org/fr/middle-east-north-afr ica/north-africa/tunisia/232-la-tunisie-de-saied-privilegier-le-dialogue-et-red resser-leconomie

Jeune Afrique. (2016). Tunisie: signature de "l'accord de Carthage" en vue d'un gouvernement d'union nationale. https://www.jeuneafrique.com/341 548/politique/tunisie-signature-de-laccord-de-carthage-vue-dun-gouvernem ent-dunion-nationale/

Jeune Afrique. (2021). Tunisie - Qui sont les nouveaux dirigeants nommés par Kaïs Saïed. https://www.jeuneafrique.com/1222201/politique/tunisie-qui-sont-les-nouveaux-dirigeants-nommes-par-kais-saied/

Kadura, J., & Jmour, Y. (2021). At the Tipping Point. *Journal of International Politics.* https://www.ipg-journal.de/regionen/naher-osten/artikel/ am-wendepunkt-5428/

Kapitalis. (2021). *Mac SA—Tunisie: la dernière notation de Fitch annonce le défaut de paiement.* https://kapitalis.com/tunisie/2021/07/09/mac-sa-tun isie-la-derniere-notation-de-fitch-annonce-le-defaut-de-paiement/

Kavaler, T. (2021). *Stalemate Between Tunisia's Prime Minister, President Continues With No End in Sight.* The Medialine. https://themedialine.org/ top-stories/stalemate-between-tunisias-prime-minister-president-continues-with-no-end-in-sight/

Khadraoui, M., & Ben Hamadi, M. (2021). *5 graphiques pour comprendre l'ampleur de la mortalité liée au Covid-19 en Tunisie.* Inkyfada. https://inkyfada. com/fr/2021/08/02/covid-19-mortalite-nombre-deces-tunisie/

Kubinec, R., & Grewal, S. (2018). When National Unity Governments Are Neither National, United, nor Governments: The Case of Tunisia. *SocArXiv.* https://doi.org/10.31235/osf.io/6z74r

L'économiste Maghrebin. (2018). Accord de Carthage 2: le 64ème point, pomme de discorde. https://www.leconomistemaghrebin.com/2018/05/ 26/chahed-suite/

Laurence, J. (2015). *Tunisia, the Courage of Compromise*. Brookings Institute. https://www.brookings.edu/opinions/tunisia-the-courage-of-compromise/

Le Monde. (2014). Constitution: la Tunisie adopte la liberté de conscience et rejette la charia. https://www.lemonde.fr/tunisie/article/2014/01/04/constitution-la-tunisie-adopte-la-liberte-de-conscience-et-rejette-la-charia_434 3130_1466522.html

Le Monde. (2020). Tunisie: le gouvernement de Habib Jemli rejeté par le Parlement. https://www.lemonde.fr/international/article/2020/01/11/tun isie-le-gouvernement-de-habib-jemli-rejete-par-le-parlement_6025484_3210. html

Le Monde Afrique. (2011). *La Tunisie va connaître de vraies élections libres*. http://www.lemonde.fr/tunisie/article/2011/04/20/la-tunisie-va-connai tre-de-vraies-elections-libres_1510254_1466522.html#94uSUV9mysvZSBE 6.99

Le Point. (2014). En Tunisie, la liberté de conscience l'emporte sur la charia. https://www.lepoint.fr/editos-du-point/mireille-duteil/en-tunisie-la-liberte-de-conscience-l-emporte-sur-la-charia-05-01-2014-1777005_239.php

Leaders. (2018). *L'échec de l'accord de Carthage. Et après*. https://www.leaders.com.tn/article/24723-l-echec-de-l-accord-de-carthage-et-apres

Lijphart, A. (2008). *Thinking About Democracy: Power-Sharing and Majority Rule in Theory and Practice*. Routledge.

Lübben, I. (2017). The Concept of the Religious Field in Bourdieu and the Reordering of the Relationship Between the Islamic and Political Fields in Tunisia and Egypt in the Context of the Arabellion. In Arabellion - Vom Aufbruch zum Zerfall einer Region? T. Demmelhuber & M. Reinkowski (Eds.), *Leviathan - Berliner Zeitschrift für Sozialwissenschaft*. Sonderband 31.

Maghreb, H. (2015). *Pour le président de la République Béji Caïd Essebsi, la "paix sociale" participe à la lutte antiterroriste*. http://www.huffpostmaghreb.com/2015/11/29/tunisie-beji-caid-essebsi_n_8678176.html

Makni, A. (2020). L'économie tunisienne face à la crise du Covid-19. In La Tunisie face à l'épreuve du Covid-19, In H. Redissi (Ed.), *Friedrich-Ebert-Stiftung, Bureau de Tunis/Observatoire Tunisien de la Transition Démocratique*.

McCulloch, A. (2021). Introduction: From Adoptability to End-Ability. In S. Keil & A. McCulloch (Eds.), *Power-Sharing in Europe: Past Practice, Present Cases, and Future Directions* (pp. 1–18). Palgrave Macmillan.

MENA Affairs. (2021). *Ennahdha Calls on Kais Saied to Promulgate the Law on the Constitutional Court*. https://menaaffairs.com/ennahdha-calls-on-kais-saied-to-promulgate-the-law-on-the-constitutional-court/

Merone, F., & Cavatorta, F. (2013). Salafist Movement and Shi'iteism in Tunisian Democratic Transition. *Middle East Law and Governance, 5*, 1–23.

Mersch, S. (2021). *We Need Separation of Powers.* Deutschlandfunk Kultur. https://www.deutschlandfunkkultur.de/staatskrise-in-tunesien-wir-brauchen-gewaltenteilung-100.html

Mezran, K., Melcangi, A., Burchfield, E., & Riboua, Z. (2020). *The Coronavirus Crisis Highlights the Unique Challenges of North African Countries.* Atlantic Council. https://www.atlanticcouncil.org/blogs/menasource/the-coronavirus-crisis-highlights-the-unique-challenges-of-north-african-countries/

Middle East Monitor. (2021a). *Tunisia: Tension Eased Between Mechichi and Saied amid Council of Ministers Crisis.* https://www.middleeastmonitor.com/20210227-tunisia-tension-eased-between-mechichi-and-saied-amid-council-of-ministers-crisis/

Middle East Monitor. (2021b). *Kais Saied: "Tunisia Needs Respectful Parliament and Responsible Government."* https://www.middleeastmonitor.com/20210410-kais-saied-tunisia-needs-respectful-parliament-and-responsible-government/

Mornagui, E. (2021). *La construction de la structure démocratique par la base: quel est le projet étatique de Kaïs Saïed?* Inkyfada. https://inkyfada.com/fr/2021/10/19/kais-saied-construction-democratie-base-tunisie/

M'rad, H. (2015). Le Dialogue National en Tunisie. *Association Tunisienne d'etudes Politiques (ATEP).* Editions Nirwana.

M'rad, H. (2016). *De la constitution à l'accord de Carthage; les premières marches de la Deuxième République.* Nirvana.

M'rad, H. (2018). *La coalition laïco-islamique à l'épreuve.* Nirvana.

Mzalouat, H., Rejbi, N., & Warda, M. (2022). *La "société civile," dans le viseur de Kaïs Saïed.* Inkyfada. https://inkyfada.com/fr/2022/03/15/kais-saied-menace-societe-civile-tunisie/

Nachi, M. (2017). *Révolutions & compromis.* Nirvana.

Nadhif, A. (2021). *Challenges and Scenarios of a Transition Roadmap in Tunisia.* Emirates Policy Centre. https://epc.ae/en/details/scenario/challenges-and-scenarios-of-a-transition-roadmap-in-tunisia

Nafti, H. (2021). *Tunisie: la bataille autour de la Cour constitutionnelle pourrait sonner la fin de la deuxième République.* Middle East Eye. https://www.middleeasteye.net/fr/decryptages/tunisie-cour-constitutionnelle-crise-bloquage-kais-saied-octroi-pouvoirs

Netterstrøm, K. L. (2015). After the Arab Spring: The Islamists' Compromise in Tunisia. *Journal of Democracy, 26*(4), 110–124.

O'Donnell, G., & Schmitter, P. C. (1986). *Transitions from Authoritarian Rule: Tentative Conclusions About Uncertain Democracies.* Johns Hopkins University Press.

Otay, D. (2020). *How Tunisia's COVID Response Demonstrates Governmental Dysfunction.* Fikra Forum. https://www.washingtoninstitute.org/policy-analysis/how-tunisias-covid-response-demonstrates-governmental-dysfunction

Reuters. (2020). *Tunisia Government Given Special Powers to Handle Coronavirus Crisis*. https://www.reuters.com/article/health-coronavirus-tunisia-parliament-idUSL8N2BR404

Safi, M. (2019). Tunisia Election: 'Robocop' Kais Saied Wins Presidential Runoff. *The Guardian*. https://www.theguardian.com/world/2019/oct/14/tunisia-election-exit-polls-point-to-landslide-win-for-robocop-kais-saied

Sasmaz, A., & Grubman, N. (2021). *The Collapse of Tunisia's Party System and the Rise of Kais Saied*. Middle East Research and Information Project. https://merip.org/2021/08/the-collapse-of-tunisias-party-system-and-the-rise-of-kais-saied/

Serrano, F. (2020). *After Successfully Managing COVID-19, Tunisia Gets Back to its Old Problems*. Middle East Institute. https://www.mei.edu/publications/after-successfully-managing-covid-19-tunisia-gets-back-its-old-problems

Siebert, L. (2020). *Tunisia's Transition Hits a Rough Patch Following COVID Lockdown*. USIP. https://www.usip.org/publications/2020/08/tunisias-transition-hits-rough-patch-following-covid-lockdown

Siebert, L., & Abouaoun, E. (2021). *What's Next for Tunisia's Transition?* USIP. https://www.usip.org/publications/2021/08/whats-next-tunisias-transition

Werenfels, I. (2022). *Time Is of the Essence: Tunisian President Consolidates Authoritarian Rule: Europe Waits and Misses Opportunities to Influence*. SWP. https://www.swp-berlin.org/en/publication/die-zeit-draengt-der-tunesische-praesident-konsolidiert-seine-autoritaere-herrschaft

Yared, C. (2021). *La construction du constitutionalisme tunisien: étude de droit comparé*. Université Bordeaux. https://tel.archives-ouvertes.fr/tel-03168107

Yerkes, S., & Yahmed, Z. B. (2019). *Tunisia's Political System: From Stagnation to Competition*. Carnegie Endowment. https://carnegieendowment.org/2019/03/28/tunisia-s-political-system-from-stagnation-to-competition-pub-78717

Yerkes, S., & Muasher, M. (2017). *Tunisia's Corruption Contagion: A Transition at Risk*. Carnegie Endowment. https://carnegieendowment.org/2017/10/25/tunisia-s-corruption-contagion-transition-at-risk-pub-73522

Zghal, A., Hénia, A., & Ben Slimane, F. (2016). *Compromis historiques et citoyenneté politique*. Diraset, Arabesques Editions.

CHAPTER 6

The Limits of Territorial Arrangements and the Relevance of Consociationalism for India

Harihar Bhattacharyya

INTRODUCTION

Federalism is an integral part of India's history. As the major country in South Asia, India became independent from British colonial rule in 1947, with the partition of the country between India and newly-formed Pakistan. A Constituent Assembly by the Indians, elected indirectly, drafted the Constitution of India between 1946 and 1949, and the Constitution was inaugurated on 26 January 1950 proclaiming India as a federal democratic republic. Article 1 (1) of the Constitution states: 'India, that is, Bharat[1] shall be a Union of States.' The Indian Union, or federation, was built from above by carving up territories left over by the British. India's federation-building by state creation since 1950

---

[1] The term Bharat is the indigenous name, mythical name for India.

H. Bhattacharyya (✉)
University of Burdwan, Bardhaman, India
e-mail: hbhattacharyya@polsc.buruniv.ac.in

© The Author(s), under exclusive license to Springer Nature Switzerland AG 2024
E. Wassim Aboultaif et al. (eds.), *Power-Sharing in the Global South*, Federalism and Internal Conflicts, https://doi.org/10.1007/978-3-031-45721-0_6

121

remains incomplete; the territory of India has been reorganized many times, and through different steps (Bhattacharyya, 2019). The Constitution of 1950 still remains in force but has been amended several times. Socially and culturally India, a country of a billion plus inhabitants—is vast with a diversity of languages, religions, tribes, regions and sub-regions. As a country of immense diversity, people in India are used to living with differences and shared cultures. However, in the realm of politics, especially after the colonial rulers introduced a semi-federal and parliamentary systems in the late 1930s by virtue of the Government of India Act 1935, a majoritarian principle ('winner takes all') has gripped the electoral democracy at federal, State and sub-State levels. What was designed in the Constitution was mostly a system of territorial distribution of powers between the Union and States with very limited scope for non-territorial power-sharing. The existing research on federation-building in India (e.g. Bhattacharyya, 2018, 2019) shows that the States in India have been the result of federation-building rather than the other way around, and behind the demand for new states are some ethno-regional and linguistic elites who are also dominant castes[2] in the States. In the case of India's North East, for example, although the tribal ethnic identity was the main factor in state creation, it has created insurmountable problems, for tribal ethnicity and territory do not coincide in most cases (Bhattacharyya, 2019).

I argue in this chapter that Indian federalism has so far resolved the issue of power-sharing territorially, but the many non-territorial issues of power-sharing remain unresolved. The territorial mode of power-sharing through federalism has worked at State and sub-State levels of the polity. At the latter level, the demand for power-sharing has been met within a pre-defined constitutional structure (often modified), and/or, by creating new structures, as appropriate. But there is limited scope for non-territorial or consociational power-sharing. The new micro-minorities as well as the old ones who may not be strong enough in territorial concentration to demand a new territory, and/or, who may be large in number but dispersed without any territorial concentration. As for Muslims (14% of India's population), power-sharing at any level remains out of reach.

---

[2] Castes still define the social and cultural hierarchies in different regions of India. The State-based dominant castes such as the Kammas and Reddys in Andhra Pardesh, and the Lingayats and Vokkaligas in Karnataka who are economically the most powerful too.

Theoretically, consociationalism as a tool of power-sharing in what is called 'deeply divided societies' is a matter of heated debates among scholars. Nagle (2020: 137–144), for example, has argued that the model leads to stalemate and dysfunctionality (what he calls zombie power-sharing), in such cases as Northern Ireland, Lebanon and Iraq. The application of the model to explain India's democracy by Lijphart (1977, 1996) has been received with scathing criticisms for the inappropriate application and has been rejected by several scholars, most recently by Adeney and Swenden (2019). But it has not lost all its appeal. McCulloch (2014, 2017) has found its relevance in understanding power-sharing in deeply divided societies. Power-sharing, McCulloch argues rightly, "is an institutional mode of governance premised on inclusion, representation and participation of all major social (ethnic or ethnonational and/or religious) groups in deeply divided societies" (2017: 405). This is an inclusive definition of power-sharing, and perhaps somewhat an ideal type. McCulloch's (2017)[3] concerns for inclusion/exclusion, representation of minorities and participation are, however, genuine, for a majoritarian political system per se has little to offer to her approach. What I seek to propose here is that the Indian parliamentary federal political system has served as the dominant and relatively successful model of power-sharing, one that is both structural and dynamic. To explain it further, India's model of federalism in which federal units and sub-units are the result of federalization of the post-colonial territory, in phases, has offered the space for contestation and negotiations between the state authorities and the aggrieved ethnic minorities (and sometimes rebels). This in turn has resulted in further territorial divisions to right-size the federal units for better representation, inclusion and participation in the political process. However, this has not resolved all problems of exclusion, representation and participation for those ethnic minorities who could be too small to demand a territorial solution, and /or who are large in number but dispersed. Finally, religious minorities such as the Muslims are not constitutionally permitted to demand a territorial solution to their exclusion; neither are they represented by any non-territorial structures. This calls for a consociational solution to the issue of power-sharing in India.

In the Indian political lexicon, federalism has stood for power-sharing. It is only at the sub-State levels that the demand for power-sharing

---

[3] See also McCulloch (2014) for the distinction between liberal and corporate consociational settlement in divided societies.

124   H. BHATTACHARYYA

has come up from the perspective of the ethnic rebels in the hilly North East. By 'power-sharing' I mean, first, the constitutionally determined and guaranteed distribution of legislative, executive and financial powers between different tiers of government. The major issue Indian power-sharing faces is how legislative, executive and financial powers are distributed between the federal government (Union government) and the federal units (the States). This conception of power-sharing is understood in territorial terms.[4] A second form of power-sharing is between the States and their sub-State units in which case it is mostly executive powers that are shared. A third form of power-sharing takes place for the aboriginal peoples, especially in India's North East (with 8 federal units) through the Constitutional pre-defined provisions for Autonomous Tribal District Councils which entitled them to have some legislative and mostly executive powers. The unit of power-sharing is a territory; however, small it might be. This model is nonetheless exclusionary. There is limited scope of non-territorial power-sharing for certain categories of people such as any religious groups. The millions of ethnic minorities in different States in India who are the offshoots of territorial power-sharing have no provision for representation in the legislative bodies and hence are deprived of taking part in decision-making. In order to accommodate some special diversity, some federal units have asymmetric statuses and powers (Jammu & Kashmir, Nagaland and Mizoram in India's North East are some examples).

In sum, power-sharing in India works at multiple levels and in different ways. First, power-sharing has worked mostly in and through the federal system which today is multi-layered. Various forms of federal asymmetry have been designed to accommodate diversity. Second, power-sharing remains mostly structural; even for the ethnic rebels in the north east of India willing to join the democratic political process through the power-sharing accords (the so-called Ethnic Peace Accords) has been understood within the parameters of the pre-determined constitutional provisions for the Autonomous Tribal District Councils as per the 6th Schedule of the Constitution for self-governance of the tribal areas. The 5th Schedule was designed to govern the tribals residing in other States of India not so far with much success though. Third, there is a democratic challenge. Whether by new state creation, or by demanding a Tribal District Council,

---

[4] On different modes of power-sharing, see Chapter 2 in this Volume.

political power is not ascriptive but something to be achieved by means of elections every five years when the incumbent leaders have a chance to get re-elected or to be rejected by the voters. Democracy, therefore, not only gives political legitimacy to the rulers, but is also a challenge to them.

I argue in this chapter that India's relatively successful mode of power-sharing, as above, is to be understood in terms of the country's evolving federalism. It is evolving in the sense that the process of federation-building is not complete since it began in the early 1950s. I also seek to highlight that there are limitations of the model based on the majoritarian principle of democracy. Minorities in India (micro-minorities; religious minorities; resultant minorities following state creation) remain excluded. As is often the case in parliamentary systems run on the majoritarian principle, parliamentary and legislative minorities are accommodated to some extent in governmental committees. Ethnic minorities might be included in some government ministries. But these are only symbolic gestures. The inherent structural limitations to power-sharing as a tool for inclusion and the promotion of democracy in a diverse democracy remain.

INDIA'S CLEAVAGES

India is evidently a deeply divided society by any terms. If we say that India is socially and culturally the world's most diverse country that still is an understatement. The country's 1.35 billion (2019) people—second largest after China—are multi-religious, multi-lingual, multi-regional and sub-regional and multi-tribal. The Hindus, contrary to conventional misunderstanding, are an amorphous and differentiated category, and largely undefined; they are the overwhelmingly majority (approximately 80%). While in a majority position, they are divided by regions, castes, sub-castes and communities, and language and dialects, and live in different regions and sub-regions. Before 1956 the ethno-linguistic cleavages in India were quite puzzling. The British rulers carved up their Presidencies and Provinces that did not follow any ethno-linguistic boundaries. For instance, in the Madras Presidency, there were, as per Census Report of India 1931, apart from the Tamil majority, 17.7 million Telegus; 4 million Oriyas; 3.7 million Malayalis; and 1.7 million Kannada speaking people (Bhattacharyya, 2018: 83). Added to it was the case of some 560 princely States[5] of different sizes and socio-cultural diversity and interspersed between the Provinces.

Today India's people live in 28 States (federal units) and 10 Union Territories (with direct control of the Union government although democratically) but then that may still be an understatement. Today's federal units, the results of India's federalization since 1956, contain in each many minorities—sub-regional; linguistic and religious. Unlike the classical federations, the Indian federation is being built from above, by the Union government unilaterally empowered by the provisions of Articles 2 and 3 of the Indian Constitution, combined with political pressures from below by ethno-regional political elites. Despite many rounds of territorial right-sizing, the states in India are explicitly unequal in terms of population ranging from about 200 million in Uttar Pradesh to Sikkim with a population of about a little over half a million. Except Assam, most of the States in India's north east have smaller populations by Indian standards. This affects, of course, power-sharing and the formation of government at the centre when coalitions have become the norm since the disintegration of the Congress Party in the late 1980s. Since 2014 though India has been governed by a majority coalition government—the National Democratic Alliance (NDA) led by the Bharatiya Janata Party (BJP), a Right-wing Hindu nationalist party, which has a majority of its own in the lower chamber of the parliament, the Lok Sabha.

Religions

India's Muslims are diverse and dispersed in the country with a majority in population in Kashmir, and Lakshadweep (UT), and have large concentration above 10% in as many as 11 States. In UP, West Bengal and Bihar, the Muslims comprise 47% of all Muslims in India. There are as many as 86 districts in India in which Muslims are 20% plus, and 19 districts where they are 50% plus. However, neither the Muslim majority state or UT, nor the districts were created as such; the Muslims have been living there for centuries. Whether a majority or not, they do not receive any benefits of territorial autonomy or reservation of seats in the Legislative Assembly or parliament. However, in India's democracy this community is very salient and determines at the State levels the political fortune of

---

[5] The princely States or kingdoms comprised of about two-thirds of India's territory and about one-third of its population with greater complexity (Menon, 1956).

6 THE LIMITS OF TERRITORIAL ARRANGEMENTS ... 127

Table 6.1 Religious composition of India's population (2011)

Religion	Population (in millions)	% of total population
Hindus	960	79.80
Muslims	170	14.24
Christians	27	2.3
Sikhs	20	1.72
Buddhists	5.76	0.8
Jains	4.4	0.7
Other religions	7.9	0.66
Religion not stated	2.8	0.24

Sources Census Reports of India 2011. Census data for 2021 not available at time of writing

political parties as vote bank. In India's lower house of parliament, Lok Sabha, the Muslims have not so far been represented in proportion to their population.[6] In the current (17th) Lok Sabha, the Muslim MPs are only 27 (about 5%) out of 543. In the Council of Ministers (56-member) led by Prime Minister Modi, there is only one Minister who is a Muslim (Table 6.1).

There are three Christian majority States—Meghalaya, Mizoram and Nagaland—in India's North East, but those States were created not on the basis of religion, but tribal ethnicity. Punjab is a Sikh majority State created in 1966 in which case a strange combination of language and religion was made. The Buddhists are predominant in Sikkim now considered as part of the North East, but then it was a kingdom until it was incorporated into the Indian Union in 1974 as an 'Associate State' to be upgraded to a full State in 1975.

Languages

Language has become an important factor for demanding territorial power-sharing in the form of new States or sub-States in India. The key to the relative success of Indian federalism and democracy in this respect is what is known in the literature as 'linguistic federalism.' This has received considerable academic attention (Bhattacharyya, 2001, 2019, 2021). There are 22 'official languages' in India (Table 6.2), which to

[6] In the State of Telangana (created in 2014) the Muslims are 13% of the population, but 40% seats in the State Assembly is occupied by the Muslim—a lone best practice.

unfamiliar eyes, may seem bizarre. First, India does not have a national language; Hindi and English are the official languages of the Union government. Second, Hindi (spoken by around 35% of the people[7]) is the largest spoken language. Third, although so far 22 languages have been declared as 'official languages' (out of some 1950 language speakers in India), for the day-to-day running of things, the States are to follow a three-language formula out of the above list, which may mean the following: the dominant regional language, Hindi and English, or English and Hindi. In practice, however, many States in the South of India follow a two-language formula neglecting Hindi.[8] In the newly created State of Telangana (2014), Telegu (77% speakers), is the official language and Urdu (12% speakers) is the second official language. Fourth, there is a constitutional provision for recognizing one or more languages as 'associate official languages' of the States in the sub-regional level (Articles 344–347 in Bakshi, 2017). Fifth, there are States particularly in India's North East, where the 8th Schedule official languages are not the languages used in day to day administration: Manipur, Meghalaya, Mizoram and Nagaland. In those States, English is the official language, for there are no commonly accepted scripts. Sixth, there are languages officially recognized as such, with a large number of speakers but they do not make any territorial claims; as these peoples are dispersed. Finally, the recognition of the languages as 'official' and their placement in the 8th Schedule of the Indian Constitution has immense symbolic significance particularly when the rights to language, script and culture are recognized as fundamental rights of the citizens and communities in the Indian Constitution, which has provided for a number of safeguards for this purpose.[9]

---

[7] Census reports have added some languages such as Maithili, Rajasthan, etc., to the category of Hindi.

[8] In Tamil Nadu, for example, Tamil is the official language, and English is the additional official language. In Kerala, Malayalam and English are the official languages of the State.

[9] There is a constitutional body named the Commissioner of Linguistic Minorities which collects data, examines the safeguards and offers recommendations to the concerned State. See Bhattacharyya (2022) for a critical examination of the failures of the States in safeguarding minority languages.

6 THE LIMITS OF TERRITORIAL ARRANGEMENTS ... 129

Table 6.2 India's official languages (2011) (8th schedule)

Hindi	528,347,193	43.63
Bengali	97,237,669	8.03
Marathi	83,026,680	6.86
Telegu	81,127,740	6.88
Tamil	69,026,881	6.70
Gujarati	55,492,554	5.70
Urdu	50,772,632	4.58
Kannada	43,706,512	3.61
Odisha[b]	37,521,324	3.10
Malayalam	34,838,819	3.10
Punjabi	33,124,726	4.79
Assamese	15,311,351	1.28
Maithili	13,583,464	1.26
Santali	7,368,192	0.61
Kashmiri	6,797,587	0.56
Nepali	2,926,168	0.24
Sindhi	2,772,264	0.23
Dogri	2,596,787	0.21
Konkani	2,256,502	0.19
Manipuri	1,761,079	0.15
Bodo	1,482,929	0.12
Sanskrit	24,821	N[a]

[a] Negligible; [b] Formerly Orissa
Source Census Reports of India (2011)

Tribes of India

The tribal population in India is quite large at about 8.6% (2011) comprising some 106 million people. There are constitutional provisions for power-sharing for the tribals especially through self-governance measures such as the Autonomous District Councils (under Sixth Schedule of the Constitution) in the North East of India. Tribals are dispersed throughout India, but comprise a majority in population in four States in India's North East—Arunachal Pradesh (1987), Meghalaya (1972), Mizoram (1987) and Nagaland (1963).[10] The internal composition of tribal population in those States except Mizoram is highly differentiated; in Nagaland, there is no one Naga group in majority; the same is true in Arunachal Pradesh; in Meghalaya, the dominant tribe (Khasis) have got power following statehood, but the Garos, the

---

[10] Figures in parenthesis indicate years of their formation as States.

second largest tribe, have been demanding a State of their own to be known as *Garoland* (Bhattacharyya, 2018). However, more tribals live in India's mainland than in the North East (Table 6.3), and not in all cases, territorial power-sharing through federalism could be followed. In some cases, other constitutional options have been utilized. For example, the 5th Schedule (Article 244 of the Indian Constitution) of the Indian Constitution was designed for the protection of interests of the tribals in the mainland of India that provides for a Tribal Advisory Council to be composed of the Members of the Legislative Assembly belonging to the tribals, and a provision for local self-government through the extension of the Panchayat Act (1996) to the tribal areas. However, the 5th Schedule provisions have not been as powerful to protect tribals' land and their right to forest produce as the 6th Schedule (Articles 244 (2) and 275 (1)), applicable only to the hill tribes of the North East, which provides for Autonomous Tribal District Council with legislative, executive and financial and some judicial powers. The District Councils are examples of territorial power-sharing. There is, in addition, provisions for quota, or reservation of seats for them in the Lok Sabha (lower house), (in other similar bodies too), but the number of seats available to them are far below their actual percentage of the population (47 out of 543 in the current Lok Sabha). This is the sole method of non-territorial power-sharing. The question remains: Even if the tribals have had proportional representation, this would not work for their interests in the absence of any minority veto provision. This is true for State Legislative Assemblies too. Even if the tribals are represented as per their number, without the provision of any veto power over the question of land alienation and loss of their livelihood due to mining operations, their legislators could do little in the face of the huge majority enjoyed by the ruling parties. There is a non-territorial provision in respect of formation of the tribal District Councils where out of 30 members, 26 are to be elected, and the State Governor has the power to nominate 4 in consideration of the communities not represented otherwise. In either case, such non-territorial measures of power-sharing pale into insignificance in the face of the majority.

Table 6.3 Distribution of tribes and their percentage contribution to the total population in States and Union Territories (2011)

States and UTs	Total population	Per cent (%)
Lakshadweep (UT)	61,120	94.8
Mizoram	1,036,115	94.4
Nagaland	1,710,973	86.5
Meghalaya	12,555,861	86.5
Arunachal Pradesh	951,821	68.8
Dadra & Naga Haveli (UT)	178,564	52.0
Sikkim	206,260	33.8
Manipur#	902,740	35.1
Tripura	1,166,813	31.8
Chandigarh (UT)	7,822,902	30.6
Chhattisgarh	7,822,902	30.6
Jharkhand	8,645,042	26.2
Odisha	9,590,756	22.8
Madhya Pradesh	15,316,784	21.1
Gujarat	8,917,174	14.8
Rajasthan	9,238,534	13.5
Assam	3,884,371	12.4
Jammu & Kashmir	1,493,299	11.9
Maharashtra	10,510,213	9.4
Andaman and Nicobar Islands (UT)	28,530	7.5
Andhra Pradesh[a]	5,918,073	5.9
West Bengal	529,695	5.5

[a] Bifurcated in 2019 to form the newest State in India, ie., Telangana. In Telangana tribals constitute 9.3% (2011)
Source http://tribal.nic.in/ST/Tribal%20Profile.pdf); # excluding 3 sub-divisions

THE ADOPTION OF POWER-SHARING IN INDIA

India's social and cultural diversity was a fact of life for centuries, and its importance was recognized both in the elite perception of India's nationhood (Bhattacharyya, 2005) and the nationalist political imagination of the future state of India after the British had left. The utmost importance in the latter was the unity of the country which was fragmented along cultural fault lines and deeply heterogeneous. Jawaharlal Nehru, as the representative of the more articulate generation of nationalists, and the main architect of post-colonial democracy in India, had recognized a decade before independence India's immense diversity and emphasized the basis of unity nonetheless:

The diversity of India is tremendous; it is obvious. It lies on the surface and anybody can see it. It concerns itself with physical appearances as well as with certain mental habits and traits. Yet, with all these differences, there is no mistaking the impress of India on the Pathans, as this is obvious on the Tamils. The Pathans and the Tamils are two extreme examples; others lie somewhere in between. All of them have their distinctive features; all of them have still the distinctive mark of India. It is fascinating to find the Bengalis, the Sindhis, the Punjabis, the Gujeratis, the Tamils, the Andhras, the Oriyas, the Assamese, the Sindhis, the Punjabis....have retained their peculiar characteristic for hundreds of years, have still more or less the same virtues and failures of which old tradition, or record tells us, yet have been throughout these ages distinctive Indian, with the same national heritage and the same set of moral and mental qualities. (Nehru, 1980/1946)[11]

The peoples mentioned by Nehru in the above quote were some of the ethno-linguistic and regional groups rooted in their territories for ages. Such acute sense of India's diversity in Nehru and other nationalist leaders were not simply the figment of their imagination. The Indian National Congress (INC) (created in 1885) was an inter-ethnic and regional political platform represented by the ethnic leaders of different regions of India who carried a dual identity: ethno-regional and pan-Indian. From the early 1910s, especially with the rise of 'Mahatma' Gandhi to the leadership of the INC, an otherwise elite organization was transformed into a mass movement, a political consensus among the historians (Chandra et al., 2008), but with a difference. With his rise to supreme leadership of the INC, the party was reorganized along ethno-linguistic lines so that the Provincial Committees of the party were re-named after the ethno-linguistic identity. This went beyond the then existing colonial provincial boundaries. For example, the Maharashtra, the Gujarat, the Tamil, the Telegu Provincial Committees, etc., were formed in order to ensure better political communication with the people; the real purpose was strategic: recognition and accommodation of ethnic identity. This was formalized in the famous Nagpur Session of the party in 1920 when a formal resolution was taken to pledge the INC to reconstitute India after independence

---

[11] The recognition of diversity by Nehru like other *nationalist* leaders of his generation was not based on any detailed understanding of the situation on the ground. A decade later at the Jaipur session of the Congress in 1948, it was admitted that the party's understanding of the ethno-linguistic situation of India was not on the basis of the concrete reality, which was more complex (see Bhattacharyya, 2019: 85).

into a federation based on linguistic Provinces. The same was reiterated in all subsequent meetings and sessions of the party till independence (Bhattacharyya, 2019: 81–93).

The path-dependent and ethnic compulsion coupled with the INC's commitment made federalism the most viable option for future India. Federalism's adoptability was beyond doubt. The task of the Constituent Assembly (CA) (1946–1949) was to debate and decide on how many Provinces would be created; how much power was to be devolved to the federal units; to what extent language could be used to demarcate provincial boundaries and so on (Austin, 1966, 1999; Bhattacharyya, 2001). The linguistic sentiments of the people were a most powerful factor behind the adoption of some kind of federalism.[12]

British colonial rule was a key influence in India's future direction to both territorial power-sharing (federalism) and democracy. India's parliamentary democracy, federalism and other methods of power-sharing were British legacies as well as the nationalist aspirations. For democracy the legacy was clearly British. The very limited nature of the same under colonial rule with highly restricted franchise based on property ownership and education was pointed out by the nationalists who demanded expansion of the franchise. From the early 1910s, the colonial rulers introduced some doses of decentralization (Morris-Jones, 1967: 19) but very little real power-sharing was guaranteed in the colonial institutional arrangements till 1935.[13]

Therefore, the Government of India Act (1935)—the landmark in the institutional development of democracy and federalism in India—provided for elected government (on limited franchise based on education, property and age so that 60% of the people could not vote) at the provincial level with limited powers, but it was not a federation in the strict sense of the term. But nonetheless it allowed significant scope of power-sharing. The Congress rejected the arrangements at the national level, but took part in elections following the Act of 1935 and formed governments in most of the Provinces in 1937. This Act provided for some a significant measure of provincial autonomy in terms of three

---

[12] In 1948 in the Jaipur session of the INC the Congress leadership was found to be self-critical of the fact that India's social and cultural diversity was more complex than what they had been harping on for decades.

[13] I have discussed the institutional developments, in detail, elsewhere (see Bhattacharyya, 2019: 81–93).

lists of the distribution of legislative and administrative powers: federal, provincial and concurrent. However, the central government enjoyed more powers and the Governor-General was given the overriding powers to declare an emergency and supremacy over provincial legislation if needed. Congress' main objection was to the manner in which a national level government with two India's (Provinces and princely States) was conceived by the colonial rulers for unity between democracy (Provinces) and medieval autocracy (of some 560 princely states). Nonetheless the key influence of British colonial rule and its legislation, particularly the Government of India Act 1935 on the future direction of India to federalism was obvious. With the onset of the Second World War, and the resignation of all Congress run provincial governments, the above system collapsed. In 1946 (16 May), the colonial rulers proposed a plan for India's constitutional transition known as the Cabinet Mission Plan—the last colonial federal experiment. The Plan provided for a Union government comprising British India and the princely states to be responsible for foreign affairs, defence, currency, communications etc., including the right to raise finance for the purposes; all subjects not enlisted in the Union List and residual powers to be vested in the Provinces; and provisions for representation in Union Legislature and Executive from British India, the princely States and two major religious communities (Hindus and Muslims) (Char, 1983: 687–689). This scheme of power-sharing was highly debated among political parties for its alleged communal character, and the motive for two India's—one for the Hindus and one for the Muslims; Congress rejected this for another reason: the Plan proposed a Union of democracy and autocracy. The colonial measures failed to resolve the religious cleavage (Hindu-Muslim relations), and the Muslim League's persistent demand for a state of their own was met in the formation of Pakistan on 14 August 1947 against India's version of secularism.

Post-independence Institutional Arrangements for Power-Sharing

Following the Government of India Act 1935, elections to form governments at the provincial level were held in 1945–1946 (on the basis of limited franchise) (about 12% of the adult population), and governments were formed in different Provinces by Congress, the Muslim League and other parties in coalition. This gave the Indians another round

6 THE LIMITS OF TERRITORIAL ARRANGEMENTS ... 135

of experience in power-sharing in colonial rule. The provincial legislative assemblies eventually formed the Central Legislative Assembly which would also act as India's Constitutional Assembly from December 1946 (Bhattacharyya, 2019: 84–88).

Legislative, financial and executive powers are shared between the Union and State governments in terms of three lists. Unlike classical federations, the Indian federation was not built from below; here the federal units are the results of federation-building in many stages which has entailed the creation of States mostly on the basis of linguistic identity of the people. But the constitution already has provided for two tiers of government, Union and State, with its defined competences ensured by three lists of distribution of powers: Union List, State List and Concurrent List. Both governments have legislative competence on their Lists and also have executive authority in matters of implementation. There are significant areas of asymmetry in the Indian federation too; but most of the States are equally placed in terms of status and distribution of powers. However, between 1950 and 1956, power-sharing arrangements were very unequal because there were three categories of States ranked A, B and C. The States A were the former British Provinces; the States B were not exactly States but 'Unions of States' (the former princely regimes), and the States C were called Commissioners' Provinces. Thus, the formation of the Indian federation would involve ample re-territorialization. The process was standardized in 1956 when India's first major reorganization of territory took place mostly on the basis of linguistic identity of the people with territorial concentration. The task, however, was not easy to recreate States simply on the basis of linguistic identity. The official Commission (States Reorganization Commission 1953–1956) was very cautious in advancing a 'balanced approach' that took into consideration language, administrative convenience and efficiency. Thus in 1956 sixteen States were created by redrawing the States' boundaries linguistically as far as possible.[14] But things took another decade to complete when in 1966 Punjab was created with one-third of its original areas as a Sikh majority State.[15] In the Indian federation, the Union government is most powerful. The Union List contains 97 items of national

---

[14] The SRC (1953–1955)'s linguistic criterion was 50 per cent speakers as the minimum, which left out large linguistic minorities.

[15] In the case of Punjab alone religion along with language was considered as the basis of State creation (Nayar 1966).

136   H. BHATTACHARYYA

and international significance: defence, military, air forces, naval forces, etc.; currency; communication, diplomacy, citizenship and extradition. However, the States were given significant powers concerning the region: (66 items in the State List), which include public order; public health; prisons; land ownership, acquisition, use and reforms and land revenue; police; local government; agricultural income tax; state public service and so on. The Concurrent List contains 47 items on which both the Union and State governments can legislate although in case of conflict the Union government authority prevails. The Concurrent List contains items such as criminal law; criminal procedure; marriage and divorce; transfer of property; civil procedure; prevention of cruelty to animals; trust and trusteeship and so on.

Power to tax mostly lies with the Union government which collects most of the taxes; the States also collects taxes levied by the Union as well as those levied by them. A Finance Commission under Articles 280 (also Art. 360) is appointed after every five years by the President of India to recommend the distribution of net tax proceeds between the State governments; the principles that govern grants-in-aid to the States; measures to augment the Consolidated Fund of India, and measures to augment the Consolidates Fund of the States to supplement the resources of the local government such as Municipalities, etc. Since 1951 the Finance Commissions of India have been regularly formed, functioned effectively by formula-based transfer of money from the Union to the States and served to give stability to India's complex federal system, thereby effectively also contributing to economic power-sharing.[16] Two very important and relevant points to be added here are: first, although the Union government collects most of the taxes, it does not spend them all. In terms of share of public expenditure, it is the State governments which spend about 55% in 2014–2015 (Reddy & Reddy, 2019: 233) of the total public expenditure. To be precise, it is not the State governments' money that they have to spend; it is by way of implementation of many Union government schemes and flagship programmes of empowerment and development. In recent years, the States' share of money by way of transfer by the Finance Commission has increased from 32% to 42% since 2014 after the BJP led NDA government under Prime Minister Modi came to power.

---

[16] On different forms of power-sharing, see Chapter 2 in this volume.

Territorial Power-Sharing for the Aboriginal Peoples and Political Exclusion

India's tribals (some 106 million in numbers) are minorities to be found all over the country. In the North East, four States have tribal majority. But most of India's tribal peoples live in the mainland of India and as many as in 12 States they constitute significant proportions of the population. Are the tribals real partners in power-sharing? Are they adequately represented? As we shall see presently, in all cases the majoritarian principle is followed. The reservation of seats at the rate of 7% in legislative bodies, government offices and admission to educational institutions run by the government is constitutional obligation. That hardly, if ever is a guarantee for their share in power at any levels. At the sub-State levels, other constitutional measures have been provided for. Two Schedules (5th and 6th) have, therefore, been designed to ensure protection of tribal interests and self-governance. A brief but critical analysis of the Constitutional provisions for the protection of tribal interests, by way of the 5th and the 6th Schedules suggests that while the latter has been successful in tribal empowerment and greater protection of their land and identity, the effectiveness of the 5th Schedule is ambiguous in nature. The Government of India's Tribal Affairs Ministry itself has sharply pointed this out.[17] No wonder there are many court cases and judicial verdicts pointing fingers at the many failures of implementation of the provision at the level of the State governments due to vested interests.

The provisions of the 5th Schedule of the Constitution (Part B Article 244 (1)) are to apply to the so-called Scheduled Areas where a Tribal Advisory Council (TAC) (not more than 20 members) is to be formed; of them three-fourths members shall be the tribal representatives in the State Legislative Assembly with the remaining seats to be filled by other members of the State Assembly concerned. The sole job of the Council is to advise the State Governor on welfare and advancement of the Scheduled Tribes. The State Governor has the power to make rules pertaining to 'peace and good government' in the area. The performance records of the Council in 13 States up to 2018 suggest that very little or nothing has been done when the Council hardly if ever met to discuss issues (*Land*

---

[17] Land and Governanc under the Fifth Schedule' a joint report by the Ministray of Tribal Affairs and the UNDP (https://tribal.nic.in/downloads/FRA/5.%20Land%20and%20Governance%20under%20Fifth%20Schedule.pdf).

and Governance Under the Fifth Schedule, Ministry of Tribal Affairs, Government of India, 2017). The Council in Chhattisgarh (tribal population about 30%) is the lone State in which there were regular annual meetings from 2012–2013 to 2017–2018. In Maharashtra and Madhya Pradesh, by contrast, there has been no annual meeting of the Councils when these two States have tribal population of 9.4% and 21%, respectively. In Gujarat, with about 9 million tribal people (15%), only one annual meeting of the Council took place in 2015–2016. This in brief is an indictment on the poor strategy of tribal welfare and identity protection. In those areas, large scale tribal land alienation, devastation on their habitat due to mining operations by the States and /or the private actors have taken place without any redress. This is one area where no power-sharing takes place except the tribals electing some representatives to the legislatures.

By contrast, the 6th Schedule of the Constitution (Articles 244 (2) and 271 (1)) has been a relative success in territorial power-sharing by the tribals (hilly) in India's North East. This provides for the formation by elected Autonomous Tribal District Council for self-government of the hill tribes in the North East of India. Such Councils (10 in number) have been functioning in the region; and in many cases the successful experience in the Council has paved the way for its upgrade to Union Territory and finally to Statehood with greater autonomy in the Indian federation. Nagaland, Mizoram and Meghalaya in India's North East are good cases in point. Even after statehood, the Autonomous Tribal District Councils have been formed regularly in the States in the region for the minority tribals. The Garo District Council (in Meghalaya), the Bru District Council and Hmar District Council in Mizoram and Tripura Tribal Autonomous Distinct Council in Tripura are cases in point. Such tribal identity-based self-governing bodies have worked and exemplars of power-sharing at the bottom of tribal society (Bhattacharyya, 2018).

The functioning of such Councils has been studied elsewhere (Mitra & Bhattacharyya, 2018). The 6th Schedule provides for formation by election on the basis of universal adult suffrage of 30-member Council of which 26 shall be elected and 4 nominated by the State Governor in every five years. The State Governor has the power to include more areas in the Council's jurisdiction. The District Council has been assigned wide ranging powers and authority: to make laws relating to allotment, occupation and use of land; forest; establishment of Village or Town Committees (as an instance of grass roots power-sharing); public health and sanitation;

trade and commerce; inheritance, marriage and divorce; land alienation; establishment of primary schools; levy taxes on land and forest, trade and calling; licensing on extraction of minerals and so on. The available records (Bhattacharyya, 2018) suggest that such Councils have been effective in protecting tribal identity (language; customs, etc.); served to ensure more participation of the common tribal folk in their development and empowerment. Much of the empowerment and development programmes of the Union and State governments targeted to the tribals are executed through the agency of the Council. Such Councils which function as kind of a State within a State have been functional for resolution of intra-tribal conflicts, to a significant extent, and added to the legitimacy of the system.[18] As a result, yesterday's rebels, as Mitra and Singh (2009) say, have been converted into the stakeholders guarding the law and territory.

LIMITS OF POWER-SHARING: CHALLENGES AND FUTURE PROSPECTS

Power-sharing arrangements in India have a number of limitations. There are significant areas where the system is very deficient. In terms of territorial power-sharing (federalism), it has worked: a dual polity (Union government and State governments) has evolved with its distinctive features (symmetrical and asymmetrical States; Special Category States; special autonomy, etc.); a sub-State level (decentralization) system since 1992 emerged as rural and urban local self-government bodies but they are very much dependent on the respective State governments for finance and staff. The (Union) Finance Commission has of late been allocating funds separately for the local bodies. Federal asymmetry in matters of status and powers in some cases, especially in the North East, has taken care of meeting the needs of special situations. For example, the States in the North East have received greater per capita federal fund transfers than the States in the mainland. On the whole, in federal terms, India is a success story in simultaneously creating newer States on some ethnic basis and allowing them the constitutionally defined autonomy as a kind of relatively sovereignty units.

---

[18] I have carried out a detailed empirical survey of the Tripura Tribal Autonomous District Council (unpub. Report submitted to the ICCSR).

However, the same cannot be said to be true in the case of non-territorial minorities, especially Muslims, India's second largest population (estimated to be around 170 million) comprising of about 14% of the total population (2011), and dispersed in different parts of India. Apart from Kashmir (Jammu & Kashmir) which remained until 2019 as India's only State with a Muslim majority,[19] there are problems of real accommodation and recognition of the tribals even in the States created in their name but not truly a State of their own.[20] Muslims are dispersed in the country with district level concentration, but a territorial recognition of them for power-sharing remains prohibited in the Constitution. Neither are there any non-territorial representation of the Muslims proportionate to their size in population. The Muslim are not only represented proportionately in the Indian parliament (about 5% in Lok Sabha currently), and they figure very poorly in the Indian state apparatuses such as the army, police, civil services and foreign service. The Sachar Committee Report (2006) of the Government of India contains detailed data on the very poor representation and participation of the Muslims: of the one million plus troops in India the Muslims are only 3% in civil services, they are only about 5% in bureaucracy, they comprise of only 2.5% in all public sectors employment and government services and they are only 7.2% (Sachar Committee, 2006: 166–170). Finally, there are other linguistic and tribal minorities in India which are yet to be accommodated and enjoy the benefits of power-sharing. As the case of India's North East shows (Bhattacharyya, 2018), the tension between territory and tribal

[19] As part of its election manifesto, the BJP, ruling party at the centre, abolished Article 370 of the Indian Constitution that provided for special autonomy to the State of Jammu & Kashmir, and made two Union Territories of Kashmir, and Jammu, and upgraded Ladhakh to a Union Territory. The abolition of the Statehood status of J & K and its demotion has been subject of many debates in India and abroad. It has also been challenged in the Supreme Court but for no effect since Article 370 was retained in the Constitution as a 'temporary and special provision'. This is how the Government of India has defended its action. The picture would have been fundamentally different and difficult if there was a provision for minority veto in India's constitutional democracy.

[20] The State of Jharkhand was created in 2000 by bifurcating as a State for the tribals who have long been demanding a State of their own. Ironically, such a State came into being at a time when the tribals comprising many tribes such as the Santhals, Ho, Munda and others were reduced to a minority (about 26 per cent) in the new State. This is another example in India when territorial power-sharing through federalization has failed to empower the concerned groups. See for further details, A. Prakash (2001).

6 THE LIMITS OF TERRITORIAL ARRANGEMENTS ... 141

ethnicity is endemic despite many institutional arrangements of power-sharing at sub-State level. The intricate division and sub-divisions among the tribes defy any neat and sensible territorial re-sizing. An unending process of territorial divisions for government formation is self-defeating, but this can hardly be a reason not to incorporate the deprived sections in power-sharing via consociationalism.

CONCLUSION: LESSONS LEARNED

India's system of power-sharing through its federalism and democracy have functioned mostly well. Most of the country's ethno-linguistic diversity has been accommodated by territorial power-sharing among the regional and sub-regional ethnic elites. Federal power-sharing in India has been backed by democratic compulsions so that some redistribution of resources percolates down to the grass roots. There have also been areas of asymmetry among the States in power-sharing for consideration of special situations. The Indian case suggests that a different federal model of power-sharing from that of consociationalism can work in complex diversity, to a large extent. However, the system is still not inclusive enough. India's democracy is yet to venture into accommodating its large Muslim minority, both territorially as well as by means of 'corporate federalism'. At the State level, there are cases of better accommodation of Muslims which help dissipate discontent and mistrust, but this has been more to do with vote bank politics than any consociational arrangement. At the national level they are a deprived and excluded minority. Institutionalization of minority veto rights over legislation concerning their interest and proportionate representation in the State structure of the minorities are the much needed reforms in India's federal democracy.

The comparative lessons the Indian experiments suggest, are the following: First, power-sharing was at the heart of India's struggle for independence from British colonial rule. India's adoption of power-sharing was backed up by an institutional evolution from the 1920s, and more particularly late 1930s, and the participation of India's elites in them—the process was carried on to the post-colonial days, and sustained with reforms. Second, while India's cultural diversity was a key factor that pushed the country to a federal mode of governance, and power-sharing, there was widespread consensus about the need for the accommodation of diversity as a value in itself. Much of India's success lies in the adaptation of power-sharing institutions to the varied and changing needs of diversity. Democracy accompanied India's federalism and power-sharing. These two were two sides of the same coin. Later-day democratic decentralization at the sub-state level of governance has added further functionality to the system despite occasional setbacks stemming from the national level regime change, and thereby linking the national to the local level. Third, given India's immense diversity, the structures of power-sharing had to be differentiated. But while this has worked relatively well for territorially rooted ethnic majorities, those without the same (non-territorial ethnic minorities) have, by contrast, struggled to receive a share of power. Fourth, the system of power-sharing in India has functioned by and large in catering to the needs of diversity accommodation, identity fulfilment and some redistribution of resources—the latter because of democratic pressures from below. Finally, India's dynamic quality is caused by the ongoing process of accommodation and power-sharing that has entailed the creation of new States as well as those with an asymmetric distribution of powers.

REFERENCES

Adeney, K., & Swenden, W. (2019). Power-Sharing in the World's Largest Democracy: Informal Consociationalism and its Decline. *Swiss Political Science Review, 25*(4), 45–75.

Austin, G. (1966). *The Indian Constitution: Cornerstone of a Nation*. Oxford University Press.

Austin, G. (1999). *Working a Democratic Constitution*. Oxford Univeristy Press.

Bakshi, P. M. (2017). *The Constitution of India*. Lexis-Nexis.

Bhattacharyya, H. (2001). *India as a Multicultural Federation: Asian Values, Democracy and Decentralization (in Comparison with Swiss Federalism)*. Institute of Federalism.

Bhattacharyya, H. (2005). *Federalism and Regionalism in India—Institutional Strategies and Political Accommodation of Identity* (Heidelberg Papers in South Asian and Comparative Politics Working Paper No. 27). https://core. ac.uk/download/pdf/32579377.pdf

Bhattacharyya, H. (2018). *Radical Politics and Governance in India's North East: The Case of Tripura*. Routledge.

Bhattacharyya, H. (2019). States Reorganisation and Accommodation of Ethno-TErritorial Cleavages in India. In Anderson, G., & Sujit Chuoudhry. (Eds.). *Territory and Power in Constitutional Transitions*. (pp. 81–99) Oxford University Press.

Bhattacharyya, H. (2021). *Federalism in Asia: India, Pakistan, Malaysia, Nepal and Myanmar*. Routledge.

Bhattacharyya, H. (2022). Pitfalls of India's Ethno-federal Model of Ethnic Conflict Management: Tension Between Tribal Ethnicity and Territory in India's North East'. *Ethnopolitics, 21*(3), 203–220.

Chandra, B., et al. (2008). *India Since Independence*. Penguin.

Char, S. D. D. (1983). *Readings in the Constitutional History of India 1757–1947*. Oxford University Press.

Land and Governance under the Fifth Schedule. (2017). https://tribal.nic.in/downloads/FRA/5.%20Land%20and%20Governance%20under%20Fifth%20Schedule.pdf sighted on 31/10/23.

Lijphart, A. (1977). *Democracy in Plural Societies*. Yale University Press.

Lijphart, A. (1996). The Puzzle of India's Democracy: A Consociational Interpretation. *American Political Science Review, 90*(2), 258–268.

McCulloch, A. (2014a). Consociational Settlements in Deeply Divided Societies: The Liberal-Corporate Distinction. *Democratization, 21*(3), 501–518.

McCulloch, A. (2014b). *Power-Sharing and Political Stability in Deeply Divided Societies*. Routledge.

Menon, V. P. (1956). *Integration of Indian States*. Orient Longman.

Mitra, Subrata K., & Singh, V. B. (2009). *When Rebels Become Stakeholders. Democracy, Agency and Social Change in India*. Sage.

Mitra, S. K., & Bhattacharyya, H. (2018). *Politics and Governance in Indian States: Bihar, West Bengal and Tripura*. World Scientific Publishers.

Morris-Jones, W. H. (1967). *The Government and Politics of India*. Hutchinson.

Nagle, J. (2020). Consociationalism Is Dead! Long Live Zombie Power-Sharing. *Studies in Ethnicity and Nationalism, 20*(2), 137–144.

Nayar, B. R. (1966). *Minority Politics in the Punjab*. Princeton University Press.

Nehru, J. (1980/1946). *The Discovery of India*. Oxford University Press.

Prakash, A. (2001). *Jharkhand: Politics of Development and Identity*. Orient Blackswan.

Reddy, Y. V., & Reddy, G. R. (2019). *Indian Fiscal Federalism*. Oxford University Press.

Sachar Committee. (2006, November). *Social, Economic and Educational Status of the Muslim Community of India: A Report*. Prime Minister's High Level Committee, Cabinet Secretariat, New Delhi.

CHAPTER 7

Power-Sharing in Nigeria's Divided Society: Structures, Conflicts and Challenges

Dele Babalola and Hakeem Onapajo

INTRODUCTION

Nigeria, an erstwhile colony of Britain, became independent in 1960. The country operates a three-tier federal system (federal, state and local governments) and an American-style presidential system, with a bicameral legislature at the federal level and a unicameral legislature at the state level. With an estimated population of about 185 million, Nigeria is the most populous country in Africa (Babalola, 2019). The country is also

---

D. Babalola (✉)
Canterbury Christ Church University, Canterbury, UK
e-mail: dele.babalola@canterbury.ac.uk

H. Onapajo
Nile University of Nigeria, Abuja, Nigeria

Institute for the Future of Knowledge, University of Johannesburg, Johannesburg, South Africa

H. Onapajo
e-mail: hakeem.onapajo@nileuniversity.edu.ng

© The Author(s), under exclusive license to Springer Nature Switzerland AG 2024
E. Wassim Aboultaif et al. (eds.), *Power-Sharing in the Global South*, Federalism and Internal Conflicts,
https://doi.org/10.1007/978-3-031-45721-0_7

the most diverse in Africa, comprising many ethnic groups that are informally estimated at 350 and largely divided across two major religious groups—Christians and Muslims (Babalola, 2020; Mustapha, 2009a; Onapajo, 2012). Nigeria's ethnic groups are broadly divided into ethnic 'majorities' which represent the three main ethnolinguistic groups—the Hausa-Fulani, Igbo and Yoruba—which are territorially concentrated in the north, east and west, respectively. The 'minorities' consist of multiple ethnic minority groups like the Kanuri, Ijaw, Nupe, Tiv and so forth spread across the country (Mustapha, 2009a: 562; Osaghae, 1991: 239). The Hausa-Fulani are predominantly Muslim; the Igbo are largely Christians, while the Yoruba are either Christians, Muslims or adherents of African traditional religion.

In Nigeria, politics is characterized by a fierce struggle among ethnic, religious and regional groups. Sometimes, ethnicity and religion interact with regionalism and territoriality. Competition for power and resources among the groups is a major source of political tension and conflicts. Mutual suspicions and continuous fear of domination have characterized relations between the groups, which have underlined Nigerian politics even before independence. The tense political relations contributed to the Nigerian Civil War (1967–1970) following claims of northern domination by the Igbo (of the eastern part of the country). Such perceptions have produced many life-threatening events for the state including the June 12, 1993, conflict, which was caused by the annulment of the presidential election of that year, and the Niger Delta violence in the 2000s. In more recent times, the state has witnessed a sudden rise in ethnic-based nationalism and secession agitations following claims of state-supported policies promoting the supremacy of the Hausa-Fulani group.

Nigeria's weak federal system has further compounded the problem. Long years of military rule entrenched a pseudo-federal system that appears more unitary in form and spirit because of its overbearing federal government over other units of government. Sadly, this has given room for more attraction to control of the center and intensified inter-ethnic and inter-religious competition. To address these concerns, there have been attempts to negotiate and create structures through power-sharing and resource-distribution arrangements. Such efforts have produced some formal and informal structures such as the federal character principle, revenue allocation principles, state creation exercises, geopolitical zoning arrangements and a rotational presidency. These structures appear as effective strategies to promote equity and justice among the competing groups in the state's federal structure. However, a lack of commitment to the power-sharing structures has worsened the situation, thereby causing conflicts and sharply increasing agitations for a restructuring of the state—which has been defined in many ways.

The above background demonstrates that Nigeria provides a rich example of the politics of power-sharing in a plural society. To accommodate the interests of competing ethnic groups, Nigeria employs the hybrid power-sharing system that combines both institutional and non-institutional mechanisms for power-sharing among competing groups. The model was a product of an elite agreement for the promotion of equity and conflict management following years of political tensions and conflict. However, the Nigerian case, as presented in this chapter, has shown that the lack of the elite's commitment to power-sharing structures can be a source of recurrent conflicts that may even lead to state collapse.

Power-Sharing: Concept and Theories

Many definitions have been advanced to capture the idea of power-sharing, but one of the most useful and comprehensive is that given by Brendan O'Leary: "[A]ny set of arrangements that prevent one agent, or organized collective agency, from being the 'winner who holds all critical power,' whether temporarily or permanently" (O'Leary, 2013: 3). Another instructive definition is that power-sharing represents "those rules that, in addition to defining how decisions will be made by groups within the polity, allocate decision-making rights, including access to state resources, among collectivities competing for power" (Hartzell & Hoddie, 2003: 320). Since power is about control, dominance, and the allocation of values, power-sharing comprises all mechanisms for including group interests in having access to power. It is for this reason that Arend Lijphart (1969, 1977) suggests that power-sharing is an embodiment of principles that provide every 'significant' identity group with a representation in the government of a multicultural society. Power-sharing is, therefore, more pronounced in plural societies for the apparent reason that it is a useful tool for conflict management among competing groups. In such societies, the elites will always engage in competition for power but if political instability is to be avoided or minimized, they must be prepared to make "deliberate efforts to counteract the immobilizing and destabilizing effects of fragmentation" by adopting power-sharing strategies (Lijphart, 1969: 212).

In conflict and peace studies, power-sharing has become popularly associated with conflict prevention and peacebuilding strategies (Trzciński, 2018a). It is used to "guarantee each of the critical players – that is, those capable of acting as spoilers – a significant payoff from cooperation and peaceful behavior" (Gates & Strøm, 2018, 2). Therefore, power-sharing in such situations becomes a sort of "elite pact between representatives of political or military parties on the division of responsibility in different fields of political and economic life" (Zanker et al., 2015: 72). Indeed, many civil wars in Africa ended through power-sharing negotiations mediated by international agencies. Power-sharing institutions help to balance power among groups and have proven to mitigate conflict since segmented groups are guaranteed some form of representation at the political center (Hartzell & Hoddie, 2003; Lijphart, 1977). McCulloch and McEvoy (2018: 469, 470) also argue that "power-sharing still holds considerable appeal" because it "seeks to regulate conflict." Likewise, as McEvoy and Aboultaif (2022) argue, "power-sharing facilitates joint decision-making between the significant groups in society" and in the case of post-conflict societies, "provides former combatants with guaranteed access to power."

Power-sharing is also relevant to discourses on democracy as it has been seen as a useful instrument to strengthen democracy and promote good governance. Power-sharing discourages dictatorial tendencies and promotes political inclusion and wider participation. As rightly noted by Krzysztof Trzciński (2018b: 17), "[b]y allowing members of the political elites of various segments to take part in the decision-making process, PS (power-sharing) helps diminish the concentration of power and the benefits derived from it by a segment that is dominant by virtue of its size and/or strength and consequently reduces the arbitrariness of power." Depending on its form, power-sharing can provide the opportunity for marginalized groups including women and youth to participate in decision-making processes. However, a rigid power-sharing structure can hinder democracy because it may limit democratic competition and the sovereign power of the people to decide their leaders (Gates & Strøm, 2018).

Three major power-sharing models are popular in the theoretical literature. The first is the classical model originating from Arend Lijphart's

7 POWER-SHARING IN NIGERIA'S DIVIDED SOCIETY ... 149

consociationalism. Lijphart has identified four elements of consociationalism: grand coalition, mutual veto, proportionality and segmental autonomy (Lijphart, 1969: 25–44). In his idea of consociational democracy, Lijiphart had argued that for cohesion and stability in plural societies, and the elites must be ready to accommodate the divergent interests and demands of the subcultures. This requires that they transcend cleavages and join in a common effort with the elites of rival subcultures (Lijphart, 1969: 216). Consociationalism, therefore, is built on the idea of formal institutional arrangements that recognize groups' rights for representation in the state's power structure. This can be actualized through the following: "segmental parties, forming grand coalitions; segmental autonomy; proportionality in elections, division of government posts, positions in public agencies or – sometimes – in the army; and a minority veto right" (Trzciński, 2018a, 89). Consociationalism "entails the representation and participation of all major social segments in the governing process" and is used in deeply divided societies (McCulloch, 2014: 501) where "it may be the only strategy to bring violent conflict to an end" (502).

Among many others, a major criticism of the approach is that it promotes ethnic divisions and intensifies unhealthy intra-ethnic competition. For example, Jarstad (2009: 42) argues that the approach "seldom solves all issues at stake... [and] often means deadlock, inefficient governments, and an institutionalisation of polarisation in already divided societies... [and] can be seen as a constraint on democracy." Another critic of the approach is Horowitz (1985: 569) who argues that consociational settlements "assume that it is necessary for ethnically divided states to live with ethnic cleavages rather than to wish them away." Another problem is the sticky nature of consociationalism. While Elazar (1985: 23) noted that consociational processes "are subject to change with relative ease when the conditions that generated them change" (Horowitz, 2014: 12) argued that consociational rules "tend to rigidify conflicts and do not lend themselves to renegotiation."

The above concerns gave birth to centripetalism, also known as integrative power-sharing, popularized by Horowitz (1985) and others. Avoiding the pitfalls of institutionalizing ethnic divisions, centripetalists advocate a formula that depoliticizes segmental differences by focusing on the creation of electoral incentives for elite cooperation (Horowitz, 2014). Contrary to the consociational approach, centripetalism prefers policies that encourage "voluntary cross-ethnic cooperation" before elections (Bell, 2018: 14). The strategies recommended include vote-pooling, decentralized voting constituencies, territorial vote distribution and other innovative strategies to promote unity (Trzciński, 2018b). Despite avoiding reinforcement of differences, centripetalism may also be criticized for creating a system that may be dominated by the major segments of a state (Trzciński, 2018a)—such as the case of Nigeria's rotational presidency that will be discussed later.

To address the weaknesses of both approaches, a combination of the two is recommended as a more practical form of power-sharing, which is referred to as the complex or hybrid power-sharing model (Trzciński, 2018b; Wolff, 2009). The aim is to use one approach to address the weaknesses in the other and create a system that guarantees more stability in a plural society. For example, the introduction of voting incentives may be added to coalition government arrangements. Recognizing how formal and non-formal power-sharing structures are used in Nigeria, Trzciński (2018a) has usefully demonstrated that Nigeria is one of the prime examples of the hybrid model.

This chapter draws on the above conceptualization of Nigeria's hybrid model by Trzciński to understand how it functions in heterogeneous societies such as Nigeria. We observe that the model has been used to establish institutional and non-institutional procedures to accommodate the interests of the groups in Nigeria. However, the problem in the Nigerian context is not because of the model but the attitude (poor commitment and desperation for power) of the political elite toward it. This has been a source of claims of marginalization, political tensions and ethno-religious conflicts and increased calls for political restructuring. It is instructive to note that power-sharing in the Nigerian context suffers from what McCulloch (2021), and McEvoy and Aboultaif (2022) describe as the problem of 'adoptability' or 'functionality' (McCulloch, 2021: 5). As McEvoy and Aboultaif (2022: 5) note, "a functional power-sharing system is one that proves useful for its intended purpose, ostensibly to promote elite cooperation…"

Power-Sharing in Nigeria

Nigeria's multiplicities manifest in its many ethnic groupings and two major religious groupings. Despite hundreds of ethnic groups, the three major ones—Hausa/Fulani, Igbo and the Yoruba—have historically dominated the minorities, which gives room to the argument that the state has a tripodal ethnic structure (Babalola, 2018). However, the more recent classification of the ethnic groups into geopolitical zones, although unofficial (as it does not appear in the constitution), has increased the prospects for other groups to negotiate and have access to power. For example, the assumption of Goodluck Jonathan, with origin from the minority Ijaw group, as president in 2011 indicates the rise of potentially new majority groups from the geopolitical zoning system.

Religion is also a significant social cleavage with high political salience in Nigeria. The Northern Region, dominated by the Hausa-Fulani, is largely composed of Muslims with a minority Christian population. Yoruba in the south-west of the country has a mixed religious population while the Igbos in the south-east and the Niger Delta peoples (in the south-south geopolitical region/zone) are mostly Christians. The intersection between religion and ethnicity in Nigeria complicates and intensifies the competition for values in the state. Thus, Nigerian politics is that of mutual suspicions, fear of domination and marginalization. The acrimonious competition for state power among ethno-religious groups has been a source of many conflicts experienced in the state.

Efforts to reduce the tension between the competing groups have produced a hybrid model of power-sharing. While some such as the federal system, state and local government creations and revenue allocation systems are institutional, others—most especially—rotational presidency and zoning arrangements are informal agreements among the elites.

Federalism

The utility of federalism and consociationalism as solutions to the problems of plural societies has been well-established in the academic literature (Elazar, 1985; Lijphart, 1979, 1985). Federalism is a power-sharing institutional mechanism that has been deployed to manage diversity-driven conflicts (McCulloch, 2021: 3–4). The federal principle, as defined by Wheare (1963: 10), is the "method of dividing powers so that the general and regional governments are each, within a sphere, co-ordinate and independent." Following on from this definition, Elazar (1987: 12) argues that the overall objective of all federations is to express "self-rule plus shared rule" through the distribution of powers between those assigned to the federal government for common purposes and those assigned to the constituent units for purposes of local autonomy and the preservation of specific identities and interests. Wheare's reference to "general and regional governments" indicates that federalism is defined as "a spatial or territorial division of power in which the component units are geographically defined" (Lijphart, 1979: 502). Thus, power-sharing in a federation has a territorial dimension. Nigeria's federal system provides the foundation for the institutional dimension of power-sharing in the state. It marks the most significant arrangement to manage diversity and ensure the protection of all the ethnic and religious groups in the country.

In a federation, political authority is territorially divided between two autonomous governments. Federalism goes beyond the constitutional division of governmental powers; it is also about the protection of territorial identities and regional autonomy. Of course, federalism cannot solve all diversity-related problems, but by "dividing power between two levels of government—giving groups greater control over their own political, social and economic affairs while making them feel less exploited as well as more secure" the system has the capacity to prevent ethnic conflict (Brancati, 2004: 7). Federalism was adopted in Nigeria because of the capacity of the system to accommodate diversity and group interests. When the federal system was adopted in Nigeria in 1954, it was not just about holding together the multiple ethnic groups but was also about creating some sort of power equilibrium between the majority and minority ethnic groups. Federations are typically products of negotiations and compromises, and the Nigerian federation is no exception. Although the multicultural nature of the Nigerian society cannot be ruled out in the motive to federalize the previously unitary state (Babalola, 2019), regional elites' cooperation was also significant. They cooperated, not only with the departing colonialists but also among themselves to work out a political framework considered suitable for the multicultural country. The system was promoted as an instrument of unity in diversity and has continued to represent the basis for the country's stability.

Federalism promotes a vertical form of power-sharing through the existence of a written constitution. Written constitutions are typically consonant with federal systems, guaranteeing the powers assigned to both governments. Lijphart (1979: 502) contends that 'the requirement of a written constitution follows logically from the primary federal principle: the division of power has to be specified, and both the central and regional governments need a firm guarantee that their allotted powers cannot be taken away.' In addition, the power assigned to regional governments "cannot be changed by constitutional amendment without their consent" (Lijphart, 1979: 503). A written constitution accommodates conflicting interests within the federal state and Nigeria's current constitution is no exception as it spells out matters on exclusive, concurrent and residual legislative lists.

In Nigeria, territorial power-sharing also occurs through the federation's bicameral legislature, which allows regional government's equal representation in the upper house of the federal legislature. Lijphart (1979: 502) argues that the legislatures of federations usually consist of two chambers, one representing the people at large and the other the component units of the federation. Lijphart's assertion is tenable. Based on the 1999 Constitution, Nigeria's upper house (the Senate), which has 109 Senators, guarantees equal representation of the 36 states irrespective of size and wealth, while the lower house (House of Representatives), consisting of 360 members, ensures proportional representation. The Senate provides for a second opinion as it guarantees the representation of the big and small political groups in the country. Members of the Senate are elected by voters in their respective senatorial districts during general elections while members of the House of Representatives are elected from their federal constituencies.

The Federal Character Principle

To ensure equitable access to national power, the political elite reached a consensus to put in place what Donald Horowitz (1985: 596) describes as a distributive policy aimed at changing "the ethnic balance of economic opportunities and rewards." The adoption of the *federal character* principle exemplifies the country's distributive policy as it provides representation for all major ethnic groups in cabinet positions and the civil service. The principle was first adopted as a state policy during the country's second experiment with democratic rule (the Second Republic, 1979–1983) and was entrenched in the 1979 constitution that heralded the

Republic.[1] According to Section 14(3) of the 1979 Constitution, the principle stipulates that:

> The composition of the government of the federation or any of its agencies and the conduct of its affairs shall be carried out in such a manner as to reflect the federal character of Nigeria and the need to promote national unity, and also to command national loyalty, thereby ensuring that there shall be no predominance of persons from a few states or a few ethnic or other sectional groups in the government (FGN, 1979).

The drafters of the 1979 Constitution were particularly convinced that the fear of domination or exclusion contributed to the Nigerian Civil War (1967–1970) which "resulted from the Eastern Nigerian protest against Northern hegemonic control over the rest of the country" (Ayoade, 1986: 82), and a repeat had to be avoided. Similarly, as Horowitz (2014: 10) has noted, this affirmative action was necessary given that the country had just emerged from a civil war and thirteen years of military dictatorship, and there was a great fear of renewed ethnic conflict. In Nigeria, the fear of domination is real. This has been aptly captured by Kirk-Greene who notes that "fear has been constant in every tension and confrontation in political Nigeria. Not the physical fear of violence, not the spiritual fear of retribution, but the psychological fear of discrimination, of domination. It is the fear of not getting one's fair share, one's dessert" (1975: 19). The 1979 constitution has been described as a 'peace treaty' as it emphasized the need to accommodate all Nigeria's ethnic groups (Ayoade, 1986: 82). It represents a step toward national unity as it reintegrated the breakaway Biafra into the country's federal power equation. More importantly, the arrangement has helped to reduce the Hausa-Fulani's stranglehold on political power. The policy was reaffirmed in the 1999 Constitution to "foster a feeling of belonging and of involvement among the various

---

[1] The post-independent Nigerian political system has been characterized by the alternation of military dictatorship and electoral politics. In the Nigerian context, 'Republic' is used to refer to the period of civilian administration. The First Republic was the period of the first civilian administration which began from independence in 1960 and came to an end in 1966 when the military sacked the civilian government and installed the first military government which terminated in 1979. The Second Republic was between 1979 and 1983, while the Third Republic was aborted through the annulment of the 1993 presidential election. The Fourth Republic is, therefore, the period of civilian rule that began in 1999 following the termination of military rule.

peoples of the Federation, to the end that loyalty to the nation shall override sectional loyalties" (Section 15(4) of the 1999 Constitution) (FGN, 1999).

As a power-sharing policy, the principle of federal character ensures that the composition of federal (national) institutions reflects the diversity (federal character) of the country. This indeed represents Lijphart's consociational principle of proportionality, which is closely connected with the grand coalition principle. Lijphart (1977: 38; 1979: 501) argues that proportionality deviates from majority rule and serves as a method of political representation, allocating civil service appointments and financial resources among the different segments in the plural society. The policy provides the different ethnic groups in Nigeria with access to national power, aligning with Lijphart's thesis that a consociational democracy requires the ability of the elites to accommodate the divergent interests of the subcultures (1969: 216). It is indeed a consociational formula engendering inclusivity (Adejumobi, 2004; Mustapha, 1986) as "every state of the federation is given a share of federal power in one form or another" (Babalola, 2019: 139). By implication, therefore, the policy recognizes the ethnic variable in the distribution of national resources, given that many states, especially in the south-west and south-east still retained a distinctive ethnic identity. Lijphart defines consociational democracy as a "government by elite cartel designed to turn a democracy with a fragmented political culture into a stable democracy" (Lijphart, 1969: 216). The policy represents a catalyst to national unity as it provides the different groups in the country equal access to the country's resources. It also breaks up the monopoly of federal power by the three major ethnic groups and promotes the empowerment of the minorities.

Another 'centripetal device' that was written into the 1979 constitution was that a presidential candidate in a general election must win a quarter of the votes in two-thirds of the Nigerian states (Nigeria was then a federation of nineteen states) (Babalola, 2020: 379; Horowitz, 2014: 10). In addition, political parties are required to have a national outlook. What this means is that they must have a presence in two-thirds of the federation. This arrangement encourages centripetal or national politics rather than ethno-regional politics. Like the federal character principle, this provision has also been replicated in the 1999 Constitution.

Political Zoning and Rotational Presidency

Another power-sharing mechanism in Nigeria is referred to as the *zoning* system. This represents an informal party arrangement in which key political positions are alternated among the ethnic, regional and religious groups. This approach reflects the pre-election party arrangement model advanced to promote national unity in the centripetalist model. Unlike the federal character principle, *zoning* is not a state policy but Akinola (1996: 21) describes it as "a realistic attempt to converge diverse interests for electoral advantage... a way of overcoming the cleavages of ethnicity, regionalism and religion..." Nigeria operates the American-style strong executive presidency and a 'top-heavy' federal system as governmental powers and other resources are exclusively concentrated at the center. The Constitution provides for the exclusive legislative list with 68 items and a concurrent list with 12 items, making the center "excessively crucial to the lives of the citizens" (Babalola, 2019: 159). The enormous power controlled by the center, and by extension, the federal executive led by the president, creates a zero-sum political competition among the regional elites, explaining why "all eyes are on the centre" (Babalola, 2019: 159). Zoning was introduced to Nigerian politics in the Second Republic (1979–1983) by the then-dominant party, the defunct National Party of Nigeria (NPN). Ethnicity dominated the politics of that era, and it is not surprising that the party embraced this arrangement. Within the NPN, presidential, vice-presidential, party chairmanship and other key political positions were zoned to different ethno-regional groups. This arrangement contributed, not only to the national outlook of the party but also to its electoral fortunes in the 1979 and 1983 elections (Babalola, 2020).

The success of *zoning* in the NPN perhaps explains the reconfiguration of the model during the military era as a component of the democratic transition program in 1995. The geopolitical zoning system was declared by General Sani Abacha, then military Head of State, in his Independence Day Broadcast of 1995 where he stated that the country was going to be divided into six regional groupings: North-East, North-West, Middle Belt (North-Central), South-West, South-East and Southern Minority (South-South). The regional grouping was against the backdrop of the recommendations of the 1994/1995 Constitutional Conference that recommended power rotation between the North and South (Agbaje, 1998). Clearly, this was aimed to encourage more representation by the minority groups and limiting of the hegemony of the three dominant ethnic groups. Given the failure of the military transition exercise that was supposed to formalize the arrangement in the 1995 (draft) Constitution, the strategy and other recommended power-sharing arrangements were excluded in the 1999 Constitution that was prepared for democratic transition in 1999, for reasons adduced to the suspicious circumstances that surrounded the General Sani Abacha-led democratic transition exercise (Mustapha, 2009a).[2]

The formalization of the geopolitical zoning is found in the People's Democratic Party (PDP) constitution.[3] In the party's constitution, it is stated that: "in pursuance of the principle of zoning, justice and fairness, the party shall adhere to the policy of rotation and zoning of party and public elective offices and it shall be enforced by the appropriate executive committee at all levels" (Section 7(2), Constitution of the People's Democratic Party, 1998). This has produced a practice of ensuring ethno-religious representation in key political offices, especially at the federal level including the president, vice-president, senate president, deputy senate president, speaker and deputy speaker at the national parliament. The key offices in the party are also zoned in consideration of the power distribution at the executive and legislative levels. Being Nigeria's dominant party for the first sixteen years of electoral democracy (1999–2015), the party's policy has significantly influenced other levels of the state and created a culture of consensus among the elites.

The PDP's adoption of the zoning arrangement could be traced to the origin of the party. The party was formed by a coalition of politicians, mostly from the southern part of the country, who opposed the annulment of the 1993 presidential election. The policy has also influenced other political parties in the country. For example, the All Progressives Congress (APC) which emerged as the governing party in 2015 after defeating the PDP also adopted its geopolitical zoning system which is more pronounced within the party structure. The constitution

---

[2] The Abacha-led military government aimed to dubiously transform itself into a democratic government by organizing the Conference to facilitate the transition. Because of the suspicions raised about the democratic transition program, the outcomes of the Conference were unpopular in civil society. The sudden death of General Abacha in 1998 finally nailed the exercise and the draft constitution.

[3] The PDP was Nigeria's dominant party for the first 16 years after the transition to democratic rule in 1999. Being the first dominant party, its principles and practices have a significant impact on politics in Nigeria.

of the party states that "[a]ll...rules, regulations and guidelines shall take into consideration and uphold the principle of federal character, gender balance, geopolitical spread and rotation of offices to as much as possible, ensure balance within the constituency covered" (Article 20(iv), Constitution of the APC).

Reflecting some critical perspectives on power-sharing, some scholars have also expressed some reservations over the idea of zoning in Nigeria because it seems undemocratic by not encouraging a level-playing field for political aspirants. Not only that, as Suberu (1988: 433) argues, the idea "points to the dangerous polarization that can arise when zoning is projected as a check on the North's political ascendancy." He argues further that "since the presidency is designed to symbolize the aspiration for national unity through the personality of a national political figure, its rotation on a geoethnic basis would tarnish the national image of an incumbent and give his mandate a sectional character" (1988: 434). These criticisms notwithstanding, the application of this informal arrangement in the current democratic dispensation has strengthened elite cooperation (and in some way promoted conflict among them). This explains why its admirers have continued to clamor for the practice to be entrenched in the constitution, at least, for the position of president. This aspect of power-sharing is referred to as rotational presidency in which the position of president is alternated between the geo-ethnic blocs in the country. The idea links to the idea of a grand coalition as highlighted by Lijphart (1977: 25), who argues that "the primary characteristic of consociational democracy is that the political leaders of all significant segments of the plural society cooperate in a grand coalition to govern the country." Summing up the argument in favor of rotational presidency, Akinola (1996: 21) argued that the idea represents a way of overcoming the cleavages of ethnicity, regionalism and religion such that each of Nigeria's ethnolinguistic groups get the opportunity to produce a president. Convinced of the usefulness of the idea, Agbu (2004: 47) argued that "short of a revolution, a rotational presidency may be the only solution to the problem of lopsided leadership by any particular segment of the dominant and ruling political classes in Nigeria." The rotational presidency tends to guarantee each region's access to the presidency and deepen political stability. Akinola (1996) has particularly posited that, given the segmented nature of the Nigerian society, in which the ethnic groups have their exclusive territories, rotational presidency will address the question of unity in the multi-ethnic country.

Rotational presidency was informally accepted by the political elite after the democratic transition in 1999. This is apparent in the emergence of President Olusegun Obasanjo in 1999 (Babalola, 2018: 29–31). Obasanjo was a product of elite consensus. But as the anti-centripetalists have posited, a rotational presidency tends to be enjoyed only by the dominant groups. Democracy is a game of numbers, and the way the majority ethnic groups have used their numerical strength as electoral value; members of the ethnic minority groups usually find it difficult to capture political power at the center. This has been a source of raging controversies around the idea of a rotational presidency. One of them is that the southern political elite favor a rotation among the current six geopolitical zones while their northern counterparts prefer the north/south rotational arrangement. Another one is the issue of what constitutes the unit of rotation and how inclusive it is for the multiple ethnic groups. Some have therefore argued that the idea of a rotational presidency is antithetical to the spirit of democracy and further promotes ethnic politics, which is the main source of disunity and political instability in the multi-ethnic country.

State Creation

At independence in 1960, the Nigerian federation had three large constituent units—the Northern, Eastern and Western Regions. The Northern Region was bigger in geographical size and population than the other two put together. The Northern Region's numerical advantage allowed it to outcompete others in the competition for national resources, including federal power. Expectedly, this structural disparity became a source of tension in the immediate post-independent period as the other two regions perceived themselves as junior partners in the union and at a disadvantage in the struggle for resources (Babalola, 2019: 135–138). By 1963, the Mid-Western Region had been carved out from the Western Region. This addition was partly in response to the minority ethnic groups' ferocious agitation for resource redistribution, and partly an attempt to diminish the political and economic strength of the Western Region.

Despite the transformation, the structural flaw in the federation remained as the Northern Region retained its numerical strength. This, however, changed at the dawn of the civil war in 1967 when the then military regime of Yakubu Gowon transformed the country into a 12-state federation (Babalola, 2019: 136). Gowon's state creation exercise weakened the political and economic dominance of the Northern Region. In its present form, Nigeria has 36 states. As Osaghae (1991: 243) has argued, one significant advantage of the division of the country into smaller units is the freeing of the minorities from the domination of the majorities and allowing them some access to the country's distributive system, especially resources that flow from the center. State creation is one of the means for negotiating increased access to national resources (Babalola & Onapajo, 2019).

Given that national resources in Nigeria are distributed based largely on the principle of equality of states, every ethnic group in the country desires a state. This interest constitutes one of the major elements of the increased agitations for political restructuring in Nigeria. For some minority leaders, what matters is the creation of more states that would represent their ethnic interests (Babalola & Onapajo, 2019). For example, one of the demands of the Igbo ethnic group's continuous agitation for federal equity is predicated on the fact that there are only five states in the south-east geopolitical region whereas other geopolitical zones have six states, and the north-west has seven. The Igbo are, therefore, promoting a restructuring in which the geopolitical regions have an equal number of states (Babalola, 2019: 145). In this light, at the end of the 2014 National Conference, 18 new states (three per geopolitical zone) and an additional state for the south-east to make the zone have an equal number of states with other zones, except for the north-west which has seven were proposed (Babalola, 2019: 145). These were to address the claims of inequity but this and other recommendations of the Conference were never implemented.

Revenue Allocation

Sharing national revenue to ensure fairness and equity has been another major issue in the politics of sharing values in Nigeria. Thus, the state's allocation system is another distributive mechanism designed not just to distribute national revenue but to ensure inclusivity. As Babalola (2019: 80) has argued, Nigeria's fiscal system revolves around three main problems: the problem of allocation of revenue to the different tiers in relation to their constitutionally assigned functions (vertical revenue sharing); the problem of sharing of revenue among the states (horizontal revenue sharing); and the problem of allocation of the oil-generated revenue between the oil-producing states and the non-oil-producing states. Just like in other federations, resource distribution in Nigeria is a daunting assignment but the federal government has, at different periods, adopted different revenue-sharing formulas aimed at ensuring national unity. The system takes cognizance of the fiscal 'need' of the people of the states in the Federation. For example, at the start of the current democratic dispensation in 1999, the Nigerian state increased the share of centrally collected oil revenues for oil-producing states to 13% based on derivation. This extra fund is in addition to whatever statutory allocation these states get from the Federation Account. With the application of the derivation principle, oil-producing states are now richer than their non-oil-producing counterparts and some even "control revenues larger than those of some neighboring countries" (Mustapha, 2009b: 78). Despite the increase in revenue, the Niger Delta region that produces the lion share of the country's oil continues to remain underdeveloped as funds meant for public goods are siphoned by regional leaders.

Nigeria's fiscal federalism has witnessed significant changes since the adoption of the federal system. Different fiscal principles have been adopted but derivation is the most contentious because each ethno-regional group wants maximum benefit from the country's wealth, the bulk being oil-generated. The derivation principle requires the Federal Government to return some proportion of the revenue generated from that state. In 1951, the principle was put at 50% while the 1953 fiscal scheme provided for 100%. In 1970, it was set at 25%, down to 3% toward the terminal end of military rule, and then raised to 13% at the start of the current democratic rule in 1999 (Babalola, 2019: 94–100). Section 162(1) of Nigeria's Constitution provides that the Federal Government deposits all centrally collected revenues into a general pool, called the Federation Account, to be shared vertically and horizontally while Section 162(2) provides that "the principle of derivation shall be constantly reflected in any approved formula as being not less than thirteen per cent (13%) of the revenue accruing to the Federation Account directly from any natural resources." Section 162(3) requires the federal government to make unconditional grants (statutory allocation) available to the states on an annual basis to allow the latter to discharge their constitutional responsibilities.

The 13% derivation represents a constitutional engineering undertaken by the departing military regime following the clamor from the oil-producing minorities of the Niger Delta for an upward review of the derivation element of the country's fiscal system. It was principally to address the claims of marginalization and exclusion usually emanating from the geopolitical region which continually claim that they contribute, in no small measure, to the economy of the country and so deserve more. In addition, the systemic downgrading of the principle, they argued, is a form of internal oppression and economic marginalization by the majority ethnic groups (Babalola, 2019: 127). They decry the inequity characterizing the country's fiscal system.

Conflict and Challenges

As discussed above, there are both formal and informal power-sharing arrangements among the Nigerian political elite, which have proven useful in the promotion of national unity. Despite the measures, it is instructive that the state is still overwhelmed by recurrent ethno-religious conflicts that come in many forms. Nigeria's power-sharing model has been applauded as one of the best frameworks to promote unity (Adejumobi, 2004), but poor implementation has rendered it more ineffective. For example, the Federal Character Commission that was established in 1996 and incorporated into the 1999 constitution to ensure compliance with the federal character principle has not been effectively implemented as expected and this has continued to fuel claims of ethnic domination.

Indeed, the issue of equal representation in major political offices which the principle of federal character intends to achieve has been a sore issue in inter-ethnic relations in Nigeria. Very often, political leaders have disregarded the principle and are seen to have favored members of their ethnic or religious groups because of a lack of trust from others. For instance, one of the major criticisms against the Buhari-led government is that key positions including those related to national security are dominated by the president's Hausa-Fulani group. Increased ethno-nationalism agitations and secessionist violence engulfing the state have, therefore, been linked to feelings of exclusion by the government. In one of its addresses, the main opposition party, the PDP claimed that "the apparent nepotism in the appointment of the top echelon of the security forces, and the commanding heights of the institutions of government further fuel agitations across the country" (Ezugwu, 2021).

Rotation of power among ethno-regional and religious groups has also been one of the most controversial issues in Nigerian politics. Although the political parties have it enshrined in their constitutions, the political actors often disregard it and make confusing interpretations of it to circumvent the principle based on prevailing interests, especially during election periods. In 2010, before the 2011 presidential election, the issue of zoning came to the fore after the sudden death of President Umar Musa Yar'Adua (a Hausa-Fulani from the Northern Region) after a protracted illness. The death of Yar'Adua had informed the emergence of his Vice President, Goodluck Jonathan (an Ijaw from the southern region), as President (as provided in the constitution). The intention of President Jonathan to contest for the presidency in 2011 was perceived as an affront to the northern political elites and a violation of the party's zoning formula because a northern president (Yar'Adua) was unable to complete his tenure, which was meant to be a slot for the North (Onapajo, 2012). Although President Jonathan scaled through and emerged the president in the 2011 presidential election, the controversy resurfaced in the 2015 electoral period when the president sought re-election. The grievance from the Northern Region over the president's disregard for the zoning principle hugely contributed to the shocking loss of the then ruling party in the 2015 presidential election, an event that was unprecedented in the political history of Nigeria (Onapajo, 2015).

The federal character principle, zoning and rotational presidency represent ethnic balancing mechanisms, but they have not prevented the continuous claims of marginalization and inter-ethnic tensions. Poor implementation of these affirmative actions has contributed to the calls for a fundamental structural reform, popularly termed *restructuring* (or true federalism) in Nigerian parlance, moves toward secession and the sudden rise of ethnic nationalism. There has not been a major agreement on what restructuring means in the circle of the elites. It means different things to the different ethnic and regional groupings in the country (Babalola & Onapajo, 2019; Onapajo & Babalola, 2021). However, the term is used to express the idea of a reconfiguration of the Nigerian state to allow for more representation and sociopolitical inclusion (Onapajo & Babalola, 2021). The agitation for restructuring has been championed by ethno-regional elites who have used the slogan to have better access to political power and other opportunities (Onapajo & Babalola, 2021).

Calls for restructuring are further taken to the extreme by new ethno-nationalist movements who agitate for a complete breakaway from the

Nigerian state. Such prominent movements include the Nnamdi Kanu-led Indigenous People of Biafra (IPOB) for the Igbo in the south-east region and the Sunday Igboho-led group advocating for a Yoruba nation-state. Chief among their grievances is the perception that the Buhari-led administration only favors his ethnic group in terms of political office appointments and has a bias toward Fulani herders causing havoc across the country.

CONCLUSION

The chapter has argued that Nigeria's power-sharing model follows the hybrid power-sharing model. This is because Nigeria has a framework for both formal and informal power-sharing models that could have been effective in promoting stability and reducing inter-ethnic conflicts. Nigeria's power-sharing institutions have attempted to address the fear of marginalization among the country's multiple ethnic, regional and religious groups but these efforts have only yielded minimal results. If well-implemented, the power-sharing structures discussed above can be an antidote to ethno-regional conflicts. Promoters of power-sharing have always seen the tool "as a preferred institutional strategy for mediating ethnic, linguistic, religious and national divisions" (McCulloch, 2021: 2). For instance, she contends that power-sharing "supports the end of violent conflict, it reduces group-based insecurities, and it supports minority inclusion in democratic processes" (2021: 2).

In Nigeria, the lack of commitment to both informal agreements and institutional provisions to entrench the system of power-sharing has been a driver of recurring conflicts. The problem has continued to threaten the corporate existence of Nigeria as there have been increased secession moves in different parts of the country. The lessons to be drawn from the Nigerian examples show that the success of power-sharing is not underlined by institutional frameworks or elite agreements, but by the commitment of the elite to implement the model they have produced. This is more so in developing societies that are characterized by weak institutions and 'Big Men' whose influence can be a stabilizing factor for politics and development.

REFERENCES

Adejumobi, S. (2004). Civil Society and Federalism in Nigeria. *Regional & Federal Studies, 14*(2), 211–231.

Akinola, A. (1996). The Concept of a Rotational Presidency in Nigeria. *The round Table: The Commonwealth Journal of International Affairs, 85*(337), 13–24.

Agbaje, A. (1998). The Ideology of Power-Sharing: An Analysis of Content, Context and Intent. In K. Amuwo et al. (Eds.), *Federalism and Political Restructuring in Nigeria*. Spectrum.

Agbu, O. (2004). Re-inventing Federalism in Post-transition Nigeria: Problems and Prospects. *Africa Development, 24*(2), 26–52.

Ayoade, J. (1986). Ethnic Management in the 1979 Nigerian Constitution. *Publius: Journal of Federalism, 16*(2), 73–90.

Babalola, D. (2018). Ethnicity, Ethnic Conflict and the Elusive Quest for Peace in Post-military Nigeria. In D. Babalola & H. Onapajo (Eds.), *Nigeria, A Country under Siege: Issues of Conflict and Its Management*. Cambridge Scholars Publishing.

Babalola, D. (2019). *The Political Economy of Federalism in Nigeria*. Palgrave Macmillan.

Babalola, D. (2020). Ethno-Religious Voting in Nigeria: Interrogating Voting Patterns in the 2019 Presidential Election. *The Round Table: The Commonwealth Journal of International Affairs, 109*(4), 377–385.

Babalola, D., & Onapajo, H. (2019). New Clamour for "Restructuring" in Nigeria: Elite Politics, Contradictions, and Good Governance. *African Studies Quarterly, 18*(4), 41–56.

Brancati, D. (2004). Can Federalism Stabilize Iraq? *Washington Quarterly, 27*(2), 5–21.

Bell, C. (2018). *Political Power-Sharing and Inclusion: Peace and Transition Processes*. University of Edinburgh.

Constitution of the All Progressives Congress (APC). (n.d.). https://www.inecni geria.org/wp-content/uploads/2019/02/APC-Constitution.pdf. Accessed 21 July 2021.

Elazar, D. (1985). Federalism and Consociational Regimes. *Publius, 15*(2), 17–34.

Elazar, D. (1987). *Exploring Federalism*. The University of Alabama Press.

Ezugwu, O. (2021, May 4). Buhari's 'Nepotism' Fueling Agitations for Secession—PDP. *Business Hallmark*. https://hallmarknews.com/buharis-nep otism-fuelling-agitations-for-secession-pdp/

Federal Government of Nigeria (FGN). (1979). *Constitution of the Federal Republic of Nigeria*. Federal Government Press.

Federal Government of Nigeria (FGN). (1999). *Constitution of the Federal Republic of Nigeria 1999*. Federal Government Press.

Gates, S., & Strøm, K. (2018). *Power-Sharing and Civil Conflict*. Center for the Study of Civil War.

Hartzell, C., & Hoddie, M. (2003). Institutionalizing Peace: Power Sharing and Post-Civil War Conflict Management. *American Journal of Political Science, 47*(2), 318–332.

Jarstad, A. (2009). The Prevalence of Power-Sharing: Exploring the Patterns of Post-Election Peace. *Africa Spectrum, 44*(3), 41–62.

Kirk-Greene, A. H. M. (1975). *The Genesis of the Nigerian Civil War and the Theory of Fear*. Nordic African Institute.

Horowitz, D. L. (1985). *Ethnic Groups in Conflict*. University of California Press.

Horowitz, D. L. (2014). Ethnic Power-Sharing: Three Big Problems. *Journal of Democracy, 25*(2), 5–20.

Lijphart, A. (1969). Consociational Democracy. *World Politics, 21*(2), 207–225.

Lijphart, A. (1977). *Democracy in Plural Societies: A Comparative Exploration*. Yale University Press.

Lijphart, A. (1979). Consociation and Federation: Conceptual and Empirical Links. *Canadian Journal of Political Science, 12*(3), 499–515.

Lijphart, A. (1985). Non-Majoritarian Democracy: A Comparison of Federal and Consociational Theories. *Publius, 15*(2), 3–15.

McCulloch, A. (2014). Consociational Settlements in Deeply Divided Societies: The Liberal-Corporate Distinction. *Democratization, 21*(3), 501–518.

McCulloch, A. (2021). Introduction: Power-Sharing in Europe—From Adoptability to End-Ability. In S. Keil & A. McCulloch (Eds.), *Power-Sharing in Europe: Past Practice, Present Cases, and Future Directions*. Palgrave Macmillan.

McCulloch, A., & McEvoy, J. (2018). The International Mediation of Power-Sharing Settlements. *Cooperation and Conflict, 53*(4), 467–485.

McEvoy, J., & Aboultaif, E. (2022). Power-Sharing Challenges: From Weak Adoptability to Dysfunction in Iraq. *Ethnopolitics, 21*(3), 38–257.

Mustapha, A. R. (1986). The National Question and Radical Politics in Nigeria. *Review of African Political Economy, 13*(37), 81–97.

Mustapha, A. R. (2009a). Institutionalising Ethnic Representation: How Effective Is Affirmative Action in Nigeria? *Journal of International Development, 21*, 561–576.

Mustapha, A. R. (2009b). Nigeria Since 1999: A Revolving Door Syndrome or the Consolidation of Democracy? In A. R. Mustapha & L. Whitfield (Eds.), *Turning Points in African Democracy*. James Currey.

O'Leary, B. (2013). Power Sharing in Deeply Divided Places: An Advocate's Introduction. In J. McEvoy & B. O'Leary (Eds.), *Power-Sharing in Deeply Divided Places*. University of Pennsylvania Press.

Onapajo, H. (2012). Politics for God: Religion, Politics and Conflict in Democratic Nigeria. *The Journal of Pan African Studies, 4*(9), 42–66.

Onapajo, H. (2015). Nigeria's 2015 General Elections: The Salience of Electoral Reforms. *The Round Table: The Commonwealth Journal of International Affairs, 104*(5), 573–584.

Onapajo, H., & Babalola, D. (2021). Restructuring, Political Gimmicks and Elite Manipulation in Nigeria. In O. Tella (Ed.), *A Sleeping Giant? Nigeria's Domestic and International Politics in the Twenty-First Century.* Springer.

Osaghae, E. (1991). Ethnic Minorities and Federalism in Nigeria. *African Affairs, 90,* 237–258.

Wheare, K. (1963). *Federal Government* (4th ed.). Oxford University Press.

Wolff, S. (2009). Peace by Design? Towards "Complex Power-Sharing." In R. Taylor (Ed.), *Consociational Theory: McGarry and O'Leary and the Northern Ireland Conflict.* Routledge.

Trzciński, K. (2018a). Hybrid Power-Sharing: On How to Stabilize the Political Situation in Multi-segmental Societies. *Politeia, 15*(56), 85–107.

Trzciński, K. (2018b). What Is Power Sharing? Consociationalism, Centripetalism, and Hybrid Power Sharing. *Studia Polityczne, 46*(3), 9–30.

Suberu, R. (1988). Federalism and Nigeria's Political Future: A Comment. *African Affairs, 87*(348), 431–439.

Zanker, F., Simons, C., & Mehler, A. (2015). Power, Peace, and Space in Africa: Revisiting Territorial Power-Sharing. *African Affairs, 114*(454), 72–91.

CHAPTER 8

Power-Sharing in Malaysia: Coalition Politics and the Social Contract

Andrew Harding

POLITICAL AND CONSTITUTIONAL ORIGINS OF THE SOCIAL CONTRACT

Faced with ethnic division and the danger of conflict between ethnic groups, societies must find ways of achieving accommodation between them that all communities consistently find operating to their overall advantage (Lijphart, 1969, 1985). In Malaysia, one of the world's most plural societies, accommodation has historically been achieved through a form of consociationalism that has come to be called the 'social contract.' The social contract was negotiated between representatives of ethnic groups, expressed in concrete terms in law and policy as a form of affirmative action, implemented and reinforced by ethnic-coalition government and rendered beyond political debate. It represents a consociational form

---

A. Harding (✉)
National University of Singapore, Singapore, Singapore
e-mail: lawajh@nus.edu.sg

University of Reading Malaysia, Johor, Malaysia

© The Author(s), under exclusive license to Springer Nature
Switzerland AG 2024
E. Wassim Aboultaif et al. (eds.), *Power-Sharing in the Global South*,
Federalism and Internal Conflicts,
https://doi.org/10.1007/978-3-031-45721-0_8

of government, as it has been not only a way of achieving peace and stability between ethnic groups, but also one that requires, and has largely achieved, inter-ethnic political support. As we shall see, this consociational arrangement is not without its challenges, and, from the perspectives of both affirmative action and coalition government, it has become increasingly difficult to maintain.

The social contract was formed in the 1950s, when the first local, then federal, elections were held, and resulted from coalition politics involving ethnic parties under the Alliance coalition (later the Barisan Nasional). It was redefined in 1971, following the inter-ethnic riots of 13 May 1969 (Comber, 1983), under the New Economic Policy (NEP) and, later, the NEP's successor policies (Gomez & Saravanamuttu, 2013). This process is explained in the next section. It was subjected to scholarly analysis for the first time by Karl von Vorys (1975), during the implementation of the social contract's revised version. In 1986, it was for the first time given the sobriquet 'social contract' by Malaysian politician Abdullah Ahmad (Tay, 2017). Since then, it has been routinely described in this way, having been in practical operation for almost 70 years, or 50 years in its second iteration following the changes effected in 1971 (Lee, 2021).

This chapter offers an analysis of the Malaysian approach to consociationalism, in which the twin goals of managing ethnic relations and creating and distributing the benefits of economic development have been brought together in the social contract (Othman et al., 2008). The chapter explains how the social contract has been implemented, the critiques it has attracted, and its status in an ongoing period of political fragmentation.

During 1956–1957 the Constitution of the Federation of Malaya was settled through extensive debates, discussions and drafting exercises, and came into force on 31 August 1957 (Fernando, 2002). This Constitution created the Federation of Malaysia with effect from 19 September 1963, when Malaysia was formed from the existing federation, together with Singapore, Sarawak and North Borneo (now Sabah). Singapore left the federation in 1965, but the ethnic dimension of Malaysian society had been altered with the addition of Sabah and Sarawak, with their largely Indigenous but also highly mixed populations (Tan, 2008).

When the 1957 Constitution came into effect, three political parties had successfully campaigned in concert, winning almost all the seats in the federal legislature in the first general election in 1955. The Alliance of parties representing the Malays (the United Malays National Organisation, UMNO), the Chinese (the Malayan, later Malaysian, Chinese Association, MCA) and the 'Indians' (citizens of South Asian heritage) (Malayan, later Malaysian, Indian Congress, MIC) proved highly attractive to the electorate, as it secured ethnically based representation while ensuring accommodation between the three main ethnic groups under the benevolent leadership of the first Prime Minister, Tunku Abdul Rahman. Indeed, the Alliance swept the board, as it had done earlier in local elections (Harding, 2022: ch1).

Over several months in 1956–1957, the Alliance parties had negotiated a common position on the future constitution. Their Memorandum on this subject—a crucial document in the drafting process—included compromise proposals that formed the basis of constitutional provision for the social contract. Under these proposals, citizenship for the non-Malays, mainly recent migrant populations, would rise, but special privileges for Malays, having origins in colonial policy, would be retained. The Memorandum also dealt with Malay as the national language, Islam as the religion of the federation, and the Malay Rulers as heads of the various states. This compromise became not just the social contract as we now see it, but in effect the political cornerstone of a newly independent country. This agreement was a social contract not in Rousseau's sense of a notional contract having explanatory value for the relationship between the individual and the state. Rather it was an actual, negotiated contract between ethnic communities planning to live together as citizens of a new state in peace and harmony rather than conflict (Harding, 2022: ch3).

The original 'terms' of this social contract, examined below, and entrenched in the 1957 Constitution, were fairly clear. The contract was concluded between leaders representing the three communities in their capacity as leaders of the three main parties in the Alliance. They presumed (and their presumption was not seriously challenged) to negotiate on behalf of their respective ethnic communities, because they had demonstrated that, collectively, they had the overwhelming support of the electorate (Tay, 2017). The agreement was in the event guaranteed by a moderate, consociational form of coalition politics under the leadership of the Tunku, and the continuing success of the Alliance (later called the Barisan Nasional) in elections after independence right up until the 14th general election in May 2018 (Wong, 2018).

The social contract should be understood in light of the deep fears (justified as the events of May 1969 showed) of inter-ethnic conflict that had occurred in the post-war years, and could reoccur at any moment. There were also economic factors. In 1957 the Malays owned about 1% of the local economy, and their poverty rate was 70%; by 1970 those figures had changed to just 2.5% of the economy and a 64% poverty rate. These figures compared unfavourably with the figures for other ethnic groups, and were naturally a source of resentment (Jomo & Chang, 2008).

It was the majority community that was dissatisfied and felt a need for special protection and special treatment, and this is unusual in comparison with other states with ethnic divisions. South Africa is one state that has attracted comparison in this aspect. In 1957, and even, one might argue, in 1969, the self-perception of the Malays was that they were in danger of losing not just their political status as masters of the country but even their aspirations for development. The non-Malays, on the other hand, also had potentially adverse positions to contemplate. They stood to lose their somewhat precarious status as migrants and their hard-won economic position. Worse, they could, under a concertedly nationalist policy, lose their cultural and language rights. However, in general, to judge by responses to the revised version of the social contract and political party alignments during 1969–1971 and beyond, the social contract was not in general seen by the minorities in terms of discrimination, but rather as a necessary compromise. Thus, under the social contract the Malays would never be treated as a minority in their own country, and their special position was given official status. For non-Malays strictly equal citizenship was surrendered in return for having citizenship at all. In spite of the inauguration in 1957 of a liberal, pluralist democracy, this group therefore accepted the status of being legally, although not economically, second-class citizens. Beyond that it was clear that the states in a federal structure and the traditional Malay monarchies, an essential feature of Malay culture, would be retained, along with the designation of Malay as the national language, and the establishment of Islam as the official religion (Mohamed Salleh, 1986).

Of course, the social contract stood in contradiction to some of the constitutional norms of decolonization, but it was nonetheless provided for in the Constitution as embodying an agreed form of affirmative action. It was reflected principally in Article 153 of the Constitution, which permitted the government to act in a manner contrary to the principle of equal protection of the law (guaranteed by Article 8), in protecting the 'special position' of the Malays, thereby giving constitutional authority to quota systems in various areas of activity. Certain practices such as the reservation to Malays of positions in the public service, and scholarships and trade licences, as well as reservation of land, had commenced during the immediate post-war period under colonial government. Article 153 clarified and extended these practices and gave them constitutional legitimacy. Other provisions, namely those on citizenship, the monarchies and religion, also embodied social contract provisions. However, Article 153 also guaranteed what it called the 'legitimate interests' of the non-Malays. The implications of this balancing concept are discussed below.

The May 13 Incident and the '*Rukunegara*' Amendments

On 13 May 1969, the most traumatic episode in Malaysian history occurred (Comber, 1983; Goh, 1973). It briefly threatened to eclipse the system of democratic, parliamentary government, with the danger also of ensuring permanent inter-ethnic conflict. In the event what emerged was a severe realignment and entrenchment of the social contract, the emergence of new redistributive policies, the instigation of emergency rule and the imposition of severe limits to free expression (Harding, 2007).

On 10 May election results for Peninsular (West) Malaysia were announced. It was clear that opposition parties had achieved considerable gains, depriving the Alliance Government of its two-thirds majority (required for a constitutional amendment), winning three of the 13 state governments, and making substantial inroads into the Alliance vote, especially amongst the non-Malays. The opposition parties staged provocative victory processions on 12 May, and on 13 May a large crowd of Malays demanded resistance to this political development. An incident involving Malay and Chinese youths sparked serious and unprecedented rioting in many parts of Kuala Lumpur. In the next few hours many people died or suffered serious injuries in an orgy of violence, looting and property damage (Goh, 1973).

The disturbances threatened to spiral further out of control and the situation was such that extraordinary measures had to be taken. Therefore, on 15 May an emergency was proclaimed under Article 150 of the Constitution that extended to the entire federation, on grounds of a threat to national security. The government suspended the elections, which were not completed until February 1971, and some 22 months after the Proclamation, was Parliament summoned. During this period Malaysia was under emergency rule and martial law (Das, 2007).

174   A. HARDING

In the wake of the riots and the emergency proclamation, a National Consultative Council (NCC), comprising a range of parties and political interests, was set up to consider ways of restoring racial harmony. The NCC agreed to a raft of amendments to the Constitution. It became clear that Parliament would not be summoned unless the government was sure that the constitutional amendments would be passed, with or without opposition support. The creation of the Barisan Nasional (BN) to replace the Alliance, with wider political support, especially with the addition of parties from Sabah and Sarawak, gave the government the likelihood of the two-thirds majority it sought. Indeed, the elections were completed, Parliament summoned and the amendments duly passed. They had the effect of fundamentally altering the social contract (Harding, 1996, 2007). Tun Abdul Razak was by that time the Prime Minister, succeeding the Tunku, and was the architect of the new social contract. One immediate effect of this was to change the leadership in 1970 from the Tunku, moderate, tolerant and regarded by some factions as rather too conciliatory, to Tun Razak, who was seen as less charismatic but a firmer supporter of Malay rights.

The return to normality saw a radically altered version of the social contract. The constitutional amendments, the so-called *Rukunegara* amendments,[1] after the national ideology which they were supposed to implement, were far-reaching (Harding, 2007). Principally, the amendments redefined the social contract so as to give more special privileges to the Malays, extend their scope to natives of Sabah and Sarawak, and entrench them even further than they had been entrenched in 1957.

The *Rukunegara* amendments added a new aspect to the social contract. The *Rukunegara* itself, promulgated on National Day 1970 by the *Yang di-Pertuan Agong*, and stressing national unity, was negotiated between political leaders representing different communities, in line with the NCC, as a concerted attempt at nation-building by forming an agreed national ideology transcending Malaysia's deeply polarized society. The amendments also expressed the social contract as a list of 'sensitive issues' that could not be discussed, except as to policy implementation, in any forum, including even the floors of the Federal and State Legislatures.

---

[1] The text of the *Rukunegara* is appended to Harding (2007), at 130–132 The word is made up of '*rukun*' (principles) and '*negara*' (nation). It can be argued that it is a milk-and-water document that few could object to. However, its principles are often reiterated.

By these amendments, policy on the so-called sensitive issues (Article 153 privileges and legitimate interests, citizenship, the national language and the monarchy) was placed beyond public debate, and even beyond parliamentary privilege, so that there was no protection of freedom of expression with regard to these issues. It was permissible, however, to debate the implementation of such policy. This was all enforced by means of the law of sedition, under which relatively small fines became usual, prison sentences much less so. In addition, the scope of the social contract was extended to include natives of Sabah and Sarawak, and admission to tertiary education was added as an area for the operation of quotas. More than this, the social contract provisions were placed under the custody of the Conference of Rulers, a constitutional body in which all nine traditional Malay Rulers meet, enjoying some limited competency under the Constitution. Their consent is required under Article 158 of the Constitution for changes to any of the social contract provisions (Harding, 2007).

This remodelling of the social contract was not done in an atmosphere of mollified public relations, but rather under the cloud of emergency rule, parliamentary democracy suspended, elections uncompleted, civil liberties severely restricted and citizens preventively detained without trial under the Internal Security Act 1960. Agreements reached behind the closed doors of inter-party meetings were placed beyond public debate. The foundations were laid for an authoritarian style of government which contradicted many of the basic assumptions of the 1957 Constitution. The amendments provided the basis for the construction of a state that entrenched the Alliance, expanded and renamed the BN, in power for more than six decades. Nonetheless, inter-ethnic peace has been kept.

THE SOCIAL CONTRACT:
IMPLEMENTATION AND CRITIQUES

It is important to understand that Article 153 is not a licence to ignore the Constitution or the rights of citizens, or to indulge generally in official or institutionalized discrimination. It obliges the *Yang di-Pertuan Agong* (head of state at the federal level), acting on advice (in other words the government), to exercise his functions under the Constitution and federal law in such manner as may be necessary to safeguard the special position of *bumiputera* and, by giving binding directions to the

176   A. HARDING

relevant authorities, to ensure the reservation for *bumiputera* of a reasonable proportion of positions in the federal public service; scholarships and other similar educational or training privileges; and permits or licences for the operation of any trade or business, where required by federal law.

Thus Article 153 represents a balanced exception to the ordinary rule of equality before the law, allowing quotas to be operated in certain public decisions affecting individual opportunities. However, there are some limitations entrenched in Article 153. It does not allow unequal treatment of federal employees of different races once they are employed (this is not of course the same as unequal *access* to public service positions); or the deprivation of a public office or scholarship already held. Similarly, it does not allow the deprivation of any licence already vested, or the refusal to renew or allow the transfer of a licence where such renewal or transfer might reasonably be expected in the ordinary course of events. Also, Parliament may not restrict business or trade only for the purpose of reservation of quotas.

With the application of Article 153 to 'natives of Sabah and Sarawak' these indigenous communities were also made in effect parties to the social contract involving the other three ethnic groups. The communities that are protected by Article 153 are referred to in Malaysia generally, although not in Article 153 itself, as *'bumiputera.'* This term includes: Malays, who are in turn defined by the Constitution as Muslims habitually using the Malay language and Malay customs and domiciled in Malaysia, and anyone with one Malay parent; natives of Sarawak, belonging to a scheduled list of indigenous groups, or having a parent belonging thereto; and similarly, natives of Sabah.

By broadening the definition of those entitled to Article 153 protection, the government was able to construct a clear bumiputera majority within Malaysia. The creation of Malaysia in 1963 followed by the departure of Singapore (with its 75% Chinese population) in 1965 made this majority possible, and it was partly the prospect of such a majority that had driven the plan to form Malaysia in the first place.

JUDICIAL RESPONSES

The courts have never had any clear interpretive occasion to pronounce on the scope and meaning of Article 153 itself, or explain the concepts of 'special position' or 'legitimate interests.' The lack of any litigation on these issues is probably attributable to their designation as sensitive issues, a fact of which lawyers would be acutely aware in providing advice. Nonetheless, religion is also a sensitive issue, yet has been a constant topic of litigation (Shah, 2017). The likelihood is that litigating rights under Article 153, whatever the circumstances, would also risk inflaming negative inter-ethnic feelings, inviting the possibility of prosecution under the Sedition Act. Nonetheless, although some litigation (see the *Merdeka University* case below, concerning the national language in the education system) has indeed concerned socially sensitive issues, Article 153 itself has not featured in such cases. The use of litigation to test the proper extent of constitutional power could of course function as a much safer means than other, more overtly political, means of raising issues with ethnic or religious implications.

The controversial case of *Merdeka University Bhd v Government of Malaysia*[2] comes the closest that any litigation has come to a conflict over the social contract (Sinnadurai, 1986). It examined the right of a private university to use a language other than the national language as the main medium of instruction. The promoting company, supported by a large number of Chinese interests, applied to the government under the Universities and University Colleges Act 1971 for permission to set up a private university, in which Chinese would be the main medium of instruction. Permission was refused on the grounds that the proposed university would conflict with the national education policy. The refusal was challenged, in judicial review proceedings, unsuccessfully, partly on the grounds of contravention of Article 152 of the Constitution, under which the use of languages other than the national language is permitted, but not for 'official purposes.' Puzzlingly, a majority of the Federal Court decided that this private university was nonetheless a public authority carrying out an official purpose, namely education.

Since the *Merdeka University* case, however, changes have been made to education policy that now allow private tertiary institutions to use English, as the medium of globalization, information technology and science; and Arabic as the medium of Islam. National primary and secondary schools, on the other hand, have always been able to use Chinese and Tamil, and even to admit pupils other than those who have these languages as their mother tongue (Tan, 2005). In a more

---

[2] [1982] 2 *Malayan Law Journal* 243.

178   A. HARDING

recent case, the courts rejected a claim that vernacular schools were unconstitutional by virtue of the same provision (Lim, 2019).[3]

The upshot is that opportunities appear to have been missed to provide juristic input to the debates around the social contract and draw limits to its operation or even simply explain its legal essence. Judicial decisions have thus had marginal impact in this area, as distinct from that of religion, which indicates the strong potential that such input might have had (Shah, 2017). In essence, this is, therefore, an area where the judiciary is unwilling to challenge government policy in any, even procedural, ways.

DURATION AND APPLICATION OF THE SOCIAL CONTRACT

There was no consensus amongst political interests in 1956–1957 on the question of the duration of the special privileges under Article 153. The Reid Commission, which drafted the constitution, concluded that after 15 years Parliament should reconsider them, but the outcome was that no specific duration was enacted. Given that the 15 years would have expired in 1972, it is probably fortunate that this benchmark was not adopted, because at that time, far from being abolished, they were increased in scope and constitutionally entrenched. This issue of duration was dealt with in the 1971 settlement not by settling a particular duration (although the NEP itself set targets, especially 30% *bumiputera* economic ownership, to be achieved by 1990), but by protecting all the changes from an easy abolition, as is explained above.

Another area of lack of clarity in the social contract is the concept of 'legitimate interests of other communities,' which, in addition to the special privileges, are also protected by Article 153. No definition has been given of this term in any judicial or statutory interpretation. However, we can probably understand it in terms of a general protection of existing vested rights, and the right to maintain minority languages and cultures. At any rate the notion of legitimate interests was at least clearly understood as implying that non-Malays would not be restricted in conducting business or having their property rights restricted; but no particular programme was implied, as opposed to some restrictions on the special privileges themselves, which are listed above.

---

[3] *Mohamed Khairul Azam bin Abdul Aziz v Menteri Pendidikan Malaysia and Anor* [2020] 1 *Malayan Law Journal* 398.

As a result, it is the quota system, which is designed to provide opportunities for *bumiputera* citizens, that principally implements the social contract as embodied in the amended Article 153. Other measures, however, are also relevant in implementing the overall policy of redistribution. Statutory boards were set up, designed to provide special economic or educational opportunities for *bumiputera*.

There are also non-statutory policies ensuring that foreign investors enter into joint ventures with *bumiputera* partners to the extent of 30% *bumiputera* ownership. The Industrial Coordination Act 1975 required both foreign and domestic investors to comply with employment policies benefiting *bumiputera*, and only 30% *bumiputera*-owned companies were allowed to be listed on the Kuala Lumpur Stock Exchange. Tax concessions and government procurement have also been used to effect employment and share allocation quotas in the private sector. Special *bumiputera* discounts of at least 7% were imposed on developers for the purchase of new housing, given effect by conditions placed on planning permissions (Harding, 2021). In relation to the public service, a formal 4:1 *bumiputera* quota for Division 1 officers was continued and applied to the unified Administrative and Diplomatic Service and the police, while a 3:1 quota applied to the Judicial and Legal Service and the Customs Department. However, the pattern of actual recruitment to Division 1 posts was varied so that almost all new recruits were *bumiputera* (Dass & Abbott, 2008).

Article 153 has had the most effect, however, on the education system, especially tertiary education. The universities had previously admitted students on merit alone, resulting in an ethnic imbalance. A Government Committee recommended that universities should ensure as far as possible that the ethnic composition of the student population within the university and within each faculty should reflect the composition of Malaysian society. This was given effect with the government giving binding directions to tertiary institutions under Article 153 to reserve admission quotas, resulting in a dramatic increase in scholarships and places for *bumiputera* students. *Bumiputera* University admissions rose from 40% in 1970 to 63% (roughly, demographically, a par figure) in 1985 (Lee, 2021: 118–119).

Success and Failure

A real problem with affirmative action programmes is the assessment of success and failure. This is especially true in cases where the entire political system is implicated. When a programme is intended to be transformative, it needs to be demonstrated that transformation has taken place, otherwise the programme's value falls into question. On the other hand, if success is demonstrated, then questions arise whether the programme is still required.

In Malaysia, the social contract presents a political programme that carries grave dangers. Non-bumiputera of previous generations had experienced 13 May, or their parents had, and understood that the social contract guaranteed security and prosperity at the cost of a measure of inequality of opportunity. After half a century of the NEP and its successor policies, non-bumiputera, born as citizens, are more likely to question whether this inequality, even if justified previously, is still justified. After all, it is to be expected that affirmative action would have succeeded in its objectives at this juncture. But at the same time, there is considerable reluctance on the part of many *bumiputera* to countenance any attempt to dismantle the social contract. Indeed, it is often seen, not as a transitional measure, but as fundamental. In 2019 an attempt by the then PH (Pakatan Harapan) government to ratify the International Convention on the Elimination of Racial Discrimination (ICERD) was abandoned in the face of hostility from Malay nationalist groups.

Therefore, there is a sense in which the NEP policy cannot be seen either to fail or to succeed, as neither outcome is politically sustainable. Even continuing with it in its current form may not prove to be politically or economically sustainable at some future juncture. The programme could possibly be dismantled, in the way in which one might play a game of pick-up sticks—very slowly and very carefully, without disturbing the pile. And in some ways changes moving away from strict application of Article 153 policies have been made. For example, in tertiary education admission quotas have been formally abandoned. And in special economic zones the 30% rule for foreign investors has been rescinded. Some politicians have made so bold as to suggest that poverty rather than race should be the criterion for affirmative action, but a far more dominant strand of opinion is represented by the discourse of '*ketuanan Melayu*' or Malay dominance, under which the political dominance of the Malays is a fundamental condition represented by the social contract (Tay, 2017).

Implicit in all of this lurk two important questions: Have the targets of affirmative action been met, or how far away from those targets are matters now? And what are the implications of the actual economic position (Yusof, 2012)?

The first point here is that Malaysia has indeed achieved economic development, and despite economic challenges, it has achieved middle-income status. Since 1970, and especially after Tun Mahathir Mohamad became Prime Minister in 1981, economic growth rates have been high, albeit not consistently so, at least up until the Covid-19 pandemic struck in 2020. Recessions in 1985/1986 and 2008/2009, in addition to the Asian currency crisis of 1997/1998, have held back economic development, but the overall trajectory represents notable achievement. Malaysia no longer appears on most lists of 'developing countries,' and poverty has been very substantially reduced (Jomo, 2005).

At the same time, the consequences of the NEP itself have by no means received universal applause. It is criticized for creating a comfortable urban Malay middle class and large numbers of state-dependent citizens, while ignoring real poverty amongst all communities. The so-called *ali-baba* phenomenon, which has become prevalent, involves *bumiputera* borrowers acting as front-men for non-*bumiputera* entrepreneurs. This has created much resentment and defeats the object of redistribution and increased opportunity. Often the government itself has stressed that the need is for thrusting new entrepreneurs pushing the economy forward, not for handouts which do not produce proportionate common benefits. Corruption and cronyism in government are other phenomena that have spurred criticism (Gomez & Jomo, 2004). One overall assessment states that Malaysia has "achieved various numerical outcomes but floundered in the ultimate goal of cultivating capability, confidence and self-reliance, towards genuinely and effectively redressing *bumiputera* socio-economic disadvantage" (Lee, 2021: 172). While this is probably true, it would be a brave politician who would seek to translate that proposition into actual policy.

The factual issues regarding success of the NEP and its successor policies, the National Development Policy and the (current) National Vision Policy, are fraught with controversy. The main objective of the NEP was to increase *bumiputera* equity ownership from 1.5% in 1969 to 30% by 1990. The other main aspect of the NEP was to reduce poverty (seen largely in practice as a rural Malay issue) from 49% in 1970 to 16%

in 1990. Officially, the poverty rate is now below 3%.[4] The NEP has without doubt succeeded in many respects, although there are still issues of uneven development. Accounts of success or failure in this objective render the issue murky, as there are no agreed criteria for assessing ownership, official statements indicating that there is still some way to go towards achieving the 30% benchmark. Some critiques doubt the 30% target in principle, while others claim that increasing equity ownership does not, as the system assumes, lead to the intended social changes. However, since there is no agreed method for benchmarking success, the true position is difficult to ascertain and objective debate has been difficult to conduct while the issue has continued to be regarded as 'sensitive.' When an NGO research unit issued a report in 2006 contradicting the government's figures, and alleging that the true percentage for *bumiputera* equity ownership might be as high as 45%, the Director of the unit, a prominent academic, was forced to resign amid serious recriminations and invective from government ministers.[5] Debate about the factual meeting of targets, moreover, has had to substitute for debate about the principles of the NEP, because it is still an offence under the Sedition Act to question the policy, albeit that such questioning has become in practice more frequent in recent years. The closer official statements have come to saying that the 30% target is being achieved, the more difficult it has been to close off debate about what comes next, whatever limitations the law imposes on freedom of speech.

Indeed, since the early 2000s government itself has cautiously addressed dysfunctional aspects of the *bumiputera*-preference policy, no doubt aware of its need to satisfy non-*bumiputera* voters, given the splintering of the Malay vote since 1999 between UMNO and newer opposition parties. The '30% rule' in foreign investment approvals was rescinded in 2009, and earlier, for all investments, in special economic zones. Quotas for university admission were abolished in 2004, and in 2008 the scholarship quota was adjusted from 90–10% to 55–45% in favour of *bumiputera*.[6]

---

[4] See https://worldpoverty.io/map (accessed 12 May 2020).

[5] *The Star*, 12 October 2006, https://thestar.com.my/news/story.asp?file=/2006/10/12/nation/15695245&sec=nation.

[6] See www.cpps.org.my/downloads/factsheets/National%20unity%20factsheet.pdf (Centre for Public Policy Studies).

There is clearly widespread belief that the social contract is outdated and changes are required. Placing an extra constitutional obstacle in the path of change (the consent of the Conference of Rulers, by amendment to Article 159 in 1971) might prove to have been unwise. The Rulers are seen as guardians of Malay rights, and consenting to them being abridged or removed would present political difficulties for the monarchy system. An alternative solution is offered by the fact that Article 153 allows the government a discretion as to when and how to exercise the powers it grants, as with the adjustment in scholarship quotas. If the government were of the view that the special position of *bumiputera* citizens is no longer in need of protection, it could simply decline to use the powers involved and rescind relevant regulations. This would be perfectly legal, but of course would also have the disadvantage of leaving the system in place for possible future use.

Any process to dismantle or replace the social contract will have to be handled carefully. There is attachment to its principle as a matter of group rights, as well as to the benefits that it has bestowed on a large proportion of the population. Many would regard their removal with dismay, and might argue with some force that the social contract and the NEP have been a success. Given the continued existence of ethnic and religious tensions, which were apparent in opposition to the PH government of 2018–2020, the social contract will continue to be a matter of sensitivity and controversy. To some advocates of Malay rights the social contract means that the state embodies a fundamental and continuing notion of Malay dominance, as is explained above. However, this view misconstrues the social contract, which is essentially a compromise which *balances* the rights and interests of different communities, and the Constitution, while preserving some traditional elements and special privileges, does not embody Malay dominance as such but a pluralist democracy (Fernando, 2002).

Apart from the visceral politics surrounding the social contract, there is scope for much disagreement about fundamental questions as to its real nature. The fact is that it is a vague and contested idea. However, the social contract is also vague. We have seen earlier its origins and purposes. But what, precisely, are its terms? Who, precisely, are its parties? How is it, or how far is it, precisely, supposed to be implemented? Most importantly, by what process can it be changed? Confusion surrounds these issues, and the lack of any real freedom to address them has proved 'not

184   A. HARDING

so much a necessity in a plural society as a dysfunctional form of political process' (Harding, 2022: xx). It is clearly a problem that the social contract is an abstraction, not contained in any particular document, and has to be construed mainly from the provisions of the Constitution itself, the circumstances surrounding their adoption, and the changing discourse on the economy and inter-ethnic relations (Othman et al., 2008).

COALITION POLITICS AND THE SOCIAL CONTRACT

Finally, this section is designed to explain briefly how the social contract and its political implications relate to the political system as it has evolved since independence.

It will have been gathered that the social contract had its origins in coalition politics. Its continuance also depended on coalition politics, and, since 2008, its critique too depends on coalition politics. This is due to the fact that in Malaysia ethnic parties, which constitute most of the political parties, cannot hope to win elections on their own. They must find allies across the ethnic divide, and in general these allies are not inclined to challenge the social contract for the political and legal reasons outlined earlier in the chapter. Given that *bumiputera* constitute more than 60% of the population and the electorate, any Malaysian government will inevitably need to present a *bumiputera* face to the electorate, but at the same time ensure that non-Malays are represented in the Cabinet, and policies developed that satisfy non-*bumiputera* voters. This has always been the case, and non-*bumiputera* parties have had to gain votes on the basis that they are the best bet to secure the interests of their ethnic group (Chinese, Indian, or indigenous) in a Malay-dominated system. Although these political norms have been persistent throughout, in recent years the Cabinet has grown to more than 70 members, as successive Prime Ministers have attempted to satisfy every kind of political supporter (race, party, faction, state) by providing ministerial jobs, or other perks such as CEO positions with government-linked companies. This need to appeal across ethnic divides applies to both governing and opposition coalitions.

The limits of multi-racial government were clearly seen with the Pakatan Harapan (PH) coalition of Tun Mahathir (in, at 94 years old, his second coming as Prime Minister, this time from the opposition), which was elected to power in May 2018, ousting UMNO from office for the first time since independence in the wake of an enormous corruption scandal (Wong, 2018). PH pulled into coalition government, for the first time, the Democratic Action Party (DAP), which is widely seen as a Chinese-dominated party, gaining most of its support from non-*bumiputera* voters. The PH government set out an ambitious reform agenda, which was on the way to being implemented when in February 2020, a faction of one of its coalition partners, PKR, the party of Mahathir's presumed heir, Anwar Ibrahim, brought the government down in what has been called the 'Sheraton move', reaching agreement with members of Mahathir's own Bersatu party and opposition MPs to deprive the PH government of a majority. During the PH reform process, a number of issues underlined the inability of the PH government to contradict large bodies of opinion supporting a nationalist agenda (Shah & Harding, 2020).

First, there was considerable opposition to the appointment of a Chinese finance minister from the DAP, the first Chinese in many decades to hold that key office. Secondly, there was disquiet at Mahathir's pick (an Indian lawyer, Tommy Thomas) as Attorney-General, expressed by the Rulers themselves, and others. It was alleged that the AG should be a guardian of Malay rights, and should always be a Malay. Mahathir nonetheless appointed Thomas, almost immediately asking for his resignation to avoid the political fallout, and then agreed for him to continue after he was prevailed upon to relent (Thomas, 2021). Thirdly, as related above, the ICERD issue raised Malay hackles on the basis that ICERD would require dismantling of the *bumiputera*-preference system. Fourthly, when the PH government proposed to sign the Rome Statute, joining the international criminal court, it was objected that this would expose the Rulers themselves to prosecution. In fact signing neither the Rome Statute nor ICERD would have these alleged consequences, but even so, the government relented in the face of extensive Malay opposition to these two measures.

With the collapse of the PH government, and the precarious survival of its successor governments under Muhyiddin Yasin (March 2020–August 2021) and Ismail Sabri Yakob (from August 2021), only latterly with a clear if small parliamentary majority, all issues relating to the social contract are off political agendas. However, problematic issues remain, as we have seen, and at some juncture Malaysia will have to confront the construction of another inter-ethnic policy, hopefully one that unites rather than divides the nation.

Conclusion

The Malaysian example of consociational government can be admired as an example of ethnic accommodation in cases where it is the majority community that is historically disadvantaged. It can also be criticized for failing to address the notion of a common citizenship that should be basic to any idea of nation-building. It shows that affirmative action over an extended period can secure peace and stability, and at the same time secure economic growth that benefits all communities. Yet clearly there are also dangers in such an approach, or at least in consistently maintaining it, as the logic of affirmative action is that redistribution of opportunity should, over time, have equalizing effects and empower the disadvantaged, rather than deepen its dependency on the state. In fact, the result has been an entrenchment of inequality as, not a temporary deviation from a perceived norm, but as a basic entitlement based on ethnic criteria. In recent years, economic under-performance has also become an issue. During the current period of political fragmentation, it should in principle be possible to rethink consociationalism. Yet there are few signs that the nettle of consociationalism is about to be grasped, or that a new formulation of it is in prospect.

References

Comber, L. (1983). *13 May 1969: A Historical Survey of Sino-Malay Relations*. Heinemann.

Das, C. (2007). The May 13th Riots and Emergency Rule. In A. Harding & H. P. Lee (Eds.), *Constitutional Landmarks in Malaysia: The First Fifty Years, 1957–2007*. Malayan Law Journal/LexisNexis.

Dass, M., & Abbott, K. (2008). Modelling New Public Management in an Asian Context: Public Sector Reform in Malaysia. *Asia Pacific Journal of Public Administration, 30*(1), 59–82.

Fernando, J. (2002). *The Making of the Malayan Constitution*. MBRAS.

Goh, C. T. (1973). *The May 13th Incident and Democracy in Malaysia*. University of Malaya Press.

Gomez, E. T., & Jomo, K. S. (Eds.). (2004). *The State of Malaysia: Ethnicity, Equity and Reform*. London.

Gomez, E. T., & Saravanamuttu, J. (Eds.). (2013). *The New Economic Policy in Malaysia*. NUS Press.

Harding, A. (1996). *Law, Government and the Constitution in Malaysia*. Kluwer and Malayan Law Journal.

Harding, A. (2007). The *Rukunegara* Amendments of 1971. In A. Harding & H. P. Lee (Eds.), *Constitutional Landmarks in Malaysia: The First Fifty Years, 1957–2007*. Malayan Law Journal/LexisNexis.

Harding, A. (2021). *Local Government in Malaysia: Responses to Urban-Rural Challenges, Report for EU Horizon Research 2020*. Institute for Comparative Federalism.

Harding, A. (2022). *The Constitution of Malaysia: A Contextual Analysis*. Hart/Bloomsbury.

Jomo, K. S. (2005). Malaysia's New Economic Policy and National Unity. In Y. Bangura & R. Stavenhagen (Eds.), *Racism and Public Policy*. Palgrave Macmillan.

Jomo, K. S., & Chang, Y. T. (2008). The Political Economy of Post-Colonial Transformation. In K. S. Jomo & S. N. Wong (Eds.), *Law, Institutions and Malaysian Economic Development*. NUS Press.

Lee, H.-A. (2021). *Affirmative Action in Malaysia and South Africa: Preference for Parity*. Routledge.

Lijphart, A. (1969). Consociational Democracy. *World Politics, 21*(2), 207–225.

Lijphart, A. (1985). Non-majoritarian Democracy: A Comparison of Federal and Consociational Theories. *Publius, 15*(2), 3–15.

Lim, W. J. (2019, December 23). The Case for the Constitutionality of Vernacular Schools. *Malaysiakini*. https://www.malaysiakini.com/news/504604.

Mohamed Salleh, A. (1986). Traditional Elements in the Malaysian Constitution. In F. A. Trindade & H. P. Lee (Eds.), *The Constitution of Malaysia: Further Developments and Perspectives*. Oxford University Press.

Othman, N., Puthucheary, M. C., & Kessler, C. (Eds.). (2008). *Sharing the Nation: Faith, Difference, Power and the State 50 Years After Merdeka*. SIRDC.

Shah, D. A. H. (2017). 'Religion, Conversions, and Custody: Battles in the Malaysian Appellate Courts', Ch.7 of A. Harding and D. A. H. Shah (eds), *Law and Society in Malaysia: Pluralism, Religion and Ethnicity*. Routledge.

Shah, D. A. H., & Harding, A. (2020, April 8). Constitutional Quantum Mechanics and a Change in Government in Malaysia. *International Journal of Constitutional Law Blog*. http://www.iconnectblog.com/2020/04/constitutional-quantum-mechanics-and-achange-in-government-in-malaysia/

Sinnadurai, V. (1986). Rights in Respect of Education Under the Malaysian Constitution. In F. A. Trindade & H. P. Lee (Eds.), *The Constitution of Malaysia: Further Developments and Perspectives*. Oxford University Press.

Tan, P. K. W. (2005). The Medium-of-Instruction Debate in Malaysia: English as a Malaysian Language? *Language Problems and Language Planning, 29*(1), 47–66.

Tan, T. Y. (2008). *Creating 'Greater Malaysia': Decolonization and the Politics of Merger*. Institute of Southeast Asian Studies.

Tay, W. T. V. (2017). Dimensions of *Ketuanan Melayu* in the Malaysian Constitutional Framework. In A. Harding & D. A. H. Shah (Eds.), *Law and Society in Malaysia: Pluralism, Religion, and Ethnicity*. Routledge.

Thomas, T. (2021). *My Story: Justice in the Wilderness*. SIRDC.

von Vorys, K. (1975). *Democracy without Consensus: Communalism and Political Stability in Malaysia*. Princeton University Press.

Wong, C. H. (2018). The Rise, Resilience and Demise of Malaysia's Dominant Coalition. *The Round Table, 107*(6), 755–769.

Yusof, Z. A. (2012). Affirmative Action in Malaysia: An Overview of Progress and Limitations. In G. Brown, F. Stewart, & A. Langer (Eds.), *Affirmative Action in Plural Societies: International Experiences*. Palgrave Macmillan.

CHAPTER 9

The Paradox of Power-Sharing in Mauritius

Sheetal Sheena Sookrajowa

INTRODUCTION

As a multi-ethnic society, Mauritius remains distinct compared to other plural settings in Africa. It has maintained democratic stability since its independence in 1968, save for the state of emergency from 1971 to 1976 and the 1999 inter-ethnic disturbance. Elections have generally been free, fair and non-violent and economic development has been promoted (Benedict, 1962; Bowman, 1991; Phaala, 2019). To what extent has consociational democracy contributed to this state of affairs?

Consociational democracy in Mauritius emerged as an institutional option from the negotiations between British colonial authorities and local political parties during the decolonization period from 1947 to 1968—an era dominated by class and communal divisions (Boudet, 2003; Simmons, 1982). This chapter sheds light on the adoption, function and potential for adaptation of power-sharing in Mauritius, beginning with the period leading up to independence. It was this period of decolonization that set the base of political accommodation between the British

S. S. Sookrajowa (✉)
University of Mauritius, Réduit, Mauritius
e-mail: s.sookrajowa@uom.ac.mu

© The Author(s), under exclusive license to Springer Nature
Switzerland AG 2024
E. Wassim Aboultaif et al. (eds.), *Power-Sharing in the Global South*,
Federalism and Internal Conflicts,
https://doi.org/10.1007/978-3-031-45721-0_9

189

190   S. S. SOOKRAJOWA

colonial authorities and the representatives of national and ethnic parties. Yet, despite the adoption of several power-sharing features, including a culture of coalition politics and a system of proportional representation known as the Best Loser System (BLS), the Mauritian political system remains highly majoritarian with the dominant rule of the Hindumajority. Mutual veto powers and segmental autonomy are weak with much power vested in the Prime Minister. There are further limitations, including, for example, the marginalization of some smaller ethnic minorities, in particular the Creole community, and the fact that ethnic representation tends to be prioritized over gender representation. In terms of adaptability, prospects for electoral reform remain slim. Thus, while power-sharing has supported political stability in Mauritius, it also raises questions of democratic quality. Consequently, this chapter aims at explaining what I refer to as the 'paradox of power-sharing'—the hybrid combination of majoritarian and consociational features in support of stability—in Mauritius.

ETHNIC PROFILE

According to Lijphart (1977: 4–5), a plural society is segregated by 'segmental cleavages' such as "religious, ideological, linguistic, regional, cultural, racial, or ethnic nature" and where its social and political institutions are likely to be formed along these differences. In the Mauritian context, Benedict (1962: 65) uses the term 'plural society' not only to refer to the different segments but also to how they can merge to form a single society. Having no native inhabitants, its population of around a million is instead derived from successive flows of migrants since 1715 (Dinan et al., 1999; Eriksen, 1994). The island was initially discovered by the Portuguese in 1513 but it remained unpopulated until 1638 when the Dutch occupied it and introduced both sugar cane and the importation of African slaves. In 1710, the Dutch deserted the island, and it was left almost entirely uninhabited when the French arrived in 1735 (Brookfield, 1957; Dinan et al., 1999; Meisenhelder, 1997). During the French period, large numbers of slaves were brought from Africa and Madagascar, as well as from India. Owing to its strategic importance, the British took over the island in 1810 and ended the legal slave trade (Allen, 2003; Brookfield, 1957). With the abolition of slavery in 1835, indentured laborers were then brought from India (Allen, 1988). Later, at the beginning of the twentieth century, the Chinese traders from China and

Muslim merchants from North India arrived in the country (Dinan et al., 1999; Eriksen, 1994).

In the contemporary period, the Hindu community (Indian descent) is the largest community on the island and comprises four different sub-ethnic groups:

(i) Hindi/Bhojpuri-speaking Hindu, the majority of whom came mostly from Uttar Pradesh (North India) and Bihar (East India);
(ii) Tamil from Southern India;
(iii) Telegu from Southern India and;
(iv) Marathis from Maharashtra, a Western state in India.

The Hindi/Bhojpuri-speaking Hindu group is further subdivided into several distinct castes: Brahmin (High Caste), Kshatriya (High Caste), Vaish (Middle Caste), Rajput (Low Caste) and Ravived (Low Caste) (Hollup, 1994).

The Muslim community (Indian descent) consists of Mauritian Muslims who also form part of the Indo-Mauritian population who came from the same regions of the Hindu community, namely Uttar Pradesh and Bihar (Eisenlohr, 2006: 397; Hollup, 1996: 288). Owing to the increasing ethno-political divisions among the people of Indian descent during the twentieth century, 'Indians' began to categorize themselves as either Hindus or Muslims, creating divergent political groups and were hence identified separately in the 1962 census for the first time (Bowman, 1991; Simmons, 1982). The Muslim community is further classified into different groupings such as sects (Memons, Surtees, Sunnis, Shiia and Ahmadiyya), profession, class and political appurtenance (Hollup, 1996).

The third community—Sino-Mauritians—is numerically a minority category of the population. A fourth community—called the General Population—consists mainly of Franco-Mauritians: the French sugar barons (the Elite), as well as the Coloreds, and the Creoles of the Black African slaves descent including the Black Creoles and the Mulatto Creoles (Fessha & Nam, 2015; Mukonoweshuro, 1991; Srebrnik, 2002). With these sub-groups, communal belonging and representation becomes an issue. For example, in 2010, to take advantage of the best loser system, a candidate declared himself as General Population instead of Sino-Mauritian. Moreover, owing to diverse implications, it would be difficult for example to replace the General Population by Creoles (Reddi,

2019). As Reddi (2019) sustains, "we all realise that ethnic categories are illogical and potentially divisive but on the other hand our Constitution makes provision for the safeguarding of both individual and group rights."

The constitution of Mauritius officially classifies the population into four communities for electoral purposes:

(i) the Hindu community,
(ii) the Muslim community,
(iii) the Sino-Mauritian community and
(iv) the General Population which is also considered as a residual category comprising of those who do not belong to the first three communities (Constitution of Mauritius, Section 31 (2)).

An approximation of the different ethnic categories according to the 1972 population census are as follows: Hindu 51%, Muslim 17%, Sino-Mauritian 1% and the General Population 31%.

The Development of Power-Sharing Under the British Colonial Rule (Adoption Phase)

All power-sharing systems evolve through a lifecycle, consisting of three phases: "adoption, implementation, and (possible) end" (McCulloch, 2021; McCulloch & McEvoy, 2020: 110). To understand how and why power-sharing features came to inform the constitutional order in Mauritius, we need to consider the country's journey to independent statehood and the role of British colonial authorities as it was during the negotiations between the British colonial authorities and local political parties about constitutional reforms, universal suffrage and the granting of independence that consociational democracy began to appear as a viable system. Although support for power-sharing was a mutual decision between British colonial authorities and local political parties, its precise institutional shape remained contentious. Moreover, the British often supported the Mauritius Labour Party (MLP) vis-à-vis other parties in the constitutional negotiations with the aim of ensuring a stable government. This section, therefore, seeks to provide a historical overview of power-sharing debates under British colonial rule and to show how the process of British decolonization had brought about the involvement of

9 THE PARADOX OF POWER-SHARING IN MAURITIUS   193

the main ethno-political actors in the development of the constitution, their participation in the design of the electoral system and their representation in the Legislative Council following the elections of 1948, 1953, 1959, 1963 and 1967.

The Division Between the Franco-Mauritians and the Indo-Mauritians, and the General Elections of 1948 and 1953

Prior to independence, the political affairs of Mauritius were managed by the Governor who was also the Queen's representative, and it was only from 1885 that the Constitution allowed members of the Legislative Council to be represented through nomination and election, with 8 official members, 9 nominated members and 10 elected members (Chan Low, 1995; Lau Thi Keng, 1991). At this time, there were nine constituencies, each able to elect one member, though the capital of Port Louis was able to return two members. Franchise was restricted to property and income prerequisites, which favored the Franco-Mauritian oligarchy (Chan Low, 1995; Simmons, 1982). Despite the end of the French administration and the introduction of British rule in 1810, Franco-Mauritians continued to dominate the economic life of Mauritius, French culture remained quite prevalent and relations with the British were quite erratic in the initial years of British control (Simmons, 1982). The British first sought the support of these oligarchs (elites of the sugar economy) but after doubting the faithfulness of the French, the British sought the support of the Creoles. Later, when faced with similar issues, the British sought the support of the Indians (Ballhatchet, 1995). Hence, in an attempt to achieve political stability, the British decision to engage with different ethnic groups reflects the divide-and-rule strategy that laid the foundation of power-sharing in Mauritius.

By the early decades of the twentieth century, the Colonial Office reckoned that many colonies needed constitutional reform (Simmons, 1982). During the 1930s, Mauritius witnessed the emergence of the MLP, a political party which aimed at regrouping the working class and the petty bourgeoisie and which campaigned for workers' rights (Chan Low, n.d.). The MLP was founded in 1936 by members of the Coloreds and the Creoles, led by Dr. Maurice Curé (supported by Emmanuel Anquetil and Guy Rozemont), and members of the Hindus namely Pandit Sahadeo, Dr. S. Ramgoolam, R. Jomadar and H. Ramnarain (Simmons, 1982; Tinker, 1977). The MLP had nationalist ideologies and was not associated to one ethnic group in the 1940s and 1950s. It was a multi-ethnic and a non-communal party for the working class. But it later became Hindu-dominated and was criticized for supporting "communalism, casteism and sectarianism" (Mannick, 1979). Workers strikes, riots and other disturbances also affected the island during the years 1937, 1938 and 1943 (Chan Low, n.d.; Croucher & McIlroy, 2013). A movement also emerged around this time to officially recognized the Indo-Mauritian community (Chan Low, n.d.). However, the then-Governor, Bede Clifford, resisted immediate constitutional reforms. The Governor Donald Mackenzie-Kennedy, the successor of Bede Clifford, acknowledged that political tensions in Mauritius were due to the restricted franchise and the mode of election. After the Second World War and during Mackenzie-Kennedy's mandate, necessary amendments were made to the constitution which were enacted in 1947 (Chan Low, n.d.; Simmons, 1982).

The 1948 general election was a turning point in the political history of Mauritius. Governor Mackenzie-Kennedy had agreed to replace the old constitution (dated 20 October 1885) with a more liberal one (La Gazettes des Iles, 1992). However, Mackenzie-Kennedy and the British authorities resisted the idea of instituting democracy in Mauritius (Chan Low, n.d.). They believed that "in a society divided horizontally into economic and social classes and vertically by racial and religious differences, there was little willingness to give due weight to the conflicting claims of race and religion or to compromise on major political issues" (Chan Low, n.d. cited Constitutional development in Mauritius, Sessional Paper, No. 3, 1956). The constitution thus made provisions for 19 elected members from 5 multi-member constituencies, 12 nominated members and 3 official members (Simmons, 1982). The new constitution also allowed for a "quasi-universal suffrage" where men and women who were 21 years above and who could read and write simple sentences in English or French would be eligible to vote (La Gazettes des Iles, 1992; Simmons, 1982). The 1948 election was historic: the MLP's victory marked "an end to sixty years of conservatism and the rule of a selected aristocratic minority" (Le Cernéen-Le Mauricien-Advance, 17 August 1948). Out of the 19 elected members, 11 were Hindus and eight were Creoles. Among the Franco-Mauritian oligarchs, only Jules Koenig was elected (Simmons, 1982). No Muslim candidate was elected and there was no representative from the Chinese community. The Muslims were upset with the 1948 constitution as they could not be represented as a community (Emrith, 2006). See Table 9.1.

9 THE PARADOX OF POWER-SHARING IN MAURITIUS   195

Table 9.1 The number of voters per ethnic group and the ratio of the members of the Legislative Council following the 1948 election

Communities	Population	Representatives	Ratio
Hindus	207,000	11	1/18,000
Coloreds	130,000	10	1/13,000
Muslims	60,000	1	1/60,000
Chinese	18,000	1	1/18,000
Whites	9500	6	1/1600
British	200	2	1/100
Rodrigues	18,000	0	
	442,700	31	1/14280

Source Un Demi-Siècle D'Elections Libres, La Gazettes des Iles No.30, Avril 1992, p. 11

To counter the emerging Hindu supremacy, the MLP's rise and the possibility of universal suffrage, the *Ralliement Mauricien* (RM) was founded in December 1952 (later renamed *Parti Mauricien* [PM] in April 1955) led by Jules Koenig (Dubey, 1997; Simmons, 1982). It was a Francophone party backed by the elites defending the interests of the Coloreds and the Creoles. It obtained the support of the newspaper, Le Cernéen, which was linked with the "metropolitan French crypto-fascist group," *L'Action Française* (Mannick, 1979). The 1953 election was another turning point, viewed by Simmons (1982: 117) as when "communalism was replacing class as the determining factor in Mauritian politics." The RM opposed universal suffrage and the establishment of a responsible government (La Gazettes des Iles, 1992). The MLP renewed its victory in the election of 1953 and only two candidates were elected from the RM: Jules Koenig and Razack Mohamed (a Muslim) (Chan Low, 1995; La Gazettes des Iles, 1992; Simmons, 1982). After its victory, the MLP appealed to the British government to review the 1948 constitution and asked for universal suffrage, a responsible government, a ministerial system, the reduction of nominated members in the Legislative Council, an increase in the number of elected members, and a Speaker in the Legislative Council. The MLP was not satisfied of the first constitutional conference which was held in London in 1955; a second conference was convened in 1957 by the British Secretary of State to discuss constitutional reforms (La Gazettes des Iles, 1992).

The paradox in the adoption phase of power-sharing in Mauritius is that although the British and the local parties were set to negotiate about constitutional reforms, it is also important to stress that colonial authorities intended to establish parliamentary institutions derived from Western civilization and as noted in the Hansard Society Report (1953: 5) "to suggest any alternative system would probably be regarded as an attempt to fob them off with an inferior article." Moreover, as elucidated in the Hansard Society Report (1953) "in most British colonies the basic structure of government is the same as in the United Kingdom." The problems in the adoption phase reflect to what Horowitz (2014: 8) would imply as "general risk aversion" where there is the tendency to adopt conversant models as "ethnic politics is a high-stakes game" and because "negotiators do not come to the table innocent and naked. They have biases that rule in some models and rule out others."

The Trustam Eve Commission and the General Elections of 1959 and 1963

Following the second meeting of 1957 in London with the MLP, the Trustam Eve Electoral Boundary Commission was established to decide on the design of electoral constituencies. In one option, Mauritius could be divided into a series of single-member constituencies up to a maximum of 40, with each having a minimum of 5,000 voters (Records of Public Hearings CO 890/15, 1957). A second option considered 11 3-member constituencies. The MLP and the PM had opposing views on electoral system design. The MLP favored 40 single-member constituencies and was opposed to any form of Proportional Representation (PR) (Records of Public Hearings CO 890/15, 1957). By contrast, the PM supported the division of the island into 11 3-member constituencies which would allow both the urban and rural regions to seek direct representation (Representations for 11 × 3 member constituencies CO 890/3, 1957). Ultimately, the Trustam Eve Commission adopted the 40 single-member constituencies and universal suffrage was obtained.

The 1959 general election was contested by four main political parties: the MLP, the PM, Independent Forward Bloc (IFB) and Muslim Action Committee (MAC). The IFB was a Hindu-dominated party led by Sookdeo Bissoondoyal. As with the PM, the IFB also aimed to overthrow the MLP (Simmons, 1982). The MAC (Muslim-dominated) was led by Razack Mohamed who was previously supporting Jules Koenig under the banner of the PM. The MLP in alliance with the MAC won an absolute majority of 23 seats and the MAC obtained 5 seats. The IFB obtained 6 seats, the PM 3 seats and the remaining 3 seats were from Labour Trade Unionists (La Gazettes des Iles, 1992). Ramgoolam was appointed by Governor Scott as the Leader of the House and Finance Minister and Razack Mohamed as the Minister of Housing (Emrith, 2006).

At the 1961 constitutional conference, the MLP made a series of requests: the granting of internal autonomy, the granting of independence in 1964, that the leader of the winning party (that is the MLP) should be titled as Chief Minister and the abolition of nominated members (La Gazettes des Iles, 1992). In the constitutional review talks held in July 1961, two stages of constitutional advance were suggested subject to the following conditions:

(i) the constitutional advance toward internal self-government was inevitable and desirable;
(ii) that after the introduction of the second stage of the constitutional advance following the next general election, Mauritius would, if all went well, be able to move toward full internal self-government before the next following election; and
(iii) that at that time it was not possible to foresee the precise status of Mauritius after full internal self-government had been achieved (Mauritius Constitutional Conference Report London DO 118/327, 1965).

The first stage was instantly applied and Ramgoolam obtained the title of Chief Minister. This led to the reduction of the prerogatives of the Governor and would henceforth require consulting the Chief Minister for the reshuffling of the Legislative Council and its dissolution. The second stage of constitutional reform was applied after the following general election. The next election was held in October 1963. But the MLP, in coalition with the MAC, did not obtain an absolute majority as in 1959. The MLP/MAC alliance won a total of 23 seats out of 40 and the opposing alliance PM/IFB obtained 15. In December 1963, the Governor Rennie announced the second stage of the constitutional reform and the Council shifted to a Legislative Assembly with Ramgoolam as Prime Minister (La Gazettes des Iles, 1992).

198   S. S. SOOKRAJOWA

The Banwell Commission and the Independence Election of 1967

In September 1965, the Mauritius Constitutional Conference was held at Lancaster House led by the Secretary of State for Colonies, Mr Anthony Greenwood, and supported by the Joint Parliamentary Under-Secretary, Lord Taylor, and represented by all the political parties in the Mauritian Legislative Council namely: Sir Seewoosagur Ramgoolam (a Hindu) of the MLP, Jules Koenig (a Franco-Mauritian) of the Parti Mauricien Social Démocrate (PMSD) (formerly the PM), S.Bissoondoyal (a Hindu) of the IFB, and Sir A. R. Mohamed (a Muslim) of the MAC. The main discussion of the conference was among the supporters of Independence and of the ongoing association of Mauritius with Britain. The Secretary of State recommended the setting up of a Commission to decide on: "the electoral system and the method of allocating seats in the Legislature, most appropriate for Mauritius, and the boundaries of electoral constituencies" (Mauritius Constitutional Conference Report London DO 118/327, 1965).

In December 1965, the Commission was eventually set up under the chairmanship of Sir Harold Banwell (Banwell Electoral Commission Report on Mauritius CO 1036/1592, 1966–1967). Again, differing opinions on electoral system design were evident. The MLP proposed 20 four-member constituencies to be elected through block voting. There would be a total of eighty-two members in the assembly, eighty members for Mauritius and two for the outer island of Rodrigues. The Muslims and the Sino-Mauritians shall be allocated reserved seats which would correspond to their population. The MLP deemed that an assembly of 82 members will ensure a broader representation (10 January 1966 record of hearing CO 961/46, 1965–1966). On the other hand, the modified party list proposed by the PMSD was rejected by all the Indo-Mauritian political parties. The Commission deemed that under a mixed system with a combination of the "first past the post" with additional quota seats as "corrective seats," there would be political participation on a national basis (Voting system CO 961/7, 1965–1966).

Finally, the Banwell Commission recommended 20 3-member constituencies and 1 two-member constituency for Rodrigues elected through block voting (see Fig. 9.1). For the representation of minorities, the Commission rejected the reserved seats suggested by the MLP and instead proposed 5 additional 'corrective seats.' However, Banwell's recommendation was criticized for the inadequate representation of the

9 THE PARADOX OF POWER-SHARING IN MAURITIUS   199

minorities. Mr. John Stonehouse (M.P, Minister, Parliamentary Under-Secretary of State), thus made the following recommendations to the Banwell report which were eventually adopted,

> There will be a fixed number of 70 seats in the Legislative Assembly. Sixty members will be elected in Mauritius by block voting (each person voting being obliged to cast his full three votes) in 20 three-member constituencies. Two members will be elected in Rodrigues by block voting in a single member constituency. In addition, there will be eight best loser seats. (Banwell electoral commission report on Mauritius CO 1036/1592, 1966–1967)

It was also agreed at the constitutional conference that the winning party at the next general election could ask officially for independence and it would automatically be granted by the British government (La Gazettes des Iles, 1992). The 1967 election was thus contested between the Independence Party (IP) (coalition between the MLP, IFB and the MAC) and the PMSD. The PMSD was led by Gaetan Duval (a Creole). The PMSD campaigned against independence, fearing that it would halt the French culture. It obtained the support of the majority of the Coloured elite, the working-class Creole population and segments of other minorities. Also, as Houbert (1992: 470) explained,

> although the Creoles thought of themselves as the first inhabitants of Mauritius, they feared that decolonisation would mean independence under 'Indian' rule because they had become an ethnic minority. After the failure of its bitter opposition to universal suffrage, the *Parti mauricien social-democrate* (P.M.S.D.) pressed for the integration of the island with Britain as an alternative to independence.

The PMSD secured 44% of the votes in the 1967 elections against the 56% of the votes obtained by the Independence Party (IP) supported mostly by Indian communities. The minorities (Muslim, General Population and the Sino-Mauritian) voted against independence whereas the Hindu-majority voted in favor of independence (La Gazettes des Iles, 1992). It is important to stress here that independence was, therefore, not the outcome of a national liberation struggle and Mauritians did not have any sense of national identity and most people identified primarily with their ethnic community, or with a narrower part of that community (Caroll & Caroll, 1999; Houbert, 1981). Once independence became a

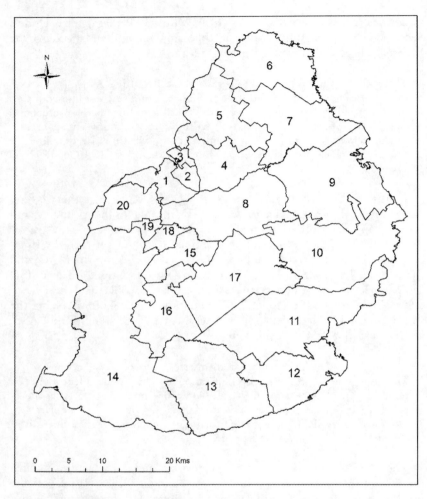

Fig. 9.1 Map of Mauritius's 20 constituencies (*Source* Couacaud, L., Sookrajowa, S. S., & Narsoo, J. [2022]. The Vicious Circle that is Mauritian Politics: The Legacy of Mauritius's Electoral Boundaries. *Ethnopolitics, 22*(1), 48–67)

reality, there were constant efforts to weld the country together, such as the formation of a coalition government in 1969 when the PMSD joined the government. The speeches on Independence Day from politicians focused on unity, economic development, and social improvement. After the racial tensions in 1968, it was observed "this temporary setback had been forgotten and leaders of the main ethnic groups have taken positive steps to cooperate and work in harmony with the overall aim of developing a unified and integrated society" (Mannick, 1979: 61). Yet, despite efforts at reconciliation, some still find it difficult to come to terms with political reality. After 1968, dissatisfaction with independence was expressed in various forms, including criticisms about the excision of Diego Garcia by the British. Mauritius had become a neo-colonial state, that is, its independence was incomplete with the brutal uprooting of the inhabitants of Diego Garcia to Mauritius where they languished in poverty.

Overall, it can be noted that the British supported the MLP to institute a new electoral system aiming at ensuring stability and cohesion. As Couacaud et al. (2022) maintain, "to understand why the British so often sided with the LP in determining what type of electoral system to use in Mauritius one must be cognisant of their desire to promote stable government in the face of efforts at decolonization." The Indian elite from the MLP were also seen by the British as a "valuable force for change" (Houbert, 1992: 470). But from a different view as Houbert (1992: 470) sustains, "the leading 'Indians' in Mauritius opted for the formula of decolonisation favoured by London as they felt that this increased their chances of obtaining state power."

Hence, with a view to ensuring a stable government, the British recommended a parliamentary system with a BLS compensatory device to ensure the accommodation of ethnic minorities. Yet, a majoritarian system has prevailed since independence mainly because of the electoral system design itself. The way in which electoral boundaries were delineated meant that half (mainly rural) out of the 20 constituencies are Hindu-dominated. Consequently, the main national political parties have become ethnicized, with voters tending to vote along ethnic lines. Meanwhile, the BLS still relies on an outdated population census (from 1972) which favors the majority and a system of mandatory declaration of a candidate's community still applies (see Couacaud et al., 2022; Sookrajowa, 2021).

Post-independence Power-Sharing (Implementation Phase)

As McCulloch and McEvoy (2020: 112) uphold, "how power-sharing is designed influences how it performs." This section, therefore, shows how power-sharing in Mauritius remains a paradox in the post-independence era where despite the adoption of consociational mechanisms, the system remains majoritarian. In this section, I review how the power-sharing features deliver majoritarian outcomes.

Coalition Politics

Post-independence politics is dominated by four main national political parties: MLP, PMSD, Mouvement Militant Mauricien (MMM) and Mouvement Socialiste Militant (MSM). Elections have always been contested between two coalitions, with the exception of the 1976 and 2019 elections which were three-cornered competitions. The tradition of coalition politics started right from 1948 by appointing nominees in addition to the elected members in the Council of Government and giving them higher responsibilities. De Smith (1968: 622) too found that a coalition government was desirable as "Mauritius can ill afford a division between 'ins' and a frustrated 'outs.'" In fact, as Kadima and Kasenally (2005: 142) rightly explain, "pre- and post-independence elections have been marked by ethnic considerations with the 'choice' of an alliance partner determined by its ethnic coefficient as opposed to its ideological proximity or compatibility." Since the establishment of the island's 20 constituencies, coalitions have always been formed by a Hindu-dominated party as the senior partner with a minority party (specifically, a General Population-dominated party) as the junior partner (Couacaud et al., 2022).

In 1969, a coalition government was formed when the PMSD joined the government led by the MLP, with the arrangement enduring until 1976 (Khan, 2019). Members of the PMSD occupied important positions in the state apparatuses and the country went through major economic transformation and development during this time. However, this later gave way to a period of discontent and the rise of the Movement Militant Mauricien (MMM) (which gradually became a General Population-dominated party). The MMM was a leftist party which challenged the political and economic order with a radical Marxist program.

This discontent culminated in a general strike in 1971. With the election postponed, a state of emergency was declared. Despite the state of emergency, the economy went through a fundamental transformation during the period with the creation of a textile industry, the Export Processing Zone, the development of tourism and public infrastructure and other state institutions as well as a proactive foreign policy that proved crucial for the development of the country.

The paradox of Mauritius's consociational system is that despite the continuation of party coalitions in ensuring the representation of the different ethnic groups, the system delivered majoritarian results, continuing to be dominated by the Hindu-majority or by a Hindu-dominated party in coalition with a General Population party as a minor partner. In 1976, the general election was contested by three main parties: (i) the IP (a coalition between the MLP and the MAC, (ii) the MMM and (iii) the PMSD. Although the MMM won the maximum number of seats of 30, it was unable to form a minority government (Le Cernéen, 22 December 1976). A post-election coalition was thus formed by the IP (Hindu-dominated) and the PMSD to prevent the MMM from being in power (Le Cernéen, 27 December 1976). Interestingly, in 1982 the MMM in alliance with Mauritian Socialist Party (PSM) (a Hindu-dominated party) won an absolute majority of 60 seats. However, the ethnic strategy of the MMM was that Sir Anerood Jugnauth (a Hindu) be the Prime Minister. The general elections of 1983, 1987 and 2010 were won by two main Hindu-dominated parties: the MLP and MSM in alliance with PMSD as the junior partner representing mainly the General Population. The 1991 election was contested by two coalition blocs: the MSM-MMM and the MLP-PMSD. The MSM-MMM alliance won the majority of seats. However, for the 1995 election, the MLP-MMM alliance came into power. Exceptionally, in 2000, there was a pre-electoral arrangement between the MSM-MMM alliance that Paul Bérenger (Franco-Mauritian) would be the Prime Minister for a period of two years. It was the first time that a Franco-Mauritian was assigned the post of Prime Minister. Otherwise, the post of Prime Minister has always been from the Hindu-Vaish community and from two families: the Ramgoolam and the Jugnauth. In 2005, the MLP, in alliance with minor parties, won. In 2014, the MSM in alliance with the PMSD and the Muvman Liberater (ML) (a minor party) won the election. The MSM, in alliance with other minor parties, remained in power further to the general election of 2019.

Proportional Representation: The Best Loser System

During the public hearings of the Banwell Commission of 1965–1966, there was much concern about majority rule and minority representation from the different political parties. The multi-member constituencies and the block voting were criticized by Duval on the basis that the MLP would intend "to consolidate and increase their majority in future assemblies." Even from the panel of the British Electoral Commissioners, Professor Leys apprehended the "desirability of the 'United Kingdom' approach to strong government with its consequential advocacy for a 'first past the post' system'." On the other hand, Sir Harold Banwell stressed that, "it probably was desirable to have a strong majority in Government in order to facilitate effective administrative control of the country's affairs" (Voting system CO 961/7, 1965–1966).

Moreover, Banwell did not favor any type of Proportional Representation (PR) as it appeared to "unduly" benefit one particular community and it was seen as a complex method (Voting system CO 961/7, 1965–1966). But, to ensure adequate representation of the minorities, the BLS as a form of PR was adopted. Among the eight best loser seats, the first four seats will be reserved for under-represented communities in the Legislative Assembly after the general election. The remaining four best losers will be attributed on "the basis of party and the community effect will be twofold;

(a) to restore the balance between, on the one hand, the leading party or party alliance, and on the other hand, all others to the extent to which this balance has been disturbed by the allocation of the first four best loser seats;
(b) to correct further any under-representation of communities after the constituency elections (Banwell Electoral Commission Report Mauritius CO 1036/1592, 1966–1968)."

In general, all candidates are required to declare their party and community on the nomination form. But the ballot form would include only the name of each candidate, the name and symbol of his/her party and not the candidate's community. The arrangement of the best loser seats would be determined by the latest published official census (Banwell Electoral Commission Report Mauritius CO 1036/1592, 1966–1968).

Although Lijphart (2012: 139) views the Mauritian case and the 3-member constituencies as a "different kind of proportionality" that "encourage the parties and party alliances to nominate ethnically and religiously balanced slates, which has resulted in better ethnic and religious minority representation than would have been achieved through single-member district elections," in fact these have led to real ethno-political issues which are merely reinforcing ethnic divisions and the marginalization of smaller ethnic minorities. The BLS is often criticized as being outdated (in that it continues to rely on data from the 1972 ethnic census), inconsistent, unrepresentative, indiscriminate, fostering ethnic identity and eventually supporting communalism in Mauritian society. For Kasenally (2011: 40) the BLS has yielded a communal system where ethnic groups compete for their own benefit and has thus limited the growth of a Mauritian national identity. Mozaffar (2005) also argues that this system urges political parties to designate candidates along ethnic lines with the aim to secure seats in parliament.

Hence, the consociational model in Mauritius remains a paradox because despite the implementation of the BLS as form of proportional representation along with the candidate's requirement to declare their party and community and the use of the outdated 1972 ethnic census, the outcome is highly majoritarian. An allocation of eight best loser seats is not sufficient to accommodate ethnic minorities as opposed to the FPTP method which is already ensuring the rule of the majority by 60 seats through direct election. With its use of outdated census data, the BLS is only a masquerade for minority representation which is indirectly favoring the rule of the majority. Over the last 12 general elections, the FPTP method has ensured the representation of the Hindu-majority in parliament ranging from 57 to 67%, to the detriment of the representation of the General Population with only 18–27% followed by the Muslim and the Sino-Mauritian. Hence, in this context, power-sharing remains a paradox because firstly the British colonial authorities already had the intent of creating a strong majoritarian government to ensure effective administration and created consociational mechanisms as the BLS to also ensure the accommodation of ethnic minorities. And secondly, since independence the system has only delivered majoritarian results and the consociational structures are not sufficiently strong enough to ensure a fair representation of the ethnic minorities.

Mutual Veto and Segmental Autonomy

In spite of the representativeness at the levels of government and the practice of coalition politics, it is the Prime Minister who wields complete control of the state apparatus with vast powers of decision-making. Cabinet decisions are taken nominally by consensus among the ministers drawn from different alliances but ultimately the final decision is taken by the Prime Minister. That is, there is no effective veto power for minority representatives, even when they are included in cabinet. Moreover, although several major institutions were intended to be independent of the executive, in reality this is not the case. Most of their presidents and chairpersons of various institutions are appointed by the President in consultation or on the advice of the Prime Minister. Even the President of the Republic is appointed by the majority party or parties in the Assembly. Although he appoints formally many members of the government and other governing bodies, these take place on the advice of the Prime Minister. In sum, the absence of veto power combined with the extensive power of the Prime Minister undermines the system's consociational elements.

Another dimension of consociation is the protection of the language, religion and culture via the introduction of cultural autonomy provisions. The promotion of these cultures, what O'Leary (2013) considers "cultural protectionism," is well-established in Mauritius. In the 1950s, the State agreed to subsidize religious organizations, such as churches (Catholic, Anglican, Presbyterian) and Hindu federations (Tamil, Telegu, Marathi and Sanathan), while the Muslim organizations were funded through the Waqf Commissioner (Dinan, 2002). However, cultures have been promoted in different circumstances and incrementally over a long period of time and stemmed also from political concessions to minority discontent in the wake of electoral campaigns. For example, the struggle for the recognition of the Creole community itself has taken more than fifty years. For example, to commemorate the end of slavery in 1835, despite a demand to celebrate the abolition of slavery, it was first celebrated in 1985 and was proclaimed a public holiday in 2001. The Nelson Mandela Centre for African Culture was set up in 1986 promoting African and Creole culture (Ramtohul, 2021). Le Morne Mountain was proclaimed as a World Heritage Site for Maroon slaves by UNESCO in 2008. A Truth and Justice Commission and subsequently a slavery Museum had also been implemented. Moreover, it was only in 2009 that the Creole language claimed by the Creole Population had been introduced in schools and later in colleges.

CHALLENGES TO POWER-SHARING FUNCTIONALITY IN MAURITIUS

As McGarry (2017: 32) expounds, "what is adoptable is not necessarily what is optimally functional." In Mauritius, although power-sharing has delivered ethnic peace and political stability, it also faces certain dysfunctionalities such as the marginalization of the smaller ethnic minorities including the Creoles, the fact that ethnic representation is often at the expense of gender representation and that there are no real prospects for electoral reform at this time.

Owing to the Hindu-majority rule since independence, the Creoles have largely been neglected in key positions (Eriksen, 2004). In 1993, in the context of the commemoration of the Abolition of Slavery, the Catholic priest, Father Roger Cerveaux, reproached the Church for its indifference toward the exclusion of the Creoles and the relapse of the Creole community—the *Malaise Créole* (La Vie Catholique, 5–7 February 1993). Even when riots took place in February 1999 after the death of a popular singer, Joseph Reginald Topize known as Kaya (a Creole/Afro-Mauritian), in police custody over claims of police brutality and causing much damage and casualties, scholars and observers attribute the main cause of the riots to the *Malaise Créole* (Commission of Inquiry Report, 1999; Miles, 1991). Paul Bérenger, the leader of the MMM, also admits that the *Malaise Créole* is a major factor explaining the 1999 riots. For him, it is "the awakening of the creoles of African and Malagasy descent to their '*retards accumulés*' in terms of education, entrepreneurship as well as to a perception of discrimination against them in terms of employment in government service, the police force, the para-statal bodies" (Commission of Inquiry Report, 1999). For Caroll and Caroll (2000) and Eriksen (2004), it is rather the marginalization of the Creole community in the country's major political and public institutions which has produced discontent.

Moreover, another power-sharing dysfunctionality in Mauritius is the low levels of women political participation where very often ethnic representation precedes gender representation (Sookrajowa et al., 2022). Over the last 12 elections, the percentage of female political representation ranges from 3% to a maximum of 25% of the total elected candidates

(Sookrajowa et al., 2022). As Yoon and Bunwaree (2006: 241) claim, "the politics of recognition and representation seems to be gender-blind in Mauritius. Accommodation and management of diversity have focused on ethnicity, not on gender." Drawing from intersectionality theory, Ramtohul (2015: 27) also concedes that "the strong emphasis attributed to ethnic and communal representation by the Mauritian political system and structures marginalises women's political citizenship." This tendency echoes the arguments of Byrne and McCulloch (2012), Kennedy et al. (2016) and Stojanović (2020), maintaining that although power-sharing has proved to be effective in delivering peace and stability, by centering on ethnic representation it precludes fair representation of those whose main political identities are not in accord with the ethnic categories of the society. The system, by emphasizing the accommodation of dominant ethnic communities, constrains opportunities for the inclusion of both small groups, like the Creoles, and for women.

Conclusion

This chapter has covered two distinct aspects of the power-sharing life-cycle in Mauritius. In terms of adoption, features of consociationalism were adopted during the British decolonization period in order to ensure a smooth transition of power to local politicians and to promote effective government in newly independent Mauritius. Power-sharing, that is, was a device deployed to allow for the exit of the British colonial powers. It involved negotiations and concessions between the British colonial authorities and the representatives of the different parties in Mauritius in the process of the constitutional development, institutional design and elections. After independence, despite a shaky start with the ethnic riot and the state of emergency in the 1970s, the power-sharing system has been well maintained throughout the years and has afforded the country a strong degree of political stability.

This stability also has consequences for system adaptability and "end-ability" (McCulloch & McEvoy, 2020). The paradox of power-sharing in Mauritius is that rather than sharing power, there is the perpetuation of Hindu majoritarianism and an ongoing marginalization of ethnic minorities, especially those from the Creole community, as well as limited representation of women. Moreover, these majoritarian tendencies disincentivizes adaptability. Major sources of discontent with the hybrid political system arise from the fact political reforms had reached a deadlock in recent years. Alongside a "relatively rigid" constitution (De Smith, 1968), any reform efforts—such as those advocating for a dose of PR—seem to be impossible as these have often been consistently opposed by the majority. The situation, therefore, remains a dead end (see Couacaud et al., 2022, Sookrajowa, 2021, Sookrajowa et al., 2022), constraining the adaptability of the system.

REFERENCES

PRIMARY REFERENCES

(1957). Records of Public Hearings. CO 890/15. The National Archives, Kew, Richmond, Surrey.

(1957). Representations for 11 × 3 Member Constituencies (le Parti Mauricien). CO 890/3. The National Archives, Kew, Richmond, Surrey.

(1965). Mauritius Constitutional Conference Report London. DO 118/327. The National Archives, Kew, Richmond, Surrey.

(1966–1967). Banwell Electoral Commission Report on Mauritius. CO 1036/1592. The National Archives, Kew, Richmond, Surrey.

(1965–1966). 10 January 1966 Record of Hearing. CO 961/46. The National Archives, Kew, Richmond, Surrey.

(1965–1966). Voting System. CO 961/7. The National Archives, Kew, Richmond, Surrey.

SECONDARY REFERENCES

Allen, R. B. (2003). *Slaves, Freedmen, and Indentured Laborers in Colonial Mauritius*. Cambridge University Press.

Allen, R. B. (1988). The Slender, Sweet Thread: Sugar, Capital and Dependency in Mauritius, 1860–1936. *The Journal of Imperial and Commonwealth History, 16*(2), 177–200.

Ballhatchet, K. (1995). The Structure of British Official Attitudes: Colonial Mauritius, 1883–1968. *The Historical Journal, 38*(4), 989–1011.

Benedict, B. (1962). The Plural Society in Mauritius. *Race, 3*(2), 65–78.

Boudet, C. (2003). *L'émergence de la Démocratie Consociative à Maurice (1948–1968)*. Annuaire des Pays de L'Océan Indien XVII. UFR Recherches Juridiques, Politiques et Sociales Université D'AIX-Marseille III.

Bowman, L. W. (1991). *Mauritius: Democracy and Development in the Indian Ocean*. Westview Press.

Brookfield, H. C. (1957). Mauritius: Demographic Upsurge and Prospect. *Population Studies, 11*(2), 102–122.

Byrne, S., & McCulloch, A. (2012). Gender, Representation and Power-Sharing in Post-conflict Institutions. *International Peacekeeping, 19*(5), 565–580.

Carroll, B. K., & Carroll, T. (1999). The Consolidation of Democracy in Mauritius. *Democratization, 6*(1), 179–197.

Carroll, B. K., & Carroll, T. (2000). Accommodating Ethnic Diversity in a Modernizing Democratic State: Theory and Practice in the Case of Mauritius. *Ethnic and Racial Studies, 23*(1), 120–142.

Chan Low, J. (n.d.). Maurice: Histoire politique de 1942 à 2005. Available online: http://www.cresoi.fr/IMG/pdf/mauricehistoiredepuis1942.pdf

Chan Low, J. L. (1995). *Great Britain and the Constitutional Evolution of Mauritius, 1954–1961* (Unpublished master's thesis). London School of Economics and Political Science.

Commission of Inquiry Report on the Death of the Popular Segae Singer Joseph Reginald Topize (Kaya) by Mr Justice Kheshoe Parsad Matadeen (1999).

Couacaud, L., Sookrajowa, S. S., & Narsoo, J. (2022). The Vicious Circle That Is Mauritian Politics: The Legacy of Mauritius's Electoral Boundaries. *Ethnopolitics, 22*(1), 48–79.

Croucher, R., & McIlroy, J. (2013). Mauritius 1938: The Origins of a Milestone in Colonial Trade Union Legislation. *Labor History, 54*(3), 223–239.

De Smith, S. A. (1968). Constitutionalism in a Plural Society. *The Modern Law Review, 31*(6), 601–622.

Dinan. M. (2002). Mauritius in the Making: Across the Censuses 1846–2000. Mauritius: Nelson Mandela Centre for African Culture, Ministry of Arts and Culture.

Dinan, M., Nababsing, V., & Hansraj, M. (1999). Mauritius: Cultural Accommodation in a Diverse Island Polity. In C. Young (Ed.), *The Accommodation of Cultural Diversity: Case Studies* (pp. 72–102). Macmillan Press.

Dubey, A. (1997). *Government and Politics in Mauritius*. Kalinga Publications.

Eisenlohr, P. (2006). *Little India: Diaspora, Time and Ethnolinguistic Belonging in Hindu Mauritius*. University of California Press.

Emrith, M. (2006). *Sir Abdul Razack Mohamed, His Life and Times*. Editions Le Printemps, Vacoas, Mauritius.

Eriksen, T. H. (1994). Nationalism, Mauritian Style: Cultural Unity and Ethnic Diversity. *Comparative Studies in Society and History, 36*(3), 549–574.

Eriksen T. H. (2004). Ethnicity, Class, and the 1999 Mauritian Riots. In S. May, T. Madood & J. Squires (Eds.), *Ethnicity, Nationalism, and Minority Rights*. Cambridge University Press.

Fessha, Y., & Nam, N. H. T. (2015). Is It Time to Let Go? The Best Loser System in Mauritius. *Afrika Focus, 28*(1), 63–79.

Hansard Society Report. (1953). *Problems of Parliamentary Government in Colonies*. The Hansard Society.

Hollup, O. (1994). The Disintegration of Caste and Changing Conceptions of Indian Ethnic Identity in Mauritius. *Ethnology, 33*(4), 297–316.

Hollup, O. (1996). Islamic Revivalism and Political Opposition among Minority Muslims in Mauritius. *Ethnology, 35*(4), 285–300.

Horowitz, D. (2014). Ethnic Power Sharing: Three Big Problems. *Journal of Democracy, 25*(2), 5–20.

Houbert, J. (1981). Mauritius: Independence and Dependence. *The Journal of Modern African Studies, 19*(1), 75–105.

Houbert, J. (1992). The Indian Ocean Creole Islands: Geo-Politics and Decolonisation. *The Journal of Modern African Studies, 30*(3), 465–484.

Kadima, D. K., & Kasenally, R. (2005). The Formation, Collapse and Revival of Political Party Coalitions in Mauritius: Ethnic Logic and Calculation at Play. *Journal of African Elections, 4*(1), 133–164.

Kasenally, R. (2011). Mauritius: The Not So Perfect Democracy. *Journal of African Elections, 10*(1), 33–47.

Kennedy, R., Pierson, C., & Thomson, J. (2016). Challenging Identity Hierarchies: Gender and Consociational Power-Sharing. *The British Journal of Politics and International Relations, 18*(3), 618–633.

Khan, I. A. (2019, August 2). The 1969 Moment. *L'Express Weekly*. https://lex press.mu/node/358302

La Gazette des Iles. (1992). Un Demi–Siècle D'Elections Libres. 1er partie – Sir Seewoosagur Ramgoolam (1948–1976).

La Vie Catholique. (1993). Quelle promotion pour la communauté créole. 5–7 February.

Lau Thi Keng, J. C. (1991). *Interethnicité et politique à l'île Maurice*, Paris, L'Harmattan.

Le Cernéen. (1976). La formation du nouveau gouvernement. 22 December 1976.

Le Cernéen. (1976). C'est official: le PT et le PMSD forment un gouvernement de coalition. 27 December 1976.

Le Cernéen-Le Mauricien-Advance. (1948). A New Chapter. 17 August.

Lijphart, A. (1977). *Democracy in Plural Societies: A Comparative Exploration*. Yale University.

Lijphart, A. (2012). *Patterns of Democracy, Government Forms and Performance in Thirty-Six Countries* (2nd ed.). Yale University Press.

Mannick, A. R. (1979). *Mauritius: The Development of a Plural Society*. Russell Press.

McGarry, J. (2017). Centripetalism, Consociationalism, and Cyprus: The Adoptability Question. In A. McCulloch & J. McGarry (Eds.), *Power-Sharing: Empirical and Normative Challenges*. Routledge.

McCulloch, A. (2021). Introduction: Power-Sharing in Europe: From Adoptability to End-Ability. In S. Keil & A. McCulloch (Eds.), *Power-Sharing in Europe: Past Practice, Present Cases, and Future Directions.* Palgrave Macmillan.

McCulloch, A., & McEvoy, J. (2020). Understanding Power-Sharing Performance: A Lifecycle Approach. *Studies in Ethnicity and Nationalism, 20*(2), 99–210.

Meisenhelder, T. (1997). The Developmental State in Mauritius. *The Journal of Modern African Studies, 35*(2), 279–297.

Miles, W. F. S. (1991). The Creole Malaise in Mauritius. *African Affairs, 98*(391), 211–228.

Mozaffar, S. (2005). Negotiating Independence in Mauritius. *International Negotiation, 10*, 263–291.

Mukonoweshuro, E. G. (1991). Containing Political Instability in a Poly-Ethnic Society: The Case of Mauritius. *Ethnic and Racial Studies, 14*(2), 199–224.

O'Leary, B. (2013). Power Sharing in Deeply Divided Places: An Advocate's Introduction. In J. McEvoy & B. O'Leary (Eds.), *Power Sharing in Deeply Divided Places* (pp. 1–64). University of Pennsylvania Press.

Phaala, E. (2019). Mauritius' Competitive Party Politics and Social Democratic Welfare Outcomes After Independence. *Strategic Review for Southern Africa, 41*(2), 1–18.

Ramtohul, R. (2015). Intersectionality and Women's Political Citizenship: The Case of Mauritius. *Journal of Contemporary African Studies, 33*(1), 27–47.

Ramtohul, R. (2021). Diaspora and Development: The Case of Mauritius. *Development in Practice, 31*(6), 828–838.

Reddi, S. (2019). General Population and the Issue of Representation. *Mauritius Times.* http://www.mauritiustimes.com/mt/general-population-and-the-issue-of-representation/

Simmons, A. S. (1982). *Modern Mauritius: The Politics of Decolonization.* Indiana University Press.

Srebrnik, H. (2002). 'Full of Sound and Fury': Three Decades of Parliamentary Politics in Mauritius. *Journal of Southern African Studies, 28*(2), 277–289.

Sookrajowa, S. S. (2021). Legibility and the Politics of Ethnic Classification of the Population in the National Census of Mauritius: A Statist Perspective. *Nationalism and Ethnic Politics, 27*(2), 128–148.

Sookrajowa, S. S., Narsoo, J., & Murday, L. (2022). The Impact of Consociationalism on Female Political Representation: The Case Study of Mauritius. *Representation,* Online First.

Stojanović, N. (2020). Democracy, Ethnoicracy and Consociational Demoicracy. *International Political Science Review, 41*(1), 30–43.

Tinker, H. (1977). *The Banyan Tree: Overseas Emigrants from India, Pakistan and Bangladesh.* Oxford University Press.

Yoon, M. Y., & Bunwaree, S. (2006). Women's legislative representation in Mauritius: 'A grave democratic deficit'. *Journal of Contemporary African Studies, 24*(2), 229–247. https://doi.org/10.1080/02589000600769983

CHAPTER 10

Lebanon: Consociationalism Between Immobilism and Reform

Drew Mikhael and Allison McCulloch

Ash-sha'b yurīd isqāṭ an-nizām/The people demand the fall of the regime! So proclaimed one of the slogans of Lebanon's 2019 October uprising, the *thawra*. On the heels of a controversial austerity budget—which included a proposed but eventually rescinded tax on Whatsapp calls—citizens collectively took to the streets in record numbers, demanding greater accountability from a political elite notorious for its clientelistic and often corrupt politics. This set off a series of interlocking and compounding crises years in the making. From an unprecedented financial collapse—characterized by hyperinflation, an exodus of young people, gas and electricity shortages, and the dramatic devaluation of life savings—to the devastating Beirut port explosion, which killed more than 200 people

---

D. Mikhael (✉)
Queen's University Belfast, Belfast, Northern Ireland, UK
e-mail: A.Mikhael@qub.ac.uk

A. McCulloch
Brandon University, Brandon, MB, Canada
e-mail: mccullocha@brandonu.ca

© The Author(s), under exclusive license to Springer Nature Switzerland AG 2024
E. Wassim Aboultaif et al. (eds.), *Power-Sharing in the Global South*, Federalism and Internal Conflicts,
https://doi.org/10.1007/978-3-031-45721-0_10

215

in August 2020 to the impact of the global COVID-19 pandemic on the country's failing infrastructure, Lebanon appears stuck in perpetuate stalemate. Even one of the "most severe crisis episodes [seen] globally since the mid-nineteenth century" (World Bank, 2021) has been unable to dislodge a firmly entrenched power-sharing elite.

What underscores this stalemate? The World Bank blames "deliberate policy inaction" and a "debilitating institutional void" for gridlock in the country (Reuters, 2021). Kelly Kimball (2021), writing in *Foreign Policy*, suggests this is a "return to crisis at the institutional level – a rot from the top down." Bassel Salloukh directly singles out the power-sharing institutions, arguing "the sectarian system is not made to reform itself, only to reproduce itself" (Al Jazeera, 2021). Indeed, this moment of extreme stalemate seems to embody what John Nagle calls zombie power-sharing, that is, a situation in which "it is almost impossible to change, reform or accommodate new policies, especially for non-sectarian issues and identities" (2020: 138). Donald Horowitz similarly refers to this state of affairs as power-sharing's immobilism problem, whereby the system is "frequently immobilized with respect to the very questions the agreement was made to settle" (2014: 12). From this, we might infer a rigidity to the political and legal architecture of the consociational state, even in the face of intense pressures for institutional and policy reform.

Is this 'inability to reform' a necessary consequence of consociational design? How do power-sharing systems reform, adapt, or transcend immobilism? Exploring the potential for consociational adaptability, we examine efforts to advance gender equality by way of legal reforms. We focus in particular on Lebanon's cultural autonomy provisions and their impact on women's rights. While segmental or cultural autonomy is designed to empower religious sects and protect their vital interests, this can come at the expense of women's rights (Byrne & McCulloch, 2018; Kennedy et al., 2016). In Lebanon, the ceding of control of sociocultural affairs to religious leaders is not historical happenstance but a deliberate expression of the power-sharing model (Dekmejian, 1978: 257). As we illustrate in this chapter, Lebanon's cultural autonomy model, a key pillar of group rights and security, not only embeds gender inequalities and maintains patriarchal norms (Joseph, 1999), but it is also inflexible in the face of attempted reforms, manifesting a form of policy immobilism. Gender equality legal reforms thus represent a hard case for assessing consociational adaptability.

We start, as others do, from the point that "not only does Lebanon's legal framework treat Lebanese women as inferior to men with regard to personal status issues (such as marriage, divorce, child custody, and inheritance), but Lebanon's pluralistic religious law system treats Lebanese women as unequal among themselves" (Dabbous, 2017: 5). Indeed, the country performs poorly on the Global Gender Gap Index, scoring 145 out of 153 countries in 2020 (World Economic Forum, 2020). Alongside severe underrepresentation in the legislature and executive, segmental autonomy provisions, a consociational cornerstone, are thought to curtail women's rights.[1] Absent a unified civil status code, religious sects regulate their own personal status laws on such issues as marriage, divorce, child custody, and inheritance.

Specifically, we study two broad reform moments geared toward changing these laws: the campaign to repeal 'marry your rapist' laws and the campaign to allow women to pass their nationality to their husbands and children. Using a structured, focused method of comparison and drawing on fieldwork interviews conducted by one of the authors with civil society activists in Lebanon between 2017 and 2019,[2] we consider whether and how the law in question forced a trade-off between religious autonomy and women's rights, the strategies employed to repeal existing laws, and whether those strategies induced policy reforms. These reform efforts highlight not only the gendered consequences of consociational design choices, but they also say something more broadly about the constraints on consociational adaptability. This relates both to how the institutions 'work' and how traditional elites perceive reform efforts, especially those that seek to uphold the sectarian balance at the heart of the power-sharing arrangement. In what follows, we consider lessons from these gender equality reform efforts that can be brought to bear on this moment of elite deadlock and intransigence; we also offer broader insights for the prospects of consociational adaptability. First, however,

---

[1] Women have been historically underrepresented in Lebanese politics; according to Carmen Geha (2019: 8), prior to 2022, only 17 women (all "wives, widows or daughters of male politicians") have ever been elected to the Lebanese parliament. Some progress was made in the 2022 election, which returned a record 8 women elected to parliament. See Mounzer (2022).

[2] Interviews were conducted as part of the "Exclusion amid Inclusion Dilemma: Power-Sharing and Non-Dominant Minorities" project, funded by the Economic and Social Research Council.

218 D. MIKHAEL AND A. McCULLOCH

we review the institutional architecture of consociational power-sharing in Lebanon.

FROM THE NATIONAL PACT TO THE TAIF ACCORDS: LEBANON'S CONSOCIATIONAL STATE

Lebanon's history is intrinsically linked with consociationalism (Aboultaif, 2019). Sectarian logic informed decision-making during the Ottoman period and the French Mandate years but it was the National Pact—a so-called gentlemen's agreement intended to usher in independence—that consolidated consociational logic as the "bedrock of Lebanese political life" (Kerr, 2005: 112). As part of the pact, political posts were allocated on a sectarian basis, with the presidency and its wide discretionary powers reserved for Maronite Christians, then in a majority position according to the 1932 census. The prime ministership was allocated to the Sunni Muslims, then the second largest community, and the Shia Muslims, then the third largest community, received the parliamentary speakership. In the legislature, Christians and Muslims were elected on a 6:5 basis (Aboultaif, 2019: 62). This arrangement remained in place from independence in 1943 until 1975, collapsing amid a myriad of internal and external factors and launching a protracted civil war (Kerr, 2005).

The Ta'if Accords ended the war and introduced a recalibrated version of consociationalism in 1989, making Lebanon one of the only countries "to adopt consociationalism twice: before and after its civil war" (Bogaards, 2017: 149). As with the National Pact, this revised consociation reserved the top three posts for Maronites, Sunnis, and Shias, respectively, though the powers of the president were curtailed, and the powers of the prime minister expanded. Muslims and Christians have parity representation in the legislature and a strong form of cultural autonomy was maintained. There are 18 recognized sects and 15 different personal status codes in operation, governing issues such as marriage, divorce, adoption, custody, and inheritance.[3] Personal status codes are arguably the longest-standing and most formalized pillar of Lebanese consociationalism, remaining in place through the different consociational

---

[3] Parsing out the differences across the estimated 15 status codes is not always straightforward. For a good primer, see Zalzal (1997).

iterations, surviving the kinds of constitutional amendments and adjustments other aspects of Lebanon's power-sharing formula have seen. Given that it uses ascriptive criteria—in this case, religious sect—to distribute power, Lebanon's system represents a case of corporate consociation.

Insights from consociational theory suggest that any effort to reform the system must confront at least two major challenges. First, consociational systems, especially corporate ones like Lebanon's, operate slowly. They are more prone to governance challenges, including a sparse legislative agenda and decision-making gridlock (Cammett & Malesky, 2012; Lijphart, 1969; McCulloch, 2022). They are also notoriously difficult to reform, with some scholars suggesting it "is almost impossible to change, reform or accommodate new policies ...[making] it extremely hard for non-sectarian groups to gain significant concessions from the state's institutions" (Nagle, 2020: 139). At best, the system results in slow, status-quo-oriented decision-making, and lowest-common denominator policymaking (Gray & Birrell, 2011); at worst, it produces crisis-ridden immobilism and gridlock (Horowitz, 2014).

Consider how the institutions are intended to work. Grand coalitions bring together parties divided by ethnicity and, often, ideology. Forming government is often protracted as parties bargain over confessional representation, portfolio allocations, and other government perks. *Custom* dictated by consociational logic are key to government formation. For example, the prime minister is expected to carry out parliamentary consultations and to seek a parliamentary vote of confidence on the ministerial program, while it is the president who issues the decree appointing members (Badran, 2021). Once formed, grand coalitions can be unwieldy. As parties come to power based on support from a single sect, they will be tempted to govern in the name of that group only, rather than for everyone. This can pit them against their power-sharing partners who, as well, will be tempted to sectarianize the legislative agenda, making it difficult to find common ground (Fakhoury & McCulloch, 2023). When combined with veto powers on a wide range of issues, the space for progressive policymaking in the consociational executive is liable to be quite small and any agreement that can be found between divergent power-sharing partners will reflect lowest-common denominator thinking.

Cultural autonomy provisions, too, push in the direction of lowest-common denominator policymaking. Devolve too much autonomy and it risks hollowing out the center, leaving very little actual power to be shared. Without enough areas of competence on which to offer reciprocal concessions, the center lacks the space for developing a coherent legislative program (Hulsey, 2010: 1139). Further, ceding too much autonomy to religious authorities comes with its own costs. The absence of an overarching civil code on personal status creates disparities and gaps in legal protection between women and girls of different sects and between those who want sectarian representation and those who do not. As to the former, an obvious example is the variance on age of marriage. The Shia code permits marriage from puberty (in some cases as young as nine) while the Catholic code set the age of consent at 14 years old (Shehadeh, 1998: 505). As it relates to child custody, meanwhile, a divorced Sunni woman will be allowed to retain custody of her child until they are 12 whereas a divorced Shia woman will automatically lose custody regardless of the child's age (Dabbous, 2017: 5). As intra-sect progress is uneven, the absence of an opt-out mechanism or civic law compels those who do not wish to align with any of the recognized sects (e.g., atheists or agonistics) to identify with their father's sect. Devolving human rights to religious sects absolves the state of its responsibility to offer universal rights protection. While cultural autonomy provisions are intended to shore up important group rights for religious communities, they risk curtailing individual rights, especially for those who may not align with any of the protected group identities.[4] Not only does this system of legal pluralism skew the balance between group and individual rights, it also sends the message that elected politicians are meant to defer to unelected religious leaders and not the other way around, thus reversing lines of democratic accountability.

Alongside this challenge of the slow pace of consociational decision-making and the lowest-common denominator policies it produces, political institutions also carry symbolic import. As Karlo Basta (2016: 948) describes it, "while institutions are rules that structure political action, they can also be imbued with symbolic meaning, encapsulating and expressing narratives about collective identities." On Basta's reading, the "symbolic weight" of an institution or formal rule can tell us something about the prospects for adaptability. Where parties see the rules in instrumental terms, compromise can be sought, but where a change to the rules is perceived to threaten a group's vital interests—understood here as those issues that affect the "well-being, survival and sense of itself" (McCulloch,

---

[4] For more on the tension between group protections and human rights in consociations, see McCrudden and O'Leary (2013).

2018: 741)—efforts to modify or change the rule will be perceived as an existential threat, closing off any amenability to reform. Adaptability, then, is contingent both on how the institutions operate and how closely they are tied to a group's sense of its vital interests. By this reading, it is not simply the legal framework and "intent" of institutions and rules that matter but also the way in which actors interpret these rules, institutions, and provisions. Dominant elites are inclined not only to forcefully protect their cultural autonomy rights but to resist any political issues they perceive as having the potential to undermine the group's sense of self. As we demonstrate below, the perception of vital interests then stretches out beyond cultural autonomy laws and encompasses even cross-ethnic agendas that employ multi-confessional mobilization strategies.

Gender Activism in a Consociational State

Through grand coalitions, veto rights, and cultural autonomy laws, corporate consociations tend to reify the status quo in support of 'sectarian balance,' inducing a system reluctant to embrace change. In this section, we consider two reform movements in Lebanon. In the first, a set of partial reforms in support of women's equality was achieved. In the other, reform remains elusive, with the system thus far able to resist change in the name of sectarian balance.

Permissible Violence: Efforts to Repeal "Marry Your Rapist" Laws

One of the most significant threats faced by women in Lebanon is gender-based violence (GBV). Between 2014 and 2018, an estimated 40 women were killed by abusive partners (Kafa, 2018). By some estimates, 66% of women had been exposed to severe physical violence (Usta et al., 2007: 208). The personal status codes contribute, both directly and indirectly, to GBV dangers faced by women. Directly, custody laws that give preferential treatment to fathers make it difficult for women to escape abusive relationships, for fear of leaving children behind (International Commission of Jurists, 2019). Some faith codes endanger young girls by continuing to sanction child marriage. Indirectly, personal status codes intersect with core provisions of the penal code to make violence against women permissible under certain conditions. Article 522 of the penal code offered a 'loophole' to men accused of rape, if they married their victim, stating: "In the event a legal marriage is concluded between the person who committed [crimes including rape, kidnapping, and statutory rape] and the victim, prosecution shall be stopped and in case a decision is rendered, the execution of such decision shall be suspended against the person who was subject to it." Other key articles on sexual violence include Article 505, where, in the case of a rape of a minor, the rapist will be exempt from punishment as long as there is a promise of marriage and Article 518, which excuses rape inside marriage.[5]

These articles of the penal code have been the subject of domestic and international condemnation.[6] By 2016, following similar moves in Tunisia and Jordan, a bill was submitted to parliament seeking to repeal Articles 505, 518, and 522, spearheaded by Lebanese Forces parliamentarian Elie Kayrouz. As the bill was being deliberated, a coalescence of women's rights NGOs, led by Abaad and Kafa, organized a public awareness campaign to put pressure on parliament. The campaign, titled 'A white dress doesn't cover the rape,' coincided with the UN-led 16 days of activism to end violence against women. At the center of the campaign was a video depicting a woman being raped and then being dressed for her marriage, which was widely shared, with 7.5 million views online.

In the face of the slowness of the system and predictable parliamentary procrastination, activists found creative ways to keep the pressure on politicians, including protests led by women in bloodied wedding dresses in front of government buildings. Flash mobs, billboards, advertisements, social media campaigns (#undress522), online petitions, art installations (such as 30 dresses hung by nooses along Beirut's seafront), sporting, and cultural events in public spaces, including the Beirut marathon, also followed (BBC, 2017). In addition to educating the Lebanese public—prior to this point, only 1% of the population was aware of the law's existence, though once they learned about it 60% supported repealing it and 85% thought it compromised the dignity of women—the campaign helped gain international media attention (Abaad, 2016; CNN, 2016). It also began to sway some domestic politicians, including then Prime

---

[5] Article 252 pertains to so-called honor killings and 'crimes of passion' allowed men in a seeming "fit of fury" to be treated with leniency for crimes "provoked" by the victim's act, such as marital infidelity, premarital sex and/or elopement.

[6] Amnesty International stated in 2016 that "it is disappointed that Lebanon rejected recommendations to enforce the Law on Protection of Women and Family Members from Domestic Violence."

Minister Saad Hariri, who tweeted his support for 522's revocation, calling the draft bill a "civilized step."

Yet, a year later, when the parliamentary committee charged with examining the bill submitted their recommendations, parliament voted to implement the original proposal only in partial form: 522 was repealed alongside only a commitment to 're-examine' 505 and 518. An incomplete victory, to which Manar Zaiter, a legal expert with the Lebanese Women's Democratic Gathering, responded: "I am not applauding the efforts of the Lebanese parliament. These are rights, and they were supposed to be granted years ago. They were extremely late in abolishing the law" (Al Jazeera, 2017).

To the extent that the campaign met with some success, this stems from networking efforts, beginning in 2014, among different civil society actors led by Kafa. Identifying amenable politicians, such as Elie Kayrouz and Jean Oghassabian,[7] to lend their support to repealing 522, 505, and 518, also contributed to reforms. When the bill was tabled by Kayrouz in July 2016, activists were ready to ratchet up the public pressure on lawmakers and were also meeting privately with other parliamentarians and religious authorities to recruit allies behind the scenes. Growing media coverage of the parliamentary debates of the bill also helped, as one former Abaad staff member, who worked on the campaign, outlined:

> Because people didn't know about this. For me, in addition to the lobbying work we did, the public support was huge. The media support was huge. Everyone was talking about article 522 and how the woman can marry the rapist. This is insane.
>
> Why now? Because we had the opportunity and because we had progressive MPs. We had Elie Kayrouz, he was very supportive in the justice committee and other MPs. We had the public support, but we wouldn't have the public support if we didn't ask them to pay attention to this issue.[8]

As support to repeal the articles grew, other, more 'fringe' voices in parliament also began to speak out. Kataeb member Elie Marouni, for example, asked publicly—if rhetorically—whether "women aren't pushing men to rape them" (Domat, 2016). There was also behind-the-scenes resistance.

---

[7] Oghassabian became Lebanon's first minister for women's affairs in December 2016.

[8] Personal interview, Beirut, 1 July 2019.

Manar Zaiter, for example, suggests that the decision to retain 505 and 518 was related to the fact that it would be "much easier to then place a cap on the minimum age required for marriage" if these articles were repealed.[9] The watering down of the bill was likely a result of a desire to protect the domain of marriage and the age of consent for the religious authorities via the cultural autonomy provisions.

How, then, was (partial) reform achieved? Rana Khoury, a key organizer with Kafa, explained the process of creating change:

> So there is work to do in lobbying with members of parliament to change laws, amend laws like the domestic violence law like 522. [...] It's very hard. Because there's a lot of calculation that these parties did, the biggest one is where the religious leader of my sect would be in line with this change of law?
> Let's say [I'm] going to take a very simple law that's not very hard to commit to, which is civil marriage. Just civil marriage. You just can't allow people to marry the way they want. And in this case a lot of politicians who got married in civil marriage and their children got married in civil marriage but still they will not vote on the civil marriage law because the religious leader of this sect would not be happy, and they want to keep control of the sects because this is the point of their existence. It's the same thing with women's issues.[10]

By this account, politicians appear to have a symbiotic relationship with religious leaders. Despite ultimate legislative power resting with parliament, activists learned that the religious leadership had to be consulted for legislative change to occur. As a local legal and political expert on women's issues explained:

> The good thing about 522 is that when they addressed the religious leaders, they didn't do it in public, they didn't name and shame them. They went and had private conversations with them. They didn't challenge them publicly, and challenge their power in public. So, when the religious leaders, they faced their people, they weren't perceived as weak.[11]

---

[9] Al-Jazeera. 2017. "Scrapping of Lebanon Rape Law 'is One Small Step,'" 18 August 2017, available at: https://www.aljazeera.com/features/2017/8/18/scrapping-of-lebanon-rape-law-is-one-small-step, accessed on 15 August 2020.

[10] Personal interview, Beirut, 1 November 2018.

[11] Personal interview, Beirut, 9 July 2019.

Women's rights activists thus had to take the critical step of consulting religious leaders prior to submission of draft Bills because, as Rana Khoury explains, parliamentarians are obliged to consult religious leaders in their constituent area regardless, to ensure that they have the "support of the leader of the sect. So, they have a lot of calculations because they are not national leaders, they are sectarian leaders, so they have to please the sect."[12] Without obtaining the blessing on specific status laws from the religious leadership, politicians risk undermining their support base.

Ultimately, the 'marry your rapist' law was abolished. A central lesson from the efforts to repeal it is that reform efforts become more feasible when the relationship between parliamentarians and religious leaders can be decoupled. This is most likely to occur when a broad, cross-sect, and public consensus is built and critical mass of support for new legislation is obtained.

Reforming Nationality Laws: The Sectarian Balance of Power

According to Maya Mikdashi, citizenship in Lebanon embodies a form of "sectarianism," which is a "modality of power that functions through the production, quantification, inheritance and management of both sexual and sectarian difference" (2018: 4). As she describes it, "you could not, and still cannot be a Lebanese citizen without a state-assigned sex and sect." Nowhere is this more apparent than in relation to nationality laws, which see women as "daughters of their fathers or wives of their husbands" (Mikdashi, 2018: 8). According to Lebanon's Nationality Law, nationality is passed from father to child with only fathers considered heads of households. Lebanese men can, without restriction, confer nationality to their children and after one year of residency in the country, to their foreign wives. By contrast, Lebanese women do not have the right to pass their nationality to their children or to their foreign husbands.

The UN conducted the most robust study of the Nationality Law, finding between 1995 and 2008 around 18,000 Lebanese women married foreign nationals; with children, there are some 77,400 persons affected by the inability to pass on their nationality to their kin (Charafeddine, 2009: 17). More recent studies show that statelessness has in fact

[12] Personal interview, Beirut, 1 Noember 2018.

worsened, with 70% of an estimated 27,000 children without nationality having been born to Lebanese women (Siren Associates, 2019). This creates a host of problems for families, ranging from difficulties in obtaining residence permits, constraints on securing work permits, limitations on the amount of property they can own in Lebanon, and other inheritance issues. For children, it affects their access to education, especially beyond the primary level: "children born of Lebanese mothers and foreign fathers are considered as foreigners [and] they are subject to the fees applicable to foreigners and do not benefit from the preferential rates given to Lebanese students, whether at public schools or universities" (Mansour & Abou Aad, 2012).

To be sure, Lebanon is not the only country to employ such nationality laws and efforts to repeal the laws actually began as a region-wide initiative, with the "Women's Rights to Nationality Campaign," in 1999. The campaign's purpose was to raise awareness regarding the discriminatory impact of nationality laws in a range of Middle East and North African countries, including Egypt, Syria, Jordan, Bahrain, and others (CRTD-A, n.d.). The campaign met with some success: several states introduced partial reforms to their nationality laws.[13] Within Lebanon, a number of domestic campaigns to amend the law have, also, met with resistance. In 2006, renewed efforts were sidelined by the July War between Hezbollah and Israel (Fakhoury & Nagle, 2018: 93). Another reform attempt failed in 2012 when a ministerial committee tasked with reviewing the law decided that changing it would not be in "the higher interest of the state" (Ghaddar, 2017: 21). In 2020, CRTD-A launched the "My Nationality, a Right for Me and My family" campaign with a renewed call to address the law.

In the face of state immobilism, more piecemeal strategies have been sought to mitigate the worst impacts of the law. For example, in 2010 decree No. 4186 gave foreign husbands and children a three-year courtesy residency permits without fees or proof of work (Human Rights Watch, 2018), and in 2012 a ministerial decision was made to correct a mistake

---

[13] In 2000, Egypt and Morocco, for example, granted women the right to confer nationality to their children, but not to spouses. In Syria and Jordan, nationality can only be granted by the state in a case-by-case basis and only when the child's father is stateless or unknown. Lebanon, along with Kuwàit and Qatar, remain the only three countries in the region with unreformed nationality laws. See Global Campaign for Equal Nationality Rights (2018).

that left a number of children without Lebanese nationality unable to enroll in school (Ghaddar, 2017: 34). While these changes are a (small) step in the right direction, they are nonetheless precarious. Decrees are not only less binding than laws, but they can also be overturned on a whim.

Why has the nationality law proven so impervious to change, with Lebanon lagging behind its regional neighbors on this issue? It is an issue traditionally bogged down in sectarian politics. To use Basta's (2016) terminology, the nationality law carries "symbolic weight." The claim is that changing the law will result in the naturalization of Palestinian refugees, in turn undermining the balance of power between sects in favor of Sunni Muslims. That is, it would "tip Lebanon's sectarian balance, challenging Lebanon's power-sharing which safeguards intercommunal coexistence" (Fakhoury & Nagle, 2018: 92).[14] The Ta'if Agreement expressly forbids the permanent settlement of Palestinians in Lebanon and by some accounts, the reluctance to reform is borne from a deep-rooted Christian Lebanese fear that they are a dwindling population (Salem, 1979: 459). The fear of a potential 'disequilibrium' caused by Palestinian men marrying Lebanese women is likely overstated; a 2009 study showed a total of 18,000 marriages, or less than 13%, involve Lebanese Christian women (Charafeddine, 2009: 19). A 2017 study of Palestinians in Lebanon found just 3,707 cases of Palestinian head of household married to a spouse of foreign nationalities (LPDC, 2018: 18). It is much more likely, as Tamirace Fakhoury (2019: 17) describes it, a case of "strategic sectarianism" confirming the Christian elite as ethno-sectarian defenders. This also works to conflate the impact of personal status codes, with sects remaining a key site of governing authority. Legal challenges to increase protection and equality for women are thus seen as a de facto challenge to the mandates of religious courts, threatening the share of power held by communal elites (Moussawi & Nasser, 2019: 65).

There are two issues to contend with here. First, the substantive content of the law is exclusionary and has negative consequences for women, their foreign husbands, and their children, and these exclusionary

---

[14] Similar arguments about the sectarian balance of power are also deployed to resist calls for civil marriage: "opponents of civil marriage view the reform as a social revolution that would progressively dismantle Lebanon's confessional system through a secularization process, which limits the autonomy of the personal status code system" (Hyndman-Rizk, 2019: 194).

effects need to be addressed within a complex and slow decision-making process. Second, the 'symbolic weight' that has been attached to the nationality laws cut to the very core of how sects define and populate their membership. As such, substantive changes to the nationality law are perceived to threaten the vital interests of sectarian elites, in turn closing off space for adaptability.

Is Reform Possible?

As we noted above, adaptability is constrained both by the nature of the consociational system as well as by the 'symbolic weight' the institutions carry in the eyes of dominant elites, who view them as means to protect their group. Consociationalism engenders a slow pace of decision-making as parties—many with veto powers—find themselves frequently at logger-heads. Change, when it does come, is likely to be the lowest-common denominator on which parties can find agreement and does not happen spontaneously, instead requiring—at least in this case—a vast transnational, cross-sectarian, and cross-sectoral coalition in support of change. As the efforts to repeal 522 underline, activists trying to create change on women's issues had to deal tactfully with the particularities and sensitivities of each sectarian pillar, because wide-ranging reform of the personal status laws was "not practically acceptable to most of the Lebanese stakeholders" (Baroud & El-Alayli, 2019: 95). While there have been some successful intra-sect initiatives, as Mariam Sfeir, Director of The Arab Institute for Women (AiW) explains, it has to come "not [from] the government that gave the rights" but from women having to make their case internally to the sects.[15] However, these intra-sect reform efforts bring their own limitations. As Wafa Abed, former head of the Progressive Socialist Party's women's department, describes it, the segmented presence of women in sectarian political parties cannot, on its own, lead to systemic change. She explained that working within a political party on women's rights was hugely problematic and she could not "fight for my rights" because the party was strategic and limiting in what positions it took publicly on women's rights.[16]

[15] Personal interview, Beirut, 29 October 2018.
[16] Personal interview, Beirut, 3 November 2018.

The challenges facing cross-sectarian, state-wide mobilization are indeed onerous. Reform-minded actors have to navigate a tight balancing act: creating national campaigns but taking each ethnic segment into account; soliciting international support, particularly on normative rights issues like women where funding and public support is in abundance, but not so much as to elicit domestic resistance. As a former Abaad campaign worker explains, "sometimes international support can backlash. Especially with Hezbollah."[17] International support can be portrayed as inviting foreign agendas and can thus be more readily dismissed out of hand. Lastly, an overarching institutional constraint faced, regardless of sect, is the lack of representation for women in legislative and executive spaces. Without a seat at the table, it becomes difficult to get your issues to the top of the political agenda.

While this first challenge—the slowness of the institutions themselves—can be managed in the ways just described, the second challenge—the symbolic weight parties attach to particular rules along with the capture of the state by political and religious elites—treads a much more fraught path to reform, as the failure to overturn the nationality law suggests. For those activists who wish to work on issues that threaten religious doctrine, they are faced with a series of binds: ensuring that their advocacy work is both in the informal sphere with religious leadership and within formal political spaces with elected officials, working to ensure that they are in lockstep on potential policies, but without the guarantee of either. The zero-sum nature of sectarian politics exercised throughout all consociational pillars only serves to enhance the policymaking influence of religious elites. These leaders will see policies that can potentially minimize the silos between sects as a threat to their vital interests (Zuhur, 2002: 180), and will work with established political elites to push back on issues like civil marriage and matrilinear nationality that could potentially reforge the sectarian status quo in favor of a "new power sharing arrangements altogether" (Zuhur, 2002). Indeed, if a unified civil code for personal status laws was to be implemented, it would fundamentally alter the power-sharing arrangement, with the introduction of a new 'civic' segment in need of accommodation.

Undoubtedly the search for gender (and sexual) equality rights is not solely a challenge of consociational states, with patriarchy and traditional

---

[17] Personal interview, Beirut, 1 July 2019.

230 D. MIKHAEL AND A. McCULLOCH

gender norms key contributors to the lack of progression in a wide variety of non-consociational settings as well.[18] But the institutional complexities of the consociational state—where sex is as integral as sect to the functionality of the system (Mikdashi, 2018)—adds an additional layer of resistance to reform along with a dominant elite who wish to ensure security for their ethnic group.

CONCLUSION

Kilon yani kilon/All of them means all of them. The 2019 protests brought people together across sect, class, and gender to push for fundamental political change. The 2019 protests provide a clear test case for assessing the extent to which cross-cutting popular mobilizations around universal claims would encourage elites to move away from representing group interests (Agarin, 2020: 26). Yet, as members of the government began to step down from their roles, including the prime minister, a protracted period of government formation soon followed, and the sweeping optimism of 2019 gave way in short order to a pessimism that Lebanon's polity is simply unreformable (Salloukh & Halawi, 2020). Yet, this resistance to reform—its adaptability problem—was clear to see in the longitudinal efforts of feminist activists before 2019. The new elites formed in the aftermath of 2019 will find a consociational system in place that is designed to constrain cross-ethnic policymaking and while the task is daunting, it is possible to create movement. The reforms discussed in this chapter were not borne from happenstance, nor were they opportunistic. Instead, they represent the culmination of decades-long efforts that sought to engage reformers on issues that transcend sect, creating pressure on both political elites and religious leadership. Whether having more 'change agents' in parliament—such as the thirteen 'reform' parliamentarians elected in 2022, many active in the 2019 *thawra*—can help

---

[18] The LGBTQ community also faces significant resistance to the pursuit of equal rights. Article 534 of the Penal Code, which prohibits sex that 'contradict the laws of nature,' places them in danger of arrest and prosecution for expressing their sexual identity. Attempts to challenge and repel 534 by LGBTQ organizations, or to organize events in support of the LGBT community, have been met with significant pressure, led by religious authorities and defended by political parties. Even with fairly wide private support from politicians in Lebanon for the abolishment of 534, very few have taken the next step in publicly supporting its repel, as LGBTQ activist Bertho Masko explains. For a comprehensive account of LGBTQ activism in Lebanon, see Fakhoury and Nagle (2021).

confront both the slowness of the system and the symbolic weight of the formal rules remains to be seen. Even if the reform parliamentarians are able to form a coherent and effective bloc that pushes reform—which is still far from guaranteed—they have a monumental uphill battle against a constitutional system that privileges ethno-sectarian state capture and immobilism.

The two reform efforts we examined in this chapter offer insights for the potential for consociational adaptability. Scholars frequently point out consociationalism's resistance to reform, especially for non-ethnic actors (Horowitz, 2014; Nagle, 2020). Our analysis offers further context to these claims. Even in conditions where the embedded elite have captured the state and sought to immobilize it to shield themselves from electoral censure, there remains space, however small, for change. Finding the best vectors for creating change in this system is tricky as reform-minded activists already struggle to be heard in a system that empowers traditional ethno-sectarian elites. Yet, activists must engage the actors most responsible for the immobilism of the system, demonstrating, through increasing public pressure on a variety of fronts, that the issue has public support and is of growing electoral importance. It is in this multi-pronged approach, both inside and outside the system, that a path lays for future policy reforms, however difficult.

REFERENCES

Abaad. (2016). *A White Dress Doesn't Cover the Rape*. https://www.abaadmena.org/programmes/advocacy-and-policy-development/project-58748b6fa56f85-59472059

Aboultaif, E. W. (2019). *Power Sharing in Lebanon: Consociationalism Since 1820*. Routledge.

Agarin, T. (2020). The Limits of Inclusion: Representation of Minority and Non-dominant Communities in Consociational and Liberal Democracies. *International Political Science Review, 41*(1), 15–29.

Al-Jazeera. (2017). *Scrapping of Lebanon Rape Law 'Is One Small Step.'* https://www.aljazeera.com/features/2017/8/18/scrapping-of-lebanon-rape-law-is-one-small-step

Al-Jazeera. (2021). *'Little Hope Is Left': Lebanon's Paralysis and a Collapsing State*. https://www.aljazeera.com/news/2021/5/24/little-hope-left-lebanons-paralysis-and-a-collapsing-state

Badran, S. (2021). Grand Coalition Government: The Case of Lebanon. *Arab Law Quarterly, 35*, 249–276.

Baroud, Z., & El-Alayli, G. (2019). Lebanon. In M. Afkhami, Y. Ertük, & A. E. Mayer (Eds.), *Feminist Advocacy, Family Law and Violence Against Women: International Perspectives.* Routledge.

Basta, K. (2016). Imagined Institutions: The Symbolic Power of Formal Rules in Bosnia and Herzegovina. *Slavic Review, 75*(4), 944–969.

BBC. (2017). *Lebanon Rape Law: Parliament Abolishes Marriage Loophole.* https://www.bbc.com/news/world-middle-east-40947448

Bogaards, M. (2017). Lebanon: How Civil War Changed Consociationalism. In A. McCulloch & J. McGarry (Eds.), *Power-sharing: Empirical and Normative Challenges.* Routledge.

Byrne, S., & McCulloch, A. (2018). Is Power-sharing Bad for Women? *Nationalism and Ethnic Politics, 24*(1), 1–12.

Cammett, M., & Malesky, E. (2012). Power Sharing in Postconflict Societies: Implications for Peace and Governance. *Journal of Conflict Resolution, 56*(6), 982–1016.

Charafeddine, F. (2009). *Predicament of Lebanese Women Married to Non-Lebanese.* UNDP. http://www.undp.org.lb/communication/publications/downloads/mujaz_en.pdf

CNN. (2016). *Lebanon Takes First Step to Abolish Marriage Rape Law.* https://edition.cnn.com/2016/12/08/middleeast/lebanon-moves-to-abolish-marriage-rape-law/index.html

CRTD-A. (n.d.). *Arab Women's Right to Nationality Campaign.* https://crtda.org.lb/project/nationality

Dabbous, D. (2017). *Legal Reform and Women's Rights in Lebanese Personal Status Laws* (CMI, Report No. 3).

Dekmejian, R. (1978). Consociational Democracy in Crisis: The Case of Lebanon. *Comparative Politics, 10*(2), 251–265.

Domat, C. (2016). Campaign Grows in Lebanon to Abolish Law Enabling Rapist to Marry Victim. *Middle East Eye.* https://www.middleeasteye.net/news/campaign-grows-lebanon-abolish-law-enabling-rapist-marry-victim

Fakhoury, T. (2019). Power-sharing after the Arab Spring? Insights from Lebanon's Political Transition. *Nationalism and Ethnic Politics, 25*(1), 9–26.

Fakhoury, T., & McCulloch, A. (2023). How Do Consociations Asylum Policy? Lebanon's Response to Conflict-Induced Displacement as an Exploratory Case. *International Studies Quarterly, 67*(3), sqad057.

Fakhoury, T., & Nagle, J. (2018). Between Co-optation and Radical Opposition: A Comparative Analysis of Power-Sharing on Gender Equality and LGBTQ Rights in Northern Ireland and Lebanon. *Nationalism and Ethnic Politics, 24*(1), 82–99.

Fakhoury, T., & Nagle, J. (2021). *Resisting Sectarianism: Queer Activism in Postwar Lebanon.* Zed Books.

Geha, C. (2019). The Myth of Women's Political Empowerment Within Lebanon's Sectarian Power-sharing System. *Journal of Women, Politics and Policy, 40*(4), 498–521.

Ghaddar, S. (2017). *Second-Class Citizenship: Lebanese Women Fight to Pass Nationality to Children and Spouses.* The Century Foundation. Retrieved August 22, 2020, from https://tcf.org/content/report/second-class-citize nship/?agreed=1

Global Campaign for Equal Nationality Rights. (2018). Middle East & North Africa, Found online at: https://equalnationalityrights.org/countries/mid dle-east-north-africa. Accessed on 9 November 2023.

Gray, A., & Birrell, D. (2011). Coalition Government in Northern Ireland: Social Policy and the Lowest Common Denominator Thesis. *Social Policy and Society, 11*(1), 15–25.

Horowitz, D. L. (2014). Ethnic Power Sharing: Three Big Problems. *Journal of Democracy, 25*(2), 5–20.

Hulsey, J. (2010). 'Why Did They Vote for Those Guys Again?' Challenges and Contradictions in the Promotion of Political Moderation in Postwar Bosnia and Herzegovina. *Democratization, 17*(6), 1132–1152.

Human Rights Watch. (2018). *Lebanon: Discriminatory Nationality Law.* https://www.hrw.org/news/2018/10/03/lebanon-discriminatory-nationali ty-law

Hyndman-Rizk, N. (2019). A Question of Personal Status: The Lebanese Women's Movement and Civil Marriage Reform. *Journal of Middle East Women's Studies, 15*(2), 179–198.

International Commission of Jurists. (2019). *Gender Based Violence in Lebanon: Inadequate Framework, Ineffective Remedies.* Retrieved August 8, 2020, from https://www.icj.org/wp-content/uploads/2019/07/Lebanon-Gender-Violence-Publications.pdf

Joseph, S. (1999). Descent of the Nation: Kinship and Citizenship in Lebanon. *Citizenship Studies, 3*(3), 295–318.

Kafa. (2018). KAFA's Clarifications on "Dissecting Lebanese Law 293 on Domestic Violence": Are Women Protected? *IFI Policy Brief.* www.kafa.org. lb/StudiesPublicationPDF/PRpdf-102-636510265940280395.pdf. Accessed 16 August 2020.

Kennedy, R., Pierson, C., & Thomson, J. (2016). Challenging Identity Hierarchies: Gender and Consociational Power-sharing. *British Journal of Politics & International Relations, 18*(3), 618–633.

Kerr, M. (2005). *Imposing Power-sharing: Conflict and Coexistence in Northern Ireland and Lebanon.* Irish Academic Press.

Kimball, K. (2021). In 2021, Lebanon Suffered While the World Looked On. *Foreign Policy.* https://foreignpolicy.com/2021/12/26/lebanon-economic-crisis-politics-covid-2021/

Lebanese Palestinian Dialogue Committee, Central Administration of Statistics, Palestinian Central Bureau of Statistics. (2018). *The Population and Housing Census in Palestinian Camps and Gatherings—2017, Key Findings Report (Population, Buildings and Housing Units)*, Beirut, Lebanon.

Lijphart, A. (1969). Consociational Democracy. *World Politics, 21*(2), 207–225.

Mansour, M., & Abou Aad, S. (2012). *Women's Citizenship Rights in Lebanon* (Working Paper Series #8). Issam Fares Institute for Public Policy and International Affairs, American University of Beirut.

McCrudden, C., & O'Leary, B. (2013). *Courts and Consociations: Human Rights Versus Power-Sharing*. Oxford University Press.

McCulloch, A. (2018). The Use and Abuse of Veto Rights in Power-Sharing Systems: Northern Ireland in Comparative Perspective. *Government and Opposition, 53*(4), 735–756.

McCulloch, A. (2022). *Getting Things Done? Process, Performance, and Decision-Evasion in Consociational Systems*. Paper presented at the Consociationalism and the State Workshop. London School of Economics.

Mikdashi, M. (2018). Sextarianism: Notes on Studying the Lebanese State. In A. Ghazal & J. Hanssen (Eds.), *Oxford Handbook of Contemporary Middle-Eastern and North African History*. Oxford University Press.

Mounzer, L. (2022). *The Smallest of Silver Linings in Lebanon's Elections: Women Candidates*. Wilson Center. https://www.wilsoncenter.org/blog-post/sma llest-silver-linings-lebanons-elections-women-candidates

Moussawi, F., & Nasser, Y. (2019). Civil Society Advocacy and Policy Entrepreneurship: Examining the Making of the Law 293 to Criminalize Domestic Violence in Lebanon. In Y. Nasser & R. Hoppe (Eds.), *Women, Civil Society and Policy Change in the Arab World*. Palgrave Macmillan.

Nagle, J. (2020). Consociationalism Is Dead! Long Live Zombie Power-Sharing. *Studies in Ethnicity and Nationalism, 20*(2), 137–144.

Reuters. (2021). *World Bank Sees Lebanon GDP Shrinking 9.5% Further, One of History's Worst Depressions*. https://www.reuters.com/world/middle-east/ world-bank-sees-lebanon-gdp-shrinking-95-further-one-historys-worst-depres sions-2021-06-01/

Salloukh, B., & Halawi, I. (2020). Pessimism of the Intellect, Optimism of the Will After the 17 October Protests in Lebanon. *Middle East Law and Governance, 12*(3), 322–334.

Salem, E. (1979). Lebanon's Political Maze: The Search for Peace in a Turbulent Land, *Middle East Journal, 33*(4), 444–463.

Shehadeh, R. L. (1998). The Legal Status of Married Women in Lebanon. *International Journal of Middle East Studies, 30*(4), 501–519.

Siren Associates. (2019). *The Plight of the Rightless: Mapping and Understanding Statelessness in Tripoli*. https://sirenassociates.com/wp-content/upl oads/2020/09/Stateless-Report_Final-Draft-March-10-1.pdf

Usta, J., Farver, J., & Pashayan, N. (2007). Domestic Violence: The Lebanese Experience. *Public Health, 121,* 208–219.

World Bank. (2021, June 1). *Lebanon Sinking into One of the Most Severe Global Crises Episodes, Amidst Deliberate Inaction.* https://www.worldbank.org/en/news/press-release/2021/05/01/lebanon-sinking-into-one-of-the-most-severe-global-crises-episodes. Accessed on 28 April 2022.

World Economic Forum. (2020). *Global Gender Gap Report 2020.* Insight Report. http://www3.weforum.org/docs/WEF_GGGR_2020.pdf

Zalzal, M. (1997). Lebanon and Syria: The Geopolitics of Change. *Middle East Report, 203,* 37–39.

Zuhur, S. (2002). Empowering Women or Dislodging Sectarianism: Civil Marriage in Lebanon. *Yale Journal of Law & Feminism, 14,* 177–208.

CHAPTER 11

Consociational Democracy Without Minority Veto? Power-sharing in Ethiopia

Yonatan T. Fessha and Biniyam N. Bezabih

INTRODUCTION

Like many African countries, Ethiopia has not managed to make ethnicity a non-issue. Ethnic-based political competition has long dominated Ethiopian politics and the political landscape is dominated by ethnic-based political parties. As can be seen from the increasing number of ethnically-branded banks, there is reason to believe that ethnicity is also permeating private socio-economic institutions. It has in fact been the source of a series of internal conflicts that have already cost hundreds of thousands of lives, further weakened communal bonds, and made the continued existence of the country more precarious than ever.

Unlike many other African countries, however, ethnic divisions have not only led to a political wrangling that aimed at capturing the center. In addition to controlling the central government, some of the ethnic claims have been about securing territorial autonomy. In fact, some have

---

Y. T. Fessha (✉) · B. N. Bezabih
University of the Western Cape, Cape Town, South Africa
e-mail: yfessha@uwc.ac.za

© The Author(s), under exclusive license to Springer Nature   237
Switzerland AG 2024
E. Wassim Aboultaif et al. (eds.), *Power-Sharing in the Global South,*
Federalism and Internal Conflicts,
https://doi.org/10.1007/978-3-031-45721-0_11

sought after the most extreme solution of secession. Ethiopia is probably one of the few countries on the continent that has faced persistent ethnic-based claims for territorial autonomy, and which has ethnic-based political groups that clamor for secession.

It should not come as a surprise then that war-torn Ethiopia adopted federalism to manage its ethnic tensions. After all, its century-old experiment to build a centralized and modernized nation-state has not succeeded. The armed struggle waged by disgruntled ethnic groups interrupted the nation-building project spearheaded by the rulers of what is now regarded as northern Ethiopia. The federalization of the Ethiopian state has entailed the provisions of territorial autonomy to ethnic groups and a constitutional guarantee that the different ethnic communities are represented in central decision-making bodies. In short, power-sharing is a central feature of the constitutional and political order the country adopted in 1995.

Following the four main ingredients of power-sharing suggested by Arend Lijphart (1977), this chapter investigates the power-sharing arrangement that Ethiopia has adopted. It investigates the segmental autonomy the constitution provides, the elements of proportionality that the constitution includes and the guarantee that the constitution provides for ensuring representation in central institutions. The constitution does not allow minority groups to veto proposals that undermine their interests and rights. The only exception is the set of self-determination rights whose amendment requires the consent of all the states that make up the federation (FDRE Constitution Article 105 of 1995).

The chapter argues that although territorial autonomy within the framework of federalism has wide support in Ethiopia, the ethnic variant that the constitution has adopted continues to be a major source of contention. The disgruntlement with the current constitutional and political dispensation is compounded by the fact that the federal government, albeit ethnically diverse in its composition, does not reflect a true representation of the diverse ethnic groups and the political formations that claim to represent them.

The chapter discusses the law and politics of power-sharing outlined in five interrelated parts. The first part briefly provides the demographic and historical context within which the scheme of autonomy and power-sharing operates in Ethiopia. The second part focuses on territorial autonomy. The third part discusses executive power-sharing. The fourth part recounts the impact of party politics on the accommodative elements of the Ethiopian constitution. Part five concludes the discussion by giving a few remarks on the future.

THE CONTEXT

With a population of more than 110 million, the ancient eastern African state is the most populated country on the continent next to Nigeria. It is also one of the most diverse countries on the continent—a multi-ethnic, multi-linguistic and multi-faith country. Although a little less than eighty ethnic groups inhabit the country, close to two-thirds of the total population belongs to three major ethnic groups. According to the 2007 population census, the Oromo are the largest ethnic group accounting for 34.49% of the population, followed by the Amhara (26.89%) and the Somali (6.2%). With no single ethnic group in the majority, Ethiopia, like most other African states, can be appropriately described as a country of minorities.

A more pronounced political mobilization of ethnic identity has gradually taken center stage in Ethiopian politics in the few decades preceding the 1974 Ethiopian revolution. The "national question," which was championed and popularized by the Ethiopian Student Movement, became one of the most important issues of mass mobilization during the revolution and the years that followed. When the military *Dergue*, which proved to be no less authoritarian and ruthless than its predecessor, effectively highjacked the revolution and crushed the multi-ethnic polit-ical groupings, the most formidable resistance against the military came from ethno-nationalist forces.

In 1991, the Ethiopian Peoples' Revolutionary Democratic Front (EPRDF), a coalition of ethnic-based liberation movements, under the leadership of the Tigray Peoples Liberation Front (TPLF), marched on Addis Ababa and removed the military government that ruled the country for 17 years. The EPRDF immediately established a transitional govern-ment that was dominated by nationalist movements. In a process that did not adequately include pan-Ethiopian political formations, the EPRDF and other ethnic-based parties played a critical role in re-organizing the Ethiopian state. The Transitional Charter, the constitutive document of the transitional government, sought to establish a political and constitu-tional order that claims to fundamentally "cut through the century-old, tangled knot of iniquitous oppressive center-periphery relations" and recognizes the right of nationalities to autonomy and self-determination. Federalism with its "multinational" variant was chosen to be the organizing principle of the state. The constitution, adopted in 1995, is presented as a "covenant" in which the self-ruling Ethiopian "nation, nationalities, and peoples" with shared institutions at the center agreed to continue living under a federally restructured Ethiopian state.

SEGMENTAL AUTONOMY

One of the important features of the power-sharing scheme, as famously developed by Lijphart (1977), includes segmental autonomy. This entails the provision of self-rule to groups, allowing them to exercise control over matters that are relevant to them. The Ethiopian constitution establishes a federation that features autonomous subnational units that are, by and large, demarcated along ethnic lines. It is the ethnic basis of the territorial autonomy that has remained to be a bone of contention even after 27 years of ethnic federalism.

The Constitutional Framework

Article 46 of the Constitution (1995) declares that the constituent units are "established on the basis of settlement patterns, language, identity, and consent of the people concerned." The act of reconfiguring the Ethiopian state, however, preceded the constitution. The constitution simply codified the geographical configuration that was taken by the Boundary Commission which was established by the transitional government. The single most important criterion that the Commission used to carve out the constituent units was "nationality."

> In practice it was current language use that became the single effective criterion applied by the commission in drafting the map. This was considered a more visible and conclusive indicator of ethnic boundaries than, for instance, historical precedent. The TGE Commission was dismissive of claims based on history, fearing their open-ended potential for dispute, and preferring to deal in currently verifiable demographics. Even this was not straightforward. (Vaughan, 2015)

The making of states, it seems, was greatly influenced by Stalin's theory of nationality (Asnake, 2009: 65). An attempt is made to carve out constituent units in such a way that the political boundary matches with cultural boundary. It seems to be driven by the belief that "nation, nationalities and peoples" need to have a "mother state" if they are to properly exercise their right to self-determination (Minute of the Ethiopian Constitutional Assembly, 1994: 80–81). Some ethnic groups are given their own state while others are given a local government in which they are in a majority (Daniel, 2003: 199). The linguistic and ethnic homogeneity of the newly created political units was, however, a myth. In fact, a study in the 1980s "found out that of the 580 woredas in the country, only around 30 were actually monolingual" (Vaughan, 2003).

Six of the original nine subnational units (the States of Tigray, Afar, Amhara, Oromia, Somali and Benshangul/Gumuz) are named after the numerically dominant nationality(ies) living in the respective states (FDRE Constitution Article 47(1) of 1995). Two "multi-ethnic" subnational units, namely, the State of the Southern Nations, Nationalities and Peoples, and Gambella, took on an ethnically neutral name given their ethnically diverse demography but the local governments that make up the states are mostly named after the numerically dominant ethnic group (ibid.). Finally, the State of Harari is named after the minority nationality of the state that is nevertheless presented as the historical owner of the area (ibid.).

The state reorganization was not without anomaly. For example, it is not clear why some numerically strong nationalities are denied the status of a state while other numerically smaller nationalities were allowed to establish their own state. The gravely inconsistent decision made in relation to the carving out of the states which granted a statehood for a tiny minority such as Harar made the arrangement unacceptable for the numerically stronger ethnic local communities (Biniyam, 2014). The population size of the then Sidama Zone, for example, is far larger than the sum of the total population of the four states established by the federal constitution (i.e., Afar, Gambella, Benishangul-Gumuz and Harari) (Fessha & Biniyam, 2019).

Economic rationalities, administrative convenience and other important factors were ignored or not seriously considered in the making of the states. The states are in many ways ahistorical (Bahru, 2008: 355). They represent "a significant and deliberate departure from the former provincial experience" (Assefa, 2008). Yet, like previous redrawing of boundaries, the process of geographically reconfiguring the redrawing of the administrative map of post-1991 Ethiopia was top-down. "When the

TGE devised the new ethnic map of the country, it was essentially drawn up on the basis of 'expert' opinion, rather than the views of the relevant populations" (Vaughan, 2003). Arguably, the federal system did not stem from below the people; nor was it the result of a broad-based bargaining (Young, 1996). It rather represents an imposition from above (Berhanu, 2009; Hassen, 1998; Vestal, 1999). It is probably because of this that scholars, like Edmond Keller, described the Ethiopian federal system as a "putting together" federation (Keller, 2002).

The constitution keeps the door open for the creation of new states. It declares that a "nation, nationality and people" within the existing member states can at any time join the federation as a fully-fledged constituent unit, provided they fulfill the constitutional requirements. The only requirement is that the demand for internal secession is supported by "a two-thirds majority of the members of the legislative council" of the community concerned and the majority vote of the concerned community in a referendum (FDRE Constitution Article 39 of 1995). Despite the relatively lax constitutional procedure to establish a new state, no community succeeded in establishing a new state in the first two decades of the federal experiment. Although there were several overt and covert demands for statehood from some ethnic communities, the internal boundary of the Ethiopian federation remained unaltered until 2021.

The Clamor for One's Own State

Things have changed. Ethiopia, which has been hailed as one of the emerging economic powerhouses of Africa and an anchor of political stability in the highly volatile region of the Horn of Africa, was rocked by widespread anti-government protests that erupted in November 2015 and lasted for three years. The power struggle within the ruling front coupled (perhaps coordinating) with the persistent political protests, primarily in the states of Oromia and Amhara, fundamentally altered the balance of power within the front and effected a change of leadership (Biniyam, 2018). Abiy Ahmed became the new Prime Minister of Ethiopia in April 2018 (Aljazeera, 2018) which marked a new dawn for the prospect of a political opening-up and economic liberalization.

The political environment opened a new window of opportunity to push the demand for statehood. In particular, the Sidama seized the moment and pushed the local government council of Sidama Zone to formally submit the demand for statehood once again (Tronvoll et al.,

2020). The Council complied and that eventually led to a referendum in which more than 98.5% of the residents of the zone voted in favor of Sidama's statehood (National Election Board of Ethiopia (NEBE), 2019). Sidama formally became the tenth fully-fledged family member of the Ethiopian federation without the need to make it to the constitutional list of federated units. The creation of the state of Sidame effectively busted the taboo against the creation of new states, "*Kilil* taboo." Statehood for ethnic local governments is no longer a pipedream.

The Sidama's renewed aggressive quest for statehood and the new political context that encouraged such a move triggered an unprecedented wave of demands for statehood and boundary redrawing. More than eleven councils of ethnic local governments in the Southern Nations, Nationalities and Peoples Regional State (SNNPRS) alone (i.e., Kaffa, Gurage, Benchi-Maji, Hadiya, Dawro, Wolayita, Gamo, Kambatta-Tambaro, South Omo, Gofa, Gedeo) submitted the demands for statehood one after the other. None of these demands were accepted by the council of SNNPRS. Some of them were silenced by force. The domino effect, at least for the time being, seems to be averted.

It immediately became clear that the federal government is not totally against the creation of new states. This is evident in the way it embraced (some would say engineered) the demand by several ethnic local governments in SNNPRS to come together and create a state. In 2021, the respective councils of several ethnic local governments located in Southwest Ethiopia submitted their demands to the House of Federation to jointly form a clearly multi-ethnic state. Unlike the dominantly mono-ethnic Sidama, the State of South-West Ethiopia is a home to 13 major ethnic groups (BBC News Amharic, 2021). Administrative convenience, it seems, is also the single most important rationale for the creation of the state of Southwest Ethiopia. Two more states were added in 2023 (Central Ethiopia and South Ethiopia) The clear emphasis given to non-ethnic factors in justifying the demand and making of the newest member of the Ethiopian federation represents a major departure from the making of states in Ethiopia. The federal constitution, as indicated earlier, does not seem to envisage the demand for the creation of new states on any basis other than ethnicity. Article 47/2 of the federal constitution states that "Nations, Nationalities and Peoples within the States enumerated … have the right to establish, at any time, their own States." The response of the federal government suggests that the constitutional promise for statehood for all ethnic groups on demand was proved to be evidently impractical and of a mere symbolic significance.

There are, however, stark similarities between the journeys that led to the creation of the new states. Major decisions relating to the endorsement of the demand for statehood, power transfer and constitution making were made by the legislative bodies that can hardly be regarded as true representatives of the communities concerned. Members of those legislative bodies made it to those institutions through election processes that were deeply flawed (Arriola & Lyons, 2016). Absent free, fair and competitive elections, it is problematic to consider the governmental institutions, which have made consequential decisions, as legitimate representatives of the will of citizens that were acting on behalf of the people.

The referenda process was also not without serious limitations. The referenda, particularly that of Sidama, were organized in a tense security environment. The political climate was too intimidating to campaign against the creation of the state. Irrespective of the noticeable popularity of the demands for the creation of the Sidama State, the voters, to make an informed decision, should have been exposed to the arguments of both the "leave" and "remain" campaigns. Finally, the constitution-making processes followed in both states were, more or less, secretive and elitist. The minimum requirements of public participation in the drafting and adoption of the constitutions were simply ignored.

Proportionality

Lijphart (1977) argues for proportional representation where segments of the society are represented in decision-making organs in rough proportion to their share of the population. Elements of proportionality are evident in the bicameral parliament of the federal government. The House of Peoples' Representatives (HPR), the lower house of the parliament, "is the highest legislative authority of the Federal Government." Although members of the HPR are expected to represent citizens as individuals, the representation of ethnic minority groups is also taken into account. The constitution reserves at least twenty seats of the HPR for minority ethnic groups (Article 54(2) of FDRE Constitution 1995).

Ethnic representation is rather the norm in the second chamber of the federal parliament, the House of Federation (HOF). Unlike many second chambers in federal countries, the HOF is not the house of member states of the federation (Fessha, 2016). Rather, it is composed of representatives of "Nations, Nationalities and Peoples," directly elected by the people or appointed by the state councils. In practice, however, members of the HOF are elected by state councils. No popular election has been conducted by any of the states to elect the members of the HOF.

The HOF has not totally avoided majoritarianism as it gives a degree of weight to the population size of the nationalities. Each ethnic group shall have one representative with an additional one more representative for each 1 million additional populations. The second chamber has no or limited role in the review of federal legislation. As one author aptly notes, its law-making power is only confined to "such specific matters as constitutional amendment, initiation of draft civil laws, approving draft procedural rules for the Constitutional Inquiry Council and adoption of its own internal administration rules" (Hashim, 2010). Unusual for an upper house, it has the power to interpret the constitution. The HOF, according to Article 62(7) of FDRE Constitution (1995), has control over other important competences, including the power to "determine the division of revenues derived from joint federal and state tax sources and the subsidies that the federal government may provide to the states." From the foregoing, it is clear that the HOF is not in a position to serve as an institution that can "constrain purely majoritarian democracy"—which is described as one of the objectives of power-sharing in multi-ethnic society (Wolff, 2005). Ethiopia's system, as a result, is clearly susceptible to tyranny of the numerically big ethnic groups.

The representation system is more complicated by the electoral system the country follows. Major federal and subnational legislative bodies are elected using the First Past the Post (FPTP) variety of the plurality electoral system, introduced by the 1995 federal constitution. This voting system, which is known for producing a clear majority for the relatively stronger parties and putting significant segments of the voting population in each constituency at disadvantage, is rarely considered to be the ideal voting system for stable power-sharing arrangement in multi-ethnic society (Wolff, 2005). The Ethiopian experience is consistent with this assessment. The electoral system embedded in the Ethiopian constitution has "exclude[d] minorities from political representation" in state and federal institutions "and may at times understate combined majority votes" (Beza, 2013). There are sections of a voting population in each constituency that do not feel represented as the plurality system effectively empowers the relative majorities at the expense of relative minorities.

EXECUTIVE POWER-SHARING

Executive power-sharing through a grand coalition is a major feature of Lijphart's model of power-sharing. According to the constitution, government in Ethiopia is not formed through a formal grand coalition. As a constitution that has adopted a parliamentary system of governance, it is the party or coalition of parties with the majority of seats in the Parliament that ordinarily form a government under the leadership of the Prime Minister. The Prime Minister, who is the highest executive power of the federal government, is elected by parliament from among its members. The President, the ceremonial head of the state, is elected when a joint session of the House of Peoples' Representatives and the House of the Federation approves the candidacy by a two-thirds majority vote.

The representation of different ethnic groups in national institutions is a constitutional requirement. Article 39(3) of the Constitution explicitly mandates the "equitable representation of the different ethnic communities in the Federal and state governments." In addition, the constitution mandates the government to ensure the representation of all ethnic communities in the national armed forces (Article 87 of the FDRE Constitution 1995). The constitutional requirement of equitable representation, as noted by Fasil (1997: 156), must "permeate the whole government in all its branches."

Consociational Coalition?

In the wake of the new dispensation, the Federal Government, under the leadership of the EPRDF, made a conscious effort to take the ethnic criterion seriously when composing the council of ministers. The council has, thus, become more diversified than ever in terms of ethnic composition, representing a departure from the past where the leadership structures of national institutions were dominated by the Amharic speaking elites. Led by a Prime Minister from Tigray, Meles Zenawi, the first cabinet that was formed after the adoption of the Constitution in 1995, was, for example, composed of four Amharas, six Oromos, three Tigreans and three ministers from other ethnic groups in the 16-member cabinet. The cabinet, which was formed after the 2005 election, was more ethnically diverse than the two cabinets that preceded it. Led by Meles Zenawi, the 21-member cabinet is composed of five Amharas, seven Oromos, two

Tigreans and one each from Somali, Gurage, Afar, Silte, Keficho, Sidama and Hadya ethnic groups.

The untimely death of Meles Zenawi, who was at the helm for some 23 years, in 2012 opened the door for then-Deputy Chairperson of the front and Deputy Prime Minister of the federal government, HaileMariam Dessalegn, to be in charge of managing both the party and the federal government (BBC, 2012). The appointment of a Prime Minister from a minority ethnic group that accounts for less than three percent of the population might be seen as an important step toward creating an inclusive Ethiopia. It should at the same time be seen against the expectation that Meles's shoes would be filled by someone that hails from one of the two major ethnic groups (i.e., Oromo or Amhara). The selection of Hailemariam Dessalegn, someone from the weakest party within the coalition (i.e., SEPDM) and a minority ethnic group (i.e., Wolayita), was regarded as a safe bet that does not threaten the status quo. Unlike Meles, who had control over the TPLF-dominated military and intelligence, loyalty of the constituting party leaders, and mastery of intra-party power politics and palace intrigue, Hailemariam wielded virtually no significant power (Biniyam, 2018).

Hailemariam kept the tradition of composing an ethnically diverse cabinet. In fact, he maintained Meles's cabinet with some adjustments. The 2010 Meles's cabinet was composed of six Amhara, six Oromo, three Tigray, two Somali, one each from six other smaller ethnic groups (Daniel, 2010). Despite TPLF's loss of the Prime Ministership, the party maintained its dominance over foreign affairs, the intelligence and the army. HaileMariam also maintained ethnic balance in the government he formed after the 2015 elections. "[His] first cabinet gives 8 positions to the OPDO (31%), 7 to the ANDM (27%), 7 to the SEPDM (27%), 2 to the TPLF (8%), and 2 to affiliated parties from the country's peripheral regions (Afar, Benishangul Gumuz, Gambela, and Somali). The ethno-regional composition of Hailemariam's 2015 cabinet is virtually identical to that of the cabinets formed by Meles in 2005 and 2010" (Arriola & Lyons, 2016: 83).

What was unusual was his decision to appoint three Deputy Prime Ministers, a notable deviation from the constitutional practice (*Addis Standard*, 2013). The arrangement, which lasted for four years, allowed the sharing of important powers of the Deputy Prime Minister among the three major ethnic groups (i.e., Amhara, Oromo and Tigrean). "In order to keep all the constituent parties at the table after Meles's death, Haile-mariam," as noted by Arriola and Lyons (2016: 83), "was compelled in 2013 to name three new deputy prime ministers—one from the ANDM, one from the OPDO, and one from the TPLF." Although some see it as a return to collective leadership, others construed it as a decision that undermined the power of the Prime Minister, leading them to consider Hailemariam as an "ineffective placeholder" (Aljazeera, 2015).

The general assessment is that representation in the post-1991 Ethiopian Federal Government is ethnically diverse. This is true not only of the national cabinet, but also of ambassadorial and other important national appointments. The question, however, is whether the individuals that are claimed to represent different ethnic groups in the cabinet represent the communities on whose behalf they are appointed. There is a need to go beyond the formal representation system and examine the true nature of their representativeness.

Responding to the question posed above requires one to investigate the formative stages of the EPRDF, the ruling party, and examine the composition of the ruling party, especially how the coalition came about. As the TPLF took control of Tigray and decided to proceed beyond south of Tigray to overthrow the military government, creating alliances with other political groupings was deemed imperative. The TPLF did not create the EPRDF by creating an alliance with existing political parties that claim to represent the different segments of Ethiopian society. The general pattern that one observes in the formation of the EPRDF is that the TPLF, its core organization, followed a policy of creating alliance which largely relied on the creation of political parties in its own image, as opposed to linking with existing parties, be it in Oromia or the Southern part of the country (Young, 1997). The general view, or at least the perception, was that these parties are not equal partners of the coalition and face legitimacy issues among the people they claim to represent. They were hardly regarded as true champions of the rights of the communities they claim to represent. This is especially damaging in a political context where there are already existing parties that claim to represent the same communities.

In 2015, the country was rocked by a series of protests. It started when the youth in Oromia, the largest state in the federation, took to the streets protesting against the Addis Ababa Master City Plan, which they believed was part of a policy to drive the Oromo out of the capital city, taking their lands and threatening their cultural survival (Chala, 2016). Political tension was heightened when members of the second-largest ethnic group, the Amhara, joined the streets in protest against the government. It quickly morphed into a protest against the domination of the Tigray People's Liberation Front (TPLF), one of the four parties that form the EPRDF. To weather the widespread protests that engulfed almost every corner of the country, Prime Minister Hailemariam Dessalegn introduced a cabinet shakeup. The Prime Minister appointed 30 ministers, only nine of whom served in the previous cabinet. Departing from the EPRDF tradition, the Prime Minister appointed prominent technocrats who were not politically affiliated with the ruling front. He eliminated ten-plus Prime Ministerial advisory positions and removed two of the three Deputy Prime Ministerial roles. Nevertheless, the need to maintain ethnic balance was not ignored. Nine from Oromo, seven from Amhara, four from Tigray, two from Somali and one each from Agew, Silite, Gurage, Hadiya, Afar, Gamo, Kembata and Sidama were included in the cabinet (Arriola & Lyons, 2016). Despite this figure, the perceived or real domination of the TPLF in federal institutions remained one of the protest issues that ignited and fueled the three-year-long anti-government riots. Further, for most of the first two decades of Ethiopia's federalism, individuals belonging to the Tigre ethnic group controlled key ministerial and other important positions, reinforcing the perception that the government was dominated by the Tigray People's Liberation Front (TPLF). The fact that the positions of Prime Minister, Ministry of Foreign Affairs, Head of National Security and Chief of Staff of the Army were in the hands of Tigrinya speakers was often used to substantiate this argument. "Down Down Woyane (i.e., TPLF)" was the most common chant of the Oromo protests. In 2018, the protests eventually led to the displacement of TPLF as the dominant member of the coalition and the emergence of OPDO as the dominant force and the emergence of Abiy Ahmed as the leader of the front and the Prime Minister of the country.

Enter Abiy Ahmed

The ascent of Abiy Ahmed to power, the first Oromo to be elected as head of government, from the Oromo People Democratic Organization, a junior partner within the ruling EPRDF, in the face of TPLF's opposition, represented a political sea change within EPRDF (Biniyam, 2018).

Consequently, the share of the political parties within the ethnic coalition that claim to represent the Oromo and the Amhara (i.e., OPDO and ANDM) in federal institutions increased both in number and "quality." In addition to the Premiership, officials from Oromo and Amhara ethnic groups were appointed to lead key federal institutions such as the Ministry of Foreign Affairs, Intelligence and the Army, posts which were previously controlled by the TPLF. With the forced retirement of army generals and other senior officers from Tigray, Oromo and Amhara officers were promoted to lead the army.

Abiy's first cabinet, formed in April 2018, was composed of 28 ministers and the Deputy Prime Minister—an ethnic Amhara. It included eight from Oromo, six from Amhara, three from Tigray, two from Somali, two from Sidama and one each from eight other ethnic groups. 18 of them were members of HaileMariam's administration. The Speaker of the lower house, who was from Oromo, was replaced by a woman from the Silite ethnic group. Apparently, the decision was motivated by the desire to avoid the concentration of the leaders of both legislative and executive authorities in the hands of a single ethnic group. Abiy's cabinet reshuffle came six months later. The cabinet consisted of 20 ministers and the Deputy Prime Minister, with six ministers from Oromo, five from Amhara, two from Tigray, one each from six other ethnic groups. What caught the attention of many was the fact that women constituted half of the cabinet, controlling important portfolios including, among others, the Ministry of Peace as well as the Ministry of Trade and Industry (BBC, 2018).

The eventual merger of the constituent parties of EPRDF to form the Prosperity Party, with the notable absence of the TPLF, further reduced the representation of TPLF, by extension that of Tigrayans, in federal institutions. The current cabinet, established after the 2021 election, is, as in the past, ethnically diverse. Abiy's new cabinet formed following the 2021 elections is made up of 22 ministers (the Deputy Prime Minister included). Seven of them are from Oromo, six from Amhara, two from Tigray and one each from seven other ethnic groups. Although the Prime Minister and Chief of Staff of the army belong to the Oromo ethnic group, the Ministry of Foreign Affairs and Head of the most powerful national security agency come from the Amhara ethnic group. Although a Tigrayan is appointed as a Minister of Defence, that cabinet member can hardly be regarded as a person that signifies the representation of the people of Tigray. In fact, he is more likely to be regarded as a sell-out in the eyes of the Tigray people (Hairsine, 2021). If anything, the individual is known for his close friendship with Abiy Ahmed. In fact, one of the noticeable things in the way that Abiy composes his cabinet and makes appointments is that he makes sure that his close friends and loyalists control key ministerial and other positions. That probably explains the appointment of Temesgen Tiruneh, an Amhara, as the Head of the important secret service.

Perhaps a notable development in post-2018 Ethiopia is that politicians from the state of Somali have taken a more prominent role in national institutions. Despite several reshuffles in the last four years, the Ministry of Finance has consistently been led by an ethnic Somali. Until recently, the Speaker of the House of Federation was an ethnic Somali. That same individual now holds the powerful role of the administrator of the Prosperity Party. A young woman from the state of Somali had also served as Minister of Women, Children and Youth. The President of the Somali Regional State touted this achievement on Twitter: "our 'claiming the center' politics is paying off! We are now the mainstream. We are the center!" (Mustaf, 2022).

Interestingly, the current cabinet that commences its term in 2021 includes three opposition leaders (Bloomberg, 2021). The last time opposition leaders made it into the cabinet was when the Transitional Government was established in 1991. None of the cabinets that were established after the adoption of the constitution in 1995 included politicians from outside the ruling party. This may make the decision of Abiy to include leaders of three political parties that have barely secured votes in the recent national election an unprecedented act of good politics. The government has also touted the decision as proof that "Ethiopia's new beginnings are marked by commitment to inclusivity."

One must not, however, exaggerate the decision of the Prime Minister to include opposition leaders. One of the leaders of an opposition party that is included in Abiy's Cabinet has been accused of leading a party that has been acting as an affiliate party that failed to act as a true opposition party. The other opposition leader comes from a political party that is a credible competitor of the ruling party, suggesting a commendable act of good politics from the part of the Prime Minister. But a closer look would reveal that it may not be the case. The opposition party in question has been divided into two factions and the individual picked by the Prime Minister to join the cabinet comes from the faction that is friendly to the Prime Minister. The longtime leader of the opposition party is, in fact, confirmed to be under house arrest for more than a year now (Amnesty, 2021).

There seems to be also an attempt to slightly deemphasize the importance of ethnicity as a criterion to nominate ministers. More precisely, it is about the explicit use of ethnicity to organize government and compose institutions. Breaking from the tradition of the last three decades, the Prime Minister, when he introduced his nominees to the parliament, did not publicly state the ethnic identities of the nominees. This break from the tradition, if sustained, suggests that Ethiopia might be joining the rank of many African countries that formally denounce ethnicity yet take it into account when composing and organizing governmental institutions. Others may interpret it as an attempt to strike a new balance between promoting ethno-cultural justice and national unity.

When Formal Institutions Do Not Matter

The operation of a political system is significantly affected by the economic, political and social contexts within which it functions (Aalen, 2002). As many studies on the Ethiopian federal experiment have repeatedly pointed out, there is a massive gulf between the constitutional promise and practice. The domineering executive has effectively weakened the legislature through a tight party discipline where party evaluation and democratic centralism play a central role (Paulos, 2007). Most important decisions, at all levels of governmental bodies, were often made within a high-level party leadership of the front that controlled the executive (Leenco, 2004; Merera, 2003). More often than not, the formal institutions are subordinated to the highly centralized informal "EPRDF's network of partner organization and affiliates" (Aalen, 2002: 99).

The dominant role the party played has undermined the equitable nature of the representative character of the federal cabinet. Irrespective of the constituencies they claimed to represent, all four constituent parties were equally represented within the major organizational bodies of the all-powerful EPRDF (i.e., the General Congress, the Council of the EPRDF and Executive Committee) (ibid.). This organizational structure, thus, artificially "equalized" the extremely unequal constituent parties whose constituency ranges from six percent to 35% of the total population of the country. This means that although the composition of the cabinet seems to comply with the constitutional mandate of equitable representation, it is undermined by the all too powerful political party whose composition is based on the principle of equality irrespective of the population size of the ethnic groups.

More importantly, the ruling front, as indicated earlier, was never a coalition of equals. TPLF, which was instrumental in the formation of the coalition and had considerable control over the birth and the evolution of the other member parties, was, as Merera (2003) succinctly put it, "the commanding real core of Ethiopia's ruling party." This asymmetric power relation within the ruling EPRDF, coupled with the flawed organizational structure, called into question the meaningfulness of representation of ethnic groups in the formal federal institutions.

The decline of democratic centralism has been occurring gradually. Despite the ruling party's transformation into a unified national party, this shift has not resulted in a federation governed by a unified and cohesive party. In fact, the current level of disputes between different levels of government surpasses what was witnessed even when the ruling party was, at least, officially a coalition of parties controlling four state governments. The federal government has increasingly resorted to utilizing its coercive powers to exert control over state governments.

The issue of census and redistricting, and in fact, its absence, has arguably interfered with the effort to ensure effective political representation. Ethiopia conducted its last census in 2007. The political instability and politicization of the census (given that some ethnic and religious groups questioned the credibility of the previous census results) led to the repeated postponement of the census which is supposed to be conducted every 10 years. This, in turn, has made redistricting of electoral constituencies impossible. This means that electoral constituencies have not been meaningfully updated for about 27 years although the Ethiopian population has more than doubled.

Conclusion

The federal option, as contentious as it initially was, is no longer a subject of political controversy in Ethiopia. There is a consensus among the political groupings on the unavoidable role that federalism has to play in managing the ethnic diversity of the country. What is still debated upon is the ethnic-based nature of the federal arrangement. The major political forces of the country disagree profoundly on the role and place of ethnicity in the federalization of the Ethiopian state. In other words, what is mostly controversial is not the decision of the TPLF/EPRDF-dominated transitional government to adopt federalism as an organizing principle of the Ethiopian state but the particular form of the federal arrangement it chose to adopt. The fact that the debate on the nature of the federal arrangement continues unabated, even three decades after its adoption, reveals how deeply divided the Ethiopian society is.

The constitution mandates the representation of the different ethnic groups in the Federal executive and other important federal institutions. The post-1991 Ethiopian governments can be generally regarded as a reflection of the diverse ethnic communities in the country. Whether these different ethnic communities see themselves represented in the higher offices of the national government is, however, another issue. Formal representation does not necessarily guarantee actual representation. In fact, as indicated above, there are grounds that cast doubt on the representative nature of the national institutions. The root of the concern lies in the political practice and, more specifically, in nature of the now defunct EPRDF and now PP, from whose rank and file the majority of the ministers and ambassadors have been appointed. The individuals that are appointed are hardly regarded as true representatives.

Further, robust power-sharing arrangements should go beyond stating the need for ensuring the representation of ethnic groups at federal level. From whichever perspective one looks at it, the importance of choosing the appropriate electoral system and putting in place fitting institutions to constrain the power of the majority, among others, cannot be ignored. The Ethiopian constitutional arrangement does not seem to adequately address these vitally important issues which clearly the power-sharing arrangement.

It is also worth noting that the translation of the constitutional mandate into reality largely depends on political practice. Under a dominant party regime, the federal system has operated as a centralized unitary system of government where the center has effectively controlled state and local governments. The real decision-making power has been concentrated in the highly centralized and disciplined ruling party and the formal institutions at federal and state levels have been subordinated to the decision of the high-level leadership of the party (i.e., the executive committee of EPRDF and now Prosperity Party). The effectiveness of the constitutional power-sharing arrangement has, thus, been significantly impacted by the anomalous evolution of the Ethiopian federal system under a dominant party regime. The power reconfiguration within EPRDF and the eventual emergence of Prosperity Party as a new ruling party has, however, unleashed a new set of political dynamics whose impact on the operation of the federal system and the power-sharing arrangement remains to be seen.

Political change that, four years ago, was expected to dawn a new era of rule of law and democracy has taken the country back to its era of civil war. Hundreds of thousands are estimated to have lost their lives as a result of the war. Millions have been displaced from their homes. As we conclude this chapter, the country seems to have got a respite from a year of brutal civil war that involved gruesome atrocities on civilians. Although there are reports of backdoor negotiations, it is not clear if we are heading to another round of devastating war or a cessation of hostilities that will eventually lead to a peace agreement. In the meantime, the federal government has established a national dialogue commission, which is supposed to facilitate conversation on the most contentious national issues. Notwithstanding the irony of establishing a dialogue commission before the guns are silenced and the warring parties are brought to the table, the process that was followed by the government to establish the commission and appoint the commissioners has drawn stern criticisms from the opposition political parties. The latter have indicated that they will not legitimize the process by participating in the activities of the commission.

The Ethiopian experience reveals that power-sharing arrangements that do not emerge from true and broadly based bargaining might not produce the desired result of peace and stability. The power-sharing arrangement in Ethiopia was an outcome of a process that only included likeminded political formations. The political forces that represent a different vision of the Ethiopian state and society were not adequately represented. True bargaining is also absent in the ruling coalition that, on the face of it, is ethnically diverse but largely includes political formations that do not have strong support among the constitutents they claim to represent. That explains why the ethnically diverse federal government may not reflect a true representation of the different ethnic groups that inhabit the country.

References

Aalen, L. (2002). *Ethnic Federalism in a Dominant Party State: The Ethiopian Experience 1991–2000*. Chr. Michelsen Institute.

Addis Standard. (2013). *A Long Awaited Cabinet Reshuffle Surprises All*. https://addisstandard.com/three-deputy-prime-ministers-indefensible-breach-of-the-constitution/

Alem, H. (2007). *Citizenship, Ethnicity and Group Rights in the Greater Horn of Africa with a Case Study of Ethiopia*. Paper Presented at the Conference on Constitutionalism and Human Security in the Horn of Africa, Addis Ababa (Inter-Africa Group).

Aljazeera. (2015). *Profile: Ethiopia's 'Placeholder' PM Quietly Holds on*. https://www.aljazeera.com/news/2015/5/27/profile-ethiopias-placeholder-pm-quietly-holds-on

Aljazeera. (2018). *Abiy Ahmed Sworn in as Ethiopia's Prime Minister*. https://www.aljazeera.com/news/2018/4/2/abiy-ahmed-sworn-in-as-ethiopias-prime-minister

Amnesty International. (2021). *Ethiopia: Opposition Politician Under House Arrest: Dawud Ibsa*. https://www.amnesty.org/en/documents/afr25/4267/2021/en/

Arriola, L. R., & Lyons, T. (2016). Ethiopia: The 100% Election. *Journal of Democracy, 27*(1), 76–88.

Asmelash, B. (1987). Some Notes on the Evolution of Regional Administration in Ethiopia. *Ethiopian Journal of Development Research, 9*(1), 21–49.

Asnake, K. (2009). *Federalism and Ethnic Conflict in Ethiopia: A Comparative Study of the Somali and Benishangul-Gumuz Regions* (Unpublished doctoral thesis). Leiden University.

Assefa, F. (August, 2008). Federalism, Diversity and the Regulation of Conflict in the Horn. In *The Second Conference on Constitutionalism & Human Security in the Horn of Africa*. Inter-Africa Group.

Bahru, Z. (Ed.). (2008). *Society, State, and Identity in African History*. African Books Collective.

BBC. (2012). *Ethiopia's Hailemariam Desalegn Sworn in as Prime Minister*. https://www.bbc.com/news/world-africa-19672302

BBC. (2018). *Ethiopia's Abiy Gives Half of Ministerial Posts to Women*. https://www.bbc.com/news/world-africa-45881004

BBC News Amharic. (2021). አንዳንድ ነጥቦች ለየት ስለሚላው 11ኛው የኢትዮጵያ ክልል[Some Points on the Unique 11th Regional State of Ethiopia]. https://www.bbc.com/amharic/news-58858519

Berhane, D. (2010). Ethiopia—Who's Who in the New Cabinet? *Horn Affairs*. https://hornaffairs.com/2010/10/12/whos-who-in-the-new-cabinet/

Berhane, D. (2016). List of PM Hailemariam's New Ministers. *Horn Affairs.* https://hornaffairs.com/2016/11/01/ethiopia-hailemariam-desalegn-new-cabinet-ministers/

Berhanu, G. (2009). *Constitutionalism in the Horn of Africa: Lesson from the New Constitution of Ethiopia.*

Beza, D. (2013). The Right of Minorities to Political Participation Under the Ethiopian Electoral System. *Mizan Law Review, 7*(1), 67–100.

Biniyam, M. (2018) ANDM And OPDO Turned Against Their Master: But Both Follow Diverging Paths. Here Is How. *Addis Standard.* https://addisstandard.com/opinion-andm-and-opdo-turned-against-their-master-but-both-follow-diverging-paths-here-is-how/

Biniyam, N. B. (2014). Federation among Unequals; Political Asymmetry and its Moderation in Ethiopia's Federal System. *Unpublished MA Thesis.* http://etd.aau.edu.et/bitstream/handle/123456789/17724/Biniyam%20Negash.pdf?sequence=1&isAllowed=y

Bloomberg. (2021). *Abiy Taps Ethiopia Opposition, Keeps Finance Head in Cabinet.* https://www.bloomberg.com/news/articles/2021-10-06/ethiopia-s-abiy-taps-opposition-retains-finance-head-in-cabinet

Chala, E. (2016). Ethiopia Scraps Addis Ababa 'Master Plan' After Protests Kill 140. *Guardian.* https://www.theguardian.com/world/2016/jan/14/ethiopia-addis-master-plan-abandoned/

Daniel, K. (2003). The Causes of the Failure of the Present Regime in Ethiopia. *International Journal of Ethiopian Studies,* 177–213.

Daniel, B. (2010). Meles Zenawi Appoints New Cabinet. *Horn Affairs.* https://hornaffairs.com/2010/10/05/meles-zenawi-appointsnew-cabinet-full-list/

De Villiers, B. (2012). Creating Federal Regions—Minority Protection Versus Sustainability. *Heidelberg Journal of International Law, 72*(2), 310–351.

Fasil, N. (1997). *Constitution for a Nation of Nations: The Ethiopian Prospect.* The Red Sea Press.

FDRE. (1995). *The Constitution of the Federal Democratic Republic of Ethiopia.* Addis Ababa.

Fessha, Y. (2016). *Ethnic Diversity and Federalism: Constitution Making in South Africa and Ethiopia.* Routledge.

Fessha, Y., & Biniyam, M. (2019). Federation Among Unequals. In P. Popelier & M. Sahadzic (Eds.), *Constitutional Asymmetry in Multinational Federalism: Managing Multinationalism in Multi-tiered Systems* (pp. 137–162). Palgrave Macmillan.

Filippov, M., et al. (2004). *Designing Federalism: A Theory of Self-Sustainable Federal Institutions.* Cambridge University Press.

Ghai, Y. (2000). Ethnicity and Autonomy: A Framework for Analysis. In Y. Ghai (Ed.), *Autonomy and Ethnicity: Negotiating Competing Claims in Multi-ethnic States.* Cambridge University Press.

Ghai, Y., & Cottrell, J. (2007, March 23–24). Federalism and State Restructuring in Nepal: The Challenge for the Constituent Assembly. *Report of a Conference organized by the Constitutional Advisory Support Unit*, UNDP, Godavari, Nepal.

Hairsine, K. (2021). Ethiopia: Aby Names Cabinet as Pressure from US, EU Mounts. *Deutsche Welle*. https://www.dw.com/en/ethiopia-abiy-names-cab inet-as-pressure-from-us-eu-mounts/a-59426272

Hashim, T. (2010). Transition to Federalism: The Ethiopian Experience. *Forum of Federations*.

Hassen, M. (1998). The Macha-Tulama Association, 1963–1967 and the Development of Oromo Nationalism. In A. Jalata (Ed.), *Oromia Nationalism and the Ethiopian Discourse: The Search for Freedom and Democracy*. The Red Sea Press Inc.

Keller, E. J. (2002). Ethnic Federalism, Fiscal Reform, Development and Democracy in Ethiopia. *African Journal of Political Science, 7*(1), 21–50.

Kinkino, K. (2019). The Quest for Regional Statehood and Its Practicability Under the Post-1991 Ethiopian Federation: The Discontents and Experience of Sidama Nation. *Global Journal of Politics and Law Research, 7*(7), 1–52.

Leenco, L. (2004). What Next in the Horn of Africa? Reconsidering the State and Self-determination. In A. Jalata (Ed.), *State Crises, Globalisation and National Movements in North-East Africa*. Routledge.

Lijphart, A. (1977). *Democracy in Plural Societies: A Comparative Exploration*. Yale University Press.

Merera, G. (2003). *Ethiopia: Competing Ethnic Nationalisms and the Quest for Democracy 1960–2000*. Chamber Printing House.

Mustaf, O. M. (2022). *We Are Now the Mainstream. We Are the Center!* Twitter. https://twitter.com/Mustafe_M_Omer/status/1503725995777576966

National Election Board of Ethiopia (NEBE). (2019). Sidama Referendum. *National Election Board of Ethiopia*. https://nebe.org.et/en/referendum

Paulos, C. (2007). *What One Hand Giveth, the Other Hand Taketh Away: Ethiopia's Post-1991 Decentralization Reform Under Neo-patrimonialism* (Unpublished Ph.D. Dissertation). The Institute of Social Studies.

Transitional Government of Ethiopia. (1994). *Minutes of the Ethiopian Constitutional Assembly*. Addis Ababa.

Tronvoll, K., Boroje, F., & Tezera, K. (2020). *The Sidama's Quest for Self-rule: A Study of the Referendum on Regional Statehood*. European Institute of Peace.

Vaughan, S. (2003). *Ethnicity and Power in Ethiopia* (Unpublished Ph.D. Dissertation). The University of Edinburgh.

Vaughan, S. (2015). Federalism, Revolutionary Democracy and the Developmental State, 1991–2012. In G. Prunier & É. Ficquet (Eds.), *Understanding Contemporary Ethiopia: Monarchy, Revolution and the Legacy of Meles Zenawi*. Oxford University Press.

Vestal, T. (1999). *Ethiopia: A post-Cold War African State*. Praeger.

Wolff, S. (2005). Electoral Systems Design and Power-sharing Regimes. In I. O'Flynn & D. Russell (Eds.), *Power Sharing: New Challenges for Divided Societies* (pp. 59–74). Pluto Press.

Young, J. (1996). Ethnicity and Power in Ethiopia. *Review of African Political Economy, 23*(70), 531–542.

Young, J. (1997). *Peasant Revolution in Ethiopia: The Tigray People's Liberation Front, 1975–1991*. Cambridge University Press.

CHAPTER 12

The Power-Sharing Arrangements in Iraq: The Instability Within

Farah Shakir

INTRODUCTION

With the introduction of federalism and a liberal consociational power-sharing arrangement in 2005, hope arose for the birth of a stable and democratic Iraq. However, this hope has faded over the last two decades, which have brought not stability and democracy but recurring political crises and violence. Consociational power-sharing was part of the political bargain between Iraqi elites and the Americans, intended mainly to accommodate the Kurds' desire for self-rule and the Shias' desire for inclusion within a unified Iraq (both groups had been marginalized during Al-Baath rule before 2003). Officially, Arend Lijphart's primary characteristics of consociational democracy—a grand coalition government and segmental autonomy—and secondary characteristics—proportionality and minority veto (Lijphart, 2000: 3)—are all included in the design of Iraq's power-sharing system.

F. Shakir (✉)
University of Kent, Canterbury, UK
e-mail: farahrose10@gmail.com

© The Author(s), under exclusive license to Springer Nature   261
Switzerland AG 2024
E. Wassim Aboultaif et al. (eds.), *Power-Sharing in the Global South,*
Federalism and Internal Conflicts,
https://doi.org/10.1007/978-3-031-45721-0_12

When analyzing Iraq's power-sharing system, it is obvious that liberal consociationalism was favored by the constitutional designers. As John McGarry and Brendan O'Leary explain, with the adoption of liberal consociation in Iraq, the problems associated with both corporate consociation and integration could be avoided (McGarry & O'Leary, 2007: 692). For them, corporate consociational arrangements would be unfair in Iraq because they would privilege certain identities and exclude others, thereby causing resentment among the excluded. These arrangements would also be unstable because they are not flexible enough to accommodate demographic shifts (McGarry & O'Leary, 2007: 691). They also have their reservations about adopting an integrational approach in Iraq as it would prevent communities that seek self-government—mainly the Kurds—from doing so, which is undemocratic and would not lead to peace and stability (McGarry & O'Leary, 2007: 677).

In this chapter, I argue that Iraq's liberal consociational power-sharing has avoided neither the problems associated with corporate consociation nor with integration, thus leading to new instability. In doing so, the chapter focuses on the sources of instability and exclusion by highlighting the absence of favorable factors for success, as well as some unfavorable outcomes of the power-sharing design. The chapter first discusses social structures of Iraqi society—politics in Iraq is based on identity and nearly all political parties form on identity bases—before turning to an evaluation of the post-2005 power-sharing arrangement and its outcomes. The chapter aims to analyze the sources of instability and exclusion that liberal consociational democracy could not avoid in Iraq. These stem from the design of the power-sharing system, the lack of factors for success and the operational outcomes of the adoption of the power-sharing arrangements.

The Social Structures of Iraqi Society

Iraq is a multi-ethnic, multi-religious and multi-linguistic country. The Constitution recognizes that Iraq is a country of multiple nationalities, religions and sects (Art.3). In terms of ethnicity, Kurds, Turkmans, Chaldeans, Assyrians and Armenians are non-Arab minorities. Arabs make up the largest ethnic group, about 75% of the population which geographically spreads across Iraqi soil. The Kurds constitute about 20% of the population, Turkmans 3% and the remaining ethnic groups 2% of the population. Minority groups are concentrated in northern Iraq with fewer groups in the central and the south of Iraq. Within each ethnic group, there is religious diversity.

Ninety-seven percent of the Iraqi population is Muslim, so we can say that it is more homogeneous in terms of religion compared to ethnicity, though there are sectarian differences. Shia Muslims, predominantly Arabs but also including Turkmans, Kurds (Faili) and others, constitute 55–60% of the population. Sunni Muslims make up approximately 40% of the population, of which Arabs constitute 24%, Kurds 15% and Turkmans 1% (DFAT, 2020: 10). The terms "Shia" and "Sunni" are mainly used to describe Shia Arabs and Sunni Arabs. Christianity, Sabaean Mandaeans, Yezidism, Zoroastrianism, Kakaeism, Shabakism, Bahai and Judaism are minority religions among the Kurds. Chaldeans, Assyrians and Armenians are Christians.

All ethnic groups have their own language and Arabic and Kurdish languages are the official languages of the state. Turkish and Syriac languages are also official languages in the administrative units in which they constitute the majority of the population (Art. 4). The 2005 Constitution guarantees the right of Iraqis to educate their children in their mother tongue.

This rich mosaic is not reflected in the administrative and territorial structures of Iraq, which is divided into 18 administrative units called governorates. Each governorate has a share of Iraq's ethnic and religious groups. Some of these ethnic and religious groups have developed their own political agendas at different times since the formation of the Iraqi state. This was reflected in the structure of opposition parties formed in the 1960s and 1970s, which later on constructed the political class that negotiated the political framework of Iraq. For example, at the time that the Shia boycotted the early stages of the political process in 1921 and formed their first religious opposition parties in the 1960s and early 1980s, both the Kurds and the Assyrians already experienced state oppression. Successive governments failed to accommodate the Kurds' political agenda, which gave rise to the "Kurdish issue" in Iraq. The Assyrians clashed with Baghdad during the 1930s, seeking self-rule. The Sunni in general had not developed any political opposition during the period between 1921 and 2003, as state authority was represented by them, and individual instances of opposition that arose were directed toward Saddam Hussein's regime and not the political process.

Iraqi society is also characterized by a strong tribal system which predates the advent of Islam. Tribal loyalties are very influential and "the largest tribal grouping in Iraqi society is the tribal federation, which can be an influential political force" (Myers, 2013: 7). The majority of Iraqis will introduce themselves according to their tribal, professional or territorial, not religious or ethnic affiliations. Some tribes have members from both Shia and Sunni religious affiliations. The large number of tribes, their different financial resources whether legal or not, and militias, make the tribes both a challenge and sometimes a tool in the hands of successive Iraqi governments. This powerful social structure did not have a role in the 2005 constitutional process, however, but at the request of the Iraqi governments and to assist in fighting terrorism, tribes played, and still play, an important role in providing security across the country.

The Iraqi rich mosaic varies in its intensity. The Arab-Kurdish and the Shia-Sunni cleavages are the most intense. However, religion, ethnicity and tribalism crosscut, subject to pressure because of their non-territorial concentration (with the exception of the Kurds). This allows for the development of blood bonds, social and economic relationships among Iraqis which enhance the formation of overarching loyalties to the state. Tolerance among Iraqis was—and still is—to a great extent society's main foundation which has resulted in moderate political and social attitudes. The evidence of this is the peaceful coexistence and absence of violence among Iraqi groups after the formation of the Iraqi state and until 2003. Before 2003, in any neighborhood, governmental institution, university or business in Baghdad or in the governorates, Iraq's different social communities lived and worked together in mutual respect. However, this foundation was shaken severely by Baath rule, the American invasion, the political class and the political process after 2003 and terrorism. The demands for integration and decentralization, as well as for protection and the articulation of differences have posed real challenges since 2003.

The Power-Sharing Arrangement in Iraq

Power-sharing provisions were embedded in the Transitional Administrative Law (TAL), the interim Constitution developed in 2004, before they were formally entrenched in the 2005 Constitution. The TAL drafting process can be considered as the initiation phase. This period, which lasted for nearly three months, was heavily influenced by the Coalition Provisional Authority (the CPA) and the two main Kurdish political parties, that controlled the drafting process. The short duration of this phase did not allow Iraqi politicians to test the power-sharing provisions nor to test each other's commitment to the new democratic process. Moving quickly to draft the permanent Constitution, the consolidation phase of power-sharing which is based on the TAL, which lasted for nearly 5 months, Shia voices started to be raised and the Sunni were brought to the process but without real influence. The constitutional process was an elite-based process coupled with pressure from the CPA to be completed within the proposed time frame of August 2005.

Power-sharing negotiations did not reach into Iraqi society, and therefore, the Iraqi people did have any influence over them. This was an expected outcome due to the heritage of the totalitarian system. Sectarian violence erupted between 2006 and 2008 and coupled with slow and complex governmental performance, this resulted in Iraqis' disappointment with the power-sharing arrangements, which in Iraq are called "Muhasasa." As a result, the formal power-sharing institutions, and the whole political process, entered a phase in which they began to wither away as represented by the Kurdistan independence referendum in 2017 and popular protests that started in 2016 and led to the government's resignation in 2020. These demonstrations were against the government's performance at both federal and local level and the political system of muhasasa.

The main aims of the consociational power-sharing arrangements have been the preservation of Iraq's territorial integrity by advancing the Kurds' aspiration for self-rule and the introduction of democracy. The constitutional approach to consociational power-sharing in Iraq has been described as liberal and temporary (Bogaards, 2019; McGarry & O'Leary, 2007), which makes it "light" (Bogaards, 2019). Moreover, Bogaards adds that consociationalism in Iraq is incomplete, informal and voluntary. Such characteristics, as the chapter explains, undermine the stability of the system mainly because of the absence of a democratic culture and poor political leadership. The four organizational principles of consociation that have been included in the Constitution are detailed below.

Grand Coalition

A grand coalition entails the participation of the representatives of all significant groups in executive decision-making (Lijphart, 2000: 3). During the transitional period, the presidency council consisted of the president of the republic and two vice-presidents. Political custom put the Kurds at the head of this council with two deputies from the Shia and Sunni communities. However, the idea of representing the three major communities was also applied to the position of prime minister and his two deputies during the same period, and it is still applied to the Speaker of the parliament and his two deputies to this day. Article 70 of the Constitution stipulates that the presidency council should exist only during the transitional period of 2005–2010. However, the political process has extended the existence of this institution until 2015.

The executive authority achieves a grand coalition through pressure from two sides. On one side, according to the Iraqi Constitution, the president should nominate the head of the largest representative bloc to form the government who would require an absolute parliamentary majority to win confidence (Art. 76, no. 1 & 4). In fact, the candidate of the largest parliamentary bloc is called the prime minister after gaining the confidence of the parliament for the nominated ministers and for the ministerial program that he/she submits. If the ministers chosen or the ministerial program do not gain the confidence of the parliament, then the nomination is withdrawn. This indicates that the authority of the prime minister in choosing the ministers is restricted by the level of political agreement inside the coalition created to form a parliamentary majority, as well as his/her own party's internal conditions.

On the other side, as political experience has shown, the president is not only committed to nominating the head of the largest parliamentary bloc but, in fact, can also reject that nominated candidate. This happened twice in 2006 when the then-president Jalal Talabani refused the candidate nominated by the United Iraqi Alliance, Ibrahim al-Jaafari, who was replaced by Nuri al-Maliki, and in 2014, when Fuad Masum refused the candidate of the National Alliance, Nuri al-Maliki, and replaced him with Haider al-Abadi. This indicates that the largest parliamentary group must nominate a candidate who is able to win the confidence of the political party, or the ethnicity, that holds the presidency position. Both pressures have led, and will lead, to political bargains over executive positions. Consequently, inclusion of the main political groups in the executive has been achieved but not on a voluntary or completely democratic basis. This contradicts the claim of the voluntary nature of consociationalism in Iraq and challenges its "light" bases argued by Bogaards, as well as the wider debate about the advantages of the liberal consociational model.

To ensure that the grand coalition is representative of the Iraqi population and all groups have a say in the decision-making and to prevent deadlock, in 2019, the Council of Ministers issued bylaw no. 2 to regulate its work. According to this bylaw, the council's quorum is complete with the attendance of the majority of its members, and decisions are taken in it by a majority of the votes of its attending members. When the votes are equal, the side that the prime minister voted for prevails (Art. 7). Moreover, decisions are taken by a majority of three-fifths of the number of attendees, including the prime minister, on issues that are strategic in nature: related to national sovereignty, including the presence of foreign forces in Iraq and how to organize their work, and the international borders of the Republic of Iraq and international relations (Al-Waqa'I Al-iraqiya, 2019). What is important in this bylaw is the right of the deputy ministers, who must be members of the council, to vote within the cabinet to achieve a quorum. The 2014 bylaw prevented the deputies from voting in the cabinet, which was an obstacle to achieving a quorum and led to deadlock.

According to Article 76 of the Iraqi Constitution, "the President of the Republic shall charge the nominee of the largest Council of Representatives bloc with the formation of the Council of Ministers within fifteen days from the date of the election of the President of the Republic." For Aboultaif, this Article is not consociational because "first, the very fact that the head of the representative bloc is automatically designated to be prime minister undermines the need for bargaining between elites in deeply divided societies to nominate a Prime Minister; second, winning a confidence vote by an absolute majority is a setback for a divided society like Iraq, because this implies that a major political group may form a coalition government with a number of insignificant groups and exclude other major ones" (Aboultaif, 2015: 6). Aboultaif might be right if we look at this article in an abstract way. However, the fact of the indirect election of the prime minister proves the dependency on political compromises. The political experience so far has demonstrated that bargains between the political elites have dominated the process of election of the heads of the three main authorities. The president cannot reach his position without a bargain that would guarantee and facilitate the election of the other heads. The two-thirds majority of the parliament that is required in order to elect the president has proven to be very difficult to achieve in Iraqi's multiparty parliamentary system where no political party alone is able to form the largest representative bloc. Therefore, compromises have and will predominate.

In addition, and in line with liberal consociationalism, the Constitution does not specify any ethnicity or sect for any position. The fear that the Shia, as the largest social group in Iraq, might form the largest representative bloc in the parliament and then a majoritarian government, has not materialized, in part because schisms among the Shia parties have resulted in cross-sectarian and cross-ethnic parliamentary coalitions with other major groups, as happened in 2010 and 2014. However, the 2018 election proved that more complicated stalemates are coming to the surface with the failure to agree on the prime minister designate within the constitutional period and the six months it took to form a government, which was forced to resign after popular demonstrations. This put the country in another stalemate and several months without a government. It took another six months of bargaining among the political parties to finally agree on Al-Kadhmi in April 2020 but not on all his chosen ministers. The same thing was repeated after the October 2021 election with the failure to agree on the president designate within the constitutional period. The winners of the 2021 elections, the Sadr bloc with 73 seats, the Sunni Sovereignty Alliance with 67 and the KDP with 31, formed a national majority government but without a consensus on the presidential candidate. When the KDP nominated Hoshyar Zebari, without an agreement with its Kurdish rival, the PUK, Sadr expressed his concerns. Usually, the Kurdish bloc in the parliament reach a consensus on the presidential candidate, however, the fierce rivalry and the superiority of the KDP in the election prevented this. Moreover, the concerns might link to the fact that Zebari was impeached from his position as a finance minister in 2016. Accordingly, the Federal Supreme Court has banned his nomination. With the insistence of the KDP on Zebari, Sadrist deputies boycotted the parliamentary presidential session in February 2022 which technically ended the national majority government. This was followed by two failed parliamentary electoral sessions. It took the political groups one year to elect Abdul Latif Rashid as the new president in October 2022; this marked the longest period without a government after an election.

Veto Rights

The minority veto offers a guarantee of political protection as the participation in the grand coalition offers no absolute and foolproof protection of a group's vital interests (Lijphart, 1977: 36–37). The application of veto rights in Iraq is conditional and formal. According to the Constitution, a veto right is given to the majority of the population in three governorates which can block a constitutional amendment. The article states that "the referendum on the amended articles shall be successful if approved by the majority of the voters, and if not rejected by two-thirds of the voters in three or more governorates" (Art.142). Bogaards states that mutual veto rights were limited to the period of Constitution adoption and the first term of the parliament from 2006 to 2010, and weakened thereafter (Bogaards, 2019). Aboultaif argues that the mutual veto is absent from both the Constitution and from political processes. He bases his opinion on the constitutional process and the referendum on the permanent Constitution in 2005 that were distinguished by the Sunnis' ineffective participation and the fact that they almost managed to block the adoption of the Constitution (Aboultaif, 2015: 8–10). The fact that a veto right is limited and conditional does not mean it is absent or weakened because, as Schneckener explains, "the right to veto could either apply unrestrictedly to all decisions (absolute veto), it could be conditional and just refer to some basic laws or it could just have a delaying effect in order to renegotiate disputed issues" (Schneckener, 2000: 5).

The Constitution's drafters might have designed the veto in this way so it can be a constructive rather than a destructive tool, a tool that must not apply to every political issue otherwise blockage would dominate the political scene, a tool that would promote the Sunni's participation in the political process and protect the Kurds' constitutional rights. However, the political reality so far proves that amending the Constitution is a complex matter. This is because the controversial articles in the Constitution are related to the essence of the power-sharing system, which the Kurds do not want to amend. Moreover, the design of veto indicates that the major social group, the Shia, can access it on equal terms to the Kurds and Sunnis, as they form the majority in more than three governorates. Therefore, political bargains among the politicians of the three groups are a must. Furthermore, minority groups other than Kurds and Sunnis, such as the Turkmans and Chaldeans, would not be able to access it as they do not form the majority of voters in three governorates. Therefore, this tool promotes a sense of security among the Kurdish politicians only, and not among all politicians as Lijphart predicted (Lijphart, 1977, 37). Political bargains are the mechanism to determine and protect groups' rights in the Iraqi political process.

Proportional Representation

Lijphart defines proportionality as "a general principle of consociational democracy that applies not only to the electoral system but also to the composition of the public service and to the allocation of public funds" (1977: 38; 2000: 15). In Iraq, and despite the absence of any explicit constitutional articles that refer to it, proportional representation is applied through the composition of the public services, the electoral system and the allocation of public funds.

Proportional representation is informal as reflected in the agreement on the composition of the heads of the main authorities. The political custom of government formation since 2005 has allocated the presidency to the Kurds, the prime minister's position to the Shia and the Speaker of the parliament to the Sunni. The positions of minister of defense and minister of internal affairs also adhere to this political custom. The former is Sunni and the latter is Shia. Proportional representation is also reflected in the composition of the public services informally and is extended to the appointment of senior public servants and the heads of independent commissions.

Article 49 of the Constitution stipulates that all components of the Iraqi people are to be represented in the parliament. To guarantee this, seats are reserved in this institution for the minorities. Previous electoral systems in Iraq were all based on proportional representation. The electoral laws of 2005, 2010, 2014, and 2018, respectively, produced a system of proportional representation in which seats were reserved for minorities in the parliament according to their proportion of the population. The electoral Law no. 9 of 2020 states that parliament consists of 329 seats, and 9 seats are reserved for religious minorities (5 for Christians, 1 for Yazidis, 1 for Faili Kurds, 1 for Shabak and 1 for Sabeans) while a 25% women's quota is assured (Articles 13 & 16). The new law is based on multiple electoral districts, 83 electoral districts, that reflect the number of seats allocated to women in the parliament (Al-waqa'i al-iraqiya). For example, the capital Baghdad, which has 71 seats in the parliament, including 17 seats reserved for women, will turn into 17 electoral districts (Sattar, 2020). It is also based on the single non-transferable vote system to address calls from the protestors to overhaul the sectarian divisions of power (Wali, 2020). This gave independent candidates the chance to win seats away from the dominant political parties in the 2021 election. Both Imtidad Movement and Ishraqit Kanon party, which represent the youth demonstrations, won 15 seats in the Parliament, demonstrating the success of these institutional provisions.

The Constitution also ensures the proportional distribution of revenues by providing a general framework of revenue-sharing. Article 111 states that "oil and gas are owned by all the people of Iraq" and Article 112 provides that the federal government along with the producing governorates and regional government will take over the management of the oil extracted from the present fields and distribute its revenue in a fair manner in proportion to the population distribution in all parts of the country. This is supposed to be organized by a law, though it has not been enacted. This is because of the conflict between Baghdad and Kurdistan over the interpretation of these articles which could "make a proportional distribution of oil and gas revenues increasingly voluntary over time" (Bogaards, 2019). Allocations to governorates are determined according to population size and through three sources: the petrodollar, regional development program and Kurdistan transfers. Conflict over oil and gas revenue-sharing resulted in a halt to the payment of Kurdistan's share of the annual budget between 2014 and 2021. In January 2023, the Federal Supreme Court ruled that the Kurdistan oil and gas law is unconstitutional and consequently the monthly remittances to the Region from the federal government are illegal.

The application of proportional representation through the above-mentioned approaches is supposed to enhance inclusiveness and trust among the Iraqi groups, necessary for building national consensus. However, it has only fueled sectarianism.

Territorial Autonomy

The majority of the Kurds are territorially concentrated in the north of Iraq and have long striven for self-rule. They were able to gain some measure of territorial autonomy through the creation of the Kurdistan Region and the Kurdistan Regional Government. Kurdistan is the only federal region in Iraq. It is founded upon an unbalanced vertical relationship with the federal government and an unbalanced horizontal relationship with the governorates. According to the Constitution, Iraq is a federal republic consisting of regions, governorates and local administrations (Art.116), and federal regions have the right to exercise executive, legislative and judicial authority in accordance with regional constitutions (Art. 121). Only a few exclusive powers of the federal government and only a few shared powers with regions are listed in the Constitution; all other powers are not stipulated as exclusive or shared with the authorities of the sub-national units of the regions or governorates (Art.109–115). Kurdistan enjoys legislative superiority over federal legislation. The Constitution provides for revenue-sharing, however, this subject, as explained earlier, has proven to be very complex due to the lack of agreement on the mechanism of how to organize it.

The complex asymmetrical relationship between Kurdistan and the federal government and the lack of an effective relationship between Kurdistan and the governorates incentivizes Kurdistan to strengthen its autonomy and to challenge the federal government in asserting its interests.

Evaluating the Power-Sharing Arrangement in Iraq

As the explanation of the political process has indicated so far, the current power-sharing arrangement provides a weak functioning of the governmental system. Some scholars explain the weakness of the arrangement by linking poor performance to absences and limitations in the four sections of formal power-sharing arrangements (e.g., Aboultaif, 2015; Bogaards, 2019). Others believe that weak adoptability has given rise to weak functionality, (e.g., McEvoy & Aboultaif, 2022). For McEvoy and Aboultaif, adoptability is linked to "the extent to which the groups support the establishment of a power-sharing polity." This support was unforthcoming by the Sunnis after 2003, meaning that not all groups were committed to sharing power. I would argue that neither approach (weak implementation of power-sharing provisions nor lack of support for power-sharing from all groups) can provide a complete and accurate explanation of the weak functionality of the power-sharing arrangement. This is because, as explained earlier, officially all the four elements of a consociational democracy are entrenched in the design of the power-sharing arrangements but the degree of implementation of each element varies depending on how crucial it is for each stage of the evolution of the political system. As for adoptability, the Sunnis' rejection of the political process and their communal veto in the 2005 constitutional referendum was temporary as they participated in the first permanent government at the end of 2005. Moreover, over 60% of the Sunnis population in their main governorates participated in the 2010 general election. It would be inaccurate to blame the system's weak functionality on their initial rejection.

Therefore, a new approach based on highlighting the sources of instability and exclusion, that liberal consociational democracy aims to avoid, would be more comprehensive. Some of these sources are the operational outcome of the power-sharing arrangements, others exist due to the lack of certain favorable factors for success and problems in the design of the arrangements. I have identified six main sources.

1. The power-sharing system is based on a mistaken assumption developed by Iraqi opposition politicians and the Americans that Iraqi society is sharply divided and there is a need to manage intergroup conflict, therefore there is a need to construct democratic institutions to end violence and build political and social contracts. However, the Iraqi people were not in conflict, the politicians were. The Iraqis did not need a social contract, although the politicians did. This is evidenced by the popular protests that took place between 2016 and 2019. Iraqis from different religious and ethnic backgrounds took part in these protests against the corrupt political class and the entire political process.

   The differences among politicians and their race to power for the sake of narrow personal interests, with Sunni initial rejection of the political process and the Americans' pressure resulted in a very fluid political contract, or "elite pact" as Bell calls it (Bell, 2018). The fluid political contract, represented by the very loose federal order and power-sharing arrangements, embodies a consensus among elites and desire for power covered up by ethnic and sectarian agendas. The Kurdish leaders' desire for self-rule has been managed in a democratic way that maintained Iraq's territorial identity. The Shia leaders' fear of more Sunni rule that would exclude them from power also pushed them toward accepting the loose federal power-sharing arrangements.

   The Iraqi governing elites have not used the national identity shared among the majority of Iraqis to consolidate democracy through a power-sharing approach. National shared identity, according to Roeder and Rothchild, is one of two conditions essential to the success of power-sharing (Roeder & Rothchild, 2005: 323). They are not seeking national stability, not cooperating to achieve a successful political process, the necessary factor, according to Lijphart, to achieve successful power-sharing. Even in governmental coalitions, elites have not been encouraged to work across their parties' narrow interests. Governmental coalitions after 2003 have been distinguished by a transfer of elites' conflicts and differences and parties' practices to national and local institutions which undermines their functionality. Political blackmail, stagnant governance and militia threats are features of the Iraqi political process. Political elites' conflicts were fueled by the power-sharing arrangements. The political situation deteriorated and the whole political process was on the verge of collapse during the popular protests in 2019 against the federal and local governments, and the political parties behind them.

2. The multiparty system in Iraq poses a challenge to the political process. As Friedrich explains, the organizational structures of the political parties tend to correspond to the governmental setup (Friedrich, 1968: 47). So the very loose multi-ethnic, multi-religious and multi-linguistic federal power-sharing system results and contributes to the formation of an extreme multiparty system—characterized by 167 parties that stood in the 2021 election—that creates a chaotic political scene which is not devoid of violence and counterviolence. No single social group in Iraq is represented by a single political party but by several parties so that the major ones are nearly equal in size and ideologically compatible. Moreover, no single major political party is represented by supporters from all segments of the Iraqi population but rather nearly all the parties are homogeneous and correspond very closely to sectarian and ethnic divisions.

While the large number of political parties might be a good sign of political pluralism within each group, practically it prevents durable government and intensifies conflicts. It complicates efforts to reach compromises. The extremely large number of political parties results in the need to form party alliances as no party is able to build a majority to form a cabinet. This coincides with McGarry and O'Leary's (2007) analysis of liberal consociation, however, the Iraqi political process has proved that both party alliances and governmental coalitions are unstable. Due to party competition for power, alliances tend to be temporary and shifting, and many of the political parties, mainly the small ones, end up being powerless and pragmatic with no clear ideology and political vision. Even when allied parties are part of the governmental coalition, they do not function as one party, or as one government with one governmental program. They function independently and follow instructions from their party heads rather than from the head of the government. Lijphart was aware of that and states that "extreme multiparty systems are conducive to governmental deadlock and paralysis" and that "a coalition cabinet tends to be less durable than one-party cabinets" (Lijphart, 1977: 63; 1999: 73).

3. Lijphart argues that proportional representation with closed lists can encourage the formation and maintenance of strong and cohesive political parties (Lijphart, 2004: 101). McGarry and O'Leary state, despite their recommendation of single transferable vote (STV) instead of list-PR in order to limit the proliferation of micro-parties (2006a: 269), that proportional representation "is far more likely to facilitate the election of non-sectarian (secular) political parties in Iraq" (2007: 693). Neither of these things have been achieved in Iraq and proportional representation is associated with many problems in the country. Several parties and governmental coalitions went through internal schism because of disputes over the distribution of governmental posts rather than any ideological motives or differences of opinion on foreign and domestic policy (Al-Jaffal, 2021). During the 2018 elections, the Dawa party formed two electoral blocs: the State of Law Coalition and Victory Alliance led by two previous prime ministers. Moreover, the split in the Patriotic Union of Kurdistan resulted in the formation of the Change Movement and the Alliance for Democracy and Justice (Yahia, 2018). In the 2021 election, the Iraqi High Commission for Elections announced that 21 coalitions participated in the election and out of 167 parties, 58 were in a coalition. The large number of coalitions complicates the possibility of finding a compromise solution in forming a government. It also undermines the chances of effective cooperation in the parliament because there is no cohesion inside a coalition and among the parties.

Furthermore, all the political parties that participated in government were identified as either religious or ethnic parties: Shia, Sunni or Kurd. Secular and non-ethnic parties failed to compete with the political Islamic and ethnic parties, thereby demonstrating that proportional representation had not facilitated their election. Sectarianism and ethnicity are the agendas that political parties are using to win power.

The list-proportional representation that applied, with a closed list in 2005, open list in 2010 and Sainte-Laguë 1.6 and Sainte-Laguë 1.9 in 2014 and 2018, led to disappointment among the population at the outcomes of the democratic process and the power-sharing. The delay between the formation of government and the declaration of election results, the quality of candidates of the parties that entered the parliament and the way that political coalitions formed after the declaration of the electoral results with no input from the voters, all contributed to popular alienation from the political process represented by a decline in turnout at elections—about 40% in the 2021 election—and popular protests in different Iraqi governorates including the ones in Kurdistan, from 2016 onwards. Younis argues "the electoral quagmire is an almost inevitable result of Iraq's system of proportional representation combined with the failure of the Constitution to enable effective coalition building" (Younis, 2011: 14).

The proportional representation arrangements, whether formal or informal, are also responsible for the rise of corruption in Iraq. Because of the lack of cohesion among the parties participating in the cabinet and the failure of the arrangements to create an overarching loyalty among the political elites to facilitate cooperation, parties have penetrated governmental ministries and special grades positions as a way to ensure power and channel resources to themselves. Elites are employing relatives and party members in these positions which enables the parties to build patronage networks and perpetrate contracts' fraud. The number of those positions held by a party depends on the party winning seats in the election. Consequently, the state's institutions are functioning as economic commissions of the parties (Nusayif, 2021). In other words, the Iraqi political system is functioning as an elite pact and the power-sharing arrangements—designed to ensure communal stability—are instead sustaining that pact (Dodge & Mansour, 2021).

Because of the incomplete proportional representation, the process of sharing revenue among the ministries, governorates and the Kurdistan is again a complex issue in a politically fragmented cabinet and parliament. The mechanism of revenue-sharing is decided annually through the country's general budget law and thus subject to yearly modifications and approval by the parliament. According to the Law of Financial Administration, the government should send the budget law in October to the parliament, which should approve it by December so that it can be implemented by January. This has never been possible due to political fragmentation, the conflict between the federal government and Kurdistan over oil and gas revenues caused by ambiguous and conflictual constitutional articles and the failure to enact the law on oil and gas. It was only in March 2021 that an agreement was reached between Baghdad and Kurdistan. However, practical obstacles are still threatening the implementation of the agreement (Abd-Al-Latif, 2021).

On the other hand, proportional representation and the idea of preserving seats in the legislature have not effectively succeeded in protecting minority rights because, according to Reilly, "there is a difference between representation and power: a minority can be fairly represented in a legislature but completely shut out of political power in government" (Reilly, 2011: 290). The Constitution confirms the ratio of one seat per 100,000 members of the Iraqi population, representing the entire population and ensuring the minority quota. However, the quota system is paralyzed in Iraq. This is because the approach used to determine the quota number is unknown. No census has been undertaken in Iraq to determine the size of population and therefore the quotas. Moreover, there are minorities that are not included in the quota system such as the Kakai, the Bahia and the Zaradishty and consequently they are not represented in the parliament. The Kakai minority was promised a seat in the provincial council of the yet unformed Halabja governorate and deprived of the opportunity to be represented in the federal institutions (Aziz, 2020). Because of the quotas, minority groups have been suffering from political exploitation and dominance by the big parties which has weakened their ability to represent the interests of their particular group. As a consequence, the quota system creates a negative attitude among minorities toward participation in the political process. This is enhanced by the schisms among the minority parties. An example of this is the Yazidi religious group. After the death of its leader, the Yazidi group split into four groups each with its own leader and its own political group. This problem is clear in Kurdistan as well. The number of seats given to ethno-religious minorities is 11 out of a total of 111 seats, five for the Turkmans, five for the Christians and one for the Armenians. According to Abdullah and Hama, "Because the electoral law of Kurdistan considers the region as a single constituency for the reserved seats, they are not specifically allocated to any of the region's governorates. This has facilitated their exploitation by the dominant ruling party in order to advance the latter's own political agenda" (Hama & Abdullah, 2020: 383).

The inclusive decision-making process has also left minority groups out of the influential ministries and with little influence on government policy and its outcomes. According to the Etihad Bayt al-Nahrain party, one of the parties that represent Christians: "The rights of the minorities are not taken into consideration at all; the majority decides on behalf of us, they impose decisions on the minorities" (Aziz, 2020).

4. According to Lijphart, it is beneficial for the consociational arrangement to be based on some kind of balance of power among the segments of a plural society in order to avoid the dominance of the majority group (Lijphart, 1977: 55). In Iraq this balance does not exist. The Shia are always going to be the major group, making up about 55–60% of the population. Therefore, the incentives for competition will always exist among the Shia leaders, and the incentives for coalition will always exist among the Sunni and Kurd leaders. The existence of these two kinds of incentive would require a very specific design of the power-sharing arrangements in order to create some kind of balance among the three groups. This explains why some of the Iraqi power-sharing arrangements and constitutional articles are still ambiguous and incomplete. Power-sharing in practice was challenging for Iraqi elites, if not impossible to properly implement. The power-sharing arrangements so far are not facilitating social balance and have consequently become a source of instability.

5. The role of external forces has complicated the chances of a smooth adoption and functioning of the power-sharing system in Iraq. O'Leary and McGarry have highlighted that classic consociational theory has failed to address the benign role of external powers and the possibility of shallow internal foundations (McGarry & O'Leary, 2006b: 48, 53). As regards the adoption of the power-sharing

system, the external role was not a benign one in Iraq. The Americans' involvement in the aftermath of the 2003 political process triggered a legitimacy issue among the Sunni and some Shia groups, such as the Sadr group, which provoked insurgencies. The outcome of the Americans' pressure on the Kurds to stay within a unified Iraq was a very loose federal system with a superior role for the region. According to Roeder and Rothchild (2005: 48), external forces usually attempt to create a balance among the different contending groups but the Americans did not do that. The result was the initial Sunni rejection of the political and constitutional processes because their role in them was limited. The highest Shia religious authority, represented by Al-Sistani, insisted that the permanent Constitution be drafted by Iraqis alone, in rejection of a role for an external force in drafting the interim Constitution. However, the Americans' role continued to be influential and they pressured politicians to submit the draft of the permanent Constitution within a specified time frame even with unfinished and ambiguous constitutional articles.

As regards the functioning of the power-sharing system, the external role was not effective either. The Americans' role also destabilized the state's authority to undertake its responsibilities toward its population. The disbanding of the Iraqi army and security forces weakened the state's ability to impose security and order, especially considering the existence of the terror threat. With de-Baathification, the state's institutions lost experienced staff which would have benefited the functioning of the new system. The same can be said regarding the Iranian role in supporting Shia militias, penetrating security institutions and influencing political decisions. The regional environment in general was not supportive of the political changes in Iraq.

6. The design of some power-sharing institutions is not conducive to effective cooperation and trust-building among elites because it is complex. For complex power-sharing institutions to function, they would require a commitment to a democratic culture by the main actors on the one hand, and well-functioning institutions on the other. Further, political elite commitment and the willingness to engage with these institutions, as well as allow them to adapt and evolve over time, are also important. All are lacking in Iraq. The executive authority is a hybrid presidential-parliamentary one. A grand coalition in the executive has been achieved but at the

expense of time and cooperation. It has been complex and weakened the role of the prime minister, who is constitutionally responsible for general policy and should enjoy the full authority to direct the council of ministers to undertake its responsibilities. While the proportional representation system requires coalitions, these have been difficult to form. As different political parties compete for power and influence, the government acts less coherently and parties are more oriented toward their own group than toward the common good. The interplay of the President and the Prime Minister, as well as the limited powers that the prime minister enjoys due to consociational restraints, further weaken central institutions. For example, according to the Constitution, the prime minister is the commander-in-chief of the armed forces. However, Al-Abbadi, and even Al-Kadhmi, struggled to control the Popular Mobilization Forces (PMF), due to its links with political parties and their militias, and was forced to be recognized as a part of state security forces. Al-Kadhmi early steps to control political parties' militias resulted in a direct threat to his life. Moreover, the different political backgrounds of the ministers are making them representatives of the interests of their political parties, not of the interest of the state as a whole. Ministers thereby have not been free to act. It has happened that some have withdrawn from the government, based on decisions by the party heads. A previous MP said that the political groups became enemies of each other because of their opposing conflicted interests (Saifuddin, 2020). Furthermore, the prime minister's authority to dismiss a minister is conditional on the parliament's approval (Art. 78) which means that the prime minister's position will always be manipulated by political compromises and the person who occupies this position will always lack the full authority to impose decisions. In sum, this translates into flawed governance and flawed institutions, and further distorts interpretations of the Constitution.

The other institutional design that is not conducive to cooperation is the imbalance between self-rule and shared-rule. The imbalanced vertical and horizontal relationship between Kurdistan and the federal government and the governorates contributes to a suspicious and competitive relationship. The superiority of Kurdistan has motivated the region to challenge the federal government, such as on the issue of sharing revenues. Under this challenge, the federal government has made concessions but has also sometimes pushed back. Controlling centrifugal and centripetal incentives has become a difficult issue in Iraq. This fits with Rothchild and Roeder's view that power-sharing institutions empower leaders of ethnic groups with means to challenge the power-sharing agreement (2005: 37). Similarly, Schneckener states that "the more competencies are delegated to self-governing bodies, the more important co-operation between the two levels becomes in order to prevent centrifugal and destabilising tendencies" and "self-governing institutions may ease tensions... But on the other hand, they need to be oriented towards the 'common good' in order not to be counter-productive as regards power-sharing" (Schneckener, 2000: 22, 25).

CONCLUSION

The Iraqi experience of power-sharing indicates that power-sharing theory has its limitations. These limitations, in addition to the particular situation that prevailed during the design of the Constitution in Iraq, have resulted in a dysfunctional power-sharing system. This chapter has depicted the sources of instability and exclusion that liberal consociational power-sharing arrangements have failed to avoid in Iraq. The outcome of applying these arrangements is a disproportion between liberal consociational power-sharing in theory and the predicted consequences of stability and inclusion and liberal consociational power-sharing in practice, that is, between normative assumptions and political practice. Liberal power-sharing systems, like other democratic systems, have their own limitations. These sources of instability and exclusion, with their different origins, are responsible for the complicated functionality of the power-sharing arrangements. These sources are blocking the development of the political process and disrupting the work of the governmental institutions and the enactment of laws.

Stability in Iraq is not about liberal consociation, corporate consociation or integration. It is not about special constitutional and institutional structures, and it is not about preventing conflict among social groups that are already distinguished by their peaceful coexistence. It is about how to create a functioning reality without compromising the state's national interest and the dignity of Iraqi people. The reality in Iraq is complicated because it is not only dependent on a real political will that would make concessions, negotiate, respect the rules and outcomes of

282   F. SHAKIR

the democratic political process and strive to serve Iraqis but also on containing regional-international conflict on Iraqi soil. Therefore, Iraq is a very special political case and the prospects of its power-sharing system functioning in the near future with any sort of consistency or reliability are weak.

REFERENCES

Abd-Al-Latif, W. (2021, September 5). *Iraqyyia Satellite Channel* [Interview].

Aboultaif, E. (2015). *The Limitations of the Consociational Arrangements in Iraq* (Ethnopolitics Papers, No. 38). https://www.psa.ac.uk/psa-communities/spe cialist-groups/ethnopolitics/blog

Al-iraqiya, A.-W. (2019). s.l. https://www.moj.gov.iq/upload/images/766740_4533.pdf

Al-iraqiya, A.-W. (2020). *Ministry of Justice: Iraqi Gazette, no 4603*, s.I. https://moj.gov.iq/upload/pdf/4603.pdf

Al-Jaffal, O. (2021). Iraq's New Electoral Law: Old Powers Adapting to Change. *Arab Reform Initiative*. https://www.arab-reform.net/publication/iraq-electi ons/

Australia Department of Foreign Affairs and Trade. (2020). *DFAT Country Information Report Iraq*. https://www.dfat.gov.au/sites/default/files/cou ntry-information-report-iraq.pdf

Aziz, A. (2020). Religious and Ethnic Minorities Quota Seats Between Fragmentations and Rivalries of Dominant Political Parties. *Kirkuk Now*. https://kir kuknow.com/en/news/62182

Bell, C. (2018). *Political Power-Sharing and Inclusion: Peace and Transition Processes*. Political Settlements Research Project. https://www.politicalsettle ments.org/wp-content/uploads/2018/07/2018_Bell_PA-X-Political-Power-Sharing-Report.pdf

Bogaards, M. (2019). Iraq's Constitution of 2005: The Case Against Consociationalism 'Light.' *Ethnopolitics, 20*(2), 186–202.

Iraq's Constitution of 2005. https://www.constituteproject.org/constitution/Iraq_2005.pdf?lang=en

Dodge, T., & Mansour, R. (2021). *Politically Sanctioned Corruption and Barriers to Reform in Iraq*. https://www.chathamhouse.org/2021/06/politically-san ctioned-corruption-and-barriers-reform-iraq/01-introduction

Friedrich, C. J. (1968). *Trends of Federalism in Theory and Practice*. Frederick A. Praeger. Inc.

Hama, H. H., & Abdullah, F. H. (2020). Minority Representation and Reserved Legislative Seats in Iraqi Kurdistan. *Contemporary Review of the Middle East, 7*(4), 381–402.

Lijphart, A. (1977). *Democracy in Plural Societies: A Comparative Exploration.* Yale University Press.

Lijphart, A. (1999). *Patterns of Democracy.* Yale University Press.

Lijphart, A. (2000). *Power-Sharing and Group Autonomy in the 1990s and 21st Century.* http://fopre.pbworks.com/f/Lijphart_Power,+Sharing.pdf. University of California.

Lijphart, A. (2004). Constitutional Design for Divided Societies. *Journal of Democracy, 15*(2), 96–109.

McEvoy, J., & Aboultaif, E. W. (2022). Power-Sharing Challenges: From Weak Adoptability to Dysfunction in Iraq. *Ethnopolitics, 21*(3), 238–257.

McGarry, J., & O'Leary, B. (2006a). Consociational Theory, Northern Ireland's Conflict, and its Agreement 2. What Critics of Consociation Can Learn from Northern Ireland. *Government and Opposition, 41*(2), 244–277.

McGarry, J., & O'Leary, B. (2006b). Consociational Theory, Northern Ireland's Conflict, and its Agreement. Part 1: What Consociationalists Can Learn from Northern Ireland. *Government and Opposition, 41*(1), 43–63.

McGarry, J., & O'Leary, B. (2007). Iraq's Constitution of 2005: Liberal Consociation as Political Prescription. *International Journal of Constitutional Law, 5*(4), 670–698.

Myers, C. N. (2013). Tribalism and Democratic Transition in Libya: Lessons from Iraq. *Global Tides, 7*(5). http://digitalcommons.pepperdine.edu/globaltides/vol7/iss1/5

Nusayif, A., & Al-Sharqiya Satellite Channel. (2021). *MP* [Interview] (15 September Al-Sharqiya Satellite Channel).

Roeder, P. G., & Rothchild, D. (2005). Conclusion: Nation-State Stewardship and the Alternatives to Power Sharing. In P. G. Roeder & D. Rothchild (Eds.), *Sustainable Peace: Power and Democracy After Civil Wars* (pp. 319–346). Cornell University Press.

Reilly, B. (2011). Centripetalism. In K. Cordell & S. Wolff (Eds.), *Routledge Handbook of Ethnic Conflict* (pp. 288–299). Routledge.

Saifuddin, A. (2020). Iraq: Efforts to Choose a New Prime Minister Failed, Which Puts Forward Several Scenarios Including Internationalization. *Alaraby.* https://www.alaraby.co.uk/

Sattar, O. (2020). Iraqi Parliament Votes on Final Version of Electoral Law. *Al-Monitor.* https://www.al-monitor.com/originals/2020/11/iraq-elections-law-parliament.html#ixzz6rAav2tm

Schneckener, U. (2000). *Making Power-Sharing Work: Lessons from Successes and Failures in Ethnic Conflict Regulation.* Institut für Interkulturelle und Internationale Studien (InIIS).

Wali, Z. Z. (2020, October 24). Iraq's New Electoral Law Allocates Constituencies Based on Women in Parliament. *Rudaw.* https://www.rudaw.net/english/middleeast/iraq/241020205

Yahia, A.-A.-G. A. (2018). Splits in the Iraqi Parties: Their Causes, Consequence and Fate. *Middle East Online*. https://middle-east-online.com

Younis, N. (2011). Set Up to Fail: Consociational Political Structures in Post-war Iraq, 2003–2010. *Contemporary Arab Affairs, 4*(1), 1–18.

CHAPTER 13

"The Unloved Child Matures": Power-Sharing in Burundi

Réginas Ndayiragije and Alexandre Wadih Raffoul

RUMORS

"In Burundi, since the 2015 crisis, everything begins with a rumor," writes Armel-Gilbert Bukenyeneza (2021: 132).[1] On 9 June 2020, the rumor is so far remote from the ordinary as to sound unthinkable: Pierre Nkurunziza is dead.

More than a President of the Republic, the man had come to incarnate the post-colonial history of Burundi. Nkurunziza was born in 1964, two

[1] Translated from French by the authors.

Authors listed in alphabetical order.

R. Ndayiragije (✉)
Institute of Development Policy, University of Antwerp, Antwerp, Belgium
e-mail: reginas.ndayiragije@uantwerpen.be

A. W. Raffoul
Uppsala University, Uppsala, Sweden
e-mail: alexandre.raffoul@pcr.uu.se

© The Author(s), under exclusive license to Springer Nature
Switzerland AG 2024
E. Wassim Aboultaif et al. (eds.), *Power-Sharing in the Global South*,
Federalism and Internal Conflicts,
https://doi.org/10.1007/978-3-031-45721-0_13

285

years after the independence of Burundi. He grew up in a country where power became increasingly monopolized by a small elite of Tutsi officers from the province of Bururi—united in the political party Uprona[2]—and where the Hutu majority was progressively marginalized (Ndikumana, 2005; Ngaruko & Nkurunziza, 2000). In 1972, Nkurunziza lost his father—Eustache Mbasha, a Uprona-affiliated MP—in Burundi's most violent purge of Hutu intellectuals and military. Similar episodes of ethnic violence shook the country in 1965, 1969, 1988, and 1991, reaching the intensity of a civil war in 1993 (Lemarchand, 1996). Nkurunziza became a professor of gymnastics at the *Université du Burundi* (BBC, 2005), where he was almost assassinated in 1995. He fled to the bush. There, he joined one of the Hutu rebel groups that had emerged to confront the government, the CNDD, which would later become CNDD-FDD[3] (Chrétien & Dupaquier, 2007).

On 28 August 2000, Burundian negotiators signed the Arusha Peace and Reconciliation Agreement (APRA). The accord used power-sharing to address the pre-war issues of political monopolization of power and ethnic marginalization (Vandeginste, 2015b). But the main rebel groups—the CNDD-FDD and the Palipehutu-FNL[4]—rejected the agreement. Violence continued. A year later, Nkurunziza became leader of the CNDD-FDD. This was his stepping stone to power. After negotiating a ceasefire agreement with the Government, he joined the transitional institutions in 2003. In 2005, the first post-conflict elections were won overwhelmingly by the CNDD-FDD. Nkurunziza was elected to the highest office. Fifteen years later, he was on the verge of stepping down when the rumors of his death were confirmed.

The ambiguities surrounding Pierre Nkurunziza's character and legacy reflect the conflicting assessments of the performance of power-sharing in Burundi. Born from a mixed marriage, Nkurunziza was celebrated by some for embodying the transition away from ethnic politics in Burundi. For others, he nevertheless remained an autocrat and a hardliner, who progressively consolidated the total control of power in the hands of the

---

[2] Union for National Progress.

[3] National Council for the Defense of Democracy—Forces for the Defense of Democracy.

[4] National Liberation Forces.

CNDD-FDD (Guichaoua, 2020). Similarly, the APRA is widely credited for succeeding to bring forth an unprecedented de-politicization of ethnicity, while failing to promote the consolidation of democracy and ending political violence in Burundi (Reyntjens, 2016).

To make sense of these conflicting assessments, this chapter argues that the evolution of power-sharing in Burundi cannot be fully comprehended if we focus exclusively on political institutions. Rather, a full account must consider *both* institutional design and the agency of the political actors sharing power, including the dynamic nature of the balance of power among political actors.

By definition, power-sharing implies joint decision-making between former enemies (McGarry & O'Leary, 2006: 63). As Byrne observes, "'power-sharing' is not called power-*shared*, or power-*divided*. (...) Sharing is a reciprocal practice that takes place through attentive dialogue" (2020: 65–66). Power-sharing can thus be understood as a process where conflict parties need to continually negotiate and find agreements on policy issues in order for the institutions to function. Effective power-sharing results from the parties' ability to successfully negotiate compromises over their disagreements in order to adopt, adapt, and operate power-sharing arrangements (Raffoul, 2019). Conversely, the shifting balance of power between adversaries can lead to institutional blockages, as powerful actors might seek to achieve a total control of power rather than continuing sharing power (Spears, 2002).

This chapter traces the history of elite controversies surrounding power-sharing through five periods, covering the adoption, functioning, and possible end of power-sharing in Burundi. It starts by showing that the *adoption* of power-sharing required a long negotiation process. In a first period (1988–1998), the Burundian elite progressively accepted the idea of sharing power. In a second period (1998–2005), the details of the power-sharing institutions were negotiated, formalized in the Arusha agreement, and inscribed in a constitution.

The chapter then turns toward the *functioning* of Burundian power-sharing. The complex institutional framework created by the 2005 constitution included both power-sharing between ethnic categories and between political parties (Vandeginste, 2015b). The varying ability of conflict parties to find agreement about these two types of power-sharing resulted in the uneven functioning of these institutions. In a third period (2005–2006), political leaders could easily accommodate ethnic power-sharing by integrating candidates from multiple ethnic backgrounds on their electoral lists, which has led to a rapid de-politicization of ethnicity in post-war Burundi. However, stark inter-elite disagreements regarding power-sharing between political parties appeared in the fourth period (2007–2015) and led to the progressive erosion of party-based power-sharing.

Finally, the chapter discusses the *adaptability* and possible *endability* of power-sharing in the fifth period (2015–2021), focusing on the 2018 revision of the Burundian Constitution. Pushed single-handedly by an all-powerful CNDD-FDD, this new constitution eliminated most party-based power-sharing and weakened ethnic power-sharing. This partial dismantlement of the Arusha framework suggests that adaptability or endability are not always positive developments, but can threaten the achievements of post-conflict power-sharing.

THE LONG ROAD TO ARUSHA (1988–1998)

When Burundian negotiators arrived in Arusha to engage in peace talks, the centrality that power-sharing would occupy in any potential agreement was clear to everyone. Indeed, the principle of sharing power had progressively become accepted—not without contestation—throughout a long history of experimentation with power-sharing (Vandeginste, 2009).

Burundi's first encounter with power-sharing took place in the context of the political opening of the early 1990s. Following an ethnic massacre in 1988, the single-party Uprona was under international pressure to open the political space (Vandeginste, 2009: 66). Toward the end of 1988, President Pierre Buyoya formed a first power-sharing government. Adrien Sibomana, a Hutu, was appointed as Prime Minister, and half of the ministerial portfolios were attributed to Hutus (Reyntjens, 1994: 68–76). While Buyoya's parity government did not include vocal Hutu activists from the diaspora in Europe or refugees in Rwanda, this move was remarkable as it marked the first attempt to significantly integrate Hutus in government as well as an important step toward the explicit recognition of ethnic identity's salience in Burundian politics.

On 9 March 1992, a new Constitution, which consecrated the transition to multi-party democracy, was adopted. This constitution stands out by its insistence on "national unity"—stressing the importance of accounting for "all components" of the Burundian population in the leadership of state institutions and political parties (Reyntjens, 1993: 565;

1994: 78–79). In addition, article 57 forbids parties' identification to any region, religion, ethnicity, or sex. This emphasis responded to a growing apprehension among the ruling Tutsi minority (14%). Largely outnumbered by Hutus (85%), they feared that elections would permanently exclude them from power. The recognition of ethnicity served as an attempt to ensure their continued representation in power.

These pre-sentiments were confirmed by the 1993 elections. The Hutu-dominated Frodebu[5] won by a landslide. To reassure Tutsis, the newly elected President, Melchior Ndadaye, formed a government of National Unity. Out of 23 ministerial portfolios, six were attributed to the Uprona, nine to Tutsi ministers, and five to ministers from Bururi. The premiership was also attributed to a Tutsi (Reyntjens, 1993: 578). Interestingly, the political field was not fully divided across ethnic lines. Even if they were not required by law, political parties had presented multi-ethnic electoral lists in an attempt to attract voters from other ethnic communities (mostly for Tutsi-dominated parties) or reassure the Tutsi minority (for Hutu parties). For instance, in a bid to look less like a Tutsi party, Uprona strategically put Hutu candidates in a top position in their electoral lists in most provinces. Because Uprona rarely won more than one seat in most of the provinces, Hutu outnumbered Tutsi in the new parliament, making this situation difficult to accept for the former ruling elite. "Even across party lines the Tutsi [did] not have a blocking minority of 20 percent, should they feel that a proposed constitutional amendment were to threaten their vital interests" (Reyntjens, 1993: 572). The proposal to reintegrate Hutu elements to the Tutsi-dominated Burundian army was a new source of uncertainty. In reaction, a group of hardline Tutsi officers launched a coup attempt in 1993 (Sullivan, 2005). While the coup failed to bring the Uprona back to power in the short run, the President and the Speaker of the National Assembly were killed, leading to a situation of a power vacuum unanticipated by the constitution. Violence spread across the country. This was the beginning of the civil war.

What they failed to obtain by taking up arms, the conspirators would eventually acquire by ruse in what Reyntjens (1996) called a "creeping coup." Uprona's remaining control of the army and the constitutional court were used to block the functioning of institutions (Reyntjens, 1996: 240). Uprona was also able to instrumentalize the

---

[5] Front for Democracy in Burundi

peace process led by the Special Representative of the UN Secretary-General, Ahmedou Ould Abdallah to effectively reverse the constitutional order and the results of the 1993 election. Indeed, the *Convention of Government* signed by the Frodebu and the Uprona on 10 September 1994 claimed supra-constitutional status and transferred most of the powers of the democratically elected presidency and the National Assembly to a new National Security Council dominated by the Uprona (Reyntjens, 1996). The Convention of Government did not survive long in this tumultuous period and its record of accomplishment is mixed. In a context where it was impossible to organize premature general elections or any orderly transition as provided for by Article 85 of the constitution, the Convention of Government resolved the political impasse. However, it weakened the party that had won the election, by pitting Frodebu leadership against its supporters, who considered the agreement a treason. On 25th July 1996, a bloodless coup brought Buyoya back to power. Using hidden and then increasingly open tactics, Uprona had eventually succeeded in achieving total control of power (Reyntjens & Vandeginste, 1997).

The regional heads of state—united since 1995 in the Great Lakes Regional Initiative for Peace in Burundi—reacted to the coup by imposing an economic embargo on Burundi. The lifting of the sanctions was conditional on the restoration of the 1992 constitutional order and the participation of the government in negotiations mediated by the former Tanzanian President Julius Nyerere (Daley, 2007). Buyoya had to engage in internal reform. An internal negotiation process, the "Parliamentary weeks" (1996–1998) resulted in the *Transitional Constitutional Act* (ACT) that transitionally replaced the 1992 constitution (Reyntjens, 1999: 8). Buyoya remained President but now accompanied by a Hutu and a Tutsi as vice presidents. A new government of national unity as well as a Transitional National Assembly (TNA) were formed, in which ethnic imbalances were corrected (Reyntjens, 1999: 9). These new power-sharing institutions paved the way for the Arusha negotiations.

While power-sharing remained continually contested over the decade, this long process of "trial-and-error" (Vandeginste, 2009) was key for conflict parties to progressively accept the idea of sharing power. The explicit recognition of ethnicity in state institutions appeared increasingly unavoidable to reassure the Tutsi minority while addressing the exclusion of Hutus and recovering institutional normalcy. Several of the institutional innovations of the ACT would also be directly transferred to the APRA: the two vice presidents, the stronger overrepresentation of minorities, and the idea of qualified majorities.

THE ADOPTION OF POWER-SHARING (1999–2005)

While the principle of power-sharing was largely accepted, it took another six years of internationally mediated negotiations—and not one, but a series of peace agreements—for Burundian leaders to progressively achieve a joint decision on the details of the institutions.

The Arusha negotiations started on 21 June 1998. The process was led by an international mediation team working under African leadership—Nelson Mandela having replaced Nyerere as lead mediator after his sudden death in 1999. The talks resulted in the adoption of the APRA on 28 August 2000. Progress in the adoption of this framework can be attributed to three factors: the existence of a complex "mutually hurting stalemate," since the demographic dominance of Hutus was counterbalanced by the Tutsis' grasp on political and military institutions; the presence of a minimal level of trust between the Uprona and Frodebu, who had learned to work together since 1994; and the important role of external third parties in facilitating negotiations and pressuring reluctant actors (Vandeginste, 2015b: 12–13).

However, when the APRA was signed, observers looked skeptically at "what was in effect a non-accord" (Reyntjens, 2006: 118). The agreement was contested on all sides (Kazoviyo, 2017). Hutu politicians were willing to sign any compromise if it had a chance to result in a multi-ethnic army and "one man, one vote" principle-based political competition. While the accord satisfied these demands, it suffered from the incomplete inclusivity of the talks. Due to important intraparty feuds and splintering, the most powerful factions of Hutu rebel groups—notably the CNDD-FDD and the Palipehutu-FNL—were not represented in Arusha (Bentley & Southall, 2005). When the APRA was signed, these rebel groups remained at war and contested the very idea of sharing power. In particular, the overrepresentation of the Tutsi minority in political institutions frustrated the CNDD-FDD who "would have preferred a representation percentage based on that of ethnic proportions of the Burundi population" (Rufyikiri, 2017: 232).

On their side, the Tutsis obtained guarantees against a total exclusion of power after elections. But many remained frustrated by the circumstances of the conclusion of the talks. Deploring slow progress in the negotiations, Mandela imposed a deadline for the end of the talks. He enforced the deadline by inviting the US President Bill Clinton and regional high-level officials to the signature ceremony—months ahead of the actual event (Francis & Tieku, 2011: 26). On the day of the ceremony, Burundian delegations, faced with Mandela's personal aura and the group of prestigious guests, felt compelled to sign (Bentley & Southall, 2005). Six Tutsi delegations however added a list of "formal reservations" on important issues (Gouvernement du Burundi, 2000). The most contentious issue was the electoral system to be used for post-conflict elections. Whereas the Accord provided for multi-ethnic parties and ethnic quotas on electoral lists, Tutsi-dominated parties would have preferred "politico-ethnic" representation, whereby Tutsi citizens would be represented by Tutsi parties exclusively. They feared that Tutsi candidates would be coopted in predominantly Hutu parties at the expense of traditionally Tutsi parties (Vandeginste, 2015b)—a scenario made particularly credible by the 1993 experience.

Faced with this difficult situation, the mediation team and the Regional Initiative understood that external involvement in Burundi could not cease after the signature of the agreement. Using coordinated threats, sanctions, and mediation, the Regional Initiative pressured the CNDD-FDD to engage in negotiations with the transitional government, which culminated in a *Global Ceasefire Agreement* on 16 November 2003 (Rufyikiri, 2017: 230). The agreement brought the CNDD-FDD into the framework of the APRA, not without conceding significant shares of power to the rebel group. Pierre Nkurunziza entered the government in the influential position of Minister of Good Governance and General Inspection of the State, and the CNDD-FDD obtained "four ministries including one Ministry of State, 15 seats in the National Assembly, three governorships, two ambassador posts, 30 positions for local Council administrators, and the directorates of 20 percent of the public enterprises" (Nindorera, 2012: 23). The agreement also provided for the replacement of the Burundian armed force (FAB) by a Burundi National Defence Force (BNDF) in which combatants form the CNDD-FDD and other Hutu rebel groups would be integrated both in file and ranks and command positions (Boshoff & Gasana, 2003).

External support was also crucial in securing the commitment of the Tutsi to the agreement. The "formal reservations" were dropped under pressure from the Regional Initiative during a Summit on 20 September 2002 (Bentley & Southall, 2005: 78). Negotiations on the electoral system continued as part of the post-conflict constitution-making process. This complex process, in which the CNDD-FDD was fully included, mixed legal work by the government and political negotiations under the aegis of South Africa and the region. A Juridical Technical Commission was formed in 2002 and established a first draft of the constitution. This draft was then negotiated by the parties in Pretoria in 2004, leading to the adoption of a *Power-sharing Agreement* outlining the future constitution. The multi-ethnic electoral lists favored by Hutu-dominated parties were maintained, which led some Tutsi parties to reject the agreement (Reyntjens, 2006: 119). The draft was nonetheless completed by the services of the president, inter-ministerial work, consultations, and parliamentary debates (Gouvernement du Burundi, 2004). A mix of arm-twisting and mediation was used to overcome Tutsi's reluctances. The then Tutsi Vice President Alphonse Kadege, critical of the draft, was removed from office and replaced. At the same time, the UN provided discreet mediation to secure the support of Tutsi parties for the draft (Jackson, 2006). The draft was finally adopted as a constitution by Parliament in 2004 via a popular referendum in 2005.

In 2005, the tumultuous process of adopting these institutions appeared to deliver outstanding results (Lemarchand, 2006). The security situation had improved. Communal and legislative elections were held, and judged relatively free and fair by international observers. The institutions could be formed without much trouble.

Functioning Power-Sharing? (2005–2006)

The 2005 constitution set up a complex power-sharing system that included both power-sharing between *ethnic categories* and between *political parties* (along with a 30% threshold of representation for women in parliament and government). The 2005 elections illustrate the functioning of the ethnic part of this arrangement, which political leaders could accommodate by integrating candidates from multiple ethnic backgrounds in their respective parties.

The 2005 constitution set up a presidential system with a bicameral parliament sustained by a complex system of quotas that enshrines power-sharing between ethnic (and gender) categories as well as between political parties (Vandeginste, 2015b). The main elements of the system can be outlined as follows.

The executive encompasses a president, two vice presidents and the cabinet (Art. 92). The president is elected via a run-off system and enjoys a five-year mandate renewable once (Art. 96). The president selects the vice presidents and his government. The vice presidents have different ethnic and party affiliations. The government respects a composition rule of 60% Hutu and 40% Tutsi, as well as a minimum of 30% women (Art. 129). Ministerial portfolios are granted proportionally to their electoral score to any political party that earned at least 5% of the votes (Art. 129).

The National Assembly (lower house) is elected via proportional representation using closed party lists in multi-member electoral districts (Art. 164–168). The National Assembly is composed of 60% Hutu and 40% Tutsi MPs, 30% of women, as well as 3 Twas, overrepresenting ethnic minorities. These quotas are achieved through distribution requirements on the electoral lists. For three candidates in a row, at least one must have a different ethnic identity (Art. 168). Should this mechanism fail to deliver the quotas as required, the electoral commission can coopt MPs to correct the equilibrium (Art. 164).

The Senate (upper house) is elected indirectly by communal councils within each province. Two representatives are selected for each province, one Hutu and one Tutsi. The Senate thereby respects ethnic parity. It also must include a minimum of 30% of women, and three Twa representatives selected among the most representative of the Twa organizations.

Qualified majorities are provided for in parliament, including a 2/3 majority for the adoption of ordinary laws and a 4/5 majority for constitutional amendments. A 2/3 quorum is also required for the National Assembly to hold votes. Taken together with ethnic quotas, they create a de facto veto power for ethnic minorities (McCulloch & Vandeginste, 2019).

The constitution also includes dispositions for power-sharing in security forces, including the army and the police. The rule is ethnic parity in both cases (Art. 257). The constitution also provides for ethnic representativity in local administration (Art. 138 and 260). Among communal administrators, a maximum of 67% can belong to the same ethnic population. The 60/40 quotas also apply to public administration and state-owned companies (Art. 143).

This design defies classification in the habitual categories of power-sharing as it serves an objective that is at odds with the logics of both consociationalism and centripetalism: incentivizing the emergence of a party system that is both itself multi-ethnic and where all parties are also multi-ethnic in composition. Raffoul (2020) proposes calling this logic "associational power-sharing." This system functions by combining guarantees for the representation of all ethnic categories (i.e., ethnic quotas and qualified majorities) with constitutional requirements and incentives for the formation of multi-ethnic parties. While the guarantees *allow* the de-politicization of ethnicity by reassuring each ethnic category against exclusion from power, the incentives *foster* the reorientation of political alliances by making them electorally profitable. These incentives are created by the quotas in parliament: should they not propose candidates for the seats reserved to both Hutus and Tutsis, political parties would fail to compete for, respectively, 60% or 40% of seats in the National Assembly, and 50% of the seats in the Senate (Raffoul, 2020).

Perhaps counter-intuitively, the sharing of power across ethnic lines thus proved the least controversial when it came to implementing the 2005 Constitution. Ethnic power-sharing could easily be dealt with by political parties by incorporating—some would say, subservient—candidates from other ethnic backgrounds. By transforming itself into a multi-ethnic party, the CNDD-FDD could appeal to the Tutsi vote and run for the parliamentary seats reserved for Tutsis, which ultimately served its electoral interests. The demographic imbalance in Burundi also meant that the locus of political competition after the war was not so much between Hutus and Tutsi than between Hutu-dominated movements.

The implementation of ethnic power-sharing was therefore remarkably smooth, especially considering the recent violent history of the country. In 2005, all major parties could present multi-ethnic candidate lists. The surprisingly rapid de-ethnicization of political parties after the war—admittedly in a minimal, descriptive sense—led to a de-politicization of the ethnic divide. In 2006, ethnic quotas were respected in institutions and ethnicity seemed to have all but vanished from politics. The CNDD-FDD party was even ostensibly hostile to the very idea of essentializing ethnicity (Rufyikiri, 2017). In speeches, Pierre Nkurunziza insisted on the necessity to "transcend ethnic and regional divisions" (Lemarchand, 2006: 16).

THE EROSION OF POWER-SHARING (2007–2015)

The early appearances were those of a honeymoon. But the initial disagreements regarding the other facet of the arrangement—party-based power-sharing—remained looming under the surface, waiting for a shift in power relations to reemerge. These enduring disagreements and the rise in power of the CNDD-FDD explain the poor functioning of party-based power-sharing in Burundi.

Paradoxically, the 2005 elections—which represented the triumph of the transition period—were also the event that recreated the imbalance of power that destabilized the system. Indeed, these elections were won overwhelmingly by the CNDD-FDD. With 58.55% of the seats in parliament, the party was now the most powerful actor, in charge of operating power-sharing institutions it supported only ambiguously. As an insider, Gervais Rufyikiri, explains, "the CNDD-FDD [had] not given up its main objective of the total control of power. Then, the strategy was to adhere to the APRA for the record and in the hope of changing it progressively once in power so as to achieve the objectives of the struggle it had not been able to attain by force of arms" (2017: 232).

While the CNDD-FDD could accommodate ethnic power-sharing by coopting Tutsi candidates, the main source of tension became party-based power-sharing. Indeed, other political forces (four parties in total) had obtained a sizable number of seats in parliament, which granted them a veto power (Vandeginste, 2011). The necessity to compromise that resulted from qualified majorities was difficult to accept for the CNDD-FDD who kept some of the reflexes of the bush and remained controlled by a group of Hutu generals (Burihabwa & Curtis, 2019; Speight & Wittig, 2018). The ruling elites developed an abhorrence for the very idea of dialogue. Any request for an inclusive dialogue, even the sincerest, was met with suspicion as intending to party-based power-sharing—a political practice CNDD-FDD soon referred to as *Intwaro z'ivyaduka* (illegitimate rule) or *Intwaro z'amagaburanyama* (sharing of the spoils).

The tensions surrounding party-based power-sharing became apparent early on. No sooner had the composition of the first cabinet been released that its compliance with the constitution was put into question. While ethnic quotas were respected, the Frodebu and Uprona representation was not commensurate with their electoral performances and some small parties were overrepresented. This composition appeared to reflect an attempt by the CNDD-FDD to weaken its most powerful opponents.

The conflict was taken to the Constitutional Court who dismissed the case as inadmissible. In reaction, the FRODEBU walked out of government in 2006. While the issue was eventually resolved relatively smoothly by a ministerial reshuffling, the government proved particularly unstable, with no less than six different cabinet reshufflings between 2005 and 2006 (Vandeginste, 2008b: 60). These events, admittedly marginal in their effects on the short term, were significant as they signaled the difficulties lying ahead operating institutions relying on consensus with parties reluctant to compromise.

It is in the National Assembly that the parties' inability to cooperate appeared the most blatantly. Between 2007 and 2008, the National Assembly was paralyzed as a result of severe disagreements between the CNDD-FDD on the one side and the Uprona and Frodebu on the other regarding, among others, the role of the parliament in the negotiations with the Palipehutu-FNL. As a sign of protestation, the opposition MPs used a veto right provided de facto by the constitution: they would not present themselves to the National Assembly, preventing it from reaching the 79 MP's quorum. The parliament was paralyzed. Only 13 out of the 63 laws planned could be adopted between February and August 2007 (Vandeginste, 2008b: 61–62).

The CNDD-FDD, who grew increasingly frustrated with this situation, quickly expressed its desire to modify the Constitution. Formally, the task was however impossible as the qualified majority required for constitutional amendments granted the opposition a veto power. The party therefore moved to more informal strategies to erode the foundations of power-sharing.

The first one was the use of CNDD-FDD's position of power to appoint loyalists to key positions of the state, such as the Constitutional Court and the National Independent Electoral Commission (International Crisis Group, 2006). Control over these institutions granted the party a large margin of maneuver in hindering any attempts to meaningfully share power in the country. The most controversial case was related to a Constitutional Court decision (RCCB 213) in 2008. The ruling followed the ousting of CNDD-FDD strongmen Hussein Radjabu and 22 MPs who supported him from the party in February 2007. At the request of the CNDD-FDD, the Constitutional Court ruled that the seats of MPs that were excluded from their party were considered vacant. This meant that any MP diverging from the party line could be excluded from their parties and lose their seat. The ruling put an end to any form of meaningful inter-party cooperation in Burundi (Vandeginste, 2008a).

Second, the CNDD-FDD displaced the locus of power from formal institutions to quasi-formal structures that could be more easily controlled or institutions that were not concerned by ethnic quotas (McCulloch & Vandeginste, 2019). For instance, the Circle of Generals—a group of high-ranked former CNDD-FDD combatants—influences the ruling party's agenda-setting and meddles in judiciary, governmental, and legislative matters. Similarly, the *Imbonerakure*, the party's youth wing, played a growing role in the intimidation of political opponents over the years (Nkurunziza, 2019). While the multi-ethnic army was kept busy by peacekeeping missions in various African conflicts, the National Intelligence Service (SNR)—which is not subjected to ethnic quotas—played an increasing role in the country. Similarly, more power was also allocated to municipal and provincial directorates of some ministries, which are not subject to ethnic quotas.

Third, the party deployed a vast authoritarian tool-kit, including the creation of an uneven playing field for political campaigns, voter intimidation, and vote-buying (Vandeginste, 2011). The strategy of "Nyakurisation," implying the splitting of opposition parties and the cooptation of some of their wings, was also widely used to neutralize the opposition (Manirakiza, 2018). In reaction, the use of violence for political purposes was trivialized (Vandeginste, 2015a), supporting Le Van's conclusion that "power-sharing often displaces norms of political competition" (Le Van, 2011: 36) and Tull and Mehler (2005)'s observation that the precedent of power-sharing can offer a motivational basis for violent endeavors. Some political leaders traditionally attuned to a peaceful political game have henceforth integrated armed struggle in their repertory of possible political strategies, leading to the ever-increasing proliferation of so-called Burundian armed insurgents' groups since 2010 (Stearns & Vogel, 2017).

The second post-conflict elections, held in 2010, were boycotted by the opposition, who denounced a climate of insecurity and election rigging. The consequence was to reinforce the CNDD-FDD grasp on political institutions, leaving virtually no checks on its power. The CNDD-FDD controlled 81% of seats in the National Assembly, with an additional 6% going to its satellite party the FRODEBU Niakuri and only 11% to the Uprona, who had rejoined the legislative course at last minute (Vandeginste, 2011: 321). The 2015 elections were the source of the biggest political crisis in the country. Following Pierre Nkurunziza's controversial candidacy to a third mandate, which many observers deemed unconstitutional, mass demonstrations were held in the capital. They were met by violent repression, pushing some 170,000 persons to flee the country (Daley & Popplewell, 2016). On 13 May, a coup attempt staged by former SNR chief Niyombare shook the country. The coup failed and ultimately backfired as it became an occasion for the ruling party to further tighten its grip on power. As coup plotters fled or were arrested, radio stations were closed by the power (Vandeginste, 2015a: 629). The election was again boycotted by the opposition.

Regional and international actors did not react decisively to prevent this degradation of the situation. For a long time, they were indeed impressed by the ease with which ethnic power-sharing was implemented in political and security institutions. Their reaction to the degradation of the situation was belated and displayed their divisions (Molenaers et al., 2017). A stronger reaction took place only from 2015, the EU imposing sanctions on Burundi. This was met by a pushback from the ruling party, who increasingly reverted to an "anti-colonial discourse" to oppose external involvement in the country, did not hesitate to ban international NGOs or declare special envoys *"persona non grata"* (Niyonkuru & Ndayiragije, 2019: 30). External actors however remained divided. During the 2015 crisis, the East African Community mediation attempt was undermined by member states disagreements and the lack of interest of regional Heads of States. Similarly, the AU Commission proposal to send an African Prevention and Protection Mission was rejected by some member states. Even the UN Security Council was blocked in its attempts to pass a resolution on the 2015 crisis by China and Russia, who echoed the CNDD-FDD's anti-interventionist discourse (International Crisis Group, 2019).

In sum, while political parties could accommodate ethnic power-sharing, party-based power-sharing became the object of growing contestations after the war. The dominance of the CNDD-FDD over the political landscape—unbalanced by external pressures—allowed it to gradually erode the foundations of party-based power-sharing (Fig. 13.1). This suggests that understanding the strategies deployed by the main political parties is thus essential to understand how power-sharing could succeed in appeasing ethnic tensions, but fail to herald the consolidation of democracy in Burundi (Reyntjens, 2016).

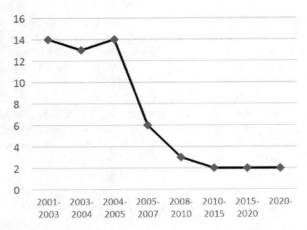

Fig. 13.1 Number of political parties in government (*Source* Compilation by Réginas Ndayiragije)

Reconfiguring Power-Sharing (2015–)

After the 2015 election, the CNDD-FDD was in such a position of force that it could formalize what was already the de facto power configuration by replacing the 2005 Constitution—a development that enables a discussion of the adaptability or endability of Burundian power-sharing. The 2018 constitution nearly eliminates party-based power-sharing and weakens the foundation of ethnic power-sharing. Because it was not the result of joint decision-making, this development toward endability can hardly be considered positive. Rather, it threatens the achievements of Burundian power-sharing.

In 2015, the domination of the CNDD-FDD over the Burundian political landscape was uncontestable. The party capitalized 86 out of the 121 National assembly seats (71%) and 33 out of 36 seats in the senate (92%) (Vandeginste, 2016: 54). Its networks were deployed and hyperactive over the country. Conversely, the opposition was largely weakened, with several opponents forced to exile. The state apparatus and the party were largely purged from potential contradictors, and the media was in tatters. Having learned its lessons from an attempt to modify the constitution in 2014 that had fallen short of one vote, the ruling party bypassed parliament and organized a popular referendum on a new constitution on 17 May 2018. The "yes" vote won with 73.24% of votes, which was unsurprising given the party's control of the process, the uneven playing field for the campaign, and the intimidations taking place (Niyonkuru & Ndayiragije, 2019: 17–18). The new constitution was promulgated by President Nkurunziza on 7 June 2018.

In line with the main line of contestation since 2005, the new constitution severely weakens power-sharing between political parties (Vandeginste, 2020). The constitution establishes the position of prime minister, designated by the president and approved by the parliament (Art. 130). No requirement is set regarding the identity of this prime minister. The position of vice president—who must have different ethnic and political affiliations as the president (Art. 124)—is maintained, but has become "totally ceremonial" (Vandeginste, 2020: 5). Perhaps most importantly, the new constitution eliminates the mandatory party-based power-sharing in government (Art. 128). Finally, the qualified majority for ordinary laws are removed—although qualified majority for organic laws and the quorum are preserved (Art. 180 & 191).

Identity-based power-sharing is preserved but weakened (Vandeginste, 2020). Ethnic and gender quotas are reconducted (Art. 128, 169, 185) and even extended to the magistrature, where they did not previously apply (Art. 123). However, the reestablishment of the prime minister and the weakening of the vice presidency limit the guaranteed representation of ethnic minorities at the highest level of the state. Similarly, the elimination of the compulsory power-sharing between political parties in parliament means that Tutsis will mostly be represented in the executive by Hutu-dominated parties. The transition toward absolute majorities to vote ordinary laws eliminates the de facto veto enjoyed by Tutsis in the National Assembly (although the quorum provides another informal veto to Tutsi MPs). Most worryingly, the SNR—an institution with a reputation for extrajudicial killings and human rights violations—is no longer classified as a "security institution," which implies that it now acts at the discretion of the president and is not required to respect ethnic quotas (Art. 268). Finally, the new constitution introduces a soft "sunset clause" as it requires the senate to reevaluate the need to preserve or eliminate ethnic quotas within five years after the implementation of the constitution (Art. 289)—a disposition that plunges the future of ethnic power-sharing in Burundi into uncertainty.

By nearly eliminating party-based power-sharing, the 2018 constitution moves toward a narrow conception of power-sharing that considers ethnicity as the only relevant fragmentation line. This perspective overlooks the contemporary political context, which—while witnessing a decreasing of political salience of ethnicity—has seen partisan identities becoming "one of the most prominent fault lines (…) along which political and economic inclusion and exclusion is organized" (Van Acker, 2015: 5). The seemingly schizophrenic relationship of the new constitution with ethnic power-sharing—reinforcing it in some places and weakening it in others—reflects the broader approach to power-sharing in Burundi. The CNDD-FDD maintains quotas where they can easily be accommodated, extends them to institutions where Hutus are still considered underrepresented (i.e., the magistrature), and weakens them where they constrain the party's unilateral exercise of power.

The constitution came into effect with the installation of the new institution after the 2020 elections (Vandeginste, 2021: 7). These elections—self-organized and self-financed by Burundi, and conducted in the absence of international observers—were held relatively peacefully, although observers question their credibility. Unsurprisingly, the results were a triumph for the CNDD-FDD, who secured 86 of the 123 seats in the National Assembly (70%) and 34 out of 36 seats in the Senate (94%) (Ndayiragije, 2021: 16). Pierre Nkurunziza did not run for a fourth mandate, and his party-designated candidate, Évariste Ndayishimiye, was smoothly elected as his successor. After the sudden death of Nkurunziza, the new institutions were installed rapidly to fill in the vacuum of power. This represents the first transfer of presidential power in the post-war history of Burundi. But the change of president did not represent a change in the political class ruling the country. On the contrary, the institutions further reinforced the CNDD-FDD's grasp on the state. Alain-Guillaume Bunyoni, a Hutu and CNDD-FDD cadre was designated prime minister (Ndayiragije, 2021: 20). The government was formed and composed for the 2/3 of CNDD-FDD members, while other ministers are not *officially* affiliated with the CNDD-FDD: civil society members, former magistrates, and a president of one of the small parties supporting the CNDD-FDD (Ndayiragije, 2021: 20). The main opposition party—the CNL—is not represented. For the first time in the history of the country, the CNDD-FDD has full control over the executive and the legislative (Vandeginste, 2021: 8–10).

It is unclear whether Burundian power-sharing is headed toward "adaptability" or "end-ability." On the one hand, the malleability of Burundian power-sharing institutions might be what prevented the arrangement from collapsing altogether. In response to institutional blockages, the CNDD-FDD was able to reshape power-sharing—first informally and then officially with the adoption of the new constitution. On the other hand, this flexibility resembles progression toward the end of power-sharing in Burundi. Along the three exit pathways from power-sharing by McCulloch (2017)—the sunset clause determining the right moment for termination, dissolution by means of judicial procedures, and dissolution via political reforms—Burundi therefore seems to have progressed quite far toward the last one.

These developments threaten minorities' representation and security, and more broadly the quality of democracy in Burundi. This suggests that, if institutional rigidity can be problematic, adaptability carries its own risks—especially when pushed single-handedly by a dominant actor rather than resulting from an inclusive dialogue process. If power-sharing can hinder governability, "endability" can hardly be considered a normative achievement in contexts where ethnic identities are durable and state power tends to be concentrated in the hands of the few.

Conclusion

The Burundian case suggests two broad lessons for power-sharing theory. The first one concerns power-sharing institutions. The institutional design devised by Burundian negotiators in Arusha defies classification in the conventional categories of the power-sharing literature. While it combined institutions typically associated with consociationalism and centripetalism, Burundi power-sharing does not fit neatly in any of these categories since these institutions pursued a novel aim: promoting the emergence of a multi-ethnic party system. This objective, which goes back to the 1992 constitution, has seemingly stood the test of time. This innovative institutional design, in line with the objective of national unity at the heart of the National unity charter, achieved a remarkable success in de-politicizing ethnicity, particularly in regard to the violent history of the country.

The second lesson is about the role assigned to the actors actually sharing power in power-sharing theory. Any understanding of Burundian power-sharing would be incomplete if our attention is focused exclusively on institutional design. A full account must broaden the analyst's attention to the dynamic of inter-elite negotiations and conflict.

The Burundian case suggests that the design of power-sharing institutions is inseparable from the historical and political trajectory of the country, as it is shaped (in its content and scope) by previous experiences of managing identity-based grievances as well as reconfiguration in the balance of power between political forces. The chapter showed that reaching a fragile inter-elite agreement was necessary for the *adoption* of power-sharing and the successful *functioning* of ethnic power-sharing in Burundi. The looming disagreements about party-based power-sharing and the rise in power of the CNDD-FDD led to the gradual erosion of this aspect of the power-sharing arrangement and its eventual elimination with the 2018 constitution. In this case, endability risks paving the way to renewed monopolization of power and ethnic exclusion—the very issues power-sharing was supposed to overcome.

Umwana yankwa niwe akura, a Burundian proverb says: "the unloved child matures." That power-sharing was—to some—a despised child of the civil war is beyond questioning. It is also clear that the enduring disagreements over power-sharing led to its transformation over time. The question that remains open is whether this lack of love helped Burundian power-sharing develop—or rather gradually turned it into little more than an empty shell.

REFERENCES

BBC. (2005). Pierre Nkurunziza, un prof de sport et ex-chef rebelle à la tête du Burundi. *BBC Afrique*. https://www.bbc.co.uk/french/highlights/story/2005/08/050819_portrait.shtml

Bentley, K. A., & Southall, R. (2005). *An African Peace Process: Mandela, South Africa and Burundi*. HSRC Press.

Boshoff, H., & Gasana, J. M. (2003). *Mapping the Road to Peace in Burundi: The Pretoria Sessions*. Situation Report. African Security Analysis Programme. https://www.files.ethz.ch/isn/136849/BURUNDI1103.PDF

Bukeyeneza, A. G. (2021). *La bible et la gâchette*. Éditions Iwacu.

Burihabwa, N. Z., & Curtis, D. E. A. (2019). The Limits of Resistance Ideologies? The CNDD-FDD and the Legacies of Governance in Burundi. *Government & Opposition, 54*(3), 559–583.

Byrne, S. (2020). Feminist Reflections on Discourses of (Power)+(Sharing) in Power-Sharing Theory. *International Political Science Review, 41*(1), 58–72.

Chrétien, J. P., & Dupaquier, J. F. (2007). *Burundi 1972, au bord des génocides*. Karthala.

Daley, P. (2007). The Burundi Peace Negotiations: An African Experience of Peace–Making. *Review of African Political Economy, 34*(112), 333–352.

Daley, P., & Popplewell, R. (2016). The Appeal of Third Termism and Militarism in Burundi. *Review of African Political Economy, 43*(150), 648–657.

Francis, D., & Tieku, T. K. (2011). *The AU and the Search for Peace and Reconciliation in Burundi and Comoros.* Centre for Humanitarian Dialogue.

Gouvernement du Burundi. (2000). *Les réserves faisant parties intégrante de l'accord et devant continuer à être négociées.*

Gouvernement du Burundi. (2004). *Exposés des motifs: Constitution du 20 Octobre 2004.* https://www.uantwerpen.be/en/projects/centre-des-grands-lacs-afrique/droit-pouvoir-paix-burundi/constitution/apercu-historique-con stitutionnel/

Guichaoua, A. (2020, June 18). Nkurunziza Left a Troubling Legacy: Burundi's New Leader has Much to Mend. *The Conversation.* https://theconversation. com/nkurunziza-left-a-troubling-legacy-burundis-new-leader-has-much-to-mend-140972

International Crisis Group. (2006). *Burundi: Democracy and Peace at Risk.* Africa Report 120. International Crisis Group.

International Crisis Group. (2019). *Running Out of Options in Burundi.* Africa Report 278. International Crisis Group.

Jackson, S. (2006). *The United Nations Operation in Burundi (ONUB): Political and Strategic Lessons Learned. Independent Study.* UN Department of Peacekeeping Operations.

Kazoviyo, G. (2017). *Entre rejet catégorique et soutien ferme de l'Accord d'Arusha: analyse de discours politiques burundais* (Discussion Paper). Universiteit Antwerpen Institute of Development Policy and Management (IOB).

Le Van, C. A. (2011). Power Sharing and Inclusive Politics in Africa's Uncertain Democracies. *Governance, 24*(1), 31–53.

Lemarchand, R. (1996). *Burundi: Ethnic Conflict and Genocide.* Cambridge University Press.

Lemarchand, R. (2006). Consociationalism and Power Sharing in Africa: Rwanda, Burundi, and the Democratic Republic of the Congo. *African Affairs, 106*(422), 1–20.

Manirakiza, D. (2018). Société civile et socialisation démocratique au Burundi. Retour sur une complicité ambiguë. *Swiss Journal of Sociology, 44*(1), 113–138.

McCulloch, A. (2017). Pathways from Power-Sharing. *Civil Wars, 19*(4), 405–424.

McCulloch, A., & Vandeginste, S. (2019). Veto Power and Power-Sharing: Insights from Burundi (2000–2018). *Democratization, 26*(7), 1176–1193.

McGarry, J., & B. O'Leary. (2006). Consociational Theory, Northern Ireland's Conflict, and its Agreement. Part 1: What Consociationalists Can Learn from Northern Ireland. *Government and Opposition, 41*(1), 43–63.

Molenaers, N., Rufyikiri, G., & Vandeginste, S. (2017). *Burundi and Its Development Partners: Navigating the Turbulent Tides of Governance Setbacks* (Working paper 2017.14). Institute of Development Policy and Management (IOB).

Ndayiragije, R. (2021). Burundi. In F. Reyntjens (Ed.), *Political Chronicles of the African Great Lakes Region 2020* (pp. 9–34). University of Antwerp Press.

Ndikumana, L. (2005). Distributional Conflict, the State and Peace Building in Burundi. *The round Table, 94*(381), 413–427.

Ngaruko, F., & Nkurunziza, J. (2000). An Economic Interpretation of Conflict in Burundi. *Journal of African Economies, 9*(3), 370–409.

Nindorera, W. P. (2012). *The CNDD-FDD in Burundi: The Path from Armed to Political Struggle. Berghof Transitions Series.* Berghof Foundation.

Niyonkuru, R. C., & Ndayiragije, R. (2019). Burundi. In F. Reyntjens (Ed.), *Political Chronicles of the African Great Lakes Region 2018* (pp. 11–40). University Press Antwerp.

Nkurunziza, A. (2019). *Burundi: Le dessous des cartes.* Editions Iwacu.

Raffoul, A. W. (2019). *Tackling the Power-Sharing Dilemma? The Role of Mediation.* Report. swisspeace.

Raffoul, A. W. (2020). The Politics of Association: Power-Sharing and the Depoliticization of Ethnicity in Post-War Burundi. *Ethnopolitics, 19*(1), 1–18.

Reyntjens, F. (1993). The Proof of the Pudding Is in the Eating: The June 1993 Elections in Burundi. *The Journal of Modern African Studies, 31*(4), 563–583.

Reyntjens, F. (1994). *L'Afrique des Grands Lacs en crise 1988–1993: Rwanda et Burundi.* Karthala.

Reyntjens, F. (1996). Constitution-Making in Situations of Extreme Crisis: The Case of Rwanda and Burundi. *Journal of African Law, 40*(2), 234–242.

Reyntjens, F. (1999). *Talking or Fighting? Political Evolution in Rwanda and Burundi, 1998–1999.* Nordic Africa Institute.

Reyntjens, F. (2006). Briefing: Burundi: A Peaceful Transition after a Decade of War? *African Affairs, 105*(418), 117–135.

Reyntjens, F. (2016). Institutional Engineering, Management of Ethnicity, and Democratic Failure in Burundi. *Africa Spectrum, 51*(2), 65–78.

Reyntjens, F., & Vandeginste, S. (1997). Burundi. Évolution politique en 1996–1997. In S. Marysse & F. Reyntjens (Eds.), *L'Afrique des Grands Lacs. Annuaire 1996–1997.* L'Harmattan.

Rufyikiri, G. (2017). The Post-wartime Trajectory of CNDD-FDD Party in Burundi: A Facade Transformation of Rebel Movement to Political Party. *Civil Wars, 19*(2), 220–248.

Spears, I. S. (2002). Africa: The Limits of Power-Sharing. *Journal of Democracy, 13*(3), 123–136.

Speight, J., & Wittig, K. (2018). Pathways from Rebellion: Rebel-Party Configurations in Côte d'Ivoire and Burundi. *African Affairs, 117*(466), 21–43.

Stearns, J., & Vogel, C. (2017, December). The Landscape of Armed Groups in Eastern Congo: Fragmented, Politicized Networks. *Kivu security tracker.*

Sullivan, D. P. (2005). The Missing Pillars: A Look at the Failure of Peace in Burundi through the Lens of Arend Lijphart's Theory of Consociational Democracy. *The Journal of Modern African Studies, 43*(1), 75–95.

Tull, D. M., & Mehler, A. (2005). The Hidden Costs of Power-Sharing: Reproducing Insurgent Violence in Africa. *African Affairs, 104*(416), 375–398.

Van Acker, T. (2015). Understanding Burundi's Predicament. *Africa Policy Briefs* (pp. 1–10).

Vandeginste, S. (2008a). *Pouvoir et droit au Burundi: un commentaire (principalement) juridique sur l'arrêt du 5 juin 2008 de la Cour Constitutionnelle dans l'affaire RCCB 213.* https://ancl-radc.org.za/sites/default/files/images/RCCB303%20commentaire.pdf

Vandeginste, S. (2008b). Burundi: entre le modèle consociatif et sa mise en œuvre. In S. Marysse (Ed.), *L'Afrique des Grands Lacs: annuaire 2007–2008* (pp. 55–75). Harmattan.

Vandeginste, S. (2009). Power-Sharing, Conflict and Transition in Burundi: Twenty Years of Trial and Error. *Africa Spectrum, 44*(3), 63–86.

Vandeginste, S. (2011). Power-Sharing as a Fragile Safety Valve in Times of Electoral Turmoil: The Costs and Benefits of Burundi's 2010 Elections. *The Journal of Modern African Studies, 49*(2), 315–335.

Vandeginste, S. (2015a). Burundi's Electoral Crisis-Back to Power-Sharing Politics as Usual? *African Affairs, 114*(457), 624–636.

Vandeginste, S. (2015b). *Arusha at 15: Reflections on Power-sharing, Peace and Transition in Burundi* (Discussion paper). Universiteit Antwerpen Institute of Development Policy and Management (IOB).

Vandeginste, S. (2016). Chronique politique du Burundi 2015–2016. In F. Reyntjens, S. Vandeginste, & M. Verpoorten (Eds.), *L'Afrique des Grands Lacs. Annuaire 2015–2016* (pp. 51–68). University Press Antwerp.

Vandeginste, S. (2020). *Burundi's Institutional Landscape after the 2020 Elections.* Egmont Institute.

Vandeginste, S. (2021). *Beyond Samuragwa's Sweet and Sour Succession: A Closer Look at Burundi's 2020 Elections* (Discussion paper). Universiteit Antwerpen Institute of Development Policy and Management (IOB).

CHAPTER 14

On the Adoptability of Power-sharing in Syria

Eduardo Wassim Aboultaif

INTRODUCTION

It has been more than a decade since the start of the war in Syria. In this time, there have been more than 500,000 deaths, more than 5.6 million people have fled the country and another 6 million have been internally displaced (USIP, 2020). The country has become territorially divided between the regime, the opposition and Kurdish forces, as well as the Turkish, Iranian, Russian militaries. President Bashar al-Assad has received military support from Iran and Russia (the former directly through the revolutionary guards and its proxies fighting in Syria, the Lebanese Hezbollah and the Iraqi Abu al-Fadl al- 'Abbas), though some regions are out of his control, like Idlib, and small pockets in Darʿa in the south. However, at the outset, the opposition groups controlling territory on the ground have multiple loyalties, and many regions on the side

---

E. W. Aboultaif (✉)
Holy Spirit University of Kaslik, Jounieh, Lebanon
e-mail: Eduardoaboultaif@usek.edu.lb

© The Author(s), under exclusive license to Springer Nature
Switzerland AG 2024
E. Wassim Aboultaif et al. (eds.), *Power-Sharing in the Global South*,
Federalism and Internal Conflicts,
https://doi.org/10.1007/978-3-031-45721-0_14

of Assad are actually under local tribal, Iranian or Russian control, rather than under the direct control of the Syrian regime.

A political resolution of the civil war has not yet matured, and the complexity of the interplay between domestic, regional and international factors has prolonged the conflict. The United Nations had an early attempt to resolve the conflict, with Kofi Annan's six-point plan for a political resolution of the war along with an end of the humanitarian crisis. This was followed by United Nations Security Council Resolution 2254, which sought to draft a new constitution by and for a political transition process. In addition, there have been several rounds of talks in Geneva, Vienna and Astana between the opposition and delegates of the Assad regime, but no agreement has been reached so far on a political transition or a new constitution. In the event of an Assad victory, it is highly unlikely that the president will be able to rule as before 2011. The resolution of the conflict will likely come about through a mixture of domestic demands with regional and international arbitration. Some form of power-sharing may be required to re-establish a stable political regime.

Prior to the civil war, ethnic and sectarian identities in Syria were not highly politicized. However, due to the atrocities committed and the intensity of the conflict, identities have become heavily politicized and securitized. This explains the mobilization strategies of communities based on identity (religious, ethnic or nationalist). For instance, Sunni groups have become influenced by political Islam, the Druze have developed their local militia to defend their community in Swaida and similarly the Kurds have established the Syrian Democratic Forces (SDC). This tribalization of Syrian society because of the war does not mean that there are no other social stratifications, but the basis of political divisions is now based primarily on religious, ethnic and tribal affiliation. As a result, it is important to reflect on their perceived existential threats by providing constitutional provisions to protect their vital interests and security at this point.

The aim of this chapter is to study the adoptability process of a power-sharing settlement in Syria. It is my contention that the adoption of power-sharing (at least for Syria) does not necessarily have to be a choice between the consociational (Lijphartian) or the centripetalist (Horowitzian) model, but it can also be a mixture of different modes of institutional power-sharing options. The discussion in this chapter revolves around the set of institutional options that the author sees best fit for a Syrian consociation. Consequently, I deal with the following questions:

1. Which system is more likely to support political stability in Syria—a corporate or a liberal consociation?
2. How should the Syrian armed forces be restructured to support peace in post-conflict Syria?

Consensus is still lacking as to what method to use in order to end the war in Syria, and the events today, along with the regional and international dimension of the conflict, make it unclear what the ultimate outcome will be. However, it is important to look at viable power-sharing options for the country and begin the discussion of a possible democratic system that can accommodate the conflicting aspirations of different segments of the Syrian population. I would like to remind many of the pessimists and critics who might look at this chapter as a "fairy tale novel," that the discussions of power-sharing in Northern Ireland took place amid "The Troubles" when no one could have thought that peace was achievable (Lijphart, 1975; McGarry, 1988; O'Leary, 1989). The same could be said for Lebanon during the civil war, 1975–1991.

This chapter follows a normative approach to the adoptability of power-sharing as the means to ending the civil war. It begins with a comparative study on the liberal and corporate types of consociationalism, and then moves on to discuss the provisions of collective-civilian control of newly reconstructed armed forces. These points represent some of the most contentious and divisive predicaments that are currently discussed between warring parties to decide on a post-war settlement, and they also highlight the importance of the interplay between security and governance. Communal political fears are often hidden in issues related to the functions of the executive, the legislative and the decision-making procedures in the armed forces. In order to implement a successful consociational democracy in Syria, each of these principles have to be contextualized according to the current regional context. Furthermore, some comparison with similar cases is necessary to avoid the mistakes that happened elsewhere being repeated in Syria.

There has been a tendency for critics to assume that analyses and recommendations toward consociational settlements mean a permanent status for power-sharing against majority rule. It is important to note here, as the work of Soeren Keil and Allison McCulloch (2021) has shown, countries have been able to move away from power-sharing as in Austria and the Netherlands. Hence, a consociational settlement for Syria does not necessarily mean a permanent status of power-sharing, but rather that it can function as a transitional tool to put an end to the civil war, enabling peace and stability until such a time that communities regain a level of trust in which they can re-establish legitimate national institutions. The only permanent arrangement suggested in this chapter should be seen in the part related to the military. No central government in a developing country with a history of ethnic bloodshed and instability should have the army under the authority of one executive office. The constitutional provision to deploy the armed forces is better to be taken by a super-majority in government.

It is important to note that the United Nations (UN), despite its many efforts to resolve the conflict, has not succeeded in establishing any sort of common ground between the Syrian opposition and the Assad regime. The latter is maneuvering to win time, use Russian and Iranian military might to achieve a military victory and avoid any sort of power-sharing. While UNSC Resolution 2254 remains the main framework for any peace negotiations, it has so far been impossible to achieve substantial progress on any of the major issues related to the conflict despite years of negotiations in Geneva and Astana. With the regime and the opposition having detrimental opposing positions and demands, and both sides featuring strong regional allies that allow them to maintain a level of control in some Syrian territories, the conflict remains ongoing without a solution in sight. Moreover, the re-integration of Syria into the League of Arab States (Al Jazeera, 2023), gives the regime further leverage to reject power-sharing proposals. Regardless of that, the chapter starts from the premise that the resolution of the conflict cannot happen comprehensively without some sort of power-sharing arrangement with consociational principles. Any kind of victory (regime or opposition) that could happen in Syria would not be enough to establish permanent and durable peace. Due to the intensity of the war, with massacres committed in all regions in Syria, one cannot expect communities to duly abandon the trauma of violence and the burden of fear that communities have against one another. Consequently, peace requires that these communities be represented in the system. That is to say that Assad (in case of his victory) will not be able to rule Syria as he did before March 2011 without accommodating the opposition, and vice versa. My argument is that the ongoing securitization of identities and the mistrust between communities that this has fostered cannot be bridged without a political safety net represented in a consociational system. Consociationalism is a form of power-sharing established in deeply divided societies that employs four main principles: grand coalition, mutual veto, proportionality and segmental autonomy (Lijphart, 1977: 25). This makes power-sharing through consociationalism an important model that is used to resolve conflicts that take an ethnic-identity-based dimension (Butenschon, 1985: 90). As a researcher, I cannot underestimate the intensity of the conflict with more than half a million killed, millions seeking refuge in neighboring countries, the use of chemical weapons several times and the rise of sectarian rhetoric. Hence, to achieve peace, consociationalism is a necessity.

On the opposite spectrum of power-sharing settlements is centripetalism. Donald Horowitz heavily criticized the consociational nature of power-sharing systems and instead proposed an integrative approach which is thought to promote minority influence on majority decision-making by specific electoral rules that create cross-ethnic moderation of party leaders (Horowitz, 2014; McCulloch, 2013). The emphasis in this integrative approach is on electoral alliances, focusing on multi-ethnic pre-electoral coalitions, a preferential electoral system and a political system based on Presidentialism. In the case of Syria, it is hard to imagine that communities would trust a president from a specific religious affiliation to enjoy a wide range of executive power. This is a point to take without prejudice as Syria is not the only country that faces obstacles to the adoption of centripetalism. Indeed, in his study of power-sharing adoptability, John McGarry (2017) has demonstrated the hardships that Cyprus faces in the adoption of a centripetal system.

Syria, like many other protracted conflicts, has struggled to reach a peace settlement. That is, despite the efforts of domestic and international actors, the country continues to face an adoptability problem when it comes to any resolution to the conflict, but especially to power-sharing as a tool to ending the violence. Adoptability, in this context, relates to the adoption of power-sharing (centripetal or consociational) institutions in which the prospects of an agreement are acceptable for the contending groups (Keil & McCulloch, 2021; McGarry, 2017). If adoptability refers to what the agreement looks like and what the parties find acceptable, the functionality question, in contrast, refers to the issue of "how" the system is working. Adoptability and functionality are closely related. In studying the case of Iraq, Joanne McEvoy and Eduardo Wassim Aboultaif (2022) point out that weak adoptability hinders the prospects of stable functionality of the system, thus creating a linkage between the two processes. This does not mean that adoptability is a pre-requisite for successful functionality. Rather, adoptability is put under heavy pressure when groups have variable support for the adoption of a power-sharing settlement, especially when group alliances converge with regional and international agendas (McEvoy & Aboultaif, 2022).

In Syria, not only have identities been securitized (Del Sarto, 2021; Robson, 2021), abuses of power for the last four decades—due to the concentration of powers in the presidential office—makes it hard to implement a centripetal solution that relies on an elected president to run the executive. Despite the fact that Sunnis compose around 74 percent of the population, many regions in Syria are homogeneous, so the impact of vote pooling to achieve moderation would be difficult to obtain in elections. Moreover, the absence of the element of political trust between communities calls into question the success of vote pooling mechanisms as citizens may be reluctant to cast their even second- or lower-order preferences for the other side. Thus, it is worth exploring the adoptability of a consociational settlement.

SYRIA'S (POSSIBLE) CONSOCIATION: THE LIBERAL-CORPORATE DEBATE

The inception of the liberal versus corporate debate in consociationalism is found in Arend Lijphart's work in which he distinguished between self-determination and pre-determination with respect to the distribution of governmental posts (Lijphart, 2007: 73; McCulloch, 2014: 504). The distinction was subsequently refined by Brendan O'Leary and John McGarry who framed the two types as liberal and corporate, respectively. Both scholars draw inspiration from Northern Ireland's Good Friday Agreement (1998) and Iraq's constitutional design (2005) (McCulloch, 2014: 504). According to McGarry and O'Leary, the corporate model accommodates groups according to ascriptive criteria, such as ethnicity or religion, on the assumption that group identities are fixed and that groups are both "internally homogenous and externally bounded" (McGarry & O'Leary, 2007). On the contrary, the liberal model rewards "whatever salient political identities emerge in democratic elections," without specifying dividing political posts according to communal identification, hence it does not provide quotas for group representation, but leaves it open to the electoral alliances (McGarry & O'Leary, 2007: 675). Consequently, a liberal consociation considers the rights of individuals and the rights of groups as well (McGarry & O'Leary, 2007: 675–676) by avoiding the association of certain political offices with a specific communal group, while corporate consociations entail constitutional entrenchments of group representation (McCulloch, 2014: 503).

McCulloch notes that academic proponents of consociationalism tend to prefer liberal versions of power-sharing. Yet, she also notes, negotiated transitions from war to democracy are more likely to produce corporate consociational pacts (McCulloch, 2014: 502). One explanation is fortified by the ethnic security dilemma that comes as a result of civil wars which strengthen social identity (Sisk, 2013: 9). The corporate mechanism is an antidote for the ethnic security dilemma, but it often comes at the expense of freezing ethnic identification. To put it in McCulloch's rationale, liberal consociationalism is often better able to avoid problems of immobilism and entrenchment, but it is less likely to be adoptable.

Any consideration of the adoptability of power-sharing arrangements must also consider the regional context. The implementation of a consociational settlement in Syria, especially one which would rely on a corporate system, could be seen as a response to the regional dynamics of identities, as a result of the Arab-Iranian struggle in the region. In today's Middle East, there is a bitter competition in the region between Saudi Arabia and Iran, taking the form of a Sunni-Shia conflict. The Syrian war has sectarianized communal identities and weakened the national one as a result of the security dilemma that these groups are facing (Hinnebusch, 2016). Sectarianism and violence make it extremely hard to adopt a liberal approach instead of a corporate one. The absence of the element of trust makes it extremely hard for a moderate politician from any sect to rely on vote pooling, and it is highly likely that concentration of powers in the executive office (president) would make political competition a win-lose scenario. Thus, corporate measures represent a more practical solution in providing security guarantees and communal political participation. It is highly unlikely that ethnic security dilemmas would evaporate once a peace settlement is reached between the warring groups without corporate provisions that guarantee communal interests. The legacy of four decades of Alawite domination through the Baath party means that the community is battling with the fear of a possible Sunni revenge in case they took over the country (for further details see Goldsmith, 2015).

Proportionality is an important factor that fortifies the proposed consociational arrangements discussed in this chapter. According to population estimates, the Sunni Arabs constitute around 74% of the population, followed by Alawites (Shia), who constitute around 12%, then the Kurds who are around 10 percent and finally the Druze who constitute 3% of the population (Syrian Civil War Map, 2017). This makes the Sunni Arabs an overwhelming majority in the country. Based on this demographic calculus, it is normal for the Sunni Arabs to take the lion share of official posts, such as the Presidency, Premiership and Speaker of the House in a majoritarian system. Such a scenario would risk becoming "a majority dictatorship" (Lijphart, 2007). Instead, in order to establish a proper balance between different groups, some degree of minority representation in high official posts would be required, preferably through an agreement to alternate some posts to soften the possibility of identity entrenchment to high-ranking posts. One way of doing so would be for Sunnis to receive the main executive office, that of the Prime Minister. From there, a ceremonial Presidency could be allocated to the Alawite, with the Speaker of the House and President of the Senate to be alternated between Druze, Kurds and Christians.

The distribution of important official posts in the political system depends on the type of the regime that will be established after the conflict ends. Because consociationalism aims at creating a balance of power between different communities, it is necessary to avoid a presidential system where the "winner-takes-all," and focus instead on a parliamentary system that can promote a grand coalition at the executive level. Here, we can learn from the Lebanese experience where the Presidency is reserved for the Maronite community, but the power of such a President is weak vis-à-vis the powers of the government, headed by a Sunni Prime Minister. For example, according to the Lebanese constitution, the President cannot vote in the governmental sessions. He can only moderate discussion, and the quorum for the meetings is two-thirds of the total number of ministers. Consequently, a grand coalition is established but also empowered by the power of veto, thanks to the two-third quorum of the total number of ministers (Taif Agreement, 1989). Above all, it is crucial to include special majority clauses in the constitution to deal with amendments, adopting organic laws, and important executive orders related to mobilizing the armed forces, war and peace, electoral law, ratifying treaties and reorganization of the administrative regions, cultural issues, language and education. These points represent vital interests for the survival and well-being of political communities in Syria.

Veto powers represent an important characteristic of modern political systems, and it is not an exclusive method used in consociational systems, as we can find it in other political regimes, too—as a main mechanism to ensure checks and balances between the executive and legislative (McEvoy, 2013). The analytical framework of veto powers provides two methods of veto: direct, and indirect, or institutional (president or parliament) and partisan (parties in a coalition government) (Tsebelis, 2002). In my proposed Syrian consociation, this would entail a combination of direct-partisan veto powers, mainly to avoid Sunni domination over the system and preserve the existential interests of smaller groups. In order to make the application of veto powers effective and avoid the excessive use of vetoes, which leads to stagnation of the political system, this should be accompanied by proportionality in all public agencies. The parliamentary and governmental seats are allocated to each community according to its size in the wider population. In this way, the threat of marginalization of the minorities by the majority will be tamed, and the corporate measures will represent a safety net to the vital interests of each community.

The executive has to be engineered around the concept of balance of power that respects communal vital interests. To do that, special majorities and quorums should be introduced. Anything that deals with communal interests, war and peace, reorganization of districts, electoral law, general mobilization and deployment of the armed forces should have national endorsement. Hence, a two-thirds majority with representatives from each community within this special majority is required to pass an executive order. This direct-partisan kind of veto preserves the interest of communities and prevents the hegemony of one group over the other. In cases that fall outside these concerns, a merely absolute majority, considering again that all communities are presented in this majority, is a quorum that allows a simple majority to pass an executive order. In this way, a veto is introduced for issues that are important but not seen as an existential threat to a community, and so the use of such a kind of political-institutional veto would not put communities against one another, instead it will rely on political alliances, enabling political actors to learn with time how to moderately compromise and bargain to pass resolutions in the government. It is also important because this political-institutional veto does not emphasize the politicization of ethnic identities and so would allow for the evolution of a civic-minded political process that could shift the pivot of the system from a communal framework to a civic one.

It is not enough to distribute posts and then claim that it is a corporate consociation. Distributing powers at the executive and legislative level requires a mechanism that clearly defines the veto powers of each community. In this context, Syria can benefit from the North Macedonian and Belgian experience of veto powers. For instance in North Macedonia, the Albanian minority under the Ohrid Framework Agreement (established in 2001) is protected by the concurrent majority voting procedures, whereby issues related to culture, language, education, personal documentation and the use of symbols must be adopted by a parliamentary majority including a majority vote among Parliamentarians who belong to the minority community (McEvoy, 2015: 171; McCulloch & Zdeb, 2022). A similar case is that of Belgium, where a language group (Dutch or French-speaking communities) may activate the alarm-bell procedure, if three-quarters of the Parliamentarians who belong to a specified language group support a motion that explains how a proposal in the Parliament harms the interests of that language group (Deschouwer, 2012: 190). As a result, discussion in parliament is stopped for 30 days, and a compromise should be reached by the government (Deschouwer, 2012). If no agreement is reached, the government will "almost certainly fail" (Adams, 2014). In the case of Syria, a synthesis of the two examples can be worked out, if three-quarters of the Members of Parliament (MPs) who belong to a certain community may trigger the alarm bell in cases specified by the constitution. If an agreement is not reached, then the bill has to be revised by a parliamentary committee, if the same outcome takes place, the bill either passes by endorsement of the three-quarters of MPs who belong to a certain community with an absolute majority in parliament. If not, then the bill should be considered annulled and cannot be reintroduced before a new parliamentary election. In this way, decisions taken in the parliament would guarantee wide support by all communities, and this process will create a balance of power between all communities.

Critics of consociationalism believe that power-sharing based on communities tends to enforce and entrench cleavages in society (Butenschøn, 1985: 98). They often argue that power-sharing arrangements are built on a primordialist view of national identity, segregate ethnic communities and accept their domination by elites (Dixon, 2011: 310). However, it is important to note that in the direct aftermath of civil wars, identities are often aggressive and sharp, presenting communal identification as a sphere of protection from other groups. Therefore, it is risky to assume that identities can be accommodated on the long run with liberal consociational provisions. Iraq is an important example here, where the partial implementation of a liberal consociational regime has not contributed to an end of communal tensions and political stability. Adoptability can be smoother with a higher chance of success when communities see that their representation in the system is guaranteed in a corporate method. Since identities are fluid and can change with time, a long process of stable accommodation and cooperation may open the door for identity transformation that can transform pillarization from communal identity into a more civic-oriented sphere of political contestation. At the moment however, it is safer to establish a corporate consociation, along the lines proposed here, as long as the aim is to end civil wars and provide a minimal level of cooperation between communities.

REFORMS OF THE ARMED FORCES

The reform of the security sector is a critical issue in deeply divided societies. However, it is under-developed in the literature on consociationalism. Caroline Hartzell and Matthew Hoodie were among the first to theorize the need for power-sharing in the military after civil wars in their seminal work, *Crafting Peace: Power-Sharing Institutions and the Negotiated Settlements of Civil Wars*. Their proposition is based on the following: integration of former combatants into a newly structured armed forces; the equal representation of antagonist combatants; the appointment of members of the armed factions that do not dominate the state (weaker militias) into key positions; the retention of antagonists of their armed forces or the creation of their private security forces (Hartzell & Hoddie, 2007). Reforms in the armed forces should be taken into account when proposing a model of conflict resolution, and in particular, when this resolution is consociational by nature. Armed forces might be used by any communal group to subdue other groups, promote their partisan vital interests at the expense of others, or even destroy the consociational provisions at hand. Hence, in order to avoid any such euphemism in Syria, reforms in the armed forces are critical.

The role, leadership and composition of the armed forces is part of the adoptability approach of consociational practices. First, in societies that suffer from ethnic, religious, cultural or linguistic divisions, armed forces may be used by the dominant group to crush, quell or ethnically cleanse people from the non-dominant community. This happened during the wars in Yugoslavia (1990–1999) and the massacres of the Kurds and Shias in Iraq by Saddam's army (Anfal 1986–1989 and Halabja 1988 against the Kurds, then 1991 against the Shias and the Kurds). The Syrian case represents an additional example of the exploitation of the armed forces by the dominant group (Alawites) to reshape the demography of the country and crush the rebellion of the non-dominant groups (Sunni as well as some Druze and Kurdish elements). Hence, in order to initiate the process of building a corporate consociational settlement, we have to look at strategies for restructuring the Syrian armed forces. We can do so by learning from the Lebanese and Iraqi cases.

The Syrian army has been dominated by the Alawites and has become a tool of oppression against the majority Sunni Arab population. According to Reva Bhalla (2011), out of the 200,000 career soldiers in the Syrian army, roughly 70% are Alawites, with some 80% of officers in the army believed to be Alawites. The Sunnis make up the majority of the 300,000 conscripts who serve for a 2–3-year period before leaving the military (Bhalla, 2011). In the air force, most of the pilots are Sunnis, but the Alawites control logistics, telecommunications and maintenance, thereby preventing potential Sunni air force dissenters from acting unilaterally. Moreover, most high-ranking officers come from the Alawite community, which puts them in control over the army. Due to the notorious reputations of the Syrian army in the Hama massacres in 1982 against the Muslim Brotherhood rebellion, along with its successive repressions of the Druze and Kurds dissents throughout the years, it is vital to reform the armed forces in Syria to achieve a successful adoptability process in the proposed Syrian corporate consociational system.

In any future agreement to rebuild the Syrian army, it is important to avoid stating that the President or Prime Minister is the commander-in-chief and can give orders to the armed forces without the approval of the government. In Lebanon, prior to the civil war, the army was put under the command of the President and he could order the army to deploy anywhere and anytime (Aboultaif, 2016: 72). President Khoury (1952), President Shamoun (1958) and President Franjiyeh (1975) used the army to try and quell the opposition (Aboultaif, 2016: 71–2). In the first two instances, Lebanon had a wise Army Commander, General Fouad Shihab, who refused such an order on the premise that the army may disintegrate. However, in 1975, the army did not object to the orders of President Franjiyeh, and once it clashed with the opposition, the army disintegrated according to confessional lines. Similarly, in Iraq, the Prime Minister is commander-in-chief and he has the right to deploy the army at will, according to Art. 78 of the Iraqi constitution (Aboultaif, 2015a, 2015b). Former Prime Minister Nouri Al-Maliki had ordered his troops to storm a Sunni protest camp in the town of Hawijah, killing about forty civilians in 2013, before sending the army a year later to crush peaceful Sunni protests in Anbar, which eventually turned the population against the army, with many joining forces with the Islamic State in Iraq and Syria (ISIS) in the takeover of Mosul and the Western part of Iraq (Aboultaif, 2015a, 2015b: 14). In addition, Al-Maliki obtained the mobile numbers of commanders all over the country and called them directly to issue orders, thus circumventing the chain of command and making those units personally answerable to him (al-Ali, 2014: 131).

These two examples reveal the complexity of governing armed forces in deeply divided societies. Syrian elites have to agree on the role, control and composition of the armed forces before moving forward to discuss the functionality of power-sharing settlements. It is advised that they avoid the mistakes of Lebanon prior to the civil war and of Iraq after the American invasion, and instead learn from the Lebanese experience in the post-Taif agreement period.

Currently, the Syrian President is commander-in-chief of the Syrian army, and he has ultimate authority over the armed forces. Even the new Russian constitutional proposal for Syria stated that the President is in control of the armed forces (Al Arabiya, 2017), a mistake that may lead to the similar episodes of unrest as previously seen in Iraq. Hence, to learn from the Lebanese case, it is important to follow the course of reform of the Lebanese armed forces, which started with the 1979 National Defence Law (Barak, 2009: 118). The Law stated that the army should be employed only on the basis of domestic consensus (Barak, 2009: 119), and reorganized responsibility for the strategic direction and day-to-day governance of the army under three new bodies: the Higher Defence Council; the Army Command; and the Military Council (Barak, 2009: 119–20). A similar law adopted for reconstructing the Syrian army can ease communal tensions and prevent the domination of the army by any communal group.

With respect to the composition of the army, any future settlement in Syria needs to clearly state that the composition of the rank and file of the Syrian armed forces should respect the demographic ratio of Syrian society; hence it is important to introduce the principle of proportionality. Rather than falling in the same trap as in Iraq, where the Iraqi army has become dominated by the Shia community (Aboultaif, 2015a, 2015b), the Syrian case can benefit again from Lebanon, where brigades are mixed so that they would not be based on religious homogeneity (Gaub, 2007: 8), with a six-month rotation of the army units between regions (Knudsen, 2014: 2). In Lebanon, soldiers are posted to areas away from where they had served during the civil war (Knudsen, 2014), and new military bodies are established in order to integrate the major communal groups into the army's decision-making (Aboultaif, 2016: 75). If the Syrian elite agrees on similar provisions for reforming the armed forces like their Lebanese counterparts, it is highly unlikely that any of the communal groups will be able to dictate their terms on the armed forces, nor will the armed forces be used against any of the communities that form the Syrian societal fabric.

The proposed security amendments for Syria require the rank and file of Syrian troops and officer corps to be proportionally representative of the demographic of Syria. Regarding the positions of battalion and squad commanders, minorities have to be represented fairly. It is important to create a balance in the high posts, particularly in the committees responsible for promoting soldiers, logistical support, and creating strategies for deploying the army. In this way, the presence of minorities in important committees will have a positive impact on the legitimacy of the army. This can be achieved by giving the position of the Army Commander to the Sunni Arab community considering that they are the biggest single population of Syria. The position of Chief of Staff can be given to the Alawite as the second-biggest community, while other high-ranking generals from the Druze, Kurdish and Christian communities will be represented in the committees that support the work of the Army Commander. In principle, one or two representatives from each community could create a balance of power between all groups. Nevertheless, if the Sunni generals represent around half of the committee members, then it is advised that members take decisions by a two-third majority.

Conclusion

The adoptability measures proposed in this chapter are linked to the Syrian context, and they should not be seen as universal models for post-conflict, deeply divided societies. These measures include a corporate consociation, with well-defined veto provisions in the constitution, and the reform of the armed forces.

The case of Iraq after the American invasion is clearly one of a liberal consociation. However, it has failed badly, and its failure has led to massacres, disintegration of the armed forces and the failure of the Arab-dominated center to properly incorporate Kurdish demands. The securitization of communal identities and the absence of a strong central state, amid mistrust between different communities, complicate any step to create a liberal consociational system. In light of this, I have recommended a power-sharing arrangement with corporate guarantees, aiming to avoid intensifying competition between different groups that could lead to democratic backlash and political instability or even violence.

Yet, it is also the case that the adoption of a consociational arrangement is not enough. In situations of heightened insecurity—as Syria surely is—security provisions are required to provide a guarantee that the armed forces would not be used for political gains by any group. This can be done through the adoption of proportionality rules that fairly reflect the demographic composition of the Syrian societal fabric. Then elites have to agree on the control of the armed forces. It is better not to have a President or Prime Minister who controls the armed forces, because they can use it for political purposes, as in the case of Lebanon prior to the civil war and in Iraq under Al-Maliki. Hence, to avoid this problem, the deployment and use of the armed forces should be done by an executive decision taken unanimously by the government. In this way, a national endorsement and cross-communal support for the role of the armed forces will strengthen the legitimacy of the army. Moreover, it will prevent any group from dominating the armed forces, which eventually will lead to the subordination of the non-dominant groups.

The adoptability of a Syrian consociation will face many challenges. It is impossible to state that successful adoption will lead to a democratic transition and a functional power-sharing system. It is critical to consider the factors that may evolve and force the system to "adapt" in a different way than intended. Also, the regional and international circumstances might change and create an environment that may hinder any previously agreed power-sharing settlement. Despite all these challenges, scholars ought not to abandon their research and academic investigation of possible solutions for power-sharing to end the misery of the Syrian people.

REFERENCES

Aboultaif, E. (2015). The Limitations of the Consociational Arrangements in Iraq. *Ethnopolitics Papers, 38*, 1–22. https://www.psa.ac.uk/sites/default/files/page-files/AbuLTaif_EP_No38.pdf

Aboultaif, E. (2015, February 9). What Iraq's Army can Learn from Lebanon. *The Daily Star*.

Aboultaif, E. (2016). The Lebanese Army: Saviour of the Republic? *The RUSI Journal, 161*(1), 70–78.

Adams, M. (2014). Disabling Constitutionalism. Can the Politics of the Belgian Constitution be Explained?. *International Journal of Constitutional Law, 12*(2), 279–302

Al-Ali, Z. (2014). *The Struggle for Iraq's Future: How Corruption*. Yale University Press.

Al Arabiya. (2017). [Online] http://www.alarabiya.net/ar/arab-and-world/syria/2017/01/26

Al Jazeera. (2023). Al Jazeera. [Online] https://www.aljazeera.com/news/2023/5/7/arab-league-agrees-to-bring-syria-back-into-its-fold

Barak, O. (2009). *The Lebanese Army: A National Institution in a Divided Society.* SUNY Press.

Bhalla, R. (2011, May 5). Making Sense of the Syrian Crisis. *Stratfor Global Intelligence*.

Butenschøn, N. A. (1985). Conflict Management in Plural Societies: The Constitutional Democracy Formula. *Scandinavian Political Studies, 8*(1–2), 85–103.

Dixon, P. (2011). Is Consociational Theory the Answer to Global Conflict: From the Netherlands to Northern Ireland and Iraq. *Political Studies Review, 9*(3), 309–322.

Del Sarto, R. (2021). Sectarian Securitization in the Middle East and the Case of Israel. *International Affairs, 97*(3), 759–778.

Deschouwer, K. (2012). *The Politics of Belgium: Governing a Divided Society* (2nd edition). Palgrave Macmillan.

Gaub, F. (2007). Multi-Ethnic Armies in the Aftermath of Civil War: Lessons Learned from Lebanon. *Defence Studies, 7*(1), 5–20.

Goldsmith, L. (2015). *Cycle of Fear: Syria's Alawites in War and Peace*. Oxford University Press.

Hartzell, C., & Hoddie, M. (2007). *Crafting Peace: Power-Sharing Institutions and the Negotiated Settlement of Civil Wars*. Pennsylvania State University Press.

Hinnebusch, R. (2016). The Sectarian Revolution in the Middle East. *Revolutions: Global Trends and Regional Issues, 4*(1), 120–152.

Horowitz, D. L. (2014). Ethnic Power Sharing: Three Big Problems. *Journal of Democracy, 25*(2), 5–20.

Keil, S., & McCulloch, A. (2021). Conclusion: The Past, Present and Future of Power-Sharing in Europe. In S. Keil & A. McCulloch (Eds.), *Power-Sharing in Europe: Past Practice, Present Cases and Future Directions* (pp. 257–273). Palgrave Macmillan.

Knudsen, A. J. (2014). Lebanese Armed Force: A United Army for a Divided Country? *CMI Insight, 9*, 1–8.

Lijphart, A. (1975). Review Article: The Northern Ireland Problem: Cases, Theories, and Solutions. *British Journal of Political Science, 5*(1), 83–106.

Lijphart, A. (1977). Consociation and Federation: Conceptual and Empirical Links. *Canadian Journal of Political Science, 12*(3), 499–515.

Lijphart, A. (2007). *Thinking About Democracy: Power Sharing and Majority Rule in Theory and Practice*. Routledge.

McCulloch, A. (2013). The Track Record of Centripetalism in Deeply Divided Societies. In J. McEvoy & B. O'Leary (Eds.), *Power Sharing in Deeply Divided Places* (pp. 67–93). University of Pennsylvania Press.

McCulloch, A. (2014). Consociational Settlements in Deeply Divided Societies: The Liberal-Corporate Distinction. *Democratization, 21*(3), 501–518.

McCulloch, A., & Zdeb, A. (2022). Veto Rights and Vital Interests: Formal and Informal Veto Rules for Minority Representation in Deeply Divided Societies. *Representation, 58*(3), 427–442.

McEvoy, J. (2013). We Forbid! The Mutual Veto and Power-Sharing Democracy. In J. McEvoy & B. O'Leary (Eds.), *Power-Sharing in Deeply Divided Places* (pp. 253–277). University of Pennsylvania Press.

McEvoy, J. (2015). *Power-Sharing Executives: Governing in Bosnia, Macedonia, and Northern Ireland*. University of Pennsylvania Press.

McEvoy, J., & Aboultaif, E. (2022). Power-Sharing Challenges: From Weak Adoptability to Dysfunction in Iraq. *Ethnopolitics, 21*(3), 238–257.

McGarry, J. (1988). The Anglo-Irish Agreement and the Prospects for Power Sharing in Northern Ireland. *The Political Quarterly, 59*(2), 236–250.

McGarry, J. (2017). Centripetalism, Consociationalism and Cyprus: The "Adoptability" Question. *Political Studies, 65*(2), 512–529.

McGarry, J., & O'Leary, B. (2005). Federation as a Method of Ethnic Conflict Regulation. In S. Noel (Ed.), *From Power Sharing to Democracy: Post-Conflict Institutions in Ethnically Divided Societies* (pp. 263–296). McGill-Queen's University Press.

McGarry, J., & O'Leary, B. (2007). Iraq's Constitution of 2005: Liberal Consociation as Political Prescription. *International Journal of Constitutional Law*, 5(2), 670–698.

O'Leary, B. (1989). The Limits to Coercive Consociationalism in Northern Ireland. *Political Studies*, 37(4), 562–587.

Robson, A. (2021). The Mobilisation of Sectarian Identities in the Syrian Civil War. *E-International Relations*. [Online] https://www.e-ir.info/2021/05/03/the-mobilisation-of-sectarian-identities-in-the-syrian-civil-war/

Sisk, T. D. (2013). Power-Sharing in Civil War: Puzzles of Peacemaking and Peacebuilding. *Civil Wars*, 15(1), 7–20.

Syrian Civil War Map. (2017). Syrian Civil War Map. [Online] https://umap.openstreetmap.fr/nl/map/syrian-civil-war-map-2017-visit-our-website-to-sup_123279#7/35.030/42.407.

Taif Agreement. (1989). Taif Agreement.

Tsebelis, G. (2002). *Veto Players: How Political Institutions Work*. Princeton University Press.

USIP. (2020). *USIP's Work in Syria*. United States Institute of Peace.

CHAPTER 15

The Pacific Islands: The Centrality of Context for Power-Sharing in the Global South

Jon Fraenkel

The Pacific Island states range from relatively homogeneous to hyper-fractionalized polities, from territories still under colonial rule to freely associated and formally independent states and from micro-states with only a few hundreds of inhabitants to Papua New Guinea (PNG), with around nine million citizens. Power-sharing arrangements have been trialed only in the bi-communal polities—New Caledonia and Fiji—both of which witnessed experiments in 'collegial' or 'multi-party cabinet' government in the new millennium. In other parts of the Pacific, linguistic diversity is mostly either so extreme as to render 'ethnicity' impossible as a basis for party formation or else polities are so homogeneous that political parties, if they emerge at all, tend not to be strongly ideologically differentiated. In PNG and the Solomon Islands, there exists no

---

J. Fraenkel (✉)
Victoria University Wellington, Wellington, New Zealand
e-mail: jon.fraenkel@vuw.ac.nz

© The Author(s), under exclusive license to Springer Nature   327
Switzerland AG 2024
E. Wassim Aboultaif et al. (eds.), *Power-Sharing in the Global South*,
Federalism and Internal Conflicts,
https://doi.org/10.1007/978-3-031-45721-0_15

328   J. FRAENKEL

societal pillarization of the type that might underpin executive power-sharing. In the eastern and northern Pacific, island micro-states either have only a single ethnic community or, as in the case of the Federated States of Micronesia, they loosely assemble groups of island sub-states (see Table 15.1). Other than in New Caledonia post-1998 and Fiji 1997–2006, central governments across the Pacific have been largely majoritarian in character.

No consensus exists in the political science literature regarding what characterizes a 'power-sharing' regime. All polities, except the most individualized of dictatorships, 'share' power in some broad sense. In Arend Lijphart's classical work on 'consociational' democracy, 'power-sharing' was understood to entail a 'grand coalition' meaning "government by elite cartel designed to turn a democracy with fragmented political culture into a stable democracy" (Lijphart, 1969: 216; Lijphart, 1975: 99). Influenced by some of his early European cases, Lijphart consistently described consociational democracies as those governed by formal *and* informal power-sharing rules. 'Power-sharing' was thus a term used to denote not only polities with legal provisions or pacts that required participation of deeply opposed parties in cabinet as in Northern Ireland in the wake of the 1998 Good Friday Agreement, Bosnia-Herzegovina under the 1995 Dayton Peace Accord or Fiji under the 1997 constitution, but also those where elites coalesced to transcend deep subcultural cleavages following "unwritten, informal and implicit" rules (Lijphart, 1968: 123). One difficulty was that it was possible to have one without the other, as we see in Fiji where a formal constitutional rule required all parties with over 10% of seats to be invited to join cabinet but this could be, and was mostly, evaded or defied in practice. Another difficulty was that Lijphart was unable to define 'plural' societies (i.e., those with a "fragmented political culture") other than in what he called an 'impressionistic' case by case way (Lijphart, 1999: 54, 56; Lijphart, 2008: 273; Lijphart, 1985: 87–88; Lijphart, 2000: 429). His later work on 'consensus' democracy, allegedly a preferable institutional framework for both plural and non-plural contexts, was in considerable part a method of avoiding that conundrum.

For the purposes of this paper, I define a power-sharing rule as one entailing a formal legal provision governing inter-communal distribution of executive positions in *segmented* settings. The relevant contexts are therefore those where group affiliations regulate party systems. Political parties are essential building blocks in Lijphart's consociational schema,

15 THE PACIFIC ISLANDS: THE CENTRALITY OF CONTEXT ...   329

which is why he so consistently recommended a closed-list proportional representation system or so-called pure PR, the most party-centric of all electoral laws. Without parties, it is possible to have power-sharing only in a limited corporate sense, with post-holders designated by ethnicity, religion or language (often without any guarantee that those post-holders are in any way *representative*). As regards the character of cleavages, Lijphart acknowledged that consociational arrangements might *not* be appropriate in either homogeneous or "the most extreme plural societies" (Lijphart, 1977a: 237–8; Lijphart, 1977b). As regards the informal/ formal distinction, he suggested that consociational democracy outside Europe, or as applied in the newer democracies, was likely to require formal rules and conversely that informal arrangements were unlikely to suffice (Lijphart, 2002: 53–54). Those various qualifications are helpful in investigating which Pacific contexts might be suitable, or unsuitable, for power-sharing configurations. I aim to show in this chapter that this finer-tuned approach to the study of power-sharing makes better sense of the Pacific cases than the more generalist perspectives, and indeed that this approach has broader applicability in the Global South. In what follows, I do however indicate where alternative definitions might encourage different interpretations of the Pacific cases.

THE CHARACTER OF CLEAVAGES

The Pacific Island states include some of the world's most and least heterogeneous polities. In linguistic and spatial terms, the region possesses one of the world's largest language families. From the coastal districts and surrounding smaller islands of PNG in the west to Rapa Nui (Easter Island) in the eastern Pacific—a distance considerably greater than that between London and Vladivostok—we find people who speak related languages belonging to a single ancestral family: Austronesian.[1] Proto-Austronesian is believed to be the language spoken by the Lapita peoples who—commencing around 6,000 years ago—migrated from coastal Asia through island New Guinea to Fiji, Tonga, Samoa and the Marquesas islands before embarking on long sea voyages north to Hawai'i, south to New Zealand (Aotearoa) and east to Rapa Nui. The Western Pacific also

---

[1] The speakers of Austronesian languages are also widely found in island southeast Asia and occasionally in mainland Asia and as far afield as Madagascar.

330   J. FRAENKEL

witnessed a much earlier wave of migration, commencing around 50–60,000 years ago, when sea levels were lower and when modern Australia and New Guinea were part of a single land mass: the Sahul. The speakers of 'Papuan' languages, a diverse grouping defined solely by their being 'non-Austronesian' languages, include most Papua New Guineans, but scattered populations of Papuan speakers are also found in the Solomon Islands.[2] Contemporary PNG has around 820 living languages, West Papua, 269, Vanuatu 109, Solomon Islands 74 and New Caledonia 39, making for a region altogether accounting for close to 20% of the world's living languages.[3] (Table 15.1).

Colonial rule deeply influenced the cleavages found in many of the modern Pacific Islands. After the establishment of a British penal colony in New South Wales (Australia) in 1788 and the signing of the Treaty of Waitangi in New Zealand in 1840, the Pacific was carved up among the colonial powers in a manner reminiscent of the nineteenth century 'scramble for Africa,' with Britain, France, Germany and the United States each establishing varying degrees of control over island states (Spain and Holland had an earlier imperial history in Oceania). Colonial importation of indentured laborers to work on plantations left a lasting legacy, particularly in Hawai'i and Fiji, but less so in Queensland from where most Melanesians were deported after the declaration of a 'white Australia' policy in 1901 or Sāmoa where nearly all were repatriated after the end of German rule in 1914. In Fiji, the descendants of indentured laborers from the Indian subcontinent outnumbered the indigenous population by the 1940s. In the New Hebrides (modern Vanuatu), which became a jointly administered Anglo-French Condominium in the aftermath of the Entente Cordiale in 1906, the distinction between 'Anglophone' and 'Francophone' political parties remained a key feature of political competition in the early years after independence in 1980. The western part of the island of New Guinea, notably the focus of Lijphart's 1963 PhD thesis, fell under Dutch control.[4] Later acquired by Indonesia after a controversial UN-recognized 1969 'act of free choice,' West Papua became another Pacific bi-communal polity owing to sizable inward

[2] It is likely to have been the case that Papuan-speaking peoples once also inhabited islands further east, including areas in modern Vanuatu (the New Hebrides) and New Caledonia.

[3] See http://www.ethnologue.com/ethno_docs/distribution.asp?by=area.

[4] Later turned into a book: Lijphart (1966).

Table 15.1 Pacific Islands population, land area, GDP *per Capita*, languages and institutions

	Population at last census 000s	Land area Km²	GDP per capita current US $	Living indigenous languages	Electoral law	Federal/ Unitary	Presidential/ Parliamentary	Formal power-sharing (executive)
Melanesia								
Fiji	888	18,333	4,274	10	OLPR	Unitary	Parliamentary	1997–2006
Vanuatu	305	12,281	3,537	109	SNTV	Unitary	Parliamentary	No
Solomon Islands	683	28,230	1,647	74	FPTP	Unitary	Parliamentary	No
Papua New Guinea	8,558	462,840	2,384	820	LPV	Unitary	Parliamentary	No
West Papua	2,221	455,405	3,510	269	OLPR	Unitary	Parliamentary	No
New Caledonia	286	18,576	31,418	39	CLPR*	Unitary	Parliamentary	1998–2022
Polynesia								
Cook Islands	15	237	19,183	1	FPTP	Unitary	Parliamentary	No
Tonga	100	749	4,024	1	FPTP	Unitary	Parliamentary	No
Samoa	197	2,934	4,208	1	FPTP	Unitary	Parliamentary	No
Tuvalu	10	26	3,537	1	FPTP	Unitary	Parliamentary	No
Niue	2	259	15,586	5	FPTP/BV	Unitary	Parliamentary	No
French Polynesia	277	3,521		1	CLPR*	Unitary	Parliamentary	No
American Samoa	57	199	11,667	1	FPTP	Unitary	Presidential	No
Micronesia								
Palau	18	444	16,262	1	FPTP	Federal	Presidential	No
Guam	154	561	37,724	1	BV	Unitary	Presidential	No
Nauru	11	21	9,393	1	Dowdall	Unitary	Parliamentary	No

(continued)

Table 15.1 (continued)

	Population at last census 000s	Land area Km^2	GDP per capita current US $	Living indigenous languages	Electoral law	Federal/ Unitary	Presidential/ Parliamentary	Formal power-sharing (executive)
Micronesia, Fed. States	105	701	3,154	8	FPTP	Federal	Parliamentary	No
Marshall Islands	56	181	4,032	1	FPTP/BV	Unitary	Parliamentary	No
Kiribati	120	811	1,533	1	TR	Unitary	Presidential	No
Comm Northern Marianas	56	457	22,298	3	FPTP	Unitary	Presidential	No

Notes 'Presidential' countries are those where the Head of Government is directly elected, whether described as 'Governor' or as 'President.' Countries with 'Presidents' elected by the legislature are listed as 'parliamentary.' OLPR = open list proportional representation, SNTV = single non-transferable vote, FPTP = first-past the-post or single member plurality, LPV = limited preferential vote or alternative vote, CLPR = closed list proportional representation, BV = block vote, Dowdall is a unique simultaneously tallied preferential system where a first vote is worth 1, a second vote 1/2, a third vote 1/3rd & etc. TR = two round system. *Electoral law for New Caledonia and French Polynesia is for the territorial assembly.

'transmigration' mostly from the islands of Java and Sumatra, which left the indigenous Papuan-speaking people in a minority.

The deepest and longest-lasting legacy of colonial rule lay in religious affinities. Protestant and Catholic missionaries fought for the hearts and minds of Polynesian, Micronesian and Melanesian peoples. The churches often tended to align either with British, French or German colonists, but some Christian creeds—like that of the South Seas Evangelical Church which emerged among Melanesian-indentured laborers in Queensland—arose independently. Newer evangelical religions arrived in the post-independence years, occasionally triggering subnational efforts by the mainstream churches to ban competitors. Several Pacific states have witnessed efforts to enshrine Christianity as the religion of state, particularly controversially in Fiji where those descended from migrants from the Indian subcontinent are mostly either Hindu or Muslim (Garrett, 1990). In Vanuatu, Protestant and Catholic loyalties were roughly coterminous with Anglophone/Francophone cleavages, sharpening the early post-independence conflict between Walter Lini's Vanua'aku Pati and the Francophone Union of Moderate Parties.

Elsewhere, efforts to forge political parties based on religious divisions have mostly been unsuccessful, perhaps surprisingly so given the extent to which Christianity defines Pacific identities. In the Solomon Islands, the Christian Fellowship Church was able to secure the election of its favored candidate on Northern New Georgia for decades (Tuza, 1977), but this was only in a single constituency (among 50 presently in total). The April 2021 election in Samoa pitted a new party, the *Fa'atuatua i le Atua Samoa ua Tasi* ('Samoa United in Faith') against the long-time governing Human Rights Protection Party (HRPP). In an ultimately unsuccessful effort to retain office after his electoral defeat, outgoing HRPP Prime Minister Tuila'epa Sa'ilele Malielegaoi claimed to have been 'appointed by god,' signaling that both parties saw themselves as inspired by religious principles but also that, in this respect, there was little to differentiate them (*Samoa* Observer, 2021). Churches have had an important influence everywhere in the Pacific Islands, but there are no post-colonial examples of national-level party differentiation closely following religious divisions.

Electoral Law and Party Systems

Most of the states of Polynesia and Micronesia have first-past-the-post or block vote electoral laws and majoritarian arrangements for government formation: Samoa, Tonga, Cook Islands, Marshall Islands, FSM, Palau, Tuvalu and Niue. The exceptions are French Polynesia, with a closed-list proportional representation system, Kiribati with a two-round electoral law and Nauru with an unusual multi-member preferential system often described as resembling the system invented by eighteenth-century French mathematician Jean-Charles de Borda (Fraenkel & Grofman, 2014). Among the Polynesian territories, only French Polynesia has a strong party cleavage roughly defined by support of, or opposition to, independence from France. Sāmoa switched in 2016 to a full first-past-the-post system, dropping its earlier use of two-member block vote districts. Uniquely across the Pacific islands, that country had a dominant party system, with the ruling Human Rights Protection Party remaining continuously in office from 1988 until its electoral defeat in 2021. In its traditional system, Sāmoa has a concept of 'power-sharing,' *Solaupule* (with *Soa* meaning 'partnership,' *Lau* meaning 'your' and *Pule* meaning 'authority' or 'rule') (Iati, 2022). Tonga too has 'power-sharing' of a sort, if that were to be defined so as to include dual power between the monarch and elected representatives. The King retains considerable authority through his Privy Council, through control over judicial appointments and powers of veto and parliamentary dissolution. Nine of Tonga's 26 MPs are selected by holders of the country's 33 noble titles, and they sit in the legislature alongside 17 MPs elected by 'commoners.' Like Sāmoa, Tonga recently switched from a multi-member district block vote system to a single-member district first-past-the-post arrangement. In the other Polynesian or Micronesian cases, parties either do not exist at all or, where they do, there exists no durable or persistent ideological differentiation between them. Nor are parliamentary factions anywhere in Polynesia or Micronesia rooted in cohesive communities of the type Lijphart saw as indispensable bases for consociational democracy.

In western Melanesia, countries have highly fluid party systems, sometimes characterized as forms of "disorderly democracy" or "unbounded politics" (May, 2003: 1; May, 2006; Steeves, 1996). Governments have regularly changed mid-term, MPs frequently switch sides and the ideological distance between those parliamentary factions often described as 'parties' is typically negligible. The Melanesian countries have devised rules regulating the formation of governments, such as PNG's 2001 Organic Law on the Integrity of Political Parties and Candidates and the Solomon Islands 2014 Political Parties Integrity Law, but these are aimed at diminishing attempted no-confidence votes and at reducing the influence of non-aligned independent MPs rather than at executive power-sharing. The Solomon Islands has a first-past-the-post system, and Vanuatu is one of the few countries in the world (alongside Afghanistan before the Taliban takeover and briefly also Iraq 2021–23) to use a single non-transferable vote system. PNG has a limited preferential vote (or 'alternative vote') system requiring voters to rank order three candidates, but it used a first-past-the-post system from independence (1975) until 2002. Under a mineral resource boom commencing in the middle of the noughties, PNG's Prime Ministers have become more likely than previously to survive a full term in office, but opposition parties remain weak and fragmented (Fraenkel, 2021). In PNG, Solomon Islands and Vanuatu, informal conventions exist regarding regional representation in cabinet and 'grand coalitions' are occasionally proposed, but government remains essentially majoritarian. In these three cases, provinces possess some local-level powers, and Bougainville (PNG) has a peace agreement that enshrines autonomy in law (97.7% of Bougainvilleans voted for independence in a non-binding 2019 referendum). A federal constitution has been under discussion in the Solomon Islands for decades but has never been implemented (Fraenkel, 2019).

Only in Fiji and New Caledonia have deep-seated communal cleavages been addressed through political compacts combined with power-sharing arrangements, and in both cases, these have been formalized in statute. We can compare the Fiji and New Caledonia institutions with respect to: how they combine proportional and majoritarian arrangements; whether they include constraints on the size of the power-sharing executive; whether they permit parties to align together in calculating cabinet portfolio entitlements; whether they possess minority veto provisions that guarantee continuity of a power-sharing executive; and, most importantly, whether central government power-sharing coexists with communal self-rule.

Fiji's Multi-Party Cabinet Experiment

Fiji was left by the departing British colonists in 1970 with a peculiar system of group representation that is occasionally but misleadingly compared to Malaysia's arrangements.[5] Until the 1987 coup, all citizens voted in ethnically reserved constituencies on separate 'Fijian,' 'Indian' and 'general voter' rolls, as well as casting three other votes in common roll constituencies where the ethnicity of candidates was reserved for 'Fijians,' 'Indians' or general voters (in an arrangement somewhat similar to Lebanon's pre-2017 system). Ratu Sir Kamisese Mara's Alliance Party governments relied largely on the indigenous and so-called 'general' voters, but he sought (largely unsuccessfully) to draw Fiji Indian politicians into cabinet particularly in the late 1970s (Premdas, 1979).[6] Although communal seats were reserved for each ethnic community, those Fiji Indian politicians elected from majority Indian constituencies always occupied the opposition benches, with only two brief exceptions. The first, in April 1977, occurred when the largely Fiji Indian-backed National Federation Party narrowly won an election, but the Governor-General controversially restored the defeated Ratu Mara as Prime Minister at the helm of a minority government pending fresh elections in September of that year (which Mara's Alliance Party won). The second, in 1987, saw a largely Fiji Indian-backed but purportedly class-based government overthrown in a military coup a month after it took office. Only a decade later, with agreement on a new 1997 constitution, did Fiji establish a formal constitutional provision requiring both Fiji Indian and Indigenous Fijian MPs to collaborate in government.

Fiji's 1997 constitution is unusual internationally in that it entailed a compact primarily agreed between opposed domestic forces.[7] External

---

[5] Horowitz correctly notes that "Fiji adopted the device of a multi-ethnic alliance directly from Malaysia" but incorrectly describes Fiji's Alliance as "basically similar" to its Malaysian namesake (Horowitz, 1985: 579, 410n). The Fijian Alliance never had the same level of support in the Indian community as its Malaysian counterpart obtained in the Chinese community. For a more careful comparison between Fiji and Malaysia, see Milne 1981.

[6] 'General voters' were those who were neither on the Fijian nor on the Indian voter rolls, i.e., Europeans, part-Europeans, Chinese and (from 1990) other Pacific islanders.

[7] John McGarry misinterprets me as arguing that "the failure of Fiji's post-1997 power-sharing experiment may be partly attributed to an absence of external involvement" (McGarry, 2017: 271). On the contrary, this was one of its greatest strengths. In

actors assisted, including the Commonwealth and the United Nations Department of Political Affairs, but the key negotiations were undertaken by Fiji's political parties. In a provision borrowed from South Africa but then modified, the 1997 constitution provided that all parties with 10% or more of seats were entitled to participate proportionally in cabinet. At the first election under the new system in May 1999, the Fiji Labour Party (FLP) secured an absolute majority (37 of the 71 seats) and formed a 'People's Coalition' cabinet with three small largely indigenous-backed parties. A critical issue was whether former Prime Minister Sitiveni Rabuka's Soqosoqo ni Vakavulewa ni Taukei (SVT) party would join the government, as it was entitled to do under the power-sharing rule. That party had secured the largest share of the indigenous first preference vote (38%), but gained only eight seats (11%), partly due to schisms among the indigenous parties and partly due to the operation of a new preferential voting system (Fraenkel, 2001; Fraenkel & Grofman, 2006). Wounded by its electoral defeat, the SVT put up conditions on accepting cabinet participation which new FLP Prime Minister Mahendra Chaudhry rejected. When that decision was challenged in the Supreme Court, the judges ruled that "what purported to be a conditional acceptance amounted to a declining of the invitation" (Supreme Court of Fiji, 1999: 22). That was a verdict that Fiji's courts later revisited, finding retrospectively that the required invitation to join a multi-party cabinet should not be a once-and-for-all offer, but rather an ongoing requirement that could have been revisited (Supreme Court of Fiji, 2003: S. 117).

Chaudhry's People's Coalition government lasted only a year in office. It was overthrown in a May 2000 coup. After a period of severe instability, Fiji's 1997 constitution was resurrected by the courts in March 2001. Fresh elections followed in August, again under the alternative vote system, which were this time won by a newly formed largely Indigenous-backed party, the Soqosoqo Duavata ni Lewenivanua (SDL). The new Prime Minister Laisenia Qarase sought to follow the 1999 precedent by issuing the required formal invitation to the FLP together with an admission that he had "already formed a coalition with like-minded parties and individuals based on consensus and voluntary agreement" (Qarase, 2001). He established a 20-minister cabinet excluding the FLP, but this was found to be unconstitutional by the Court of Appeal (2002). No

---

Bosnia, by contrast, the externally appointed Office of the High Representative intervened continuously after 1997 in ways that diminished the likelihood of effective power-sharing.

reconfigured government was established. Dispute continued over the extent of the FLP's entitlement to cabinet portfolios (Supreme Court of Fiji, 2003, 2004). In its final decision in 2004, the Supreme Court watered down the power-sharing provision, allowing the SDL to retain its majority in cabinet by appointing independents or unaffiliated senators outside its formal party entitlement and therefore unconstrained by the power-sharing rule. With a new election looming in 2006, the FLP chose not to join government.[8]

In 2006, a third election under the 1997 constitution saw the SDL again emerge victorious. This time Qarase did form a multi-party cabinet, albeit under the revised 2004 rules. Nine FLP MPs joined the government, but party leader Mahendra Chaudhry preferred to remain outside cabinet and sought, unsuccessfully, to become Leader of the Opposition. In its eight months in existence, Fiji's multi-party cabinet took steps to resolve critical issues of inter-ethnic dispute (Green, 2009).

The destruction of Fiji's power-sharing experiment did not arise directly from differences between those parties in government, but as a result of extra-parliamentary action. During the multi-party cabinet controversies of 2002–4, military commander Frank Bainimarama had assumed an increasingly belligerent stance toward the SDL government (Firth & Fraenkel, 2009). In December 2006, the Republic of Fiji Military Forces overthrew the Qarase-led administration. A military-backed interim government formed in January 2007 initially included several FLP ministers. Chaudhry became Minister of Finance, and—using his trade unionist background—played a pivotal role in crushing a strike by teachers and nurses later that year (Lal, 2008: 4). Chaudhry was sacked as a minister in 2008, and subsequently reinvented himself as a bitter opponent of the post-coup government. Only seven years after the coup was a new 2013 constitution promulgated, now without the power-sharing requirement or the preferential voting system. Instead, Fiji adopted an open-list proportional representation system and reverted to majoritarian arrangements for government formation. Bainimarama formed a FijiFirst Party, which was able to win semi-democratic elections in 2014 and, with a reduced majority, in 2018, although that government was narrowly defeated at polls held in December 2022 by a three-party multi-ethnic opposition coalition. The orientation of the 2006–22 governments was

---

[8] The court controversies regarding Fiji's power-sharing provisions are reviewed at greater length in Fraenkel (2017).

integrationist or even anti-consociational in vision, with a military-backed government seeking to transcend ethnic divisions first by a period of dictatorship and subsequently through semi-authoritarian rule.

COLLEGIALITY IN NEW CALEDONIA

New Caledonia's power-sharing arrangements stem from compacts agreed in 1988 and 1998 aimed at ending a period of acute civil strife in the 1980s. Since the late 1970s, the French territory has had a bifurcated configuration, with a cleavage between largely Indigenous Kanak supporters of independence and mostly non-Kanak loyalists determined to keep the territory under French rule. The 1988 Matignon-Oudinot Accords and the 1998 Nouméa Accord aimed at bridging political differences over the issue of whether to remain under French sovereignty. The 1988 Matignon-Oudinot Accords included provisions for a referendum on independence to be held a decade later, some autonomy for each of the territory's three provinces and a program of 'rééquilibrage' ('rebalancing') to improve well-being in the predominantly Kanak Northern and Loyalty Islands provinces. When the Matignon Accord's ten-year deadline fell due, both sides agreed to delay the scheduled referendum for a further 15–20 years. The 1998 Nouméa Accord strengthened the Matignon Accord's provincial autonomy arrangements but also provided for a phased devolution of powers from France, a Kanak customary Senate, a power-sharing government and continued affirmative action for the poorer and predominantly Kanak-Indigenous Northern and Loyalty Islands provinces.

New Caledonia's post-1998 institutional arrangements are classically consociational. The territory uses a closed-list proportional representation system for simultaneously elected five-yearly provincial administrations and has a 54-member territorial congress, with zipper lists applying the French 'Law on Parity' that ensures that close to 50% of legislators are women. The provincial government arrangements offer Indigenous Kanaks a considerable degree of autonomy in the north of the main island and on the smaller Loyalty Islands, both areas where they form a majority of the population. All slates in the territorial congress with more than six representatives are entitled to executive positions, but smaller parties can align with others to obtain portfolios. New Caledonia's government has between 5 and 11 ministers. Once government is formed, its president is chosen by majority rule. A strong minority veto exists because

340 J. FRAENKEL

any minister who resigns from the executive, if not replaced by his or her party, precipitates the fall and reconstitution of the government out of the assembly. That provision was used by the pro-independence Front de Libération Nationale Kanak et Socialiste (FLNKS) to bring down a loyalist-led government in February 2021. When recomposed, a small party mainly backed by settlers from the islands of Wallis and Futuna, L'Éveil Océanien (Oceanian Awakening) switched sides enabling the FLNKS to secure its first ever President in July 2021. Until 2021, loyalists had led the territorial executive. By convention, from 2001 to 2021 the Vice President had come from the FLNKS. As of July 2021, the positions are switched: the President is now an Indigenous Kanak and the Vice President comes from one of the loyalist parties.

Although classically consociational, New Caledonia's agreement—like those in the former Sudan under the 2005 Comprehensive Peace Agreement and in Bougainville—centrally featured a core majoritarian provision with a firm time horizon.[9] In all three cases, peace accords were reached by agreement on a delayed independence referendum. New Caledonia's Nouméa Accord provided for three consecutive votes. By agreement, the New Caledonia electorate was restricted to the Indigenous population and those who arrived in the territory before 1994 (In recognition that French loyalists had engineered a population shift over the 1960s–1990s that potentially disadvantaged the Indigenous Kanaks and longer-term settlers). In the first referendum held in November 2018, 56.7% voted against independence, and 43.3% in favor. In the second vote in October 2020, 53.3% were opposed and 46.7% in favor (Chauchat, 2019). That narrowing margin, together with the restrictions on the franchise and new alignments within the territorial assembly, suggested that the vote might eventually sway in favor of independence (Maclellan, 2021). The third required referendum was held on 12 December 2021, with the timing dictated by Paris in line with the preference of the anti-independence parties. The FLNKS refused to participate owing to the Covid-19 pandemic which had hit the Indigenous community particularly severely (*France24*, 2021). The other reason was that scarcely a year had passed since the second referendum in contrast to the two-year gap between the first two. The result was a 96.5% majority against independence for New Caledonia, but with turnout at only 43.9%, only marginally over half of

---

[9] In Bougainville's case, the outcome was not binding on the PNG government.

the 85.6% who cast ballots at the previous referendum held in October 2020. In the majority Kanak areas in the northern part of the *grand terre* (Main Island) and on the outer islands, the polling booths were empty and eerily quiet.

Despite the 'no' vote, the Nouméa Accord provides that the power-sharing institutions and devolved powers remain in place, but with negotiations scheduled on a new agreement.[10] Fearing that the tide may be turning against them, some of the Loyalist politicians have mooted a potential secession of the majority-settler Southern Province, also the richest part of the territory, but the Nouméa Accord prohibits breaking the territory up into constituent parts.[11] The loyalists also want to revisit the restricted franchise, which if abandoned would solidify the anti-independence majority. That too is strongly opposed by the FLNKS. The Macron government now wants a fresh statute for New Caledonia to replace the Nouméa Accord, but the FLNKS is unlikely to agree unless there is a possibility of a further referendum this time with Kanak participation.

New Caledonia and Fiji Compared

Fiji's 1997–2006 power-sharing arrangements worked far less effectively than those in New Caledonia after 1998. In New Caledonia, proportionality governs both provincial and territorial elections as well as the

---

[10] 'Tant que les consultations n'auront pas abouti à la nouvelle organisation politique proposée, l'organisation politique mise en place par l'accord de 1998 restera en vigueur, à son dernier stade d'évolution, sans possibilité de retour en arrière, cette "irréversibilité" étant constitutionnellement garantie' (Accord de Nouméa, 1998), [English translation: "If the consultations [or referendums] have not resulted in the proposed new political organization, the political organization established by the 1998 agreement will remain in force, at its last stage of development, without the possibility of going back, this 'irreversibility' being constitutionally guaranteed"].

[11] 'Le résultat de cette consultation s'appliquera globalement pour l'ensemble de la Nouvelle- Calédonie. Une partie de la Nouvelle-Calédonie ne pourra accéder seule à la pleine souveraineté ou conserver seule des liens différents avec la France, au motif que les résultats de la consultation électorale y auraient été différents du résultat global', (Accord de Nouméa, 1998), [English translation: "The result of the poll will apply comprehensively to New Caledonia as a whole. It will not be possible for one part of New Caledonia alone to achieve full sovereignty, or alone to retain different links with France, on the grounds that its results in the poll differed from the overall result"].

composition of cabinet whereas Fiji (1997–2006) had a majoritarian electoral law for general elections coupled with a proportionality rule for the formation of the multi-party government. Fiji's single-member district-based alternative vote system generated severe inequities in parliamentary representation and was ultimately abandoned. In New Caledonia, small parties in the territorial assembly could coalesce to boost joint entitlements to cabinet portfolios, but in Fiji they could not. New Caledonia's arrangements set limits on cabinet size (maximum 11) whereas the size of Fiji's power-sharing cabinet remained unconstrained (encouraging Qarase to respond to court rulings enforcing power-sharing by expanding cabinet size to 36 ministers in a 71-member government and offering tokenistic portfolios to the FLP). Fiji retained the Westminster convention of a Prime Minister first having to form a government that commands a majority in the house but subsequently supplemented a power-sharing rule requiring all parties with over 10% of seats to receive an invitation to join the cabinet thereby building a predictable tension into government formation.[12] New Caledonia's smoother arrangement was that the formation of the power-sharing executive precedes the decision on the territory's president.

In Fiji's case, the power-sharing rules themselves became a key focus of inter-ethnic discord over 2001–6. FLP leader Mahendra Chaudhry had little desire to share power with the major ethnic Fijian party, as shown by his unsuccessful effort to lead the opposition in the aftermath of the 2006 election, but he gamed the court controversies over the multi-party cabinet provision to undermine the legitimacy of the Qarase government. During those years, the Republic of Fiji Military Forces assumed an ever more interventionist stance. Other more accommodating leaders of the FLP joined the multi-party cabinet of May-December 2006, but they were left in the political wilderness after the military coup of December 2006. In New Caledonia, leadership of the territorial executive was an important focus of political competition, but—for the Kanak politicians—control over the Northern and Loyalty Islands provincial assemblies offered some autonomy at the local level. In unitary

---

[12] As Fiji's Supreme Court found in 2002, "there remains an element of discordance between the mandatory language of s. 99 and the terminology of s. 6(g) which states 'if it is necessary or desirable to form a coalition government from among competing parties.'" The latter had been the original intent of the Reeves Commission, but it was inconsistent with the multi-party cabinet rule (Supreme Court of Fiji, 2002: S. 126).

Fiji, political competition was always focused on the central government. Provincial and municipal governments existed, but the former were exclusively Indigenous-controlled (with conjoined powerless 'Indian advisory councils') and the multi-ethnic municipal councils were subordinate to the central government. As the Bosnia-Herzegovina and Belgium cases demonstrate, local-level autonomy can potentially serve as an alternative to central government power-sharing (Fraenkel, 2020; Popelier, 2021). In the aftermath of her victory in the 2019 New Caledonia provincial elections, the key loyalist leader Sonia Backès notably assumed the post of President of the Southern Provincial Assembly rather than joining the territorial executive. That decision signaled a preference for majoritarian sub-territorial control over executive power-sharing at the central territorial level.

Conditionalities and Contextual Blindness

In Lijphart's work on 'consociational democracy,' power-sharing was understood as a specific form of institutional arrangement suitable for 'segmented,' 'plural' or 'pillarized' polities. It was not necessarily suitable for homogeneous polities where cleavages revolved around issues other than ethnic identity, although Lijphart did later elaborate a defense of 'consensus democracy' allegedly suitable also for homogeneous contexts. In *Democracy in Plural Societies*, he ruled out "any hope" for democracy in the most hyper-fractionalized polities even if accompanied by consociational arrangements (Lijphart, 1977a: 237–8). In later work, he advanced a less pessimistic verdict about one such highly diverse polity, India, which he argued was in fact 'consociational' in character (Lijphart, 1991). This has not been broadly accepted or, when it has been accepted, it has been with reference largely to the inclusiveness of the post-war Congress governments (Adeney, 2002; Adeney & Swenden, 2019; Mcmillan, 2008; Wilkinson, 2000). Many hyper-diverse polities have indeed fallen under authoritarian rule, but some have remained democracies, including PNG, the Solomon Islands and Vanuatu. Lijphart's work offers little guidance for highly heterogeneous countries, unless one extracts from this only a very vague recommendation for inclusiveness or devolution of power away from the central government.

In the Pacific Islands, we find numerous highly diverse polities where cultural or linguistic differences are not highly politicized. PNG, Solomon Islands and Vanuatu are hyper-fractionalized, and they have weak and fluid party systems that are neither defined by ethnicity nor ideology (with the rider that 'ethnicity' is of course itself deeply ideological). In Vanuatu, an Anglophone/Francophone cleavage dominated the party system that emerged in the wake of the Santo Rebellion of 1980, when secessionist groups emerged on the islands of Santo and Tanna, leaving the predominantly Anglophone Vanua'aku Pati in a bi-communal competition with the Francophone Union of Moderate Parties. By the 1990s, schisms had emerged on both sides and the centrality of the Francophone/Anglophone cleavages faded over time (Morgan, 2008; Van Trease, 2005). None of these three Western Melanesian countries could, or should, have adopted 'power-sharing' regimes simply because such arrangements presuppose the existence of cohesive and segmented groups represented by powerful actors on the national stage.

In other island states, critical constitutional controversies center on the distribution of power between central and local government rather than on power-sharing at the center. Federal arrangements or devolved autonomy are either embedded in constitutions (FSM, Palau), or peace agreements (Bougainville, 2001, New Caledonia, 1988, 1998), or have some informal de facto presence (Solomon Islands, Tuvalu, Kiribati). In the Solomon Islands, pressure for 'state government' was an important feature both of the Western breakaway movement of the 1970s and of the Isatabu rebellion on the island of Guadalcanal in the later 1990s (Fraenkel, 2004; Premdas et al., 1984). Tuvalu is formally a unitary state, but the 1997 Falekaupule Act gives considerable powers to the island councils. Vanuatu's ceremonial President is elected by an electoral college comprising MPs as well as Presidents of the regional councils (Levine & Roberts, 2005: 282). The Federated States of Micronesia began existence as a residual state, the remaining part of the US-controlled United Nations Trust Territory of the Pacific Islands after the secession of the Commonwealth of the Northern Marianas, the Republic of the Marshall Islands and Palau. It combines the states of Yap, Pohnpei, Chuuk and Kosrae, with continuing pressures for independence by Chuuk, FSM's most populous and poorest state. Palau too has a federation, but with a population of only 18,000 it is a 'Lilliputian' arrangement, combining sixteen separate states. Palau, FSM, Kiribati, Marshall Islands, Nauru and Tuvalu have been described as "democracies without parties," although factional groupings have occasionally emerged that adopt party monikers (Anckar & Anckar, 2000; Veenendaal, 2016).

Power-sharing is of potential relevance in French Polynesia. Colonized by France in 1842, the islands of Tahiti and Mo'orea have a long tradition of inter-mixing between Polynesians and settlers of French descent.[13] Those islands account for 88% of the French Polynesian population, with the remainder dispersed across the scattered Marquesas, Tuamotu, Gambier and Austral Island groups. The territory was re-inscribed on the United Nations list of non-self-governing territories in 2013. The main division has been between the supporters of independence and those who prefer greater autonomy from France. Oscar Temaru's pro-independence Tavini Huiraatira fought a long-running battle with Gaston Flosse's Tahoeraa Huiraatira during the 2000s, but Edouard Fritch's ruling Tapura Huiraatira subsequently assumed the mantle of being the major anti-independence party while Flosse (having been briefly imprisoned for corruption) has fallen out with Paris (Gonschorr, 2020: 233). Coalitions have arisen between the major parties, but there exists no formal power-sharing agreement. Temaru's party has sought a New Caledonia-style arrangement for French Polynesia, including a referendum on self-determination (Fisher, 2018). Even if Paris were to agree on a Nouméa Accord-style consociational arrangement for French Polynesia, the dilemma remains that—as in New Caledonia 1998 and Sudan 2006—such an agreement would ultimately entail a simple-majority vote on the core constitutional question (which the pro-independence side would be likely to lose).

In West Papua, some agreement on devolved powers and/or power-sharing is feasible, but the predominantly Melanesian pro-independence movement remains highly fragmented (Fraenkel & Aspinall, 2012; Mietzner, 2007). With a population of 1.3 million, including large numbers of Indonesian migrants, West Papua accounts for only 1.7% of Indonesia's overall population but 24% of its land mass (Elmslie, 2017). Migrants have flocked to vast palm oil plantations, laid out on land cleared of tropical forests. The Grasberg gold and copper mine employs close to 20,000 and is the largest tax paying entity in Indonesia. The indigenous population forms a majority only in the mountainous interior, not in the lowland coastal or urban areas. Indigenous areas are just as linguistically diverse as those in neighboring PNG (See Table 15.1).

---

[13] The 1988 census was the last to report ethnicity. It identified 66.5% of the population as Polynesian, and the remainder as either European (11.9%), Asian (4.7%) or mixed (16.4%) (Brami Celentano, 2002).

The UN-recognized 1969 'act of free choice' was conducted by only 1,000 or so government-selected delegates but was rejected by the Free Papua Movement (OPM) which has conducted a sporadic insurrection against Indonesian authorities ever since. The government passed a special autonomy law for West Papua in 2001, promising affirmative action for indigenous Papuans but not self-government. The autonomy statute was unilaterally renewed in 2021 (Reuters, 2021), but this offers only tokestic concessions to pro-independence politicians. There have been no peace negotiations both due to Jakarta's unwillingness to make concessions and the lack of centralized leadership among Papuans. The relative strength of the Indonesian state coupled with the fragmentation of the West Papuan independence movement has precluded any constructive dialogue around a non-imposed autonomy statute for West Papua.

CONCLUSION

The Pacific Island states and territories have a wide range of internal cleavage configurations: between center and periphery, between Indigenous peoples and the descendants of indentured laborers, and between intra-country trans-migrants and metropolitan settlers. Only in Fiji and New Caledonia was societal segmentation and conflict addressed through power-sharing compacts, but Fiji's hybrid combination of Westminster and proportionality in the executive worked poorly. In New Caledonia, provincial autonomy allowed Kanak self-rule in the Northern and Loyalty Islands provinces whereas in Fiji conflict was ever focused on control over central government. In West Papua and French Polynesia, there have been efforts to resolve conflict through autonomy arrangements, rather than power-sharing deals, but these have not been greatly successful. Elsewhere, party systems were either absent altogether or too fluid and personalized to encourage compacts aimed at balancing the distribution of executive authority. Constitutional deliberations have instead centered on the extent of island or provincial autonomy, particularly for Bougainville, the Solomon Islands and the Federated States of Micronesia.

Two implications for investigations of power-sharing in the Global South flow from this analysis. The first is the importance of context: one needs to carefully analyze the character of cleavages (or their absence) to establish where power-sharing agreements might be appropriate or workable. In highly heterogeneous settings without robust party systems, including those polities that Thomas Carothers once described as "feckless" democracies (Carothers, 2002), there is no place for 'power-sharing' of the type discussed by Lijphart or the consociational theorists.

Second, Lijphart's formal/informal distinction glides over a critical difference between polities that prioritize inclusion. It owes its origin to his original sequence of investigation. Initially, Lijphart was engaged in establishing typologies of democracy and identifying countries that departed from the Anglo-American majoritarian model, including Switzerland, Austria and the Netherlands (Liphart, 1969; Lijphart, 1977a: 1–24). Later, as the wave of post-Cold War experiments in institutional design got under way, 'consociational democracy' was advanced as a constitutional recommendation for countries such as South Africa, Bosnia and Fiji which were adopting new institutional arrangements intended to mitigate conflict. In the former cases, power-sharing denoted a specific behavioral type. In the latter, it was an institutional device anticipated to be uniquely capable of sustaining democracy in deeply divided settings. Yet it was entirely possible to have formal executive portfolio distribution rules in place without behavioral power-sharing, as we saw in Fiji over 1999–2000 and 2001–2006 or Bosnia after 1995 regarding relations between the Republika Srpska and the Bosnia-Herzegovina-level government.[14] Only in the formal cases was it possible to test the efficacy of power-sharing arrangements through an investigation of what these delivered in practice. For the Global South, at least in appropriate contexts, power-sharing rules are likely to need to be codified in law or placed within constitutions.

[14] Even in those European cases that had both formal rules and behavioral power-sharing, as in Belgium, it has been the propensity to seek consensual solutions at critical junctures rather than the formal legal rules that has most contributed to the survival of consociational democracy (Deschouwer, 2006: 895, 905-6). The price of failure to reach agreement was just too high.

References

Accord de Nouméa. (1998, May 5). http://www.ac-noumea.nc/sitevr/NC/AccdsN.html.

Adeney, K. (2002). Constitutional Centring: Nation Formation and Consociational Federalism in India and Pakistan. *Commonwealth & Comparative Politics, 40*(3), 8–33.

Adeney, K., & Swenden, W. (2019). Power-sharing in the World's Largest Democracy: Informal Consociationalism in India (and its Decline?). *Swiss Political Science Review, 25*(4), 450–475.

Anckar, D., & Anckar, C. (2000). Democracies without Parties. *Comparative Political Studies, 33*(2), 255–247.

Brami, C. A. (2002). Frontières Ethniques et Redéfinition du Cadre Politique à Tahiti. *Hermès, 32–33*, 367–375. https://www.cairn.info/revue-hermes-la-revue-2002-1-page-367.htm.

Carothers, T. (2002). The End of the Transition Paradigm. *Journal of Democracy, 13*(1), 5–31.

Chauchat, M. (2019). New Caledonia Remains French for Now: The Referendum of 4 November 2018. *Journal of Pacific History, 54*(2), 253–267.

Court of Appeal (Fiji). (2002, January 22). *In re the Constitution, Chaudhary v Qarase [2002] FJCA 28; Miscellaneous 1.2001.* http://www.paclii.org/fj/cases/FJCA/2002/28.html

Deschouwer, K. (2006). And the Peace Goes On? Consociational Democracy and Belgian Politics in the Twenty-First Century. *West European Politics, 29*(5), 895–911.

Elmslie, J. (2017). The Great Divide: West Papuan Demographics Revisited; Settlers Dominate Coastal Regions but the Highlands Still Overwhelmingly Papuan. *The Asia-Pacific Journal, 15*(2), 1–11.

Firth, S., & Fraenkel, J. (2009). The Fiji Military and Ethno-nationalism: Analysing the Paradox. In J. Fraenkel, S. Firth, & B.V. Lal (Eds.), *The 2006 Military Takeover in Fiji: A Coup to End All Coups?* ANU EPress.

Fisher, D. (2018, May 8). *New Caledonia's Independence Referendum: Local and Regional Implications.* Lowy Institute.

Fraenkel, J. (2001). The Alternative Vote System in Fiji; Electoral Engineering or Ballot-Rigging? *Journal of Commonwealth and Comparative Politics, 39*(2), 1–31.

Fraenkel, J. (2004). *The Manipulation of Custom: From Uprising to Intervention in the Solomon Islands.* Pandanus Books & Victoria University Press.

Fraenkel, J. (2017). Power-sharing in Coup Prone Fiji. In A. McCulloch & J. McGarry (Eds.), *Power-Sharing: Empirical and Normative Challenges* (pp. 103–123). Routledge.

Fraenkel, J. (2019, October 30). Solomon Islands: A Federation that Never Was. *50 Shades of Federalism*. http://50shadesoffederalism.com/case-studies/solomon-islands-a-federation-that-never-was/?fbclid=IwAR02NOe0GB8CZeeDF3fY2wClTXYFwzjJ7DaXXLc4jNitLx5Dmga0CKTTTrs.

Fraenkel, J. (2020). The 'Uncle Tom' Dilemma: Minorities in Power-Sharing Arrangements. *International Political Science Review, 41*(1), 124–137.

Fraenkel, J. (2021, September 16–17). *Zapping the Yo-Yo Man: OLIPPAC and the Consolidation of Executive Power in Papua New Guinea.* Paper delivered at Ron May's Festschrift, Learning about Papua New Guinea and How it Works. Australian National University.

Fraenkel, J., & Aspinall. E. (2012). *Comparing Across Regions: Parties and Political Systems in Indonesia and the Pacific Islands.* Centre for Democratic Institutions, Discussion Paper, 2. http://archives.cap.anu.edu.au/cdi_anu_edu_au/.AP/2012-13/2013_04_3_RES_IPD_AP_Frnkl_Aspnll_CBR.html.

Fraenkel, J., & Grofman, B. (2006). Does the Alternative Vote Foster Moderation in Ethnically Divided Societies? The Case of Fiji. *Comparative Political Studies, 39*(5), 623–651.

Fraenkel, J., & Grofman, B. (2014). The Borda Count and its Real World Alternatives: Comparing Scoring Rules in Nauru and Slovenia. *Australian Journal of Political Science, 49*(2), 186–205.

France24. (2021, October 21). *New Caledonia Separatists Call for Boycott of Independence Referendum.*

Garrett, J. (1990). Uncertain Sequel: The Social and Religious Scene in Fiji since the Coups. *The Contemporary Pacific, 2*(1), 87–111.

Gonschorr, L. (2020). Political Reviews: French Polynesia. *The Contemporary Pacific, 32*(1), 232–239.

Green, M. (2009). *Fiji's Short-lived Experiment in Executive Power-Sharing.* May-December 2006, State, Society & Governance in Melanesia, Discussion Paper, 2.

Horowitz, D. L. (1985). *Ethnic Groups in Conflict.* University of California Press.

Iati, I. (2022). Are Sāmoa's Political Institutions Democratic? A Critical Examination of the Fa'amatai and the 2021 General Election. *Journal of Pacific History, 57*(4), 451–473.

Lal, B. V. (2008). *One Hand Clapping: Reflections on the First Anniversary of Fiji's December 2006 Coup.* State Society & Governance in Melanesia, Discussion paper, 2008/1.

350   J. FRAENKEL

Levine, S., & Roberts, N. (2005). The Constitutional Structures and Electoral Systems of Pacific Island States. *Commonwealth & Comparative Politics, 43*(3), 276–295.

Lijphart, A. (1966). *The Trauma of Decolonization: The Dutch and West New Guinea*. Yale University Press.

Lijphart, A. (1968). *The Politics of Accommodation: Pluralism and Democracy in the Netherlands*. University of California Press [Revised edition 1975].

Lijphart, A. (1969). Consociational Democracy. *World Politics, 21*(2), 207–225.

Lijphart, A. (1975). The Northern Ireland Problem: Cases, Theories, and Solutions. *British Journal of Political Science, 5*(1), 83–106.

Lijphart, A. (1977a). *Democracy in Plural Societies: A Comparative Exploration*. Yale University Press.

Lijphart, A. (1977b). Majority Rule versus Democracy in Deeply Divided Societies. *Politikon, 4*(2), 113–126.

Lijphart, A. (1985). *Power-sharing in South Africa, Institute of International Studies*. University of California Press.

Lijphart, A. (1991). The Puzzle of Indian Democracy: A Consociational Interpretation. *American Political Science Review, 90*(2), 258–268.

Lijphart, A. (1999). *Patterns of Democracy: Government Forms and Performance in Thirty-Six Countries*. Yale University Press.

Lijphart, A. (2000). Definitions, Evidence and Policy: A Response to Matthijs Bogaards' Critique. *Journal of Theoretical Politics, 12*(4), 425–431.

Lijphart, A. (2002). The Wave of Power-Sharing Democracy. In A. Reynolds (Ed.), *The Architecture of Democracy: Constitutional Design, Conflict Management, and Democracy*. Oxford University Press.

Lijphart, A. (2008). *Thinking about Democracy: Power Sharing and Majority Rule in Theory and Practice*. Routledge.

Maclellan, N. (2021, June 15). Third Time Lucky in New Caledonia. *Inside Story*. https://insidestory.org.au/third-time-lucky-in-new-caledonia/.

May, R. (2003). *Disorderly Democracy: Political Turbulence and Institutional Reform in Papua New Guinea* (p. 3). Society & Governance in Melanesia Discussion Paper.

May, R. (2006). Papua New Guinea: Disorderly Democracy or Dysfunctional State? In D. Rumley, V.L. Forbes and C. Griffin (Eds.), *Australia's Arc of Instability: The Political and Cultural Dynamics of Regional Security*. Springer.

McGarry, J. (2017). Conclusion: What Explains the Performance of Power-sharing Settlements. In A. McCulloch & J. McGarry (Eds.), *Power-Sharing: Empirical and Normative Challenges*. Routledge.

Mcmillan, A. (2008). Deviant Democratization in India. *Democratization, 15*(4), 733–749.

Mietzner, M. (2007). Local Elections and Autonomy in Papua and Aceh: Mitigating or Fueling Secessionism. *Indonesia, 84*, 1–39.

Milne, R. S. (1981). *Politics in Ethnically Bipolar States: Guyana, Malaysia, Fiji.* University of British Columbia Press.

Morgan, M. (2008). The Origins and Effects of Party Fragmentation in Vanuatu. In L. Hambly, M. Morgan & R. Rich (Eds.), *Political Parties in the Pacific Islands.* ANU Press.

Popelier, P. (2021). Power-sharing in Belgium: The Disintegrative Model. In S. Keil & A. McCulloch (Eds.), *Power-Sharing in Europe: Past Practice, Present Cases, and Future Directions.* Cham: Palgrave Macmillan.

Premdas, R. (1979). Elections in Fiji: Restoration of the Balance in September 1977. *The Journal of Pacific History, 14*(4), 194–207.

Premdas, R., Steeves, J., & Larmour, P. (1984). The Western Breakaway Movement in the Solomon Islands. *Pacific Studies, 7*(2), 34–67.

Qarase, L. (2001, September 10). *Qarase to Chaudhry, letter.* [Included as annex in Supreme Court of Fiji 2003].

Reuters. (2021, July 15). *Indonesia Parliament Passes Revised Autonomy Law for Restive Papua.*

Samoa Observer. (2021, May 12). *Tuilaepa: An Incapable Democrat.*

Steeves, J. (1996). Unbounded Politics in the Solomon Islands: Leadership and Party Alignments. *Pacific Studies, 19*(1), 115–138.

Supreme Court of Fiji. (1999). *President of the Republic of Fiji Islands and Kubuabola, Chaudhry & Speed,* Miscellaneous Case No 1 of 1999, p. 22.

Supreme Court of Fiji. (2003, July 18). *Qarase, President of the Republic of the Fiji Islands & Attorney General Vs Chaudhry,* Civil Appeal No. CBV 0004/2002S. http://www.paclii.org/fj/cases/FJSC/2003/1.html

Supreme Court of Fiji. (2004, July 9). *In re the President's Reference, Qarase v Chaudhry—Decision of the Court. FJSC 1; MISC 001.2003.* http://www.paclii.org/fj/cases/FJSC/2004/1.html.

Tuza, E. (1977). Silas Eto of New Georgia. In G. Trompf (Ed.), *Prophets of Melanesia: Six Essays* (pp. 65–87). Institute of Papua New Guinea Studies, Port Moresby.

Van Trease, H. (2005). The Operation of the Single Non-transferable Vote System in Vanuatu. *Commonwealth & Comparative Politics, 43*(3), 296–332.

Veenendaal, W. (2016). How Democracy Functions without Parties: The Republic of Palau. *Party Politics, 22*(1), 27–36.

Wilkinson, S. (2000). India, Consociational Theory, and Ethnic Violence. *Asian Survey, 40*(5), 767–791.

CHAPTER 16

Conclusion: The Power-Sharing Lifecycle across the Global South

Allison McCulloch and Joanne McEvoy

From Burundi to Lebanon, from Colombia to New Caledonia,[1] political elites in divided places often find it hard to agree to the terms of a power-sharing settlement, hard to share power with one another, and hard to reform the terms of their settlements over time. It is no wonder that, as Brendan O'Leary once argued, power-sharing systems "are difficult to love and celebrate" (2005: 36). Grand coalition governments very often succumb to political crises, stalemate, and instability. Citizens often lament that power-sharing dysfunction dashes their hopes for stable democratic government, in some cases taking to the streets to air their

[1] Also referred to as Kanaky New Caledonia.

A. McCulloch (✉)
Department of Political Science, Brandon University, Brandon, MB, Canada
e-mail: mccullocha@brandonu.ca

J. McEvoy
University of Aberdeen, Aberdeen, Scotland
e-mail: j.mcevoy@abdn.ac.uk

© The Author(s), under exclusive license to Springer Nature   353
Switzerland AG 2024
E. Wassim Aboultaif et al. (eds.), *Power-Sharing in the Global South*,
Federalism and Internal Conflicts,
https://doi.org/10.1007/978-3-031-45721-0_16

grievances with the state of the regime. Moreover, little clarity exists on how to move beyond such arrangements; that is, "no one has yet specified the location of the exit" (Horowitz, 2014: 12). Yet despite such challenges, international mediators and domestic elites often find their way to power-sharing as the best option to realize peace and democracy while also accommodating communal divisions, especially so after violent conflict.

In light of these difficulties of adoption, function, and reform, the contributors to this volume were asked to consider three broad questions: How do power-sharing systems come in and out of being? How do power-sharing systems 'work,' that is, how do they resolve political crises and other forms of deadlock between governing partners? What are the major challenges facing power-sharing systems? They approached these questions from different perspectives and emphasized different stages of the power-sharing lifecycle. Some focus more on the adoption stage. For example, in Chapter 3 Derek Powell emphasizes how ideas of power-sharing influenced the transition away from apartheid in South Africa. In Chapter 9, Sheetal Sheena Sookrajowa revisits the historical record on the adoption of consociational features in Mauritius, which coincided with independence from the United Kingdom. In Chapter 14, Eduardo Wassim Aboultaif reflects on a would-be case of power-sharing, proposing a set of institutions that might help Syria to get over the adoptability hurdle after more than a decade of civil war.

Others emphasize the implementation phase and the quest for functionality, as Ana Sánchez Ramírez and Madhav Joshi do in the case of Colombia (Chapter 4), Andrew Harding does for Malaysia (Chapter 8), Yonatan Fessha and Biniyam Bezabih do for Ethiopia (Chapter 11), and Farah Shakir does for Iraq (Chapter 12). Others still emphasize the 'coming out of being' side of the equation, including those cases where power-sharing has ended or is being constrained by authoritarian revival, as in Tunisia (Chapter 5 by Julius Dihstelhoff and Moritz Simon) or Fiji (covered in Chapter 15 by Jon Fraenkel). In Chapter 13, Réginas Ndayiragije and Alexandre Wadih Raffoul, too, deal with the possible end of power-sharing with their discussion of the erosion of power-sharing in Burundi in the face of deepening authoritarianization under CNDD-FDD rule. Adaptability is emphasized in those cases where some constitutional reforms have occurred. In Chapter 6, Harihar Bhattacharyya explains how an "evolving" form of federalism helps to manage territorial cleavages in India. Nigeria, covered by Dele Babalola and Hakeem Onapajo in

Chapter 7, has evolved from a 3-state federal parliamentary system to its current configuration as a 36-state federal presidential arrangement. A further set of chapters deal with those cases that appear unable to update their agreements to enhance functionality, as in Lebanon (Drew Mikhael and Allison McCulloch, Chapter 10), Mauritius (Sookrajowa, Chapter 9), and, perhaps, New Caledonia (Fraenkel, Chapter 15).

Indeed, the chapters, collectively, highlight the diverse trajectories of power-sharing across the Global South. From federations to consociations to hybrid forms of power-sharing, including those with centripetal or integrative features, the institutional manifestation of power-sharing is highly variable. As Soeren Keil and Eduardo Wassim Aboultaif note in the Introduction to this volume, there is not one form of power-sharing, but many. While much has been written on consociationalism as the premier form of power-sharing (so much so that Arend Lijphart (1985) has suggested that the terms can be used interchangeably),[2] the chapters instead underscore the full range of institutional tools in the power-sharing toolbox. A focus on cases from across the Global South thus requires a reorientation away from thinking of consociation and power-sharing as synonyms towards a more fulsome understanding of the different ways power can be shared. Indeed, several of the cases embody what Christina Murray (2016) has labelled a "mix and match approach." While acknowledging the "real danger in bits and pieces of various schemes being pasted together with inadequate attention to the whole or to their practical implications," she also points out that, given the very real difficulties and constraints facing the pursuit of peace, stability, and democracy, policy-makers should make use of "all the tools in the constitutional toolbox" (2016: 531). Stefan Wolff's (2009) conception of 'complex power-sharing' in which power-sharing settlements "no longer depend solely on consociational theory," nor "solely upon integrative theory" would fit this description as would Krzysztof Trzciński's (2022) articulation of hybrid power-sharing, which Babalola and Onapajo use to describe Nigeria in their chapter. As part of the trend towards 'mix and match' approaches, it remains important to distinguish, as Rene Lemarchand once did in relation to the countries of the Great Lakes, between those cases which are instances of "improvised bricolage, aimed at coopting the bad guys" and those that reflect "a set of carefully calibrated constitutional norms" (Lemarchand, 2007: 3), a

---

[2] For an important rebuttal, see Bogaards (2000).

distinction that will matter when the power-sharing trajectory shifts from adoption to function. The case studies here give credence to these claims necessitating a wider and richer conception of power-sharing.

Indeed, the chapters offer considerable insight into *what* gets adopted, that is, they shed light on the specifics of diverse power-sharing designs. In Nigeria, as Babalola and Onapajo outline, power-sharing rules can be formal (via federal structures) and informal (e.g., the convention of a rotational presidency). Harding's chapter on Malaysia highlights a potentially novel approach to managing group diversity and tensions. In this case, a 'negotiated social contract' has been in operation since the 1950s, intended to manage ethnic relations and guide the distribution of economic development. Revised following post-electoral violence in 1969, the principle takes the form of affirmative action policies to protect communal groups, acting as a balancing force between group interests and the wider constitution. Notably, power-sharing can evolve as something of a mélange, as per the experience in Burundi, which is part consociational, part centripetal, part 'associational power-sharing,' which is explained by Ndayiragije and Raffoul as owing to the pursuit of a multi-ethnic party system. Mauritius embodies the 'mix and match' approach through its combination of majoritarian and consociational features as might India's form of federalism.

Beyond the diversity of institutional forms, the cases also vary by temporality and performance. Some were short-lived, others long-lasting; some have proven amenable to reforms, others now appear 'stuck' with systems that have outlived their usefulness. Some have performed reasonably well; others may be qualified as failures. Beyond their relationship to power-sharing, the cases also exhibit differences in demographic composition, economic development, ideological positionality, and experience of violent conflict. This variability could only ever be thus. The Global South—which is after all "most of the world" (Chatterjee, 2004)—is not a single monolithic entity, nor do we aim to treat it as such.

Despite their variability, a point of commonality shared by many of the cases is the colonial encounter and other "transnational entanglements" (Berger, 2021: 2002). Across the Global South, colonial legacies loom large and continue to reverberate. In some cases, power-sharing operated as a device for achieving independence, either via a 'coming together' dynamic vis-à-vis the colonial powers, as in Lebanon, or such institutions were encouraged by the outgoing colonizers, as in Mauritius and India. As described by Sookrajowa, "features of consociationalism were adopted during the British decolonization period in order to ensure a smooth transition of power to local politicians and to promote effective government in newly independent Mauritius. Power-sharing, that is, was a device deployed to allow for the exit of the British colonial powers" (Chapter 9). Some, of course, are compelled to continue the efforts to detach from colonial rule, as in New Caledonia, where the Indigenous Kanak people have voted for independence from France in the referendums agreed as part of the Nouméa Accord but where their sovereignty aspirations thus far remain elusive (Chapter 15). Even for those cases that arrived at their power-sharing agreements later in the post-colonial period, they continue to deal with the fallout from colonial choices, whether in the assemblages of diverse states cobbled together by colonizers for their own ends, the exploitation of natural resources for personal profit, or the hollowing out or elite capture of state institutions for communal gain.

Moreover, some contemporary cases continue to arrive at power-sharing under duress, with Iraq a notable instance of this trend. As Shakir shows in Chapter 12, the American invasion not only precipitated a legitimacy crisis among the different communities, especially the Sunnis who ultimately eschewed the constitution-writing process, but it also undermined, through policies such as de-Baathification, "the state's authority to undertake its responsibilities towards its population." Shakir's chapter demonstrates how external actors can exert pressure on domestic elites to arrive at a reconfigured polity including power-sharing institutions. A line can be drawn from political choices made in the early stages of invasion to the anti-government Tishreen protests in 2019 (Mako & Edgar, 2021). Meanwhile, in Syria, the prospect of an "inclusive Syrian-led process," as envisioned by the United Nations, grows dimmer with time, considering increasing Arab rapprochement towards Syria and other international interventions.

Though external actors have been involved in establishing and maintaining power-sharing structures across many of the cases considered in this volume, it is unclear whether this trend in place for several decades will continue in the future. As Caroline Hartzell and Vanessa Igras note in Chapter 2, with the resurgence of major power rivalries between the US and Russia, as well as a "growing disenchantment on the part of the international community with the results of some negotiated peace agreements, and fluctuating funding for peacemaking and peacekeeping in the wake of global economic crises," the tide may be turning against the kinds of international interventions that give way to power-sharing agreements.

Whatever the geopolitical future holds, the impact of outsiders—colonial, neocolonial, and imperial—affects processes of state formation and statebuilding, and thus highly influences the trajectory of power-sharing across the Global South (for an exploration of these issues in Lebanon and Iraq, see Dodge & Salloukh, 2024). If we take Tobias Berger's understanding of the Global South as "a relational category that describes a subdued position in a structural relationship of domination between interconnected entities within a global system" (2021: 2002), then it becomes clear that power-sharing theory has failed to reckon with the colonial encounter and its reverberations as it should.

The variability of the cases presents us with something of a quandary, tasked, as we are, with distilling a set of insights from across this geographically, institutionally, and temporally diverse landscape. Here, we utilize the three stages in the power-sharing lifecycle—adoption, function, and (possible) end—to reflect on the power-sharing journeys captured by the authors in their respective chapters. We have argued elsewhere that a lifecycle approach to power-sharing can direct scholarly attention in productive ways to better understand the sequencing and subsequent performance of power-sharing (McCulloch & McEvoy, 2020). A lifecycle appraisal views the sharing of power as an ongoing process, not an event. As such, it requires sustained commitment and recommitment to ensuring functional performance. It also asks us to take a longue durée perspective, to see the conditions under which the agreement came into being as intimately connected to how it operates over time, as well as to where it might lead in the future. Starting at the beginning, the process by which a power-sharing government comes into being influences its operational performance. Yet, power-sharing theory often obscures or glosses over some of these starting conditions, assuming strict application will deliver similar outcomes regardless of context. The cases considered in this volume warn against such assumptions and invite critical reflection on some of the theory's foundational assumptions regarding the *what*, the *how,* and the *who* of power-sharing adoption (Hartzell with Igras, Chapter 2).

Similarly, a lifecycle approach suggests that how power-sharing partners respond to implementation difficulties indicates whether efforts at institutional revision promote compromise or brinkmanship. Such an approach highlights shifts in adoptability, helping to see what moves parties towards accepting power-sharing and what might make them turn away from it at different points over an agreement's lifecycle. Choices made at the point of adoption and over the life of the agreement will also tell us something about power-sharing 'endability.' Such choices—either in aggressing institutional reform or by addressing wider contentious policy issues—may lead to better democratic governance but could also set the scene for protracted dysfunctionality or even pave the way for renewed violence. In simplified heuristic form, then, a power-sharing lifecycle has three stages: adoption, function, and end. In practice, however, it can be marked by repeated regressions, erosions, and impasses. Indeed, lifecycles are often "fraught with contestations and reversals" with "different behavioural logics" dominating different stages (Finnemore & Sikkink, 1998: 888; Krook & True, 2010: 106). The trajectory is never linear, but is marked by ups and downs, and goes back and forth, including in some cases, starting over again, as in Lebanon and Colombia, both of which experienced a return to power-sharing after civil war. In what follows, we review how the cases covered in this volume inform the adoption, function, and reform of power-sharing settlements.

ADOPTABILITY

The adoption of power-sharing settlements has been a key puzzle for power-sharing theory and practice. Why and how does power-sharing come into being? For some time, scholarship has sought to explain why, against the odds, opposing communal actors decide to put down their weapons and govern a contested polity together, channelling their differences through political institutions instead of violence (Sisk, 2013). Once considered "as rare as the arctic rose" (Horowitz, 2002: 197), inter-group agreement to establish consociational institutions overcomes majority and minority preferences that are often poles apart. As the former will likely favour majoritarianism and the latter demands independence, autonomy, or, at minimum, a stake in government, agreeing to govern together might be considered wishful thinking. Elsewhere we have argued for a need to better clarify the challenges of getting to a power-sharing settlement and that doing so will help explain the variable performance of power-sharing across cases. In addition to understanding 'why power-sharing,' we posit that the adoption process has implications for power-sharing performance (McCulloch & McEvoy, 2020). There are two key elements to power-sharing adoption: the process by which the settlement is negotiated and agreed; and the prospect of specific institutional arrangements being acceptable to the main communities. As John

McGarry (2017) argues in an earlier consideration of the power-sharing adoption conundrum, adoptability should be understood as the condition under which parties agree to share power or come to see power-sharing as an acceptable arrangement for managing their differences.

Thus, the book's focus on adoptability speaks not just to how and why power-sharing comes into being, but also to the institutional choices made, highlighting diversity beyond the core package of executive power-sharing and autonomy, sometimes hybrid combinations of formal and informal, partly consociational and partly centripetal, and sometimes a mix of power-sharing and majoritarian rules. To some extent, the diversity of rules adopted across the cases may arguably reflect the considerable variation in terms of internal cleavage characteristics, group relations with the centre, and dynamics of inter-communal relations, as evidenced by the complexity explored in Jon Fraenkel's chapter on the Pacific Islands. This finding regarding a mix of institutional choices raises questions: what explains diverse or hybrid institutional choices? And in what ways might a mix of institutional rules (including seemingly incoherent power-sharing packages) matter for functionality?

So, what do the book's chapters on cases of the Global South tell us about the adoptability of power-sharing? The first, and obvious, benefit is that these contributions help illuminate the adoption of power-sharing beyond Europe and build knowledge on the full universe of power-sharing cases. With considerable geographical spread, diverse historical backgrounds, and varied political trajectories, the cases considered in this volume have much to say about why actors turn to—and also away from—power-sharing. Providing insights for the development of power-sharing theory, commonalities are found in the motivations for power-sharing adoption: ending violent inter-group conflict, addressing insecurity on the part of both minority and majority communities, and as part of wider processes of constitutional change including decolonization. Moreover, the cases eschew any sense of an institutional blueprint. Rather than institutional experimentation as an exception, the adoption of power-sharing across cases in the Global South has produced a mix of institutional rules, formal and informal, consociational and centripetal variants in tandem, and power-sharing co-existing with majoritarian rules.

The variety of cases explored in this book demonstrates that power-sharing has often been adopted as a means to end violent political conflict. These cases share an expectation that shared government by former foes will help a war-stricken society move beyond conflict and instability and induce a degree of political stability. For example, as Ndayiragije and Raffoul detail, such hope was apparent at various junctures in Burundi where power-sharing was first introduced following ethnic violence in 1988 with the objective of bringing Hutu representatives into government. When the main parties came to negotiate the Arusha Accords of 2000, facilitated by international mediation, power-sharing was an expected central element of the deal (Chapter 13). Moreover, as Aboultaif's chapter on Syria shows, power-sharing continues to be considered a potentially feasible mechanism for facilitating war to peace transitions, despite the many challenges in reaching agreement.

The power-sharing adoptions experienced in the Global South also show that societies which have relapsed into violent conflict despite some earlier effort to accommodate groups, later seek to cement power-sharing to avoid future conflict recurrence. In some sense, power-sharing might be said to reside in the institutional memory of many conflict-affected societies, re-emerging amidst renewed effort to end conflict. Lebanon, for example, has a historical legacy of accommodation with the National Pact of 1943 whereby political posts were allocated on a sectarian basis, if not further back to the *mutasarifiya* system of the nineteenth century in Mount Lebanon (Aboultaif, 2019). Following the collapse of these arrangements and the onset of civil war in 1975, a revised consociational system was finally established with the Ta'if Agreement of 1989. In Colombia, as Sánchez Ramírez and Joshi demonstrate, there is a long temporal horizon with a history of power-sharing going back to the mid-nineteenth century, with power-sharing deals secured between the then dominant identities, conservatives, and liberals (Chapter 4). In later peace talks with various insurgent movements throughout the 1980s and 1990s, power-sharing was a key element of negotiations, proposed as an incentive for groups to disarm. The subsequent cycles of conflict were broken with the 2016 peace agreement with FARC, including multiple forms of power-sharing: political power-sharing with provisions for FARC to share legislative power for two electoral cycles; an element of military power-sharing with the creation of the Security and Protection Corps; and some economic power-sharing including provisions relating to land title distribution. By investigating how power-sharing has commonly been adopted to end inter-group violence in cases across the Global South, the book adds to our understanding of the perceived value of power-sharing at extremely challenging moments of conflict to peace transitions.

As witnessed in cases in the Global North, beyond the urgency to end violent conflict, power-sharing is often adopted to address group insecurity by affording access to power for groups hitherto excluded, marginalized, and even oppressed (Chapter 2; Hartzell & Hoddie, 2007; Mattes & Savun, 2009). Power-sharing adoption thus becomes an attractive and viable institutional prospect when groups view the arrangement as providing assurance that they will have a (potentially guaranteed and ongoing) stake in government. Notably, though most cases of power-sharing in the Global South are designed to address minority insecurity, some cases have had a majority community historically excluded from power. Power-sharing is therefore used in an attempt to undo the injustice of the historical exclusion of minorities and majorities depending on the case specifics. The chapters on Burundi, South Africa, Malaysia, and Iraq all attest to the particular context of creating more legitimate political institutions when majority communities have been marginalized and deprived of a governing role. Power-sharing thus comes to be adopted as it provides greater security for both minority and majority communities.

The case studies highlight that power-sharing adoption should also be seen as part and parcel of wider processes of constitutional transformation in the Global South. As one of us has argued elsewhere, to better understand power-sharing adoption, we need to consider both "the agreement's constituent parts as well as the wider environment in which power is to be shared" (McCulloch, 2021: 5; see also McGarry, 2021). The wider political environment in several transitional states of the Global South has been shaped by constitutional change processes, often arriving at power-sharing and group autonomy in the process. Such constitutional change might be designed as transitional and limited (e.g., South Africa), it might be intended to have longevity (e.g., Ethiopia, Nigeria) but later backslide (e.g., Tunisia, Fiji), it might come about in the context of decolonization (e.g., Mauritius, India) or largely imposed by external actors (as in Iraq). As Powell outlines in his chapter on South Africa, the constitutional transition was shaped by ideas of power-sharing that did not appear out of the blue, but had been in circulation for some time. The Government of National Unity established after the 1994 elections was a "pivotal transitional arrangement that made an orderly and managed transition" (Chapter 3). The Tunisian experience, in contrast, was driven by an urgent need to find a political solution amidst the political vacuum brought about by the fall of Ben Ali. In their chapter, Dihstelhoff and Simon sketch how the elite 'rapprochement' between the secular-laicist

Nidaa Tounes and the Islamist Ennahda led to a participatory constitutional reform process and to the new constitution of January 2014. The conditions of the particular moment of political instability required an elite compromise in the spirit of national dialogue and conciliation. However, the "consensual milestone" of the new Tunisian constitution started to unravel when concerted moves were made to shore up power in the presidency.

The case of Mauritius, where aspects of consociational power-sharing were agreed for the newly independent state, speaks to how group accommodation was a key element in negotiations between the British colonial authorities and the local political parties on constitutional change. Sookrajowa demonstrates how power-sharing in Mauritius was intended to secure political stability and improve inter-group relations by building a culture of coalition politics (Chapter 9). The degree of power shared was limited, however, given the dominance of the Hindu majority and the ongoing marginalization of ethnic minorities, especially the Creole community. In Chapter 6, Bhattacharyya describes how the adoption of federalism in India "was beyond doubt" in the transition to independence from the United Kingdom. In this instance, the pursuit of democracy and elements of power-sharing were informed by thinking on the part of both the independence movement and the British colonial powers. And the case of Iraq provides yet another context in which power-sharing was adopted as part of a wider constitutional transformation process: a new constitutional order based on federalism and power-sharing at the centre in the wake of the US-led invasion. Shakir's chapter argues that the adoption of power-sharing in Iraq was central to the political bargain reached between Iraqi elites and the US, facilitating the Kurds' ambition for autonomy in a federal structure and the Shia demand for inclusion in a unified Iraq (Chapter 12). Across different contexts of political instability and transformation in the Global South, power-sharing has been a central element of institutional design for new constitutional orders, arguably seen to provide a way to reimagine a contested polity based on more legitimate and inclusive political structures, leaving behind exclusionary structures and practices of the past.

Power-sharing has been adopted in the context of fragile conflict dynamics and politically charged constitutional change. Understanding power-sharing adoptability as pertaining to the process of getting to a deal, and the prospect of an institutional package being acceptable to the main groups, the book's chapters highlight the significance of the adoption phase for the power-sharing lifecycle. Though the starting conditions of a power-sharing settlement are not determinative, we suggest that the case study chapters underscore how the adoption 'moment' matters for power-sharing maintenance. The specific context of the starting conditions will have ramifications not just in terms of 'what' gets adopted but also for the prospect of effective and stable governance, the question of functionality.

FUNCTIONALITY

In lamenting the lack of scholarly attention to power-sharing adoptability, McGarry points to the "primacy of the functionality question in academic writings" (2017: 17). We concur with his point that a focus on functionality at the expense of adoptability might lead to, as he puts it, "time wasted" if we end up prescribing institutions that are "arguably functional [but] that are not adoptable." Yet, we also recognize why the literature has tended to emphasize functionality. As one of us has argued elsewhere, "if power-sharing governments are unable to provide sufficient levels of good governance, the whole post-agreement edifice will likely be at stake" (McEvoy, 2017: 211). How to measure functionality remains contested. While there remains a preoccupation in the wider power-sharing literature with the ability of such systems to deliver peace and stability, there is increasing focus on its ability to deliver on broader governance goals, including robust public service provisions, economic development and redistribution, social justice and a full legislative and policy-making agenda. The chapters here speak to both the concern with peace and stability and, as described by Hartzell and Igras, to the "effects stemming from the exercise of power via power-sharing institutions."

A first functionality theme that is evident across the cases is a concern with quality governance (or lack thereof). Power-sharing institutions, like grand coalitions and mutual vetoes, are intended to slow the decision-making process in order to ensure all voices are heard. Yet rather than just slowing the decision-making process, such institutions can sometimes actually grind it to a halt. Arend Lijphart once argued that because "decision-making that entails accommodation among all subcultures is a difficult process," the success of the system is bolstered by "a relatively low total load on the decision-making apparatus" (1969: 219). Yet, this expectation of a lighter load is seemingly in tension with the post-conflict

16 CONCLUSION: THE POWER-SHARING LIFECYCLE ... 365

peacebuilding agenda, characterized as it is by a plethora of competing issues in urgent need of attention and resolution. The protracted and intersected crises in Lebanon and Iraq, which are characterized by the state's limited ability to provide basic public goods provisions, wrapped up in deep-rooted clientelism and corruption, bring this tension into stark relief. Here, the chapters by Mikhael and McCulloch and Shakir recall the point that "though peace and stability are undoubtedly important—and arguably are pre-requisites for effective state action on these other issues—how different settlements fare in terms of their governing capacity and ability to confront and ameliorate societal problems needs to be a bigger part of assessing performance records than is often the case" (McCulloch & Aboultaif, 2023).

The chapter by Harding, too, reminds us that power-sharing must mean more—deliver more—than just stability (Chapter 8). Malaysia, he suggests, demonstrates how affirmative action programmes can help to shore up peace and stability, as well as economic growth. Yet, he cautions: "there are also dangers in such an approach, or at least in consistently maintaining it, as the logic of affirmative action is that redistribution of opportunity should, over time, have equalizing effects and empower the disadvantaged, rather than deepen its dependency on the state" (Chapter 8). This potential disconnect between institutional design and intended outcome reflects a wider question raised by the chapters: what does power-sharing do for citizens? Without question, moving society out of violent conflict will likely be a vast improvement on what went before. But citizens also want to feel they are recipients of a peace dividend, that power-sharing improves their daily lives and not just in security terms.

A second key theme on functionality raised by the chapters concerns the disposition of political actors to share power. It is perhaps unsurprising that in the context of violent conflict and/or deep communal divisions, political actors will be reluctant to share much, never mind the trappings of state power. Yet for the reasons discussed above, the great compromise to govern together has happened time and again across cases. Yet it is also clear, as shown, for example, in the Ethiopian experience (Fessha and Bezabih, Chapter 11), that if inter-elite bargaining and group representation are confined to a narrow range of actors, then the prospect of enduring peace and stability may be limited. This problem speaks to the risk of 'weak adoptability' when a deficient level of inclusion harms power-sharing's potential (McEvoy & Aboultaif, 2022). The book's chapters also highlight that due to a shifting balance of power in the post-settlement phase, support for power-sharing fluctuates over time. As Ndayiragije and Raffoul recount in relation to Burundi (Chapter 13), the scope for actor agency matters a great deal, with political party behaviour continually shaped by the shifting balance of power, at times cooperating and at other times reneging on commitments in an effort to derail or control. Such dynamics have also been obvious in Tunisia where power-sharing was initially supported by key parties to secure some stability amidst considerable uncertainty but came undone as powerful actors moved to monopolize power, unravelling the "pacted transition" of the post-Arab Spring constitutional moment (Dihstelhoff and Simon, Chapter 5). Conversely, as witnessed by elites' obstinate commitment to power-sharing rules in Lebanon, preference for the status quo does not guarantee smooth inter-group cooperation and the provision of good governance (Mikhael and McCulloch, Chapter 10). Much depends, then, on the extent to which actors choose to remain faithful to the terms of the settlement, with power-sharing at risk of becoming an undertaking they may seek to depart from, should a changed political environment provide parties room for manoeuvre to capitalize on power.

As evident across the cases, functionality does not exist independently of its environment. How power-sharing works is often a product of how it came into being and the extent to which actors continue to regard power-sharing as meeting their interests. It is these dynamics of elite commitment, we submit, that influence power-sharing functionality and its future prospects of either adaptation or transformation.

ADAPTABILITY AND ENDABILITY

As the cases demonstrate, power-sharing agreements come into being via a range of different pathways, and they perform variably over time. So too might they take different exits at power-sharing's end. The cases in this volume speak to several different patterns of power-sharing dissolution, or its 'endability,' by which we mean "the ability of a polity to reform its power-sharing rules and to move beyond such a system" (McCulloch, 2021: 6). One such pathway entails moving to new governance forms democratically and by consensus, if and when the governing partners agree to do so; South Africa continues to be the textbook example. For several cases discussed in the volume, however, the end of power-sharing is a consequence of authoritarian revival or the descent into civil war. Tunisia and Fiji are emblematic cases here; Burundi looks set to follow them. There are worrying signs too in India with pressures on its democratic quality in the context of Hindutva nationalism. In both Lebanon and Colombia, meanwhile, civil wars ended power-sharing, and power-sharing later ended civil wars. We can also observe those cases which have amended their agreements and retained some power-sharing features, such as India, Ethiopia, and Nigeria. Another category of cases is populated by those that are unable to do either, that is, where power-sharing has not ended but nor have the parties been able to effectively reform it. Lebanon is the stand-out case here, but Mauritius, Iraq, and New Caledonia are also examples demonstrating the resilience or 'stickiness' of power-sharing settlements. Together, the cases point towards the need for further exploration of what Stef Vandeginste (2022) astutely refers to as the "shelf-life" of power-sharing (see also O'Driscoll & Costantini, 2024). This is meant both in the sense that power-sharing provisions may have an expiry or 'best before' date, after which the arrangement begins to outlive its usefulness and the time is ripe to move towards a new institutional settlement, but also those situations where the institutions may no longer align with their original rationale "without however dissolving them" (2022: 265). Vandeginste writes: "While institutional design shapes political behavior by shifting incentives and cost–benefit calculations, the real life meaning of institutions is vice versa also determined by strategic interests and changing power relations" (2022: 265).

Ndayiragije and Raffoul detail precisely this turn of events in Burundi between 2007 and 2015, which they label as a period of erosion of power-sharing, characterized by the rise of the CNDD-FDD (Chapter 13). As part of its authoritarian turn during this period described by Ndayiragije and Raffoul, the CNDD-FDD followed a three-pronged approach of appointing loyalists to key government positions, shifting power away from the formal power-sharing institutions and towards quasi-formal structures or those outside the bounds of ethnic quotas, and drawing from the classic authoritarian toolkit (vote-buying, voter intimidation, attacks on the opposition). The rollback of some of the power-sharing institutions in the 2018 constitution comes once those provisions had already been weakened in practice. With the sunset clauses introduced in that new constitution due to lapse in 2023, Burundi finds itself, as Ndayiragije and Raffoul rightly note, in a situation where "endability risks paving the way to renewed monopolization of power and ethnic exclusion—the very issues power-sharing was supposed to overcome." Babalola and Onapajo likewise emphasize the dynamic between political institutions and those who design and populate them, noting that in the case of Nigeria, "the success of power-sharing is not [only] underlined by institutional frameworks or elite agreements, but by the commitment of the elite to implement the model they have produced."

Lijphart (1977) once argued that consociational arrangements can "render themselves superfluous." Nonetheless, a common thread weaved through the case studies, is that, regardless of institutional form, power-sharing is often "sticky." The question of endability follows a familiar refrain across the cases: everyone agrees on the need to reform the institutions; no one can agree on the shape such reforms should take. Sookrajowa sees the resistance to reform in Mauritius stemming from the system's majoritarian tendencies, suggesting that while there is widespread dissatisfaction with the system, which still employs 1972 census data as the basis for electoral representation, any move towards reform has been resisted by the majority, thus leading to perpetual stalemate. This recognition of the need to reform combined with the lack of agreement on the form those reforms should take surely resonates in Ethiopia. There might be broad agreement on "territorial autonomy within a federal framework" but there is less consensus on its ethnic manifestations which have proven to be "a major source of contention." Part of the challenge in Ethiopia—as elsewhere—is that the process of adoption only included "likeminded political forms," thus highlighting how choices made at earlier stages of the lifecycle impact later functionality and adaptability. As Fessha and Bezabih (Chapter 11) note "the Ethiopian experience reveals that power-sharing arrangements that do not emerge from true and broadly-based bargaining might not produce the desired result of peace and stability." In Lebanon, the urgency of institutional reforms consistently expressed by the public, as highlighted most recently in the 2019 *thawra*, sits in tension with the elites' laissez-faire attitude to the magnitude of the political, economic, and humanitarian crisis facing the country. But as Mikhael and McCulloch detail in Chapter 10 "this resistance to reform—its adaptability problem—was clear to see in the longitudinal efforts of feminist activists before 2019." They trace the source of Lebanon's adaptability problem both to the deliberate slowness of the institutions as well as to the 'symbolic weight' attached by political actors to those institutions.

Meanwhile, in New Caledonia, the fight for independence and decolonization butts up against referendum results split on the country's sovereignty. A yes/no referendum question, in which the choice is drawn starkly—full and immediate independence "with a total break with the past" versus full integration into the French state "without examining in any way the possibility of free association"—does not lend itself to the sharing of power or other forms of compromise (Chauchat, 2022: 470). Instead, it risks pitting two visions of the future, one articulated by the island's Indigenous people and one by its settlers as "incompatible struggles" (Tutugoro, 2020). While the current arrangement allows for some degree of Kanak autonomy in the Northern and Loyalty Islands provinces (Fraenkel, Chapter 15), its 'shelf-life' is currently under debate. With the set of referendums agreed as part of the Nouméa Accord now completed (though, contentiously so in the case of the 2021 vote which saw a Kanak boycott of the poll), decolonization remains radically unfinished. Independence—when it comes—will also likely require some degree of power-sharing for all those who call Kanaky/New Caledonia home.

As a whole, the chapters speak to a need for future investigation into how to pursue reforms to power-sharing, or even its (democratic) dissolution. If earlier power-sharing scholarship could be taken to task for "not specifying the location of the exit" (Horowitz, 2014), this volume takes some tentative steps towards theorizing departures from power-sharing. To be sure, there are some worrying trends highlighted by the authors, on susceptibility to authoritarian revival, conflict resumption, or regression on minority rights. Still, other cases are 'sticky,' locking—or attempting to lock in—a specific balance of power even in the face of political and demographic shifts. To switch back to the shelf-life metaphor, some cases remain seemingly impervious to change while simultaneously exhibiting signs of decay. The chapters emphasize differences in the speed and extent of reforms, from time-bounded agreements (e.g., South Africa), incremental reforms (e.g., as pursued by activists in Lebanon), to wholesale constitutional revisions (e.g., Nigeria's different constitutional iterations). The effect of generational turnover on power-sharing performance is another line of inquiry worth pursuing. While evidence suggests that support for power-sharing will fluctuate with turnover in party leadership, with the emergence of new parties, and when citizens born after the power-sharing arrangement was agreed come of political age, there is more to learn about how this might open windows of opportunity for enhancing power-sharing's 'reform capacity' (Lindvall, 2010). Finally, given the full range of power-sharing rules employed in the Global South, the cases also suggest further research into the adaptability and endability of mix-and-match power-sharing configurations. Much of the literature on 'unwinding' power-sharing (McCulloch, 2017, McCrudden & O'Leary, 2013) is focused on consociationalism, but in keeping with the wider theme of this book—many forms of power-sharing, not one—we would do well to consider how the interplay between different power-sharing logics affects the wider ability of the system to adapt, reform, and evolve.

CONCLUSION

This book has explored a wide set of cases, covering an expansive global remit, and yet has only just begun to capture the complex and frequently uneven trajectories of power-sharing in the Global South. The contributions tell us much about why power-sharing is difficult to adopt, why it struggles to do well, and why it has trouble reforming over time. The case study chapters, read in conjunction with the thematic overview in Chapter 2, tell a story of institutional diversity and variability, of compromise and collapse, of hope, and for some, despair. The book thus serves as a reminder that power-sharing agreements are reached for different reasons and come into being via different pathways, with some commonalities around the impetus of ending conflict, addressing insecurity, and finding solutions to political and constitutional crises. Such arrangements take different institutional shape and they have performed variably, across both time and space. They have also followed different pathways towards the dissolution of power-sharing, sometimes sliding back into conflict or authoritarianism, sometimes getting stuck with institutions that no longer serve their intended purposes, sometimes adapting and evolving according to societal conditions. In capturing this variability, the authors in this volume help to chart the power-sharing lifecycle, lending vital comparative insights into the adoption, function, adaptation, or even end of one of the leading forms of governance for diverse and divided settings the world over.

References

Aboultaif, E. W. (2019). *Power Sharing in Lebanon: Consociationalism since 1820.* Routledge.

Berger, T. (2021). The 'Global South' as a Relational Category—Global Hierarchies in the Production of Law and Legal Pluralism. *Third World Quarterly, 42*(9), 2001–2017.

Bogaards, M. (2000). The Uneasy Relationship Between Empirical and Normative Types in Consociational Theory. *Journal of Theoretical Politics, 12*(4), 395–423.

Chatterjee, P. (2004). *The Politics of the Governed: Reflections on Popular Politics in Most of the World.* Columbia University Press.

Chauchat, M. (2022). Kanaky New Caledonia. *The Contemporary Pacific, 34*(2), 466–473.

Dodge, T., & Salloukh, B. (Eds.). (2024). *Consociationalism and the State: The Cases of Lebanon and Iraq.* Special issue. *Nationalism and Ethnic Politics, 30*(1), 1–172.

Finnemore, M., & Sikkink, K. (1998). International Norm Dynamics and Political Change. *International Organization, 52*(4), 887–917.

Hartzell, C., & Hoddie, M. (2007). *Crafting Peace: Power-Sharing Institutions and the Negotiated Settlement of Civil Wars.* Penn State Press.

Horowitz, D. L. (2002). Explaining the Northern Ireland Agreement: The Sources of an Unlikely Constitutional Consensus. *British Journal of Political Science, 32*(2), 193–220.

Horowitz, D. L. (2014). Ethnic Power Sharing: Three Big Problems. *Journal of Democracy, 25*(2), 5–20.

Krook, M. L., & True, J. (2010). Rethinking the Life Cycles of International Norms: The United Nations and the Global Promotion of Gender Equality. *European Journal of International Relations, 18*(1), 103–127.

Lemarchand, R. (2007). Consociationalism and Power Sharing in Africa: Rwanda, Burundi, and the Democratic Republic of the Congo. *African Affairs, 106*(422), 1–20.

Lijphart, A. (1969). Consociational Democracy. *World Politics, 21*(2), 207–225.

Lijphart, A. (1977). *Democracy in Plural Societies: A Comparative Exploration.* Yale University Press.

Lijphart, A. (1985). *Power-Sharing in South Africa.* University of California Press.

Lindvall, J. (2010). Power-Sharing and Reform Capacity. *Journal of Theoretical Politics, 22*(3), 357–376.

Mako, S., & Edgar, A. (2021). Evaluating the Pitfalls of External Statebuilding in Post-2003 Iraq (2003–2021). *Journal of Intervention and Statebuilding, 15*(4), 425–440.

Mattes, M., & Savun, B. (2009). Fostering Peace after Civil War: Commitment Problems and Agreement Design. *International Studies Quarterly, 53*(3), 737–759.

McCrudden, C., & O'Leary, B. (2013). *Courts and Consociations: Human Rights versus Power-Sharing.* Oxford University Press.

McCulloch, A. (2017). Pathways from Power-Sharing. *Civil Wars, 19*(4), 405–424.

McCulloch, A. (2021). Introduction: Power-Sharing in Europe—From Adoptability to Endability. In S. Keil & A. McCulloch (Eds.), *Power-Sharing in Europe: Past Practices, Present Cases, and Future Directions.* Palgrave Macmillan.

McCulloch, A., & Aboultaif, E. W. (2023). *Territorial and Institutional Settlements in the Global South.* Oxford University Press.

McCulloch, A., & McEvoy, J. (2020). Understanding Power-Sharing Performance: A Lifecycle Approach. *Studies in Ethnicity and Nationalism, 20*(2), 109–116.

McEvoy, J. (2017). Power-Sharing and the Pursuit of Good Governance: Evidence from Northern Ireland. In A. McCulloch & J. McGarry (Eds.), *Power-Sharing: Empirical and Normative Challenges.* Routledge.

McEvoy, J., & Aboultaif, E. W. (2022). Power-sharing Challenges: From Weak Adoptability to Dysfunction in Iraq. *Ethnopolitics, 21*(3), 238–257.

McGarry, J. (2017). Centripetalism, Consociationalism and Cyprus: The 'Adoptability' Question. In A. McCulloch & J. McGarry (Eds.), *Power-Sharing: Empirical and Normative Challenges.* Routledge.

McGarry, J. (2021). Why Has Cyprus Been a Consociational Cemetery? In S. Keil & A. McCulloch (Eds.), *Power-Sharing in Europe: Past Practice, Present Cases and Future Directions.* Palgrave Macmillan.

Murray, C. (2016). Constitutional Design in Africa: Is Mix and Match OK? *Ethnopolitics, 15*(5), 528–532.

O'Driscoll, D. & Costantini, I. (2024). Conflict Mitigation versus Governance: The Case of Consociationalism in Iraq. *Nationalism and Ethnic Politics, 30*(1), 65–84.

O'Leary, B. (2005). Debating Consociational Politics: Normative and Explanatory Arguments. In S. Noel (Ed.), *From Power-Sharing to Democracy: Post-Conflict Institutions in Ethnically Divided Societies.* McGill-Queen's University Press.

Sisk, T. (2013). Power-Sharing in Civil War: Matching Problems to Solutions. *Civil Wars, 15*(1), 7–20.

Trzciński, K. (2022). Consociationalism meets Centripetalism: Hybrid Power-Sharing. *Nationalism and Ethnic Politics, 28*(3), 313–331.

Tutugoro, A. (2020). Incompatible Struggles? Reclaiming Indigenous Sovereignty and Political Sovereignty in Kanaky and/or New Caledonia. *Department of Pacific Affairs* Discussion Paper 5/2020.

Vandeginste, S. (2022). Reserved Seats and Cooptation in Burundi (2000–2020). *Nationalism and Ethnic Politics.*, *28*(3), 249–268.

Wolff, S. (2009). Complex Power-Sharing and the Centrality of Territorial Self-Governance in Contemporary Conflict Settlements. *Ethnopolitics, 8*(1), 27–45.

INDEX

A

adaptability, 3, 7, 11, 13, 190, 208, 209, 216, 217, 220, 221, 228, 230, 231, 288, 300, 302, 303, 354, 368, 369

adoptability, 3, 7, 8, 13, 87, 105, 106, 133, 150, 272, 354, 358, 360, 363–365

Africa, 2, 31, 40, 43, 44, 47–49, 51, 52, 54, 55, 58, 102, 145, 148, 189, 190, 242, 330

African National Congress (ANC), 9, 23, 24, 38–40, 46, 54, 55, 59, 74, 75, 90

apartheid, 3, 23, 38, 39, 41–44, 46, 51–53, 55, 57–59, 354

Arab spring, 10, 85–88, 90, 96, 104–108, 366

armed forces, 12, 22, 23, 78, 246, 280. *See also* militias

Art. 153, 172, 173, 175–180, 183. *See also* Malaysia

Arusha Peace and reconciliation Agreement (APRA), 286, 287, 291, 292, 296. *See also* Burundi

autonomy
cultural, 4, 206, 216, 218–221, 224
regional, 23, 152
segmental, 11, 19, 47, 149, 190, 217, 238, 240, 261

B

Banwell commission, 198, 204. *See also* Mauritius

bipartisan system, 64

Bosnia and Herzegovina, 328, 343, 347

British colonial rule, 121, 133, 134, 141, 192

bumiputera, 175, 176, 178–185

Burundi, 2, 3–5, 8, 10, 12, 21, 23, 25, 285–290, 292, 295, 296, 298, 299, 301–304, 353, 354, 356, 361, 362, 366, 367. *See also*

© The Editor(s) (if applicable) and The Author(s), under exclusive   375
license to Springer Nature Switzerland AG 2024
E. Wassim Aboultaif et al. (eds.), *Power-Sharing in the Global South*,
Federalism and Internal Conflicts,
https://doi.org/10.1007/978-3-031-45721-0

376 INDEX

Arusha Peace and reconciliation
Agreement (APRA)

C

centripetalism, 8, 13, 149, 150, 295,
303
Christian, 127, 146, 151, 218, 227,
263, 270, 278, 333
civil war, 6, 12, 18, 20–22, 24–26,
28, 30–33, 63, 64, 66, 70, 74,
75, 77, 148, 154, 159, 218, 255,
286, 289, 304, 354, 359, 361,
366, 367
coalition politics, 170, 171, 184, 190,
202, 206, 363. See also grand
coalition
Colombia, 3, 7, 9, 10, 22, 28, 33,
64, 65, 67–69, 71, 74, 75,
78–80, 353, 354, 359, 361, 367
conflict, 2, 3, 5, 6, 8, 9, 11, 12, 17,
18, 20, 21, 25, 26, 29–33,
37–42, 47–49, 52, 53, 55–57,
64, 67–69, 71, 75–80, 86, 101,
107, 136, 139, 146–151, 158,
162, 164, 169, 171, 177, 271,
273, 277, 281, 286–288, 290,
292, 297, 303, 333, 346, 347,
354, 356, 360–363, 365, 369,
370
  management, 18–20, 26, 27, 67,
147, 271
  prevention, 79, 107, 136, 148
consensus, 9, 10, 18, 19, 27, 40, 42,
45, 47, 48, 51, 76, 87, 90–92,
94, 96–100, 132, 141, 153, 157,
159, 178, 206, 225, 253, 268,
271, 273, 297, 328, 337, 343,
366, 368
consociational democracy, 5, 8, 19,
149, 155, 158, 189, 192, 261,
262, 270, 272, 273, 329, 334,
343, 347

consociationalism, 2, 5, 6, 8, 13, 19,
20, 40, 42, 51, 53, 123, 141,
149, 151, 169, 170, 186, 208,
218, 228, 231, 265, 266, 268,
295, 303, 355, 356, 370
  liberal, 5. See also consensus;
consociational democracy
constitution, 7, 38, 39, 41, 42, 45,
46, 48, 49, 51–55, 59, 74, 76,
86, 87, 90–94, 101, 103, 104,
121, 122, 124, 126, 128–130,
135, 137, 138, 140, 151–158,
161–163, 170–178, 183, 184,
192–195, 209, 238, 241–246,
251, 254, 262–272, 276, 277,
279–281, 287–290, 293–297,
300–304, 328, 335–338, 356,
357, 363, 367
  Ethiopian, 239, 240, 242, 243,
245, 253, 254
Constitutional Court, 38, 94, 97,
101, 103, 289, 297
constitutional democracy, 38, 55–59,
140
convention of Government, 290
cooperation, 4–6, 22, 26, 86, 98,
148–150, 152, 158, 275, 276,
279, 280, 298, 366
corporate model, 5. See also liberal
model
Creole community, 190, 206–208,
363
cultural autonomy, 4, 206, 216,
218–221, 224
cultural protectionism, 206

E

Elazar, D., 6, 149, 151
elite compromise, 10, 85–88, 91–94,
96, 98, 101, 105–107, 363
end-ability, 3, 9, 13, 87, 105, 107,
302

Ennahda, 86, 87, 90–102, 106, 107, 363
Ethiopia, 3–6, 10, 12, 237–239, 241–243, 245–247, 249, 251–253, 255, 354, 362, 367, 368
Ethiopian Peoples' Revolutionary Democratic Front (EPRDF), 239, 246, 248–250, 252–254
ethnic conflict, 152, 154, 164, 171, 173
ethnicity, 50, 58, 122, 127, 141, 146, 151, 156, 158, 208, 219, 237, 243, 252, 253, 262–264, 266, 268, 276, 287–290, 295, 302, 303, 327, 329, 336, 344, 345. *See also* ethnic conflict; ethnic nationalism
ethnic nationalism, 163
conflict, 152, 154, 164, 171, 173

F
federalism, 4, 6–8, 12, 51, 64, 121–123, 125, 127, 130, 133, 134, 139, 141, 142, 151, 152, 163, 238, 240, 249, 253, 254, 261, 354, 363
fiscal, 160, 161. *See also* federation
federation, 121, 122, 125, 126, 133, 135, 138, 151–155, 159, 161, 170, 171, 173, 206, 238, 240, 242, 243, 245, 248, 264, 344, 355
Fiji, 3, 5, 13, 26, 327–330, 333, 335–338, 341–343, 346, 347, 354, 362, 366. *See also* Pacific Islands
first-past-the-post (FPTP), 198, 204, 205, 245, 334, 335
functionality, 10, 13, 87, 105, 106, 142, 150, 230, 272–274, 281, 354, 355, 360, 364–366, 368

G
Gandhi, 132
gender, 28, 93, 158, 208, 216, 217, 221, 229, 230, 294, 301
representation, 190, 207. *See also* women's rights
Government of National Unity (GNU), 9, 37–41, 56, 59, 95, 289, 290, 362
grand coalition, 4, 19, 39, 40, 48, 56, 149, 155, 158, 219, 221, 246, 261, 265, 266, 268, 279, 328, 335, 353, 364. *See also* coalition politics

H
Hindu, 11, 126, 134, 190–192, 194–196, 198, 201–203, 205–208, 333, 363
House of Federation (HOF), 243–245, 251
House of Peoples' Representatives (HPR), 244, 246
Hutu, 23, 286, 288–296, 301, 302, 361
Horowitz, Donald, 6, 39, 153, 216, 313

I
immobilism, 6, 30, 216, 219, 226, 231
India, 2–6, 8, 10, 121–142, 190, 191, 343, 354, 356, 362, 363, 367
institutional rigidity, 303
integration, 6, 8, 23, 40, 94, 199, 262, 264, 281, 369. *See also* integrationalist power-sharing
integrationalist power-sharing, 6
interim constitution of 1993, 38, 40, 42, 46, 57

378　INDEX

Iraq, 3, 4–8, 10, 12, 23, 30, 123,
　　261–279, 281, 335, 354, 357,
　　358, 362, 363, 365, 367. *See also*
　　Kurds; Shia; Sunni

K

Kurds, 261–265, 269–271, 279, 363

L

Lebanon, 2, 3, 5, 7, 8, 10, 11, 25,
　　30, 123, 215–219, 221–227,
　　230, 336, 353, 355, 356, 358,
　　359, 361, 365–369
liberal model, 314
Lijphart, Arend, 2, 4–6, 8, 19, 20,
　　38–42, 48, 49, 51, 53, 63, 86,
　　123, 147, 148, 151–153, 155,
　　158, 169, 190, 205, 219, 238,
　　240, 244, 246, 261, 265,
　　268–270, 274, 275, 278,
　　328–330, 334, 343, 347, 355,
　　364, 368

M

majoritarian rule, 360
Malaysia, 3, 4–6, 10, 11, 26, 169,
　　170, 173, 174, 176, 180, 181,
　　184, 185, 336, 354, 356, 362,
　　365. *See also* Art. 153,
　　Rukunegara,bumiputera
Mandela, Nelson, 38, 46, 54, 206,
　　291, 292
Mauritius, 3, 7, 8, 10, 11, 26, 189,
　　190, 192–195, 197–203,
　　205–208, 354–357, 362, 363,
　　367, 368. *See also* Banwell
　　commission; Mauritius Labour
　　Party (MLP)
Mauritius Labour Party (MLP),
　　192–199, 201–204

militias, 264, 279, 280
minority, 9, 11, 19, 23, 29, 32, 39,
　　53, 55–58, 76, 128, 138, 140,
　　141, 146, 151, 152, 157, 159,
　　160, 164, 172, 178, 191, 194,
　　199, 202–206, 238, 241, 244,
　　247, 263, 269, 277, 278,
　　289–291, 333, 336, 359, 360,
　　362, 369
　veto, 4, 40, 130, 140, 141, 149,
　　　206, 261, 268, 335, 339
minority veto, 130, 140, 141, 149,
　　261, 268, 335, 339
multiculturalism
　multicultural society, 147
　plural society, 18–20, 39, 45, 50,
　　　147, 149–151, 155, 158, 169,
　　　184, 190, 278, 329. *See also*
　　　cultural autonomy; cultural
　　　protectionism
multi-party Cabinet, 327, 337, 338,
　　342
Muslims, 122, 123, 126, 127, 134,
　　140, 141, 146, 151, 176, 191,
　　194, 198, 218, 227, 263
Myanmar, 3

N

National Party of Nigeria (NPN), 156
New Caledonia, 7, 13, 327, 328, 330,
　　335, 339–342, 344–346, 353,
　　355, 357, 367–369
Nigeria, 3, 4–6, 8, 10, 145–147,
　　150–158, 160–164, 239,
　　354–356, 362, 367–369. *See also*
　　National Party of Nigeria (NPN);
　　oil

O

O'Leary, Brendan, 5, 147, 206, 220, 262, 265, 274, 275, 278, 353, 370
oil, 24, 161, 271, 277, 345

P

paced transition, 102
Pacific Islands, 13, 330, 333, 334, 343, 344, 360
People's Democratic Party (PDP), 157, 162
personal status laws, 217, 228, 229
polarization, 90, 94, 97, 101, 107, 149, 158
power, 1–13, 17–33, 37–39, 41, 42, 45, 46, 48, 51, 53, 54, 56–59, 63–70, 74, 75, 77–80, 86–88, 93, 95, 96, 98–100, 103–108, 122–125, 129, 130, 133–142, 146–159, 162–164, 175, 177, 183, 184, 190, 192, 193, 195, 201–203, 205–208, 216–219, 224, 225, 227–229, 238, 240, 242, 244–247, 249, 253–255, 261, 262, 264, 265, 270–274, 276–282, 286–304, 327–330, 334–339, 341–347, 353–370
power vacuum, 85, 87, 93, 101, 289
power-sharing
  complex, 3, 8, 136, 141, 150, 265, 269, 279, 287, 293, 355, 370
  economic, 2, 11, 18, 21, 24, 25, 28, 30, 31, 64, 65, 70, 75, 76, 79, 80, 136, 148, 276, 302, 356, 361, 365
  hybrid, 147, 150, 151, 164, 190, 346, 355, 360
  military, 21–25, 28, 70, 78–80, 148, 157, 361

territorial, 3, 6, 10, 12, 21, 23, 25, 28, 64, 70, 76, 79, 80, 122, 124, 127, 130, 133, 138–141, 152, 153, 238, 265, 342, 343
presidential monopolization, 10, 86, 96
proportional representation, 4, 19, 21, 22, 30, 39, 65, 130, 153, 190, 205, 244, 270, 271, 275–277, 280, 294, 329, 334, 338, 339

R

religion, 4, 91, 122, 127, 135, 146, 151, 156, 158, 171–173, 177, 178, 194, 206, 262–264, 289, 329, 333
resources, 21, 24, 28, 29, 31, 32, 64, 75, 79, 136, 141, 142, 146, 147, 155, 156, 159–161, 264, 276, 335, 357
restructuring, 147, 150, 160, 163
revenue
  allocation, 146, 151, 160, 161
  horizontal revenue sharing, 161
  vertical revenue sharing, 160
rotational presidency, 146, 150, 151, 158, 159, 163, 356
Rukunegara, 174. *See also* Malaysia

S

secession, 146, 163, 164, 238, 242, 341, 344
  secessionist violence, 162
Shia, 218, 220, 261, 263–265, 268–270, 273, 275, 278, 279, 363
social contract, 11, 169–180, 183–185, 273, 356
South Africa, 2, 3, 5, 6, 8, 9, 21, 23, 37–39, 41–46, 48–50, 53,

380 INDEX

57–59, 172, 293, 337, 347, 354, 362, 366, 369
Sunni, 218, 220, 227, 263–266, 268–270, 273, 275, 278, 279
Suriname, 3
Syria, 3, 4, 7, 12, 32, 226, 354, 357, 361

T

Transitional National Assembly (TNA), 290
Trustam Eve Commission, 196
Tutsi, 23, 286, 289–296, 301

V

veto rights, 4, 141, 149, 221, 269, 297. *See also* minority veto

W

women's rights, 216, 217, 222, 225, 228

Z

Zimbabwe, 3
zoning, 146, 151, 156–158, 163

Printed in the United States
by Baker & Taylor Publisher Services